Issues in
Labor Policy

Issues in Labor Policy

A Book of Readings

edited by

Sanford Cohen

The University of New Mexico

55692

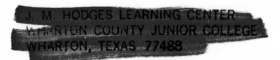
Charles E. Merrill Publishing Company
A Bell & Howell Company
Columbus, Ohio

Published by
Charles E. Merrill Publishing Company
A Bell & Howell Company
Columbus, Ohio 43216

This book was set in Helios and English.
The production editors were Linda Lowell and James Leeke.
The cover was designed by Will Chenoweth.

International Standard Book Number   0–675–08517–9

Library of Congress Catalog Card Number   76–23338

1   2   3   4   5   6   7   8   81   80   79   78   77

Printed in the United States of America

Preface

The readings presented in this book are concerned with contemporary issues which pose questions for labor policy. All of the selections deal directly with such issues or provide background for them. The selections also represent the editor's best guess as to the labor policy problems which will continue to be troublesome in the years immediately ahead. Whenever it appeared to be appropriate, an effort was made to present opposing views on disputatious issues.

The general guiding principle followed in the selection of specific readings was that the material be sufficiently sophisticated to be useful to the labor specialist but not so technical as to be incomprehensible to the undergraduate student or general reader. This is a difficult gap to bridge and, if the effort has not been wholly successful, I hope that it is largely so. The search for readable and pertinent materials brought me into contact with numerous publishers and authors and I would like to express my appreciation for their cooperation.

This book is designed as a supplementary book for a number of courses. It can be used in a labor economics course, a labor relations course, or a collective bargaining course. The book can be used in any management course where there is a strong emphasis on labor issues and problems.

to:
Julia
Beth
Melanie

Contents

I

Industrial Relations Law

Background

Since the enactment of the National Labor Relations Act of 1935 (The Wagner Act), employees who are covered by the Act and who choose to organize and negotiate with employers through their bargaining representatives have been protected against job pressures and other employer influences when exercising their choices. The Labor-Management Relations Act of 1947 (The Taft-Hartley Act) and the Labor-Management Reporting and Disclosure Act of 1959 (The Landrum-Griffin Act) are statutory elaborations and modifications of the 1935 Act which, among other objectives, place various limitations upon union activities. One of the major problems in the administration of this body of industrial relations law has been that of shaping the statutory language to the circumstances of specific disputes. Literally thousands of decisions have been issued by the National Labor Relations Board and the federal courts as a consequence of disputes involving allegations of illegal actions on the part of management or unions, an experience that is not altogether surprising in view of the detailed nature of the law and the vast variation in types of union-management relationships which characterize the American system of industrial relations.

In recent years, new questions of law have arisen as a result of the widespread union-management practice of referring unresolved grievance disputes to binding arbitration. The essence of the legal question which has developed is found in the fact that some grievances may involve violations of both the collective bargaining agreement and provisions of federal law and, thus, may be adjudicated either through arbitration or through the filing of charges with the National Labor Relations Board. By way of clarifying the question, we shall note, first, changes in the legal status of arbitration which have resulted from Supreme Court rulings and, next, certain problems which derive from the interrelationship between the role of the National Labor Relations Board and the authority of the arbitrator. At a later point in this section, a somewhat analogous situation, which has characterized the interrelationship between civil rights legislation and private arbitration of labor disputes, will be examined.

3

The Growth of Labor Arbitration

Arbitration was rarely used as a method of grievance dispute settlement prior to 1940. At the present time, a popular estimate is that 95 percent of all labor-management agreements call for binding arbitration of those grievance disputes which the parties are unable to resolve. One factor which encouraged the growth of arbitration was the policy of the War Labor Board between 1942 and 1945. In a wartime situation when most unions had voluntarily relinquished the right to strike, the Board encouraged labor and management to adopt contract clauses providing for arbitration of disputes over the interpretation and application of their agreements. By late 1945, when the Board was disbanded, a peaceful alternative to the strike had come to be widely accepted. Since that time, the popularity of grievance arbitration has increased. In recent years, over 4,000 arbitration awards have been issued annually by arbitrators selected from panels provided by the Federal Mediation and Conciliation Service, and it is probable that at least that many have been issued by arbitrators selected through the American Arbitration Association or directly by the bargaining parties.

The Supreme Court and Arbitration

The Wagner Act of 1935 did not address the question of the enforceability of the labor-management agreement. This changed in 1947 with the passage of the Taft-Hartley Act. Section 301 (a) of Taft-Hartley reads as follows:

> Suits for violations of contracts between an employer and a labor organization representing employees in an industry affecting commerce as defined in this Act, or between any such labor organizations, may be brought in any district court of the United States having jurisdiction of the parties, without respect to the amount in controversy or without regard to the citizenship of the parties.

Section 301 (b) provides that a labor organization covered by the Act shall be bound by the acts of its agents and may sue or be sued as an entity and in behalf of employees whom it represents in courts of the United States.

An important interpretation of Section 301 came in the *Lincoln Mills* case which involved an employer's refusal to arbitrate an unsettled grievance. Speaking for the Court, Justice Douglas observed that the agreement to arbitrate grievances was a *quid pro quo* for an agreement not to strike. Viewed in this light, the legislation (Taft-Hartley Act) expressed the federal policy that federal courts should enforce these agreements on behalf of or against labor organizations.

Textile Workers Union v. Lincoln Mills
353 US 448 (1957)

Petitioner-union entered into a collective bargaining agreement in 1953 with respondent employer, the agreement to run one year and from year to year thereafter, unless terminated on specified notices. The agreement provided that there would be no

strikes or work stoppages and that grievances would be handled pursuant to a specified procedure. The last step in the grievance procedure—a step that could be taken
by either party—was arbitration.

This controversy involves several grievances that concern work loads and work
assignments. The grievances were processed through the various steps in the grievance procedure and were finally denied by the employer. The union requested arbitration, and the employer refused. Thereupon the union brought this suit in the District
Court to compel arbitration.

The District Court concluded that it had jurisdiction and ordered the employer to
comply with the grievance arbitration provisions of the collective-bargaining agreement. The Court of Appeals reversed by a divided vote, 230 F2d 31. It held that,
although the District Court had jurisdiction to entertain the suit, the court had no
authority founded either in federal or state law to grant the relief. The case is here on
a petition for a writ of certiorari which we granted because of the importance of the
problem and the contrariety of views in the courts, 352 US 821.

The starting point of our inquiry is Section 301 of the Labor Management Relations
Act of 1947. . . .

There has been considerable litigation involving Section 301 and courts have construed it differently. There is one view that Section 301 (a) merely gives federal district
courts jurisdiction in controversies that involve labor organizations in industries affecting commerce, without regard to diversity of citizenship or the amount in controversy. Under that view Section 301 (a) would not be the source of substantive law; it
would neither supply federal law to resolve these controversies nor turn the federal
judges to state law for answers to the questions. Other courts—the overwhelming
number of them—hold that Section 301 (a) is more than jurisdictional—that it
authorizes federal courts to fashion a body of federal law for the enforcement of these
collective bargaining agreements and includes within that federal law specific performance of promises to arbitrate grievances under collective bargaining agreements.
. . . That is our construction of Section 301 (a) which means that the agreement to
arbitrate grievance disputes, contained in this collective bargaining agreement,
should be specifically enforced.

From the face of the Act it is apparent that Section 301 (a) and Section 301 (b) supplement one another. Section 301 (b) makes it possible for a labor organization,
representing employees in an industry affecting commerce, to sue and be sued as an
entity in the federal courts. Section 301 (b) in other words provides the procedural
remedy lacking at common law. Section 301 (a) certainly does something more than
that. Plainly, it supplies the basis upon which the federal district courts may take
jurisdiction and apply the procedural rule of Section 301 (b). The question is whether
Section 301 (a) is more than jurisdictional.

The legislative history of Section 301 is somewhat cloudy and confusing. But there
are a few shafts of light that illuminate our problem.

The bills, as they passed the House and the Senate, contained provisions which
would have made the failure to abide by an agreement to arbitrate an unfair labor
practice. S Rep No 105, 80th Cong, 1st Sess, pp. 20–21, 23; H R Rep No 245, 80th
Cong, 1st Sess, p. 21. This feature of the law was dropped in Conference. As the Conference's Report stated, "Once parties have made a collective bargaining contract,
the enforcement of that contract should be left to the usual processes of the law and
not to the National Labor Relations Board." H Conf Rep No 510, 80th Cong, 1st Sess,
p. 42.

Both the Senate and the House took pains to provide for "the usual processes of the law" by provisions which were the substantial equivalent of Section 301 (a) in its present form. Both the Senate Report and the House Report indicate a primary concern that unions as well as employees should be bound to collective bargaining contracts. But there was also a broader concern—a concern with a procedure for making such agreements enforceable in the courts by either party. At one point the Senate Report, supra, p. 15, states, "We feel that the aggrieved party should also have a right of action in the Federal courts. Such policy is completely in accord with the purpose of the Wagner Act which the Supreme Court declared was 'to compel employers to bargain collectively with their employees to the end that an employment contract, binding on both parties, should be made. . . .' "

Congress was also interested in promoting collective bargaining that ended with agreements not to strike. The Senate Report, supra, p. 16 states:

> If unions can break agreements with relative impunity, then such agreements do not tend to stabilize industrial relations. The execution of an agreement does not by itself promote industrial peace. The chief advantage which an employer can reasonably expect from a collective labor agreement is assurance of uninterrupted operation during the term of the agreement. Without some effective method of assuring freedom from economic warfare for the term of the agreement, there is little reason why an employer would desire to sign such a contract.
>
> Consequently, to encourage the making of agreements and to promote industrial peace through faithful performance by the parties, collective agreements affecting interstate commerce should be enforceable in the Federal courts. Our amendment would provide for suits by unions as legal entities and against unions as legal entites in the Federal Courts in disputes affecting commerce.

Thus collective bargaining contracts were made "equally binding and enforceable on both parties." Id., p. 15. As stated in the House Report, supra, p. 6, the new provision "makes labor organizations equally responsible with employers for contract violation and provides for suit by either against the other in the United States district courts." To repeat, the Senate Report, supra, p. 17, summed up the philosophy of Section 301 as follows: "Statutory recognition of the collective agreement as a valid, binding, and enforceable contract is a logical and necessary step. It will promote a higher degree of responsibility upon the parties to such agreements, and will thereby promote industrial peace."

Plainly the agreement to arbitrate grievance disputes is the *quid pro quo* for an agreement not to strike. Viewed in this light, the legislation does more than confer jurisdiction in the federal courts over labor organizations. It expresses a federal policy that federal courts should enforce these agreements on behalf of or against labor organizations and that industrial peace can be best obtained only in that way. . . .

It seems . . . clear to us that Congress adopted a policy which placed sanctions behind agreements to arbitrate grievance disputes, by implication rejecting the common-law rule, discussed in *Red Cross Line* v. *Atlantic Fruit Co.,* 264 US 109, against enforcement of executory agreements to arbitrate. We would undercut the Act and defeat its policy if we read Section 301 narrowly as only conferring jurisdiction over labor organizations.

The question then is, what is the substantive law to be applied in suits under Section 301 (a)? We conclude that the substantive law to apply in suits under Section 301 (a) is federal law which the courts must fashion from the policy of our national labor laws. See Mendelsohn, Enforceability of Arbitration Agreements Under Taft-Hartley Section 301, 66 Yale LJ 167. The Labor Management Relations Act expressly furnishes some substantive law. It points out what the parties may or may not do in certain situations. Other problems will lie in the penumbra of express statutory mandates. Some will lack express statutory sanction but will be solved by looking at the policy of the lesgislation and fashioning a remedy that will effectuate that policy. The range of judicial inventiveness will be determined by the nature of the problem. . . .

The judgment of the Court of Appeals is reversed and the cause is remanded to that court for proceedings in conformity with this opinion.

Reversed.

The Trilogy Cases

Three Supreme Court decisions involving the United Steelworkers Union and since referred to as *the trilogy* clarified the role of the courts in actions for specific performance of agreements to arbitrate disputes over contract interpretation. The rules laid down in these cases can be summarized as follows: (1) the role of the court is limited to determining whether the party seeking arbitration is making a claim which, on its face, is covered by the contract; (2) the courts are not to consider the merits of a grievance under the guise of interpreting the arbitration clause of a contract; (3) in suits for performance of an arbitration agreement, arbitration should be ordered unless it is clear beyond doubt that the dispute is not covered by the contract's arbitration clause—doubts should be resolved in favor of coverage; and (4) an arbitrator's award is enforceable under Section 301 of the Taft-Hartley Act. In suits for enforcement of such awards, the courts may not overrule the arbitrator simply because their interpretation of the contract is different from his. A court, however, may refuse to enforce an arbitration award that is not based on the collective-bargaining contract.

United Steelworkers of America v. American Manufacturing Company
363 US 564 (1960)

This suit was brought by petitioner union in the District Court to compel arbitration of a "grievance" that petitioner, acting for one Sparks, a union member, had filed with the respondent, Sparks' employer. The employer defended on the ground (1) that Sparks is estopped from making his claim because he had a few days previously settled a workmen's compensation claim against the Company on the basis that he was permanently partially disabled, (2) that Sparks is not physically able to do the work and (3) that this type of dispute is not arbitrable under the collective agreement in question.

The agreement provided that during its term there would be "no strike" unless the employer refused to abide by the decision of the arbitrator. The agreement sets out a detailed grievance procedure with a provision for arbitration. . . . of all disputes between the parties "as to the meaning, interpretation and application of the provisions of this agreement."

The agreement reserves to the management power to suspend or discharge any employee "for cause." It also contains a provision that the employer will employ and promote employees on the principle of seniority "where ability and efficiency are equal." Sparks left his work due to an injury and while off work brought an action for compensation benefits. The case was settled, Sparks' physician expressing the opinion that the injury made him 25 percent "permanently partially disabled." That was on September 9. Two weeks later the union filed a grievance which charged that Sparks was entitled to return to his job by virtue of the seniority provision of the collective bargaining agreement. Respondent refused to arbitrate and this action was brought. The District Court held that Sparks, having accepted the settlement on the basis of permanent partial disability, was estopped to claim any seniority or employment rights and granted a motion for summary judgment. The Court of Appeals affirmed, 264 F2d 624, for different reasons. After reviewing the evidence it held that the grievance is "a frivolous, patently baseless one, not subject to arbitration under the collective bargaining agreement." *Id.*, at 628. The case is here on a writ of certiorari, 361 US 881.

Section 203 (d) of the Labor Management Relations Act, 1947, states, "Final adjustment by a method agreed upon by the parties is hereby declared to be the desirable method for settlement of grievance disputes arising over the application or interpretation of an existing collective bargaining agreement. . . ." That policy can be effectuated only if the means chosen by the parties for settlement of their differences under a collective bargaining agreement is given full play.

. . . The collective agreement requires arbitration of claims that courts might be unwilling to entertain. In the context of the plant or industry the grievance may assume proportions of which judges are ignorant. Yet the agreement is to submit all grievances to arbitration, not merely those that a court may deem to be meritorious. There is no exception in the "no strike" clause and none therefore should be read into the grievance clause, since one is the *quid pro quo* for the other. The question is not whether in the mind of the court there is equity in the claim. Arbitration is a stabilizing influence only as it serves as a vehicle for handling any and all disputes that arise under the agreement.

The collective agreement calls for the submission of grievances in the categories which it describes, irrespective of whether a court may deem them to be meritorious. In our role of developing a meaningful body of law to govern the interpretation and enforcement of collective agreements, we think special heed should be given to the context in which collective bargaining agreements are negotiated and the purpose which they are intended to serve. . . . The function of the court is very limited when the parties have agreed to submit all questions of contract interpretation to the arbitrator. It is confined to ascertaining whether the party seeking arbitration is making a claim which on its face is governed by the contract. Whether the moving party is right or wrong is a question of contract interpretation for the arbitrator. In these circumstances, the moving party should not be deprived of the arbitrator's judgment when it was his judgment and all that it connotes that was bargained for.

The courts, therefore, have no business weighing the merits of the grievance, considering whether there is equity in a particular claim, or determining whether there is particular language in the written instrument which will support the claim. The agreement is to submit all grievances to arbitrators, not merely those which the courts will deem meritorious. The processing of even frivolous claims may have therapeutic values of which those who are not a part of the plant environment may be quite unaware. . . .

Reversed.

United Steelworkers of America v. Warrior and Gulf Navigation Company
363 US 574 (1960)

. . . A number of employees signed a grievance which petitioner presented to respondent, the grievance reading:

We are hereby protesting the Company's actions of arbitrarily and unreasonably contracting out work to other concerns, that could and previously has been performed by Company employees.

This practice becomes unreasonable, unjust and discriminatory in lieu (*sic*) of the fact that at present there are a number of employees that have been laid off for about one and one-half years or more for allegedly lack of work.

Confronted with these facts we charge that the Company is in violation of the contract by inducing a partial lockout, of a number of employees who would otherwise be working were it not for this unfair practice.

The collective agreement had both a "no strike" and a "no lockout" provision. It also had a grievance procedure which provided in relevant part as follows:

Issues which conflict with any Federal statute in its application as established by Court procedure or matters which are strictly a function of management shall not be subject to arbitration under this section.

Should differences arise between the Company and the Union or its members employed by the Company as to the meaning and application of the provisions of this Agreement, or should any local trouble of any kind arise, there shall be no suspension of work on account of such differences but an earnest effort shall be made to settle such differences immediately in the following manner:

A. For Maintenance Employees:
  First, between the aggrieved employees and the Foreman involved;
  Second, between a member or members of the Grievance Committee designated by the Union, and the Foreman and Master Mechanic. . . .
  Fifth, if agreement has not been reached the matter shall be referred to an impartial umpire for decision. . . . The decision of the umpire shall be final.

Settlement of this grievance was not had and the respondent refused arbitration. This suit was then commenced by the union to compel it. . . .

We held in *Textile Workers* v. *Lincoln Mills,* 353 US 448, that a grievance arbitration provision in a collective agreement could be enforced by reason of 301 (a) of the Labor Management Relation Act and that the policy to be applied in enforcing this type of arbitration was that reflected in our national labor laws. The present federal policy is to promote industrial stabilization through the collective bargaining agreement. A major factor in achieving industrial peace is the inclusion of a provision for arbitration of grievances in the collective bargaining agreement.

. . . The grievance machinery under a collective bargaining agreement is at the very heart of the system of industrial self-government. Arbitration is the means of solving the unforeseeable by molding a system of private law for all the problems which may arise and to provide for their solution in a way which will generally accord with the variant needs and desires of the parties. The processing of disputes through the grievance machinery is actually a vehicle by which meaning and content are given to the collective bargaining agreement.

Apart from matters that the parties specifically exclude, all of the questions on which the parties disagree must therefore come within the scope of the grievance and arbitration provisions of the collective agreement. The settlement of disputes by the parties through the machinery of arbitration, the judicial inquiry under 301 must be strictly confined to the question of whether the reluctant party did agree to arbitrate the grievance or did agree to give the arbitrator power to make the award he made. An order to arbitrate the particular grievance should not be denied unless it may be said with positive assurance that the arbitration clause is not susceptible of an interpretation that covers the asserted dispute. Doubts should be resolved in favor of coverage.

We do not agree with the lower courts that contracting out grievances were necessarily excepted from the grievance procedure of this agreement. To be sure the agreement provides that "matters which are strictly a function of management shall not be subject to arbitration." But it goes on to say that if "differences" arise or if "any local trouble of any kind" arises, the grievance procedure shall be applicable.

Collective bargaining agreements regulate or restrict the exercise of management functions; they do not oust management from the performance of them. Management hires and fires, pays and promotes, supervises and plans. All these are part of its functions, and absent a collective bargaining agreement, it may be exercised freely except as limited by public law and by the willingness of employees to work under the particular unilaterally imposed conditions. A collective bargaining agreement may treat only with certain specific practices, leaving the rest to management but subject to the possibility of work stoppages. When, however, an absolute no-strike clause is included in the agreement, then in a very real sense everything that management does is subject to the agreement, for either management is prohibited or limited in the action it takes or, if not, grievance procedure is, in other words, a part of the continuous collective bargaining process. It, rather than the strike, is the terminal point of a disagreement.

The labor arbitrator performs functions which are not normal to the courts; the considerations which help him fashion judgments may indeed be foreign to the competence of the courts. . . .

The labor arbitrator's source of law is not confined to the express provisions of the contract, as the industrial common law—the practices of the industry and the shop—is equally a part of the collective bargaining agreement although not expressed in it. The labor arbitrator is usually chosen because of the parties' confidence in his knowledge of the common law of the shop and their trust in his personal judgment to bring to bear considerations which are not expressed in the contract as criteria for judgment. The parties expect that his judgment of a particular grievance will reflect not only what the contract says but, insofar as the collective bargaining agreement permits, such factors as the effect upon productivity of a particular result, its consequences to the morale of the shop, his judgment whether tensions will be heightened or diminished. . . . The ablest judge cannot be expected to bring the same experience and competence to bear upon the determination of a grievance because he cannot be similarly informed.

The Congress, however, has by 301 of the Labor Management Relations Act, assigned the courts the duty of determining whether the reluctant party has breached his promise to arbitrate. For arbitration is a matter of contract and a party cannot be required to submit to arbitration any dispute which he has not agreed so to submit. Yet, to be consistent with congressional policy in favor of it is protected from interference by strikes. This comprehensive reach of the collective bargaining agreement does not mean, however, that the language, "strictly a function of management," has no meaning.

"Strictly a function of management" might be thought to refer to any practice of management in which, under particular circumstances prescribed by the agreement, it is permitted to indulge. But if the courts, in order to determine arbitrability, were allowed to determine what is permitted and what is not, the arbitration clause would be swallowed up by the exception. . . .

Accordingly, "strictly a function of management" must be interpreted as referring only to that over which the contract gives management complete control and unfettered discretion. Respondent claims that the contracting out of work falls within this category. . . . A specific collective bargaining agreement may exclude contracting out from the grievance procedure. Or a written collateral agreement may make clear that contracting out was not a matter for arbitration. Here, however, there is no such provision. Nor is there any showing that the parties designed the phrase "strictly a function of management" to encompass any and all forms of contracting out. In the absence of any express provision excluding a particular grievance from arbitration, we think only the most forceful evidence of a purpose to exclude the claim from arbitration can prevail, particularly where, as here, the exclusion clause is vague and the arbitration clause quite broad. Since any attempt by a court to infer such a purpose necessarily comprehends the merits, the courts should view with suspicion an attempt to persuade it to become entangled in the construction of the substantive provisions of a labor agreement . . . when the alternative is to utilize the services of an arbitrator.

The grievance alleged that the contracting out was a violation of the collective bargaining agreement. There was, therefore, a dispute "as to the meaning and application of the provisions of this agreement" which the parties had agreed would be determined by arbitration.

. . . Whether contracting out in the present case violated the agreement is the question. It is a question for the arbiter, not for the courts.

Reversed.

United Steelworkers of America v. Enterprise Wheel & Car Corporation
363 US 593 (1960)

Petitioner Union and the respondent during the period relevant here had a collective bargaining agreement which provided that any differences "as to the meaning and application of the agreement should be submitted to arbitration and that the arbitrator's decision should be final and binding." The agreement stated:

Should it be determined by the Company or by an arbitrator in accordance with the grievance procedure that an employee has been suspended unjustly or discharged in violation of the provisions of this agreement, the Company shall reinstate the employee and pay full compensation at the employee's regular rate of pay for the time lost.

The Agreement also provided:

. . . It is understood and agreed that neither party will institute civil suits or legal proceedings against the other for alleged violation of any of the provisions of this labor contract; instead all disputes will be settled in the manner outlined in this Article III—Adjustment of Grievances.

A group of employees left their jobs in protest against the discharge of one employee. A union official advised them at once to return to work. An official of respondent at their request gave them permission and then rescinded it. The next day they were told they did not have a job any more "until this thing was settled one way or the other."

A grievance was filed; and when finally refused to arbitrate, this suit was brought for specific enforcement of the arbitration provisions of the agreement. The District Court ordered arbitration. The arbitrator found that the discharge of the men was not justified, though their conduct, he said, was improper. In his view the facts warranted at most a suspension of the men for 10 days each. After their discharge and before the arbitration award the collective bargaining agreement had expired. The union, however, continued to represent the workers at the plant. The arbitrator rejected the contention that expiration of the agreement barred reinstatement of the employees. He held that the provision of the agreement above quoted imposed an unconditional obligation on the employer. He awarded reinstatement with back pay, minus pay for a 10-day suspension and such sums as these employees received from other employment.

Respondent refused to comply with the award. Petitioner moved the District Court for enforcement. The District Court directed respondent to comply. 168 F Supp 308. The Court of Appeals, while agreeing that the District Court had jurisdiction to enforce an arbitration award under a collective bargaining agreement, held that the failure of the award to specify the amounts to be deducted from back pay rendered the award unenforceable. That defect, it agreed, could be remedied by requiring the parties to complete the arbitration. It went on to hold, however, that an award for back pay subsequent to the date of termination of the collective bargaining agreement could not be enforced. It also held that requirement for reinstatement of the discharged employees was likewise unenforceable because the collective bargaining agreement had expired. 269 F 2d 327. We granted certiorari. 361 US 929.

The refusal of courts to review the merits of an arbitration award is the proper approach to arbitration under collective bargaining agreements. The federal policy of settling labor disputes by arbitration would be undermined if courts had the final say on the merits of the awards. . . .

. . . The question of interpretation of the collective bargaining agreement is a question for the arbitrator. It is the arbitrator's construction which was bargained for; and so far as the arbitrator's decision concerns construction of the contract, the courts have no business overruling him because their interpretation of the contract is different from his.

We agree with the Court of Appeals that the judgment of the District Court should be modified so that the amounts due the parties may be definitely determined by arbitration. In all other respects we think the judgment of the District Court should be affirmed. . . .

The National Labor Relations Board and Arbitration

While the trilogy cases enhanced the legal status of the arbitration process, they did not provide direct guidance to the National Labor Relations Board, which administers the National Labor Relations Act as amended. As noted at an earlier point, in certain grievance disputes, the union or the management may pursue a remedy either by filing an unfair practice charge through the NLRB or by taking the dispute to arbitration. Over time, the

NLRB has moved in the direction of deferral to arbitration, affirming a federal policy of favoring voluntary settlement of labor disputes through arbitral processes, as the Supreme Court did in the trilogy cases.

A comprehensive statement of this policy, which includes a review of earlier relevant Board decisions, is provided by the NLRB decision in the *Collyer* case. The NLRB Trial Examiner had found that the Company committed an unfair labor practice when it made certain unilateral changes in wages and working conditions, thus violating the Company-Union Agreement. Among other contentions, the Company argued that any of its actions in excess of contractual authorization should properly have been remedied by grievance and arbitration proceeding as provided in the Contract.

Citing an earlier Board ruling, the NLRB gave the following rationale for deferral to arbitration at the discretion of the Board:

> There is no question that the Board is not precluded from adjudicating unfair labor practices even though they might have been the subject of an arbitration proceeding and award. Section 10(a) of the Act expressly makes this plain and the courts have uniformly so held. However, it is equally well established that the Board has considerable discretion to respect an arbitration award and decline to exercise its authority over alleged unfair practices if to do so will serve the fundamental aims of the Act.

Collyer Insulated Wire and Local Union 1098, International Brotherhood of Electrical Workers, 192 NLRB 150, August 20, 1971

. . . We find merit in Repondent's (Employer's) exceptions that because this dispute in its entirety arises from the contract between the parties, and from the parties' relationship under the contract, it ought to be resolved in the manner which that contract prescribes. We conclude that the Board is vested with authority to withhold its processes in this case, and that the contract here made available a quick and fair means for the resolution of this dispute including, if appropriate, a fully effective remedy for any breach of contract which occurred. We conclude, in sum, that our obligation to advance the purposes of the Act is best discharged by the dismissal of this complaint.

In our view, disputes such as these can better be resolved by arbitrators with special skill and experience in deciding matters arising under established bargaining relationships than by the application by this Board of a particular provision of our statute. The necessity for such special skill and expertise is apparent upon examination of the issues arising from Respondent's actions with respect to the operator's rates, the skill factor increase, and the reassignment of duties relating to the worm gear removal. . . . The determination of these issues, we think, is best left to discussions in the grievance procedure by the parties who negotiated the applicable provisions or, if such discussions do not resolve them, then to an arbitrator chosen under the agreement and authorized by it to resolve such issues.

The Board's authority, in its discretion, to defer to the arbitration process has never been questioned by the court of appeals or the Supreme Court. Although Section 10(a) of the Act clearly vests the Board with jurisdiction over conduct which constitutes a violation of the provisions of Section 8, notwithstanding the existence of methods of "adjustment or prevention that might be established by agreement," nothing in the Act intimates that the Board must exercise jurisdiction where such methods exist. On the contrary in *Carey* v. *Westinghouse Electric Corporation,* 375 US 261, 271 (1964), the Court indicated that it favors our deference to such agreed methods by quoting at length and with obvious approval the following language from the Board's decision in *International Harvester Co.:*

> There is no question that the Board is not precluded from adjudicating unfair labor practice charges even though they might have been the subject of an arbitration proceeding and award. Section 10(a) of the Act expressly makes this plain, and the courts have uniformly so held. However, it is equally well established that the Board has considerable discretion to respect an arbitration award and decline to exercise its authority over alleged unfair labor practices if to do so will serve the fundamental aims of the Act.
>
> The Act, as has repeatedly been stated, is primarily designed to promote industrial peace and stability by encouraging the practice and procedure of collective bargaining. Experience has demonstrated that collective bargaining agreements that provide for final and binding arbitration of grievance and disputes arising thereunder, "as a substitute for industrial strife," contribute significantly to the attainment of this statutory objective.

In an earlier case, *Smith* v. *Evening News Assn.,* 337 US 195, the Supreme Court had likewise observed that, "the Board has, on prior occasions declined to exercise its jurisdiction to deal with unfair labor practices in circumstances where, in its judgment, federal labor policy would best be served by leaving the parties to other processes of law." . . .

The question whether the Board should withhold its process arises, of course, only when a set of facts may present not only an alleged violation of the Act but also an alleged breach of the collective-bargaining agreement subject to arbitration. Thus, this case, like each such case, compels an accommodation between, on the one hand, the statutory policy favoring the fullest use of collective bargaining and the arbitral process and, on the other, the statutory policy reflected by Congress' grant to the Board of exclusive jurisdiction to prevent unfair labor practices.

We address the accommodation required here with the benefit of the Board's full history of such accommodations in similar cases. From the start the Board has, case by case, both asserted jurisdiction and declined, as the balance was struck on particular facts and at various stages in the long ascent of collective bargaining to its present state of wide acceptance. Those cases reveal that the Board has honored the distinction between two broad but distinct classes of cases, those in which there has been an arbitral award, and those in which there has not.

In the former class of cases the Board has long given hospitable acceptance to the arbitral process. In *Timken Roller Bearing Company,* 70 NLRB 500, the Board refrained from exercising jurisdiction, in deference to an arbitrator's decision, despite the fact that the Board would otherwise have found that an unfair labor practice had been committed. The Board explained "It would not comport with the sound exercise of our administrative discretion to permit the Union to seek redress under the Act after having initiated arbitration proceedings which, at the Union's request, resulted in a determination upon the merits." The Board's policy was refined in *Spielberg Manufacturing Company,* 112 NLRB 1080, where the Board established the now settled rule that it would limit its inquiry, in the presence of an arbitrator's award, to whether the procedures were fair and the results not repugnant to the Act.

In those cases in which no award has issued, the Board's guidelines have been less clear. At times the Board has dealt with the unfair labor practice, and at other times it has left the parties to their contract remedies. In an early case, *Consolidated Air-*

craft Corporation, 47 NLRB 694, the Board, after pointing out that the charging party had failed to utilize the grievance procedures, stated:

> It will not effectuate the statutory policy of encouraging the practice and procedure of collective bargaining for the Board to assume the role of policing collective contracts between employers and labor organizations by attempting to decide whether disputes as to the meaning and administration of such contracts constitute unfair labor practices under the Act. On the contrary we believe that parties to collective contracts would thereby be encouraged to abandon their efforts to dispose of disputes under the contracts through collective bargaining or through settlement procedures mutually agreed upon by them, and to remit the interpretation and administration of their contracts to the Board. We therefore do not deem it wise to exercise our jurisdiction in such a case, where the parties have not exhausted their rights and remedies under the contract as to which this dispute has arisen.

The Board has continued to apply the doctrine enunciated in *Consolidated Aircraft,* though not consistently.

Joseph Schlitz Brewing Company, 175 NLRB 23, is the most significant recent case in which the Board has exercised its discretion to defer. The underlying dispute in *Schlitz* was strikingly similar to the one now before us. In *Schlitz* the respondent employer decided to halt its production line during employee breaks. That decision was a departure from an established practice of maintaining extra employees, relief men, to fill in for regular employees during breaktime. The change resulted in, among other things, elimination of the relief man job classification. The change elicited a union protest leading to an unfair labor practice proceeding in which the Board ruled that the case should be "left for resolution within the framework of the agreed upon settlement procedures." . . .

The circumstances of this case, no less than those in *Schlitz,* weigh heavily in favor of deferral. Here, as in *Schlitz,* this dispute arises within the confines of a long and productive collective bargaining relationship. The parties before us have, for 35 years, mutually and voluntarily resolved the conflicts which inhere in collective bargaining. Here, as there, no claim is made of enmity by Respondent to employees' exercise of protected rights. Respondent here has credibly asserted its willingness to resort to arbitration under a clause providing for arbitration in a very broad range of disputes and unquestionably broad enough to embrace this dispute.

Finally, here, as in *Schlitz,* the dispute is one eminently well suited to resolution by arbitration. The contract and its meaning in present circumstances lie at the center of this dispute. In contrast, the Act and its policies become involved only if it is determined that the agreement between the parties, examined in the light of its negotiating history and the practices of the parties thereunder, did not sanction Respondent's right to make the disputed changes, subject to review if sought by the Union, under the contractually prescribed procedure. That threshold determination is clearly within the expertise of a mutually agreed-upon arbitrator. In this regard we note especially that here, as in *Schlitz,* the dispute between the parties is the very stuff of labor contract arbitration. The competence of a mutually selected arbitrator to decide the issue and fashion an appropriate remedy if needed, can no longer be gainsaid. . . .

We are not compelling any party to agree to arbitrate disputes arising during a contract term, but are merely giving full effect to their voluntary agreements to submit all such disputes to arbitration, rather than permitting such agreements to be sidestepped and permitting the substitution of our processes, a forum not contemplated by their own agreement.

Nor are we "stripping" any party of "statutory rights." The courts have long recognized that an industrial relations dispute may involve conduct which, at least arguably, may contravene both the collective agreement and our statute. When the parties have contractually committed themselves to mutually agreeable procedures for resolving their disputes during the period of the contract, we are of the view that those procedures should be afforded full opportunity to function. The long and successful functioning of grievance and arbitration procedures suggests to us that in the overwhelming majority of cases, the utilization of such means will resolve the underlying dispute and make it unnecessary for either party to follow the more formal and sometimes lengthy combination of administrative and judicial litigation provided for under our statute. At the same time, by reservation of jurisdiction, we guarantee that there will be no sacrifice of statutory rights if the parties' own processes fail to function in a manner consistent with the dictates of our law. . . .

Equal Employment Opportunity and Arbitration

In view of the deferral by both the Supreme Court and the National Labor Relations Board to private arbitration of grievance disputes, the Court's 1974 ruling in *Alexander* v. *Gardner-Denver Company* was something of a surprise to students and practitioners in the area of industrial relations law. Reversing the lower courts, the Supreme Court held in *Gardner-Denver* that an employee's statutory right to trial *de novo,* under Title VII of the Civil Rights Act of 1964, was not foreclosed by prior submission of a claim to arbitration under a nondiscrimination clause of a collective-bargaining agreement. In so ruling, the Court recognized a difference between the law of the shop, a contract right interpreted through arbitration, and the law of the land, which placed final responsibility for enforcement of Title VII in the federal courts.

Alexander v. Gardner-Denver
415 US 36 (1974)

Mr. Justice Powell delivered the opinion of the Court.

This case concerns the proper relationship between federal courts and the grievance-arbitration machinery of collective-bargaining agreements in the resolution and enforcement of an individual's right to equal employment opportunities under Title VII of the Civil Rights Act of 1964. Specifically, we must decide under what circumstances, if any, an employee's statutory right to a trial *de novo* under Title VII may be foreclosed by prior submission of his claim to final arbitration under the nondiscrimination clause of a collective-bargaining agreement.

I

In May 1966, petitioner Harrell Alexander, Sr., a black, was hired by respondent Gardner-Denver Company (the "company") to perform maintenance work at the company's plant in Denver, Colorado. In June 1968, petitioner was awarded a trainee position as a drill operator. He remained at that job until his discharge from employment on September 29, 1969. The company informed petitioner that he was being discharged for producing too many defective or unusable parts that had to be scrapped.

On October 1, 1969, petitioner filed a grievance under the collective-bargaining agreement in force between the company and petitioner's union, Local No. 3029 of the United Steelworkers of America (the "union"). The grievance stated: "I feel I have been unjustly discharged and ask that I be reinstated with full seniority and pay." No explicit claim of racial discrimination was made.

Under Art. 4 of the collective-bargaining agreement, the company retained "the right to hire, suspend or discharge [employees] for proper cause." Art. 5, 2 provided, however, that "there shall be no discrimination against any employee on account of race, color, religion, sex, national origin, or ancestry," and Art. 23, 6(a) stated that "[n]o employee will be discharged, suspended or given a written warning notice except for just cause." The agreement also contained a broad arbitration clause covering "differences aris[ing] between the Company and the Union as to the meaning and application of the provisions of this Agreement" and "any trouble aris[ing] in the plant." Disputes were to be submitted to a multi-step grievance procedure, the first four steps of which involved negotiations between the company and the union. If the dispute remained unresolved, it was to be remitted to compulsory arbitration. The company and the union were to select and pay the arbitrator, and his decision was to be "final and binding upon the Company, the Union, and any employee or employees involved." The agreement further provided that "[t]he arbitrator shall not amend, take away, add to, or change any of the provisions of this Agreement, and the arbitrator's decision must be based solely on an interpretation of the provisions of this Agreement." The parties also agreed that there "shall be no suspension of work" over disputes covered by the grievance-arbitration clause.

The union processed petitioner's grievance through the above machinery. In the final prearbitration step, petitioner raised, apparently for the first time, the claim that his discharge resulted from racial discrimination. The company rejected all of petitioner's claims, and the grievance proceeded to arbitration. Prior to the arbitration hearing, however, petitioner filed a charge of racial discrimination with the Colorado Civil Rights Commission, which referred the complaint to the Equal Employment Opportunity Commission on November 5, 1969.

At the arbitration hearing on November 20, 1969, petitioner testified that his discharge was the result of racial discrimination and informed the arbitrator that he had filed a charge with the Colorado Commission because he "could not rely on the union." The union introduced a letter in which petitioner stated that he was "knowledgeable that in the same plant others have scrapped an equal amount and sometimes in excess, but by all logical reasoning I . . . have been the target of preferential discriminatory treatment." The union representative also testified that the company's usual practice was to transfer unsatisfactory trainee drill operators back to their former positions.

On December 30, 1969, the arbitrator ruled that petitioner had been "discharged for just cause." He made no reference to petitioner's claim of racial discrimination. The arbitrator stated that the union had failed to produce evidence of a practice of transferring rather than discharging trainee drill operators who accumulated excessive scrap, but he suggested that the company and the union confer on whether such an arrangement was feasible in the present case.

On July 25, 1970, the Equal Employment Opportunity Commission determined that there was not reasonable cause to believe that a violation of Title VII of the Civil Rights Act of 1964 had occurred. The Commission later notified petitioner of his right to institute a civil action in federal court within 30 days. Petitioner then filed the present action in the United States District Court for the District of Colorado, alleging that his discharge resulted from a racially discriminatory employment practice in violation of paragraph 703 (a) (1) of the Act.

The District Court granted respondent's motion for summary judgment and dismissed the action. 346 F Supp 1012 (1971). The court found that the claim of racial discrimination had been submitted to the arbitrator and resolved adversely to petitioner. It then held that petitioner, having voluntarily elected to pursue his grievance to final arbitration under the nondiscrimination clause of the collective-bargaining agreement, was bound by the arbitral decision and thereby precluded from suing his employer under Title VII. The Court of Appeals for the Tenth Circuit affirmed *per curiam* on the basis of the District Court's opinion. 466 F 2d 1209 (1972).

We granted petitioner's application for certiorari. 410 US 925 (1973).

We reverse.

II

Congress enacted Title VII of the Civil Rights Act of 1964 to assure equality of employment opportunities by eliminating those practices and devices that discriminate on the basis of race, color, religion, sex, or national origin. Cooperation and voluntary compliance were selected as the preferred means for achieving this goal. To this end, Congress created the Equal Employment Opportunity Commission and established a procedure whereby existing state and local equal employment opportunity agencies, as well as the Commission, would have an opportunity to settle disputes through conference, conciliation, and persuasion before the aggrieved party was permitted to file a lawsuit. In the Equal Employment Opportunity Act of 1972, Congress amended Title VII to provide the Commission with further authority to investigate individual charges of discrimination, to promote voluntary compliance with the requirements of Title VII, and to institute civil actions against employers or unions named in a discrimination charge.

Even in its amended form, however, Title VII does not provide the Commission with direct powers of enforcement. The Commission cannot adjudicate claims or impose administrative sanctions. Rather, final responsibility for enforcement of Title VII is vested with federal courts. The Act authorizes courts to issue injunctive relief and to order such affirmative action as may be appropriate to remedy the effects of unlawful employment practices. Courts retain these broad remedial powers despite a Commission finding of no reasonable cause to believe that the Act has been violated. *McDonnell Douglas Corp.* v. *Green,* 411 US at 798–799. Taken together, these provisions make plain that federal courts have been assigned plenary powers to secure compliance with Title VII.

In addition to reposing ultimate authority in federal courts, Congress gave private individuals a significant role in the enforcement process of Title VII. Individual grievants usually initiate the Commission's investigatory and conciliatory procedures. And although the 1972 amendment to Title VII empowers the Commission to bring its own actions, the private right of action remains an essential means of obtaining judicial enforcement of Title VII. In such cases, the private litigant not only redresses his own injury but also vindicates the important congressional policy against discriminatory employment practices.

Pursuant to this statutory scheme, petitioner initiated the present action for judicial consideration of his rights under Title VII. The District Court and the Court of Appeals held, however, that petitioner was bound by the prior arbitral decision and had no right to sue under Title VII. Both Courts evidently thought that this result was dictated by notions of election of remedies and waiver and by the federal policy favoring arbitration of labor disputes, as enunciated by this Court in *Textile Workers Union* v. *Lincoln Mills,* 353 US 448 (1957), and the *Steelworkers Trilogy.* See also *Boys Markets, Inc.* v. *Retail Clerks Union,* 398 US 235 (1970); *Gateway Coal Co.* v. *United Mine Workers of America, et al.,* US (1974). We disagree.

III

Title VII does not speak expressly to the relationship between federal courts and the grievance-arbitration machinery of collective-bargaining agreements. It does, however, vest federal courts with plenary powers to enforce the statutory requirements, and it specifies with precision the jurisdictional prerequisites that an individual must satisfy before he is entitled to institute a lawsuit. In the present case, these prerequisites were met when petitioner (1) filed timely a charge of employment discrimination with the Commission, and (2) received and acted upon the Commission's statutory notice of the right to sue. There is no suggestion in the statutory scheme that a prior arbitral decision either forecloses an individual's right to sue or divests federal courts of jurisdiction.

In addition, legislative enactments in this area have long evinced a general intent to accord parallel or overlapping remedies against discrimination. In the Civil Rights Act of 1964, Congress indicated that it considered the policy against discrimination to be of the "highest priority." *Newman* v. *Piggie Park Enterprises, Inc.,* 390 US at 402. Consistent with this view, Title VII provides for consideration of employment-discrimination claims in several forums. And, in general, submission of a claim to one forum does not preclude a later submission to another. Moreover, the legislative history of Title VII manifests a congressional intent to allow an individual to pursue independently his rights under both Title VII and other applicable state and federal statutes. The clear inference is that Title VII was designed to supplement, rather than supplant, existing laws and institutions relating to employment discrimination. In sum, Title VII's purpose and procedures strongly suggest that an individual does not forfeit his private cause of action if he first pursues his grievance to final arbitration under the nondiscrimination clause of a collective-bargaining agreement.

In reaching the opposite conclusion, the District Court relied in part on the doctrine of election of remedies. That doctrine, which refers to situations where an individual pursues remedies that are legally or factually inconsistent, has no application in the present context. In submitting his grievance to arbitration, an employee seeks to vindicate his contractual right under a collective-bargaining agreement. By contrast, in filing a lawsuit under Title VII, an employee asserts independent statutory rights accorded by Congress. The distinctly separate nature of these contractual and statutory rights is not vitiated merely because both were violated as a result of the same factual occurrence. And certainly no inconsistency results from permitting both rights to be enforced in their respectively appropriate forums. The resulting scheme is somewhat analogous to the procedure under the National Labor Relations Act, as amended, where disputed transactions may implicate both contractual and statutory rights. Where the statutory right underlying a particular claim may not be abridged by contractual agreement, the Court has recognized that consideration of the claim by the arbitrator as a contractual dispute under the collective-bargaining agreement does not preclude subsequent consideration of the claim by the National Labor Relations Board, as an unfair labor practice charge or as a petition for clarification of the union's representation certificate under the Act. *Carey* v. *Westinghouse Corp.,* 375

US 261 (1964). Cf. *Smith* v. *Evening News Assn.*, 371 US 195 (1962). There, as here, the relationship between the forums is complementary since consideration of the claim by both forums may promote the policies underlying each. Thus, the rationale behind the election of remedies doctrine cannot support the decision below.

We are also unable to accept the proposition that petitioner waived his cause of action under Title VII. To begin, we think it clear that there can be no prospective waiver of an employee's right under Title VII. It is true, of course, that a union may waive certain statutory rights related to collective activity, such as the right to strike. *Mastro Plastics Corp.* v. *NLRB*, 350 US 270 (1956); *Boys Markets, Inc.* v. *Retail Clerks Union*, 398 US 235 (1970). These rights are conferred on employees collectively to foster the processes of bargaining and properly may be exercised or relinquished by the union as collective-bargaining agent to obtain economic benefits for unit members. Title VII, on the other hand, stands on plainly different ground; it concerns not majoritarian processes, but an individual's right to equal employment opportunities. Title VII's strictures are absolute and represent a congressional command that each employee be free from discriminatory practices. Of necessity, the rights conferred can form no part of the collective-bargaining process since waiver of these rights would defeat the paramount congressional purpose behind Title VII. In these circumstances, an employee's rights under Title VII are not susceptible to prospective waiver. See *Wilko* v. *Swan*, 346 US 427 (1953).

The actual submission of petitioner's grievance to arbitration in the present case does not alter the situation. Although presumably an employee may waive his cause of action under Title VII as part of a voluntary settlement, mere resort to the arbitral forum to enforce contractual rights constitutes no such waiver. Since an employee's rights under Title VII may not be waived prospectively, existing contractual rights and remedies against discrimination must result from other concessions already made by the union as part of the economic bargain struck with the employer. It is settled law that no additional concession may be exacted from any employee as the price for enforcing those rights. *J.I. Case Co.* v. *Labor Board*, 321 US 332, 338–339 (1944).

Moreover, a contractual right to submit a claim to arbitration is not displaced simply because Congress also has provided a statutory right against discrimination. Both rights have legally independent origins and are equally available to the aggrieved employee. This point becomes apparent through consideration of the role of the arbitrator in the system of industrial self-government. As the proctor of the bargain, the arbitrator's task is to effectuate the intent of the parties. His source of authority is the collective-bargaining agreement, and he must interpret and apply that agreement in accordance with the "industrial common law of the shop" and the various needs and desires of the parties. The arbitrator, however, has no general authority to invoke public laws that conflict with the bargain between the parties:

> (A)n arbitrator is confined to interpretation and application of the collective bargaining agreement; he does not sit to dispense his own brand of industrial justice. He may of course look for guidance from many sources, yet his award is legitimate only so long as it draws its essence from the collective bargaining agreement. When the arbitrator's works manifest an infidelity to this obligation, courts have no choice but to refuse enforcement of the award. (*United Steelworkers of America* v. *Enterprise Wheel & Car Corp.*, 363 US at 597.)

If an arbitral decision is based "solely on the arbitrator's view of the requirements of enacted legislation," rather than on an interpretation of the collective-bargaining agreement, the arbitrator has "exceeded the scope of his submission," and the award will not be enforced. Thus the arbitrator has authority to resolve only questions of contractual rights, and this authority remains regardless whether certain contractual rights are similar to, or duplicative of, the substantive rights secured by Title VII.

IV

The District Court and the Court of Appeals reasoned that to permit an employee to have his claim considered in both the arbitral and judicial forums would be unfair since this would mean that the employer, but not the employee, was bound by the arbitral award. In the District Court's words, it could not "accept a philosophy which gives the employee two strings to his bow when the employer has only one," 346 F Supp at 1019. This argument mistakes the effect of Title VII. Under the *Steelworkers Trilogy,* an arbitral decision is final and binding on the employer and employee, and judicial review is limited as to both. But in instituting an action under Title VII, the employee is not seeking review of the arbitrator's decision. Rather, he is asserting a statutory right independent of the arbitration process. An employer does not have "two strings to his bow" with respect to an arbitral decision for the simple reason that Title VII does not provide employers with a cause of action against employees. An employer cannot be the victim of discriminatory employment practices. *Oubichon* v. *North American Rockwell Corp.,* 482 F 2d 569, 573 (CA9 1973).

The District Court and the Court of Appeals also thought that to permit a later resort to the judicial forum would undermine substantially the employer's incentive to arbitrate and would "sound the death knell for arbitration clauses in labor contracts," 346 F Supp at 1019. Again, we disagree. The primary incentive for an employer to enter into an arbitration agreement is the union's reciprocal promise not to strike. As the Court stated in *Boys Markets, Inc.* v. *Retail Clerks Union,* 398 US 235, 248 (1970), "a no strike obligation, express or implied, is the *quid pro quo* for an undertaking by an employer to submit grievance disputes to the process of arbitration." It is not unreasonable to assume that most employers will regard the benefits derived from a no-strike pledge as outweighing whatever costs may result from according employees an arbitral remedy against discrimination in addition to their judicial remedy under Title VII. Indeed, the severe consequences of a strike may make an arbitration clause almost essential from both the employees' and the employer's perspective. Moreover, the grievance-arbitration machinery of the collective-bargaining agreement remains a relatively inexpensive and expeditious means for resolving a wide range of disputes, including claims of discriminatory employment practices. Where the collective-bargaining agreement contains a nondiscrimination clause similar to Title VII, and where arbitral procedures are fair and regular, arbitration may well produce a settlement satisfactory to both employer and employee. An employer thus has an incentive to make available the conciliatory and therapeutic processes of arbitration which may satisfy an employee's perceived need to resort to the judicial forum, thus saving the employer the expense and aggravation associated with a lawsuit. For similar reasons, the employee also has a strong incentive to arbitrate grievances, and arbitration may often eliminate those misunderstandings or discriminatory practices that might otherwise precipitate resort to the judicial forum.

V

Respondent contends that even if a preclusion rule is not adopted, federal courts should defer to arbitral decisions on discrimination claims where: (i) the claim was before the arbitrator; (ii) the collective-bargaining agreement prohibited the form of discrimination charged in the suit under Title VII; and (iii) the arbitrator has authority to rule on the claim and to fashion a remedy. Under respondent's proposed rule, a court would grant summary judgment and dismiss the employee's action if the above conditions were met. The rule's obvious consequence in the present case would be to deprive the petitioner of his statutory right to attempt to establish his claim in a federal court.

At the outset, it is apparent that a deferral rule would be subject to many of the objections applicable to a preclusion rule. The purpose and procedures of Title VII indicate that Congress intended federal courts to exercise final responsibility for enforcement of Title VII; deferral to arbitral decisions would be inconsistent with that goal. Furthermore, we have long recognized that "the choice of forums inevitably affects the scope of the substantive right to be vindicated." *U.S. Bulk Carriers* v. *Arguelles*, 400 US 358, 359–360 (1971) (Harlan, J., concurring). Respondent's deferral rule is necessarily premised on the assumption that arbitral processes are commensurate with judicial processes and that Congress impliedly intended federal courts to defer to arbitral decisions on Title VII issues. We deem this supposition unlikely.

Arbitral procedures, while well suited to the resolution of contractual disputes, make arbitration a comparatively inappropriate forum for the final resolution of rights created by Title VII. This conclusion rests first on the special role of the arbitrator, whose task is to effectuate the intent of the parties rather than the requirements of enacted legislation. Where the collective-bargaining agreement conflicts with Title VII, the arbitration must follow the agreement. To be sure, the tension between contractual and statutory objectives may be mitigated where a collective-bargaining agreement contains provisions facially similar to those of Title VII. But other facts may still render arbitral processes comparatively inferior to judicial processes in the protection of Title VII rights. Among these is the fact that the specialized competence of arbitrators pertains primarily to the law of the shop, not the law of the land. *United Steelworkers of America* v. *Warrior & Gulf Navigation Co.*, 363 US 574, at 581–583. Parties usually choose an arbitrator because they trust his knowledge and judgment concerning the demands and norms of industrial relations. On the other hand, the resolution of statutory or constitutional issues is a primary responsibility of courts, and judicial contruction has proven especially necessary with respect to Title VII, whose broad language frequently can be given meaning only by reference to public law concepts.

Moreover, the fact-finding process in arbitration usually is not equivalent to judicial fact-finding. The record of the arbitration proceedings is not as complete; the usual rules of evidence do not apply; and rights and procedures common to civil trials, such as discovery, compulsory process, cross-examination, and testimony under oath, are often severely limited or unavailable. See *Bernhardt* v. *Polygraphic Co.*, 350 US 198, 203 (1956); *Wilko* v. *Swan*, 346 US 427, 435–437 (1953). And as this Court has recognized, "(a)rbitrators have no obligation to the court to give their reasons for an award." *United Steelworkers of America* v. *Enterprise Wheel & Car Corp.*, 363 US 593, at 598. Indeed, it is the informality of arbitral procedure that enables it to function as an efficient, inexpensive, and expeditious means for dispute resolution. This same characteristic, however, makes arbitration a less appropriate forum for final resolution of Title VII issues than the federal courts.

It is evident that respondents' proposed rule would not allay these concerns. Nor are we convinced that the solution lies in applying a more demanding deferral standard, such as that adopted by the Fifth Circuit in *Rios* v. *Reynolds Medals Co.*, 467 F 2d 54 (1972). As respondent points out, a standard that adequately insured effectuation of Title VII rights in the arbitral forum would tend to make arbitration a procedurally complex, expensive, and time-consuming process. And judicial enforcement of such a standard would almost require courts to make *de novo* determinations of the employees' claims. It is uncertain whether any minimal savings in judicial time and expense would justify the risk to vindication of Title VII rights.

A deferral rule also might adversely affect the arbitration system as well as the enforcement scheme of Title VII. Fearing that the arbitral forum cannot adequately protect their rights under Title VII, some employees may elect to bypass arbitration and institute a lawsuit. The possibility of voluntary compliance or settlement of Title VII claims would thus be reduced, and the result could well be more litigation, not less.

We think, therefore, that the federal policy favoring arbitration of labor disputes and the federal policy against discriminatory employment practices can best be accommodated by permitting an employee to pursue fully both his remedy under the grievance-arbitration clause of a collective-bargaining agreement and his cause of action under Title VII. The federal court should consider the employee's claim *de novo*. The arbitral decision may be admitted as evidence and accorded such weight as the court deems appropriate.

The judgment of the Court of Appeals is *Reversed*.

The Gardner-Denver Decision and Labor Arbitration

Sanford Cohen   Christian Eaby

The federal law of labor arbitration as established by the three Supreme Court decisions in 1960 known as the "Steelworkers Trilogy"[1] remained virtually unchanged for 14 years. The 1974 Court decision in the *Gardner-Denver* case has been interpreted as a major change in the Court's position.[2] Before examining this case, aspects of the history of labor arbitration and some of the judicial interpretations that anticipated *Gardner-Denver* will be reviewed.

Prior to 1940, arbitration was rarely used to settle grievance disputes. Today, arbitration of grievances arising under a collective bargaining agreement is widely accepted by labor and management. Ninety-five percent of the labor-management agreements in the private sector provide for binding arbitration of grievance disputes and similar provisions are not unusual in public sector agreements.

The activity of the War Labor Board from 1942 to 1945 was an important factor which accelerated the use of grievance arbitration. In a situation where most unions had voluntarily given up the right to strike, War Labor Board policy encouraged the adoption of contract clauses which provided for the arbitration of disputes over the interpretation and application of agreements. This policy was a strong influence in

Reprinted from the *Labor Law Journal* 27, no. 1 (February 1976): 18–23, with the permission of the publisher.

the direction of making binding arbitration by a neutral third party the final step in the grievance procedure. By the end of 1945, when the War Labor Board terminated its activities, a peaceful alternative to the strike had come to be widely accepted in American industrial relations. Binding arbitration involved a significant exchange of rights. The union gave up the right to strike for the life of the agreement and management gave up its final authority over many personnel questions.

Before the passage of the Taft-Hartley Act in 1947, the Congress had made no provision for the enforcement of collective bargaining agreements. In that Act, officially the Labor-Management Relations Act, Congress set the stage for the enforcement of agreements in the federal courts. In essence, Sections 301 (a) and (b) of Taft-Hartley say that both parties are responsible for the acts of their agents, that they can be sued for contract violations when these occur in an industry affecting interstate commerce, and that such suits are to be brought through the United States District Courts.

Until 1957, the courts played a minimal role in the evolution of the arbitration process. The parties and the arbitrators, many of whom had served on the War Labor Board, shared the responsibility for developing criteria for the interpretation and application of collective bargaining agreements. A decision by the Supreme Court in the *Lincoln Mills* case of 1957 began to lay the groundwork for a federal law of labor arbitration under Section 301.[3]

In the *Lincoln Mills* case, the parties had negotiated an agreement providing for arbitration of grievances and prohibition of strikes and work stoppages during the life of the agreement. The union attempted to bring a grievance to arbitration and the company refused, claiming that the issue was not arbitrable. The union then sued in federal court under Section 301 seeking enforcement of the contract and the arbitration provisions. In upholding the applicability of Section 301, the Court affirmed that either party could sue through the federal courts for the enforcement of a labor-management agreement and that agreements to arbitrate disputes were enforceable in the federal courts.

The Court, in *Lincoln Mills,* differentiated labor arbitration from commercial arbitration. Arbitration of disputes in the business sector, according to the Court, is a substitute for protracted and expensive litigation. Grievance arbitration in labor-management disputes, in contrast, is not a substitute for litigation but is, rather, a substitute for the strike.[4]

Speaking for the Court, Justice Douglas declared that ". . . the agreement to arbitrate grievance disputes is the *quid pro quo* for an agreement not to strike." Labor gives up the right to strike for the life of the contract, and, in return, management surrenders certain rights that previously were exclusive managerial prerogatives. The arbitration of grievances, as part of a collective bargaining agreement, is a binding contract agreed upon by the parties and as such is enforceable in the courts.

The Trilogy Cases

On June 20, 1960, the Supreme Court issued three important decisions on labor arbitration. These were the "trilogy cases" referred to above. In these decisions, the Court established guidelines for arbitration and arbitrators and presented a doctrine of court deferral to arbitration that recognized the authority and expertise of the arbitrator. The basic elements of the Court opinions in the trilogy are summarized as follows.

The role of the courts is limited to determining whether the party seeking arbitration is making a claim which on its face is covered by the contract. The courts are not to consider the merits of a grievance under the guise of interpreting the arbitration clause of a contract. In suits for performance of an arbitration agreement, arbitration should be ordered unless it is clear beyond doubt that the dispute is not covered by the contract's arbitration clause, and doubts should be resolved in favor of coverage. Finally, an arbitrator's award is enforceable under Section 301. In suits for enforcement of such awards, the courts have no business overruling the arbitrator because their interpretation of the contract is different from his. A court, however, may refuse to enforce an arbitration award that is not based on the collective bargaining contract.[5]

These decisions established a strong basis for judicial deferral to arbitration awards. In many cases, the courts have refused to review the merits of an arbitration decision and have ordered it enforced unless there has been a showing of irregularities or bias in the arbitration hearing. The Court position in the *Gardner-Denver* case would, at first glance, appear to be a major shift in the federal law concerning deferral to arbitration.

The *Alexander* v. *Gardner-Denver* case involved the discharge of an employee for alleged poor performance. The employee contested his discharge through the negotiated grievance procedure, where he claimed that he had been discharged because of his race. At the same time, he filed a complaint with the local Equal Employment Opportunity Commission charging racial discrimination. The employee lost at arbitration and the EEOC found that there were no reasonable grounds for finding that he had been discriminated against. Following these two decisions, the employee carried his complaint to the federal courts.

The Supreme Court ruled that the arbitration award had not exhausted the grievant's legal remedies. This conclusion was based on the fact that an individual can pursue multiple avenues of remedy in civil rights cases. Rights arising out of the Civil Rights Act of 1964 rather than the collective bargaining agreement do not require judicial deferral to arbitration. This is true even though remedy is originally sought under the grievance arbitration procedures of a collective bargaining agreement.

A number of the points made by the Court in *Gardner-Denver* were not new and the direction toward which the decision pointed was anticipated in a number of earlier decisions. A few of the significant issues—multiple remedies and limited deferral in civil rights cases, distinctions between the rights of an individual and those of the union organization, and distinctions between contractual rights and statutory rights—require further examination.

In *Smith* v. *Evening News,* the Supreme Court in 1962 ruled in favor of multiple remedies for an alleged breach of a collective bargaining agreement that was, at the same time, an unfair practice under the National Labor Relations Act.[6] The Court there held that "the authority of the Board (The National Labor Relations Board) to deal with an unfair labor practice which also violates a collective bargaining agreement is not displaced by Section 301, but it is not exclusive and does not destroy the jurisdiction of the courts in suits under Section 301." The Supreme Court in the *Smith* case also upheld the right of an individual to bring suit under Section 301 on the basis that an individual might have a claim which differs from that of the union organization and that the rights of an individual "are a major focus of the negotiation and administration of collective bargaining contracts." Thus, some twelve years before Gardner-Denver, the Court recognized the possibility of multiple remedies in certain types of disputes as well as the existence of individual rights distinct from those of the union organization.

The court appeal in *Gardner-Denver* was based on Title VII of the Civil Rights Act of 1964. While some lower federal courts had ruled against multiple remedies in civil rights cases,[7] other decisions had allowed for appeals after proceedings which were usually considered to be final. In *Cooper* v. *Philip Morris* the Circuit Court held that the bringing of a claim of discriminatory employment practices in state proceedings did not preclude bringing federal action under Title VII.[8] In another case, it was held that a determination by an NLRB trial examiner that an employee was not dismissed because of racial bias did not prevent the employee from subsequently bringing an action under Title VII of the Civil Rights Act.[9] Another court ruled that bringing a case to the federal EEOC or a state human relations commission, both of which rejected the charge, did not preclude going into the Federal courts.[10] The court ruled that the "civil rights suit was not rendered moot by labor arbitrator's decision . . . (and) . . . judicial review of administrative decisions is the rule—not the exception. . . ."

Circuit Court Cases

Cases in the United States Circuit Courts have dealt specifically with grievance arbitration and deferral in cases of discrimination brought under Title VII. In *Hutchens* v. *United States Industries,* the court held that pursuing a contractual remedy of grievance arbitration to final determination did not prevent action under Title VII.[11] In an arbitration proceeding, the arbitrator's role is to determine contract rights of the employees, as distinct from the constitutional rights afforded by federal legislation. The doctrine of election of remedies that would preclude multiple remedies in other cases applies only in so far as the person bringing suit is "not entitled to duplicative relief in public and private forums that would result in an unjust enrichment or windfall." The court also ruled that the judiciary ought to examine arbitration awards and the evidence on their merits in cases involving public policy assertions.

In an earlier case in 1963, the Supreme Court upheld the decision of a lower court that enforced an arbitration award reinstating an employee discharged for gambling on company property, but also observed that "when public policy is interposed as a bar to enforcement of an arbitration award, a court must evaluate its asserted content."[12] Obviously, when the grievance dispute concerns rights of the parties established in the collective bargaining agreement, the courts will defer to the award of the arbitrator as bargained for in the contract, but when the grievance concerns rights established by statute, the courts reserve the authority to make final judgment.

In the case of *Rios* v. *Reynolds Metals,*[13] the circuit court dealt with the questions of deferral and the distinction between contractual and statutory rights. The court held that in civil rights cases brought under authority of Title VII, the courts may, under limited circumstances, defer to the arbitration award. However, there may be no deferral unless the contractual right coincides with the statutory right, and it must be plain that the arbitrator's decision is in no way a violation of the private rights guaranteed by the Civil Rights Act of 1964, or of the public policy inherent in the Act. An employee may seek relief under Title VII without first invoking or exhausting available legal or contractual remedies, and even when an employee pursues an alternative remedy the federal court has final authority in cases of alleged discrimination.

A list of conditions to be considered for possible deferral to a prior arbitration award are included in the decision and these go beyond those outlined in the Steelworkers Trilogy: (1) The factual issues before the court are identical to those decided by the arbitrator. (2) The arbitrator had the power under the agreement to decide the issue of discrimination. (3) Evidence at the arbitration hearing dealt fairly with all the factual issues. (4) The arbitrator actually decided the issue presented to the court. (5) The hearing was fair and regular.

The federal courts have overturned labor-management contract provisions found to be in violation of expressly granted civil rights deriving from federal law. In a suit brought by the United States, the court overturned a provision establishing a particular seniority system on the basis of its violation of Title VII.[14] That case concerned a contract between the United Paperworkers Union and the Crown Zellerbach Corporation. Before 1966, the agreement had provided for segregated lines of progression for black and white employees. After 1966, the segregation clause was eliminated from the contract, but the existing job seniority system was retained. In the case brought alleging discrimination, the court held "where a seniority system has the effect of perpetuating discrimination . . . that present result is prohibited. . . . We agree . . . that present discrimination cannot be justified . . . because Title VII refers to an effective date and because present discrimination is caused by conditions in the past."

New Standards

Grievance arbitration is a contractual right open to judicial review in civil rights cases in the same manner as seniority provisions or other sections of a labor-management agreement. The Civil Rights Act of 1964 establishes new standards for judicial review of arbitration awards that were not present in 1960, but as shown by the opinions reviewed above, the decision in *Gardner-Denver* is not that wide a departure from the earlier federal law of arbitration.

The Supreme Court in *Gardner-Denver* held that civil rights guaranteed by the Civil Rights Act of 1964 are not part of the collective agreement, and that while a union may waive certain statutory rights related to the progress of collective bargaining, there can be no waiver of employee rights under Title VII of the Civil Rights Act. Individual employees have a statutory right to trial under Title VII that is not foreclosed by submission of a claim to final arbitration under the nondiscrimination clause of a collective agreement. The Congressional intent was to allow individuals to pursue their rights independently under Title VII and all other applicable state and federal statutes. The Court recognized a difference between the law of the shop, a contract right interpreted through arbitration, and the law of the land, a statutory right brought through the federal courts.

The *Gardner-Denver* decision suggested guidelines for judicial deferral to arbitration awards. The arbitration decision itself can be submitted as evidence and accorded such weight as the courts may deem appropriate. Relevant factors in considering deferral include the existence of provisions in the agreement that conform with the intent of Title VII; the degree of procedural fairness in the arbitration hearing; the adequacy of the record with respect to discrimination; and the special competence of particular arbitrators. If the arbitration decision gives full consideration to an employee's Title VII rights, it may be accorded great weight in the courts, but the federal courts will have ultimate authority for resolution of such disputes, this authority having been given by the will of Congress.

The reach of the *Gardner-Denver* case is limited to labor disputes which involve alleged violations of the 1964 Civil Rights Act and, even in this area, the actual impact of the decision remains uncertain. While a number of industrial relations practitioners have argued in favor of abandoning arbitration in discrimination cases, the argument would appear to be premature in view of the Court's suggestion that the awards of arbitrators be given appropriate weight in judicial proceedings. There are, furthermore, distinct advantages to labor arbitration and, over time, these advantages may become as apparent in civil rights disputes as they are elsewhere. The economy and efficiency of arbitration, for example, may prove to be sufficiently attractive so as to assure that arbitration will, in fact, be the final step in many disputes over civil rights at the workplace.

NOTES

1. *United Steelworkers* v. *American Manufacturing,* 363 US 564 (1960), 40 LC 66,628. *United Steelworkers* v. *Warrior and Gulf Navigation,* 363 US 574 (1960), 40 LC 66,629. *United Steelworkers* v. *Enterprise Wheel and Car,* 363 US 593 (1960), 40 LC 66,630.

2. *Alexander* v. *Gardner-Denver,* 415 US 36 (1974), 7 EPD 9418.

3. *Textile Workers Union* v. *Lincoln Mills,* 353 US 448 (1957), 32 LC 70,733.

4. See Paul Prasow and Edward Peters, *Arbitration and Collective Bargaining* (New York: McGraw-Hill, 1970), p. 247.

5. See ibid., pp. 256–57, for further elaboration on this point.

6. 371 US 195 (1962), 46 LC 17,962.

7. *Dewey* v. *Reynolds Metals,* 429 F 2d 324 (1970).

8. 464 F 2d 9 (1972).

9. *Tipler* v. *duPont deNemours,* 443 F 2d 195 (1971), 3 EPD 8216.

10. *Fekete* v. *United States Steel,* 424 F 2d 331 (CA-3, 1970), 2 EPD 10,201.

11. 428 F 2d 303 (CA-5, 1970), 63 LC 9465.

12. *International Union of Electrical Workers* v. *Otis Elevator,* 314 F 2d 25 (CA-2, 1963), 46 LC 18,111; cert. denied, 373 US 949 (1963), 47 LC 18,286.

13. 467 F 2d (CA-5, 1972), 5 EPD 7976.

14. *United States* v. *United Papermakers Union,* 282 F Supp 39 (1967), 57 LC 9120.

II

Conditions of Work

Occupational Injury and Illness

Industrial injury and work-related illness continue to exact a massive toll. Although statistics on these matters are far from accurate, available data suggest that approximately 14,000 persons die each year as a result of industrial injury or illness and that 90,000 persons are permanently disabled. The number who suffer lesser disability is, of course, much larger.

Public policy relative to occupational illness and injury is expressed primarily in the Occupational Safety and Health Act of 1970 and in the Workmen's Compensation laws of the states. The stated purpose of OSHA is "to assure so far as possible every working man and woman in the nation safe and healthful working conditions and to preserve our human resources." The state workmen's compensation laws establish social insurance programs to provide compensation and medical benefits to persons who suffer work related injuries or illnesses.

The controversy over OSHA, intense during the time of congressional consideration, continues with union and management spokesmen arguing that the law is either too lax or rigid. The selections which follow present a description of the extent and consequences of industrial injury and disease, the general nature of OSHA, and representative labor and management reactions to the law. The final selection in this section reviews the details and background of the state workmen's compensation laws and presents a number of objectives for modernizing the existing programs.

Industrial Injuries and Their Consequences

National Commission on State Workmen's Compensation Laws

In 1970 about 14,000 workers died from a work-connected injury or disease; another 90,000 were permanently disabled; and more than 2,100,000 were temporarily dis-

Reprinted from National Commission on State Workmen's Compensation Laws, *Compendium on Workmen's Compensation* (Washington, D.C.: U.S. Government Printing Office, 1973), chapter 1.

abled. Although these deaths and disabilities were only one-fifth of the total accidental injuries from all causes, the numbers are disturbing. Furthermore, another 6 or 7
million persons were injured on the job although they did not miss a day's work.
These injured workers and their families suffered bodily injuries and emotional strain
as well as substantial economic losses. Their employers and society also suffered size-
able economic losses.

Work-related Injuries: Trends and Characteristics

The number of disabling work injuries has fluctuated within a fairly narrow range
during the past three decades. The peak year in recent history was 1943 when the
special demands of World War II (e.g., high employment, inexperienced workers,
inadequate training, and constantly changing supervision) moved the number over
2.4 million. The best year was 1958 when the number dropped to about 1.8 million.
The number of injuries declined following World War II, rose again during the
Korean conflict, continued to decline during the middle fifties, increased gradually
from 1958 to 1966, and has remained almost constant since that year. Deaths, permanent disabilities and temporary disabilities were all higher in 1970 than in 1958.

Because of the inadequacies of accident reporting these data on work injuries are
subject to a considerable margin of error. The reporting requirements of the Occupational Safety and Health Act of 1970 will provide more accurate data in the future.

Sources of Work Injuries

Industrial injuries occur most frequently in association with (1) handling some object
manually or (2) falling. Those two classes account for about 43 percent of all com-
pensable work injuries. Other events associated with more than 10 percent of these
injuries are: Being struck by a falling or moving object and contact with machinery
other than vehicles.

Vehicle accidents are the most important factor in fatal or permanent total injuries,
followed by falls and manual handling of objects. Accidents involving machinery,
falling moving objects, and falls are the three most frequent factors in permanent
partial disabilities.

Data are not available on the reason why the person fell, what he did wrong while
handling an object manually, and so on. Some special studies are available that
analyze the hazardous or unsafe conditions that gave rise to work injuries in selected
industries.

Economic Consequences

When a worker dies, is disabled, or merely requires medical attention because of a
work-connected injury or disease, the economic consequences affect the worker, his
family, his employer, and society.

The Worker and His Family

The worker and his family may suffer two types of economic losses: (1) a loss of earnings and (2) extra expenses.

Loss of earnings. If a worker dies because of a work-related injury or sickness, his
survivors lose the income he would otherwise have earned less the amount that he
would have spent to maintain himself during the remainder of his working career and

his retirement years. This loss can be substantial. For example, according to a Bureau of the Census report, in 1968, the average male, aged 30, who had completed 1 to 3 years of high school, had an annual income of about $5,827. The present value of his expected lifetime earnings, assuming an annual discount rate of 4 percent, was about $125,000. In a typical family about 20 percent of this annual income would have been needed to meet the worker's own maintenance expenses. Reducing the lifetime earnings loss by this 20 percent leaves the still substantial loss of about $100,000.

These estimates ignore any expected gains in annual income per worker because of higher productivity and inflation. Assuming an annual increase of 3 percent per year would raise the 1968 net earnings loss to $154,000. For a worker, aged 50, the potential earnings loss would have been less, about $71,000, because he was nearer retirement.

Total and permanent disability causes an even greater earnings loss than death because the worker must be maintained. If the two males, aged 30 and 50, discussed above had been totally and permanently disabled instead of killed, their earnings losses would have been $193,000 and $89,000 respectively.

Variation Among Industries

Selected industry data show how injury frequency rates and severity measures varied in 1970. The frequency rate is the number of disabling work injuries per 1 million man-hours worked. Two severity measures are shown: The average number of days lost per injury and a "severity rate" which is the number of days lost per million man-hours worked. Because this "severity rate" is the product of the injury frequency rate and the average number of days lost per injury, it reflects both injury frequency and the severity of those injuries that occur.

Injury frequency rates were highest in the police protection (45.6), fire protection (41.7), and coal mining industries (41.6). The industries with the lowest rates were communication (2.5), electric, gas, and sanitary services (6.7), miscellaneous business service (6.0), and educational services (6.7). The average number of disabling days per injury exceeded 100 for the low-frequency electric, gas, and sanitary services industry, fire protection, and the four mining groups. For only three industries (tobacco manufactures, textile products, and ordinance and accessories) were the average disabling days per injury under 30. The figure on average days per injury includes schedule charges for death and permanent impairment as well as the number of full calendar days lost to temporary total disability.

Severity rates, reflecting both injury frequency and severity, exceeded 2,000 for eight groups: lumber and wood products, contract construction, fire protection, police protection, and the four mining groups. Coal mining had the highest severity rate (7,792), the highest average disabling days per injury (187), and the third highest injury frequency rate (41.6).

Work injury frequency rates in manufacturing industries increased from 12.0 in 1960 to the 1970 level of 15.2. Every manufacturing industry except lumber and wood products had a higher rate in 1970 than in 1960. A possible explanation is a rise in new hires and more overtime in most of these industry groups coupled with rapid technological change. Fortunately, however, because of a decline in the average number of days per injury, the severity rate for all manufacturing increased only slightly over this 10-year period from 753 to 759.

The experience in most nonmanufacturing and mining industries has been more favorable. Employment increased in many of these industries as it did in manufacturing, but in construction an increase in mechanization apparently eliminated many injuries formerly caused by manual handling.

Because injury and severity rates are not available for all industries, no rates are calculated for all industries combined. It is probable, however, that these overall rates, though still disturbingly high, have declined somewhat over the past decade.

Permanent partial disability causes some fraction of the permanent total disability loss, depending upon the proportion of annual earnings lost. A worker who is totally disabled for a temporary period loses his income for a specific number of weeks or months. Loss of even a month's earnings is a serious loss for the typical worker. In addition to these earnings losses, the deceased or disabled worker may no longer provide valuable household services that must now be foregone or replaced at some additional expense.

Extra expenses. In event of death, the earnings loss generally is much greater than the extra expenses associated with death, but these expenses are still substantial. They include funeral and burial expenses, probate costs, lawyer's fees, federal estate taxes, and state inheritance taxes.

Not all injured workers are disabled but almost all require some form of medical attention. Hospital bills, doctors' and nurses' fees, and other medical expenses follow. For all injuries combined, medical expenses are less than the total earnings loss but for most injured workers their medical expenses exceed their earnings loss.

The Worker's Employer

Part or all of the worker's economic loss may be transferred to the worker's employer under workmen's compensation laws or employers' liability statutes. For example, in New York State the employer of a totally and permanently disabled worker would be responsible for all of his medical expenses and a lifetime weekly income equal to two-thirds of his wage at the time he was disabled subject to a weekly maximum of $80. Most employers are required by law to purchase workmen's compensation insurance to secure their obligations to their employees. Through this insurance, certain premium payments, which include an expense and profit or contingency allowance, replace uncertain benefits to employees. In 1970 workmen's compensation cost employers $4.9 billion or 1.13 percent of covered payrolls.

Less apparent to employers are the other losses, often called indirect losses, associated with industrial accidents. One source lists ten examples of such losses:

1. Cost of wages paid for working time lost by workers who were not injured.
2. Net cost to repair, replace, or straighten up material or equipment that was damaged in an accident.
3. Cost of wages paid for working time lost by injured workers, other than workmen's compensation payments.
4. Extra cost due to overtime work necessitated by an accident.
5. Cost of wages paid supervisors while their time is required for activities necessitated by the accident.
6. Wage cost due to decreased output of injured worker after return to work.
7. Cost of learning period of new worker.
8. Uninsured medical cost borne by the company.
9. Cost of time spent by higher supervision and clerical workers on investigations or in the processing of compensation application forms.
10. Miscellaneous unusual costs (e.g., loss of profits on contracts canceled, public liability claims, and cost of excess spoilage by new employees).

According to H.W. Heinrich, a pioneer in developing scientific approaches to industrial accident prevention, on the average these indirect costs are about four times the employers' share of their employees' earnings losses and medical expenses.

In a more recent study Simonds and Grimaldi have argued that, although Heinrich should be commended for dramatizing the importance of indirect costs, the ratio of these costs to direct costs (1) varies markedly among employers and overtime and (2) on the average may be less than four to one. Instead of a ratio approach, these two authors favor the following formula:

Insurance costs

      A times number of lost-time cases
+ B times number of doctors' cases
+ C times number of first-aid cases
+ D times number of no-injury cases
= Total costs

In the formula A, B, C and D represent constants indicating the average uninsured cost for each of these categories of cases.

Society

In addition to the losses described above, society loses the taxes that would have been paid by the injured employees, the products or services they would have produced, and the costs of commissions and courts administering workmen's compensation and employers' liability. Some injured employees and families become public assistance beneficiaries and are supported by other members of society.

The Federal Role in Job Safety and Health: Inspection and Enforcement at the Workplace

Joe Collier

Its full name is the Occupational Safety and Health Administration but it is better known as OSHA—the acronym appearing in ads promoting employer compliance with the Occupational and Safety Health Act of 1970.

OSHA officially began life as an arm of the Department of Labor on April 28, 1971, the effective date of the act. Its mission is to assure safe and healthful conditions for working men and women in the nation. It works closely with the states, encouraging their full participation in the nation's first comprehensive worker protection program.

Since its beginning, OSHA has stirred controversy. At the heart of the conflict has been the OSHA mandate to provide effective enforcement of job safety and health standards with the strong tools provided by the act.

Reprinted from the *Monthly Labor Review,* August 1973, pp. 35–42.

Under a delegation of authority from the Secretary of Labor, OSHA has congressional authorization at two critical points, which most Federal and State job safety and health programs have not had in the past. The first is the right to enter a workplace without giving advance notice to the employer and inspect for compliance with the act. The second is the authority to propose penalties for violations of standards, or of the "general duty clause" (barring all "serious recognized hazards") upon discovery of the violation. Most earlier Federal and State laws either made no provision for penalties or authorized them only if an employer failed to obey an order to correct a violation. The act makes mandatory a proposed penalty of up to $1,000 upon discovery of a serious violation, which involves "a substantial probability that death or physical harm could result" (except when an employer could not reasonably have known of the violation). It permits, but does not require, the same penalty when the violation is not regarded as serious in this sense. These provisions are significant not so much in any punitive effect they may have on an employer after an inspection of his establishment as in the motivation they provide for the employer to correct violations in his workplace before an inspection occurs.

OSHA may still order the correction or "abatement" of violations discovered by an inspector, as was permitted in many States prior to passage of the act. However, that authority extends over many more employers and permits much more stringent penalties—up to $1,000 a day—for failure to comply with such an order. In addition, the act provides for much more severe penalties in cases where violations of the act are clearly willful or repeated. Such violations may result in a civil penalty of up to $10,000. A willful violation resulting in the death of an employee may result in a criminal charge. For a first conviction, it may occasion a penalty of up to $10,000 and/or a year in prison.

OSHA may issue citations ordering abatement of a violation and propose penalties on its own administrative authority, without going to court. Only when a citation or penalty is contested does the case go to the Occupational Safety and Health Review Commission, an independent agency. This reduces the time required to achieve compliance with the occupational safety and health standards and the general duty clause. As a last resort, the case may go to the U.S. Court of Appeals. Complementing this administrative authority is the right of OSHA's compliance officers to question privately any employer, employer agent, or employee involved at the worksite. Likewise, OSHA may require the testimony of witnesses and the production of evidence to carry out its inspections and investigations. The compliance officers have access to employer records, required by the act, of occupational illnesses and injuries as well as records which may be required by standards under the act regarding employee exposure to toxic materials and harmful physical agents.

It is necessary for OSHA to seek a court order when it finds an uncorrected "imminent danger," one which could be expected to cause death or serious injury. The court may issue, without hearing from the employer, a temporary restraining order effective up to 5 days, requiring immediate abatement of the danger and prohibiting the presence of all persons in the area except those necessary to remedy the condition. If the court rules against the employer after he presents his case, it may issue an injunction requiring similar action. These cases are heard by the U.S. district courts, which can be called into session on short notice.

Employee Rights

The Act does not leave the entire job of identifying hazards to OSHA, however. No matter how sizable its staff, OSHA could never be in as good a position to identify some workplace as another group of people—workers on the job. Therefore, as an integral part of the compliance system, complementary to OSHA's responsibility and authority, the act gives employees certain rights in assuring their own job safety and health.

Parallel to the OSHA authority to enter and inspect a workplace, the act empowers the worker to trigger an inspection, through a written complaint, when he thinks a condition threatens physical harm or poses an imminent danger in violation of the act. In accord with OSHA's authority to cite employers and propose penalties for violations, the act assures workers the right to have a representative accompany the OSHA compliance officer in his examination of the workplace and to point out alleged hazards. Employees or their representatives may also submit written complaints to the compliance officer before or during his walk through the workplace. Where there is no employee representative, a reasonable number of employees must be interviewed by the compliance officer about safety and health in their workplace. The initiatives in protecting their own safety and health which are permitted to employees through these mechanisms go well beyond any opportunities given in earlier legislation.

The act permits any employee or his representative to participate in hearings before the Commission and to appeal the length of time allowed by OSHA for abatement of a violation. The act does not, however, provide the opportunity for an employee to appeal to the Review Commission if OSHA refuses to inspect or to issue a citation in response to his complaint, nor does it permit him to appeal the size or the lack of a penalty proposed by OSHA.

In addition, when an employee believes he is exposed to an imminent danger and that OSHA has arbitrarily or capriciously failed to seek court action, he may turn to the U.S. district court to compel OSHA to seek such action.

As a safeguard against reprisals, an employee may have his name withheld from any copy of his complaint given to his employer or otherwise made public. In addition, he may file a complaint with OSHA if he feels he is victim of discrimination. OSHA may seek relief for him in the U.S. district court, including rehiring or reinstatement with back pay.

Employer Rights

Employers, too, are often better equipped than OSHA to identify and correct hazards in their establishments. The act, therefore, assures them of certain rights in the enforcement system which not only protect them against undue OSHA action but at the same time encourage them to give careful attention to the safety and health of their workers.

When an employer surveys his workplace for hazards, he may find a situation which technically violates a standard but which represents no real hazard, only an alternate way of achieving safe and healthful results. Or he may find a violation which does reflect a hazard but which, for one of several reasons, cannot be corrected quickly. In either of these circumstances the employer may apply for a "variance" (permission to differ) from the standard involved. He would apply for a permanent variance where conditions are safe, a temporary variance where he needs more time to correct a hazard. He is not subject to citation for violations covered by a variance, though even under a temporary variance he must take all available steps to provide for his employees' safety. As noted, he may contest any citation, penalty, or abatement period to the Review Commission, and may appeal an adverse Commission decision to the U.S. Court of Appeals.

Like the employee, the employer has a right to have a representative accompany the OSHA compliance officer during his walk through the workplace. In the setting of penalties, he is due consideration for any good faith he has shown in attempting to assure a safe workplace, as well as for the gravity of the violation, the history of previous violations, and the size of his business. Thus, his efforts to comply voluntarily with the act have a significant bearing on his treatment if violations are still found.

Employers are also entitled to the protection of any trade secrets which an inspector must learn in order to carry out his inspection. Many small businesses may qualify for loans from the Small Business Administration to permit them to come into compliance with the act.

Program Implementation

In keeping with a general policy of decentralization, OSHA has placed the responsibility for administering the enforcement program with 10 regional administrators and 50 area directors. To reduce administrative delays to a minimum, area directors have authority to schedule inspections, investigate complaints, issue citations, and propose penalties. They must consult with regional administrators prior to action on certain critical matters, as for example, willful violations.

By June 1973, there were about 450 compliance safety and health officers in OSHA's 50 area offices, including 65 industrial hygienists. Since January, they have been supplemented by nearly 200 State safety and health inspectors serving under special agreements with 18 States. . . .

The first standards under the Williams-Steiger Act were issued on May 29, 1971. These included national consensus standards and some existing Federal standards. Most became effective 90 days after adoption. But the standards were effective immediately for those employers—for example, in the construction and maritime industries—who were already subject to existing Federal safety laws. Until August 27, 1971, only limited compliance activity was undertaken. Disasters, fatalities, and complaints were investigated in all industries and regular inspections were made in industries previously covered by Federal statutes. The first citation and penalty for a serious violation was issued on May 28, 1971, under the "general duty clause," as a result of the first complaint of imminent danger filed with OSHA. The citation was, significantly, for an occupational health violation, involving excessive airborne concentrations of mercury in a Moundsville, West Virginia, chlorine plant.

Because the demands upon OSHA far exceeded its manpower resources, a list of priorities was established to govern the use of its inspection time. Those priorities are still in effect. First priority goes to the investigation of disasters, fatalities, and imminent danger situations. A series of disasters, beginning with a tunnel explosion at Sylmar, California, and continuing through the collapse of the center of a 24-story building under construction in Alexandria, Virginia, has led to the development of a list of specialists who may be called immediately to assist in investigating such circumstances. OSHA standards committees have initiated studies intended to develop means to prevent such accidents. . . .

OSHA moved early in developing programs to make an immediate impact on some industries with the most significant problems. The first program has dealt with five industries whose injury frequency rates—under old standards—were twice as high as the average rate for manufacturing industries. . . . Other factors considered were the number of employees involved, the distribution of the industries throughout the country, and the existence of viable standards. The industries selected, rate of injuries per million man-hours worked in 1969, and number of employees:

Marine cargo handling	69.9	112,00
Roof and sheet-metal work	43.0	115,000
Meat and meat products	43.1	356,000
Miscellaneous transportation equipment (primarily manufacture of mobile homes)	33.3	116,000
Lumber and wood products	34.4	597,000

In addition to OSHA's own compliance activity, a basic feature of the program is the effort to stimulate voluntary compliance in the industries through work with trade associations and employee organizations to insure the existence of industry safety and health committees, to encourage the development of safety and health programs within these industries, and to spread information to employers and employees throughout the industries.

Each of the target industries has responded to the program. The fact that in about 45 percent of the facilities inspected from July 1972 through January 1973 no violations were found suggests progress in complying with the act. . . .

The longshoring industry had reduced its rate almost by half between 1960 and 1969, under a safety program authorized by Congress in 1958. Yet its rate was still among the highest in American industry. . . . Additional regulations have been issued since the inception of OSHA, including the requirement that hard hats and other personal protective equipment be worn. Injuries to the head from falling objects, low ceilings, hanging hooks and other equipment are among the most common and the most serious in the industry. Compliance officers conduct relatively frequent longshoring inspections, since the ships they inspect move in and out of port rapidly. Though 77 percent of inspections in the first 7 months of 1973 revealed no violations, data are not yet available regarding the industry's injury frequency rate since the beginning of OSHA.

The Perils of Logging

The lumber and wood products industry involves a number of rugged environments. . . . OSHA has special standards for sawmills and pulpwood in addition to its general industry standards. Specific standards apply to such operations as felling, limbing, skidding, loading and sawing logs, as well as to the proper guarding and use of the saws and other equipment which are peculiar to the lumber industry. The sawmill standard was the 12th most frequently cited during the first 6 months of fiscal 1973. Similarly, the standard for woodworking machinery, used in the production of other wood products, was among the five most cited standards both for serious and nonserious violations. However, it is notable that many of the safety standards cited for this target industry are the same as those for other industries. . . .,

The other three target industries also have their distinctive hazards, but each shares the more common hazards as well. Roofers, and even mobile homebuilders, often slip or fall because of poor "housekeeping" on walking and working surfaces. Roof workers are frequently burned by hot tar. Sheet-metal workers are cut by tin and other metals. Meatpackers are often injured by hand-held knives. Yet a recent inspection of a meatpacking plant revealed some of the same standards violated as were found in the sawmills: walking and working surfaces (slippery floors); National Electric Code (uncovered receptacles); portable fire extinguishers (none present);

mechanical power transmission apparatus (unguarded belt and sprocket). In addition, there were violations of the standards regarding general requirements for industry (a grinder was not anchored to keep it from "walking"), guarding wall and floor openings (unguarded loading platform), and powered industrial trucks (no horns). Each of these standards was among the 10 most cited during the last 6 months of 1972. Of the 10, only abrasive wheel machinery and woodworking machinery standards were not cited in either the sawmill or the meatpacking plant.

Zeroing in on Health Hazards

The second major special program of OSHA focuses on five target health hazards and the ability to measure the exposure involved. This program began in January 1972, in response to the fact that more than 50 percent of the employee complaints during the earlier period were related to occupational health issues. Selected were five of the more hazardous substances on the list of over 8,000 toxic substances identified by the National Institute for Occupational Safety and Health of the Department of Health, Education and Welfare. These substances, and estimates of the number of employees exposed to them, were asbestos (over 200,000), cotton dust (800,000), silica (1.1 million), lead (1.6 million), and carbon monoxide (unknown, but highest).

Health hazards such as these are usually much more difficult to identify and authenticate than most safety hazards. The substances are either invisible or in miniscule particles, and the effects of overexposure to some of them may not be felt until years later. They require carefully calibrated instruments and considerable time to measure human exposure to them. And many new substances have been developed, compounding the problem.

Asbestos has become increasingly recognized as a cause not only of asbestosis, a debilitating lung disease, but also of cancer of the lungs and adjacent parts of the body. Its effects may first be felt 20 to 30 years after initial exposure. Most disturbing is the evidence that a relatively short and light exposure may be enough to precipitate asbestosis over the 20 to 30 years. Silica and cotton dust may also cause serious lung diseases called silicosis and byssinosis. Lead can do severe damage to the gastrointestinal, blood, and central nervous systems. Carbon monoxide may cause serious brain damage and probably results in many more deaths than are attributed to it.

The basic OSHA requirements in regard to these hazards appear in one standard, on air contaminants. Asbestos is addressed in a separate section of the standard. The asbestos provisions resulted from a petition for an emergency standard on asbestos from the Oil, Chemical and Atomic Workers. The emergency standard was issued on December 7, 1971, and a permanent section was added to the existing standard for air contaminants effective July 7, 1972. The standard for air contaminants provides that employees shall not be exposed to concentrations of the toxic materials which exceed a certain level. The levels are expressed in terms of the average exposure of an employee to the substance during an 8-hour day. This "time-weighted average" is determined by regular (usually hourly) sampling of the substance concentrations near an employee's breathing zone. The samples are usually obtained by sensitive instruments attached to several employees as they go through their normal duties. However, the carbon monoxide detector must be carried by the industrial hygienist near the employee's breathing zone. In addition to the "time-weighted averages" there is for asbestos a ceiling above which an employee may not be exposed at any time without suitable personal protective equipment.

The means for keeping employee exposure to these contaminants within permissible limits is required, whenever feasible, to be engineering controls such as isolation of the employees, enclosure of equipment, exhaust ventilation, or dust collection. Rotating employees in and out of the exposure areas and the use of respirators and other personal protective equipment are acceptable as an interim measure where engineering controls are not feasible or while such controls are being installed. In addition, for asbestos, when an employee is exposed to a concentration higher than the ceiling level, his employer must provide special clothing covering his entire body, and special locker and laundry facilities to avoid contamination of his own clothes. Various kinds of respirators are required for different concentration levels of asbestos. The standard also requires employers to monitor and keep a record of employee exposures to asbestos and requires regular medical examinations.

OSHA has begun its attack on these hazards, making almost 1,400 inspections in the first 7 months of fiscal 1973. Almost 500 of these were done by State inspectors under agreement with OSHA. . . .

OSHA has also developed short-term special programs in response to hazards which demonstrate critical dimensions. An emphasis on the inspection of fireworks manufacturing plants resulted after a series of explosions in such plants. A special emphasis on trenching hazards was begun in April (1973) as a result of more than 100 deaths from trench and excavation cave-ins in 1972. The trenching emphasis includes an effort to encourage voluntary compliance much like the target industry and target health hazard programs. It is notable that the first criminal charge filed under the act is a result of a trenching cave-in. An employer in Omaha was initially cited for failing to shore a trench being dug for sewer pipes. Ten days later an extension of the trench caved in and killed an employee. The Justice Department has charged the employer on three criminal counts: failing to shore a trench, failing to provide a means of escape for his employee, and storing excavated material too close to the edge of the trench and thereby weighing it down.

The fourth priority in OSHA inspection activity is given to the random inspection of industries according to a formula which ensures that a representative number of large and small worksites will be inspected within each industry subgroup over an appropriate geographical spread. Though last in priority, a significant number of industries are inspected under this formula. Since the target industries and target health hazards are only relatively deserving of special attention, the violations discovered in random inspections may be as significant as any other. After inspecting a construction site at Miami International Airport, an OSHA compliance officer issued a citation for a serious violation because no safety net had been placed below employees working over 80 feet above ground. The contractor installed the net and a few months later an iron worker fell 18 feet into it and escaped serious injury. . . .

Summary of Experience

Based on figures for July 1971 to January 1973, and other data for July 1972 to January 1973, OSHA has assumed the following dimensions:

During the 19 month period, OSHA compliance officers and their counterpart State inspectors made an initial Federal inspection of over 45,800 establishments, about 1 percent of the establishments covered by the act. Over 8.5 million workers—14 percent of the covered force—were employed in the inspected establishments. Of the initial inspections, 8 percent were in response to employee complaints. About 40 percent were related to target industries and about 3 percent to target health hazards. Most of the remaining were directed toward the fourth priority, though a small percent involved investigations of violations of regulations other than standards. . . .

Sixty percent of the complaints . . . were from employees themselves and 30 percent from employee representatives. . . . About 7 percent of the complaints received involved a claim of imminent danger, though most were found to be less than an imminent danger or were abated immediately. Only five situations resulted in a court order. Most imminent danger situations have been abated quickly without a court order. About 35 percent of the complaints were related to health issues. . . .

Taking account of initial and followup inspections, more than 167,300 violations were alleged. During the 7 month period, nearly 72 percent of the citations were in manufacturing industries and 13 percent in construction. Five percent were in the maritime industry. More than 25 percent were issued in the five target industries. . . .

Even with a projected 1,000 state inspectors conducting State inspections under plans approved by OSHA or which may be approved in the near future and with the anticipated growth of OSHA's own compliance staff, the enforcement effort will have just started. Many industries, of course, may not merit intensive inspection activity, as, for example, some service industries. But in many industries the Nation has barely begun to take account of the occupational sources of many diseases.

The Federal Role in Job Safety and Health: Forging a Partnership with the States

Sally Seymour

While the Federal Government has a large role in setting and enforcing safety and health standards, the Occupational Safety and Health Act of 1970 clearly encourages the States to take the initiative. Federal enforcement action, in fact, will phase out in States whose programs gain U.S. approval.

Since the law went into effect in April 1971, considerable Federal effort has been directed at encouraging State participation and helping States to improve their own programs.

The history of Federal-State cooperation under the act is far from complete; in some ways, the most critical tests of the program's success remain several years distant. However, the record to date may provide some useful insights about the development of a "joint" enforcement program, as well as how States are conducting their own operations.

Prior to passage of the act, inspection staffs and budgets varied widely among Federal safety programs; by most criteria they were deemed inadequate. In addition, enforcement powers were weak; sanctions could be imposed only for failure to correct a violation. Thus, the burden of work fell on limited inspection staffs to ferret out violations and demand remedial action.

Reprinted from the *Monthly Labor Review*, August 1973, pp. 28–34.

The situation in the States presented an erratic composite portrait. Most States covered a substantial proportion of their labor forces, but standards, coverage of hazards, staff and budget resources, and enforcement powers varied widely and were usually inadequate. As with Federal laws, State laws lacked any systematic array of incentives for employers to remove hazards *before* an enforcement visit.

Given the size of the problem . . . the authors of the act designed a system which would do what prior laws had failed to do—effectively encourage employers to eliminate hazards prior to an inspection visit.

The incentive is explicitly embodied in the penalty system; employers are subject to fines upon *discovery* of violations, rather than for failure to abate violations once discovered. This approach enhances the effectiveness of a small number of inspectors. . . .

It is this incentive for private action which is, perhaps, the key to the act's effectiveness. Further, it is precisely this type of radical departure from past approaches which States must follow to participate under the act. Combining this type of incentive structure with other program improvements will enable States to help provide labor force protection, in partnership with the Federal Government.

Measuring Up

The States must come up with a program which is at least as good as the Federal effort. Approval of this program, however, is not the last word. Once a plan is accepted, the act requires that the State must then put it to work, under the watchful eye of Federal evaluation. If, after a minimum of 3 years of operation, the State plan satisfies Federal performance criteria, the Federal Government will formally relinquish its enforcement authority to State jurisdiction. Up to that point, the Federal Government retains discretionary authority to exercise its enforcement powers, if necessary, simultaneously with exercise of State powers. State failure to perform adequately during the evaluation period can result in withdrawal of plan approval and Federal preemption. In addition, failure to maintain performance *after* relinquishment of Federal authority can also lead to reassertion of Federal jurisdiction.

To carry out the Federal function, the Occupational Safety and Health Administration was established in the Department of Labor. OSHA was charged with the responsibility of encouraging the States, with widely different philosophies and histories of enforcement efforts, to develop programs "at least as effective" as the Federal program. This problem was futher compounded by the fact that the Federal program was itself a moving target; OSHA was busily engaged in trying to give written and operational meaning to the act's mandate for development and enforcement of Federal standards. Out of this welter of activity had to be gleaned an understanding of the essential parts of a Federal model against which States could gauge their development of approvable plans. How much of the Federal model should be drawn from its written program and how much from the operational results? What did "at least as effective" mean? How different could States be, at what points was divergence from the Federal program possible?

The strategy adopted by OSHA to achieve full State participation under the act rested on three fundamental assumptions. First was the premise that *all* States would be given full assistance and encouragement. Past performance, good or bad, was rejected as a criterion. In effect, the act was viewed as setting new ground rules, with room for full participation. To this end, a separate OSHA staff was established at both national and regional office levels to help the States develop plans.

Second was the premise that "at least as effective" permitted substantial State flexibility in developing and operating approvable standards enforcement. Approaches differing from the Federal model were to be encouraged, if the States could show theirs were as good as OSHA's attack on the problem. This point was tempered somewhat by the realization that a few attributes of the Federal program as defined by the act would probably prove essential to any enforcement effort.

The third assumption was a commitment to a thorough assessment of State participation, including both written plans and the operation of these plans. This entailed the development of a plan review system. Further, the creation of a system for evaluating plan *operation* assumed major importance; it needed to produce adequate, *timely* evaluation data without impeding the running of both Federal and State programs. An additional point deserves mention. Decentralization received substantial stress in setting up the program. Heavy emphasis was placed on regional staff involvement in dealing with State officials. With these assumptions, the first steps were: (1) to stimulate interest and get the States moving toward plan development, and (2) to start defining the nature of an approvable plan. . . .

Planning Grants

A substantial tool for moving the States toward approvable plans was the act's planning grant authority. This section provided for matching grants of up to 90 percent for identifying needs, developing State plans, developing record keeping programs, enhancing personnel capabilities, and generally improving safety and health programs. Authority to grant these funds expired on June 30 (1973). . . .

An additional stimulus to State participation was developed in two experimental inspection programs: the Target Industry Program and the Target Health Hazards Program.

To supplement Federal resources, States with substantial concentrations of high hazard establishments (and with good enforcement staffs) were invited to participate, supplying staff to act as Federal inspectors, with reimbursement for "services rendered." . . .

Plan Criteria

What were the criteria for an approvable State plan? OSHA decided two types of plans would be acceptable. The first is a *complete* plan. In this case, a State provides assurances that it is already at least as effective as the Federal program, in all relevant areas. This means, among other things, that the State already has sufficient statutory enforcement authority, adequate standards, full enforcement staff, and so forth. In the case of a complete plan, approval would be followed by immediate entry into the minimum 3-year period of operational evaluation.

The second type of plan is *developmental.* In this case, the State is *not,* at the time of written plan submission, at least as effective as the Federal program in all areas. . . . In a developmental plan, a State must identify its deficient areas, and specify the remedial steps it proposes to take. If the plan contains adequate assurances that these steps can be completed within 3 years, it receives approval. Operations are then evaluated while program development continues; at least one year of evaluation must be devoted to the plan's operation at full effectiveness.

The regulations anticipated that most States would fall into the developmental category for one of three reasons. First, many States lacked adequate standards coverage, and promulgation of new standards can be time consuming. Second, many States needed time to recruit and train staff. Third, and perhaps most important, many States lacked adequate enforcement authority. With many legislatures having only odd-year sessions, passing new laws can also become a lengthy process.

Through the vehicle of developmental plans, several important objectives could be served. States could ease into running comprehensive programs, with the assistance of operational (up to 50 percent) Federal grants. In addition, the transition to a full cooperative program could be smoothed by providing this means for participating States and OSHA to build strength together.

The regulations elaborated on the requirement for "at least as effective" standards development and enforcement. This was done by identifying the essential ingredients of the Federal standards-setting and enforcement apparatus, and listing these points as indices, each of which the State must address in its plan, in a manner at least as effective as the Federal approach. In all, there were 20 such indices—7 for standards development and 13 for enforcement.

These regulations, then, provided the main touchstone for States in developing plans. Their issuance helped make some points clear about the growth of the program. First, the Federal model was, and would continue to be, a moving target. It combined both written and operational elements, and as these were improved the States would have to keep pace in their plans. Second, while imitation of the Federal program was one avenue to approval, *effective* alternatives would be accepted, although the responsibility for demonstrating the acceptability of alternate approaches fell fully on the States. . . .

Evaluation

Once plans are approved, two problems acquire major significance: how are plans to be evaluated, and how will State and Federal operations be integrated? The evaluation system which OSHA has devised is designed to serve numerous goals. It will help OSHA determine appropriate Federal enforcement levels to supplement State programs during developmental phases. It will provide information for decisions about continuation or withdrawal of plan approval, both during the minimum 3-year trial period and after relinquishment of Federal authority. It will provide a basis for supplying technical assistance to States as needed.

The Post (Plan) Approval Evaluation System will involve a combination of written reports and analyses, on-site visits, and investigation of any complains received about State administration. Particular attention will be given to State enforcement techniques and outcomes, although all program areas will be examined. The bulk of evaluative work will be handled by regional staffs, in close cooperation with State personnel, although critical decisions, especially on continued acceptability of plans, will be made by the Secretary.

Program Integration

The problem of integrating Federal and State efforts is intricate. The basic tenets for coordinating activities with plan States have been devised through a combination of benchmark staffing levels and assessments of each State's current enforcement power.

States are at varying developmental stages which requires different combinations of Federal efforts in each jurisdiction. Basically, a State which is very close to being completely "as effective" will have a low level of Federal enforcement presence; States at the other end of the spectrum will have a higher concentration of Federal enforcement staff. Some minimum degree of Federal enforcement staff will be a relatively permanent fixture, to cover areas *not* included in State plans, and to perform evaluative work.

As can be guessed from the futuristic description of plan evaluation and program integration, some of the most critical phases of the program are yet to be faced. To date, most States have put forth a vigorous effort to measure up to Federal criteria.

Developmental plans, however, presume a continued uphill struggle, at least in the near future. The problem confronting States is one of program improvement; in particular, new enabling legislation may be a substantial hurdle. For OSHA, the question is twofold: how to devise new and relevant supports for the States in this process, and how to insure that the *total* program, Federal *and* State, meets the act's mandate to "provide . . . safe and healthful places of employment. . . ."

"Big Mother" and the Businessman

G. John Tysse

It would be a gross understatement to say that American employers were not satisfied with the Occupational Safety and Health Act when it was signed into law almost five years ago. Businessmen realized that OSHA would have an immediate impact on company operations. Prior to the law's passage, industry had voiced its concerns that OSHA would allow too much scope for arbitrary government interference into management decision making with the result that occupational safety and health problems in the context of real working conditions would get buried in the federal bureaucracy.

Be that as it may, the U.S. Congress proceeded to enact OSHA, thereby taking another step in the direction of "Big Motherism." Under "Big Motherism" the federal government functions as an omnipresent benign protector in order to minimize societal risks to its citizens. However, as already observed, this protector role can tend to interfere with traditional concepts of free enterprise, since industry is often targeted as the perpetrator of the risks.

Notwithstanding the non-punitive language in Section 2 of the Act, which proposes to encourage and stimulate employers in instituting new, and perfecting existing, safety and health programs, OSHA has operated much like a policeman. The reasons for this enforcement posture are easily discernible. OSHA is given form and substance by the package of mandatory occupational safety and health standards with which industry must comply. To determine compliance, OSHA must inspect, and in cases where al-

Reprinted from *Trial Magazine* 11, no. 5 (September/October 1975), with the permission of the publisher.

leged violations are discovered, OSHA must issue citations and proposed penalties This is the most tangible way for OSHA to determine its job performance.

This is not to say that OSHA has not made efforts to educate employers on improving their safety and health programs. On the contrary, OSHA has conducted training courses, has issued many educational publications, and has even expressed a willingness to personally consult with employers in an effort to encourage improved safety and health awareness. Unfortunately, OSHA has difficulty in determining the effectiveness of these cooperative programs, particularly in comparison to the relative ease with which standard compliance can be determined. Thus, there is a strong tendency on the part of OSHA to downgrade voluntary compliance activities.

A few months ago, OSHA issued a new program through which small employers could request the assistance of government experts to advise them in meeting OSHA requirements. Rather than maintaining a clear separation between this "consultation" and its normal enforcement activities, OSHA devised the final program so that enforcement personnel could beome too easily involved in the consultations. In other words, OSHA was telling the small businessman: "Our consultant is here to help you. However, if you don't listen to his or her advice, then we're going to bring our enforcers in and they'll make you listen."

A serious limitation exists in a philosophy built exclusively around determining standards compliance. Even if OSHA were successful in achieving absolute compliance with its standards, it is highly unlikely that totally hazard-free workplaces would result. Indeed, there are studies that indicate that only one out of five industrial injuries will be prevented through maximum control of physical factors.

By now it can be seen that all of industry's OSHA concerns are related in varying degrees to standards' compliance. During the first two years of the Act, the Secretary of Labor was given almost unlimited statutory authority to incorporate by reference any national consensus standards or already existing federal safety/health standards. Seizing upon this broad mandate, the Secretary proceeded to adopt a package of standards, limited to general industry alone, that filled more than 250 pages in the *Federal Register*.

In all fairness, many of the national consensus standards were adopted at the urging of industry, perhaps because employer representatives had been active on the drafting committees which originally drew up the standards. Yet very few people realized that these consensus standards had been designed and drafted exclusively as advisory guidelines in order to prescribe optimal workplace safety and health conditions. They were never intended to have the force and effect of law.

Based on the above, it should not be hard to understand industry's frequent complaint that the OSHA standards are complex, difficult to interpret, and in many cases impossible to comply with. While OSHA has made a few passes at revising or eliminating some of the more obscure or antiquated standards, a substantial majority of that initial standards package remains on the books as a legal requirement for industry.

There is one curious anomaly which exists in the area of OSHA standards interpretation. It is a general industry view that the standards should be performance-type. In other words, standards should be expressed in terms of objective criteria for the performance desired. Yet there are employers who complain that many of the OSHA standards are vague and unenforceable. A leading example cited is the standard which requires that personal protective equipment shall be used "whenever it is necessary, by reason of hazards (which are) capable of causing injury or impairment." (See *Ryder Truck Lines Inc.* v. *Brennan,* 497 F 2d 230.) On balance, it would appear that

American industry is better off with a performance-type standard which may be subject to complaints of vagueness, than with the alternative of a rigid specification of standard which can so severely limit the employer's option for innovation in creating a safe or healthful work condition.

It is becoming increasingly apparent, as evidenced by the recent action taken with respect to the chemical vinyl chloride, that the future emphasis of OSHA will be on the promulgation and enforcement of occupational health standards rather than safety standards. A major concern of business is the feasibility of compliance with these OSHA standards designed to prevent exposures to hazardous substances.

Many of OSHA's occupational health standards have originated and will continue to originate out of criteria documents sent to OSHA from the National Institute for Occupational Safety and Health (NIOSH). This procedure has tended to increase the political pressure on OSHA, however, because the NIOSH scientists are not required to consider economic impact or the state of the technology when preparing their criteria. The NIOSH recommendations often take the form of a standard, which, should it be adopted and implemented, would provide absolute protection for employees. If OSHA subsequently modifies the standard to account for feasibility considerations, the agency is criticized for selling out on the health protection of American workers. Yet the Act explicitly directs the Secretary to consider feasibility when setting occupational health standards. (See *AFL-CIO* v. *Hodgson,* 499 F 2d 467.)

It is impossible to overstate the difficulty involved in trying to establish what is feasible. Economic impact, technological achievability, production interference potential, magnitude of risk—all of these are relevant factors that must be considered in determining feasibility. To say there are simple solutions to the dilemma of providing total protection to the worker versus accepting a possible risk of exposure in order to permit continuing production is to be ignorant of the problem. However, until such time as this nation decides that American industry shall provide a workplace absolutely free from harmful exposure (a concept explicitly rejected by the Occupational Safety and Health Act) then it must be willing to look at the problem in the terms of an "acceptable risk." Therefore, the Secretary's ultimate determination as to feasibility is of critical importance to both the employer and the worker.

There is another very important factor relating to feasibility, i.e., who has the burden of proving it? Up until recently, the Occupational Safety and Health Review Commission and the federal courts have held that the Secretary of Labor has the burden of proof as to feasibility in contested OSHA enforcement actions. (See *National Realty and Construction Company* v. *OSHARC,* 489 F 2d 1257.) Perhaps stung by the frequent failure to carry this burden, the Solicitor of Labor has introduced a clever manipulation of words in several of the recently proposed OSHA standards, most notably the noise standard, which would appear to switch the burden of proof to the cited employer by making him prove infeasibility. This backdoor legal maneuver, if successful, would tremendously enhance the Solicitor's odds in proving violations against a cited employer.

Another major concern to industry arising out of OSHA is the proliferation of record-keeping requirements. Included in these are not only the standard OSHA record-keeping forms relating to injury and illness statistics, but also the numerous specific requirements such as inspection and maintenance records on mechanized equipment. OSHA is now proposing extensive record-keeping as well as monitoring and medical surveillance requirements on virtually all new and existing health standards.

The Act directs the Secretary to obtain record-keeping information with a minimum burden upon employers. . . . However, it is becoming increasingly clear that unless something is done to alleviate the growing cumulative effect of occupational health standards' record-keeping requirements, there will not be enough medical, clerical, and industrial hygiene personnel within this country to perform the duties required by the standards.

The problem to employers which has received the most publicity and attention, even though it is subordinate in impact to the issues already discussed herein, is the way in which OSHA has enforced the law. Complaints of "Gestapo tactics" were not unfamiliar to OSHA officials in the first months of the law's operation, and are still voiced occasionally.

Much of the criticism directed at OSHA enforcement results from the way the Act has been administered. Federal compliance officers, as noted previously, are instructed to cite any alleged hazard which they discover upon a workplace inspection. If the gravity of the hazard warrants it, then monetary penalties are proposed against the employer. The federal inspectors are not permitted to advise employers on compliance, nor are they allowed to give any dispensation to an employer who corrects a violation immediately after it is pointed out by the inspector.

There are two serious drawbacks to this enforcement system. First, it doesn't permit good faith credit to the employer who wants to comply with OSHA's requirements but simply doesn't know them all. Thus, when an inspection takes place, this employer is basically treated the same as the employer who has totally rejected OSHA. Secondly, the size of the penalties proposed by OSHA has been negligible in comparison to the costs associated with abatement thereby serving to harass rather than motivate the cited employer.

While space limitations prohibit a detailed discussion, there are other specific concerns that American industry has experienced arising out of OSHA. For example, jurisdictional conflicts exist with other federal regulatory agencies, as evidenced by the railroad industry, where the U.S. Department of Transportation has also claimed occupational safety and health jurisdiction. Rather than exercising the authority . . . of the Act to recommend legislation to avoid unnecessary duplication between OSHA and other federal laws, the Secretary of Labor has asserted broad jurisdiction for OSHA, while leaving resolution of the avoidable conflicts of authority up to the tedious process of litigation.

Another area of concern to industry is OSHA's complicated and extremely burdensome variance procedures. This cumbersome process not only discourages employers in requesting variances from OSHA standards requirements, it also seriously hinders the Secretary of Labor in acting expeditiously on valid variance applications.

It should be obvious by now that OSHA has not been accepted by American industry in the spirit of cooperation and dedication which is necessary in order for the law to accomplish its stated purpose, i.e., to assure so far as possible safe and healthful working conditions for every working man and woman in the nation. The attitude taken by the law's administrators has been to view industry as the bad guy. Thus OSHA has attempted to achieve industry compliance through enforcement rather than through encouragement. Similarly, the U.S. Congress, which has the power to amend the law to make it less punitive and more amenable to industry, has been content to do nothing. As long as this climate remains unchanged, OSHA will never achieve its hoped-for success.

The Continuing Fight for Job Safety

John R. Oravec

Nearly 63 million American workers are seeking refuge under the federal occupational safety and health umbrella that was unfurled three years ago. Enacted late in 1970 and effective in April 1971, the safety law was hailed as the blueprint for development of the best possible safeguards against hazards in the nation's 5 million workplaces.

As the Labor Department got down to the routine of administering the act, some of the expectations of job safety did materialize. But the full potential of the law has not been reached.

Underfunding, delays, partial solutions and weak enforcement have diluted the total effectiveness of the law. Minute loopholes are being dilated by employer interests and their friends in the Nixon administration. Every session of Congress since passage has a load of bills dumped on it that would weaken or repeal the act.

Progress is being made against day-to-day hazards. But progress has at times come in teaspoon proportions and often been shadowed by setbacks.

Employer groups such as the U.S. Chamber of Commerce fought enactment of the safety bill . . . from the start and are leading the fight against effective enforcement and funding of the law.

Washington lobbyists representing smaller businessmen have been particularly active in the campaign to cripple or kill the law. In 1972, they managed to push through Congress a measure that would exclude federal enforcement for firms with 15 or fewer workers. Organized labor was successful in whittling down the exclusion to three or fewer workers when the legislation got to the conference committee. . . .

Subsequent efforts by business and right wing groups to bury the law have emerged in Congress. But the National Association of Manufacturers, which had opposed the safety legislation, now appears to be softening its position. The NAM and substantial elements of large interstate business have shown indications that a uniform federal safety program would be more palatable than a potpourri of state plans.

Consequently, the tug-of-war over job safety and health is not a classical struggle between labor and management. Many large corporations are aware of productivity losses resulting from disabling job injuries or illnesses that eventually erode profits.

Smaller business looks at job safety as an investment problem: job safety carries a price tag that cuts into profits. But for workers, job hazards encompass the horrors of serious injury and occupational disease that carry the burden of lost wages, hardships and added expense:

Reprinted from the *American Federationist*, June 1974, pp. 1–6, with the permission of the AFL-CIO.

An estimated 14,500 workers are killed annually in on-the-job accidents.

Another 2.2 million are permanently or temporarily disabled by occupational injuries and disease.

One of every 10 workers suffers a work-related injury or illness each year.

The annual mandays lost to job injuries and illness totals 25 million for those covered by OSHA alone.

An estimated 25,000 chemical and physical agents are regularly used in industry, and each year more new materials are being introduced. Workers are exposed to these materials without any assurance that they are not hazardous to their health.

Independent studies have detected that many more job accidents are not reported. For example, the Jerome B. Gordon study commissioned by the Labor Department and published in 1971 found that 25 million serious injuries and thousands of deaths go uncounted each year.

To thwart record keeping in some industries it's a common practice to bring disabled workers back on the job—still in the cast if necessary—so they can check in and get off the list of on-the-job injuries.

Occupational disease often goes undetected because of the latency of the appearance of illness in workers after chronic exposure to low-level doses of toxic materials and because doctors in general practice do not have the expertise to determine that a worker's illness may be caused by a hazard on the job. Factory doctors, while well versed in their profession, are at times under employer pressure from reporting findings which would leave companies open to legal suits or additional payments to workmen's compensation programs.

Once the federal safety law emerged in 1970, the main battlefield for job safety shifted to the Occupational Safety and Health Administration where the standards are developed.

Ironically, OSHA has been attacked by smaller business groups, claiming that federal inspectors use "gestapo" tactics in enforcing the law. Labor has viewed these charges as a smokescreen to pave the way in Congress for weakening amendments that would neutralize the law. Unions have found that OSHA has not fulfilled its enforcement role.

Much of the agency's problems stem from the lack of adequate funds and manpower. . . . While the fight goes on in Congress for the needed increase in OSHA spending, the agency is also stirring strong opposition to its long-range efforts to return safety enforcement programs to the states.

It was because of shoddy state programs and weak enforcement that Congress enacted the federal safety law. Yet, since the law has been in effect, the agency has approved 25 state plans that would replace much of the enforcement in those jurisdictions. None of the 25 plans meets the test of quality specified by Congress.

Section 18 of the law does provide for the development of state safety programs, but it insists that they be "at least as effective" as the standards under the federal law.

Although some state proposals come close, none provides the effectiveness of federal protection for workers. What could result is a crazy-quilt patchwork of state plans, like the current mishmash of state workmen's compensation programs.

Companies located in several states have problems with different interpretations, adjudication procedures and court systems—all of which add to the expense of doing business.

Under such a disjointed set-up, companies that find safety standards too restrictive in one state could shift operations to another where regulations are lax. This could lead to a form of political and legislative blackmail whereby companies pressure the state to relax safety enforcement under the threat of shutting down their plants and moving the business elsewhere.

More than 40 states have submitted plans to OSHA for approval. If past patterns are followed, even the most inferior ones will be cleared, along with half the grant-in-aid funds needed for "development." The state provides the other half of the funds.

OSHA approved the 25th state plan earlier this year and legal action against the Labor Department to check further erosion has been brought by the AFL-CIO, asking a federal court to block the Secretary of Labor from "abdicating federal enforcement responsibilities." . . .

While traveling to Capitol Hill annually to seek more funds for federal safety programs, labor has been urging Congress to plug the drain of money for the state plans, as favored by the administration.

President Nixon's fiscal 1975 budget would provide an appropriation of $102.5 million for OSHA. Although this is a $32 million increase over the current fiscal year, all but $9 million of that would be used to boost the funding of state programs. The budget calls for doubling the spending for state programs from the current $23 million to $46 million, surpassing the funds proposed for federal inspection by $9 million. Funds for federal inspection in the coming fiscal year would be $37 million, an increase of $8.8 million, which would help pay for expanding the federal enforcement staff from 800 to 920. Labor's position is that $23 million of the $46 million should be re-allocated from the state plans to federal enforcement, making possible the addition of nearly 11,000 inspectors.

Even with added manpower, that would leave one inspector to cover an average of 2,200 work places. Workers in more than 4 million plants, shops, construction sites and other establishments come under the federal safety jurisdiction. . . .

A critical past of the budget will seriously affect the National Institute of Occupational Safety and Health (NIOSH), a branch of the U.S. Department of Health, Education and Welfare. The President proposes to cut the direct operations of NIOSH from the current level of $26.8 million to $23.5 million—less than was spent on occupational health by HEW before OSHA was enacted. The AFL-CIO is asking $16.7 million more for fiscal year 1975.

The HEW agency has the responsibility for handling the research of the health hazards faced by workers on the job, but it has been severely crimped by underfunding. No other government agency has enough expert manpower to investigate occupational health hazards. Consequently, little research of this type is conducted in the United States.

Of the 3,000 new chemical and physical agents introduced each year, the burden of proof of whether a chemical is safe is not on the employer. The government, with limited research facilities on occupational disease, provides little control over the introduction of new chemicals.

While the safety law provides that the government can take immediate action to protect workers from the imminent danger of death or serious disease, it is seldom applied. No government agency has the expertise to determine serious health hazards. Consequently, action comes only on the brink of disaster.

Typical of this situation is the current vinyl chloride threat in the plastics and related industries. Liver cancer and other serious disorders have been linked directly to the chemical gas, commonly used to make polyvinyl chloride or PVC, a solid plastic that has wide industrial and consumer application.

Thirteen cases of the liver cancer—angiosarcoma—have been found among vinyl chloride workers in the United States. Eleven of those are dead. Another dozen cases have been diagnosed in other countries.

When the vinyl chloride deathers were reported at a B. F. Goodrich plant in Louisville, Kentucky, earlier this year, concentrations of the gas were permitted up to 500 parts per one million parts of air. (500 ppm)

Largely on the basis of findings by an Italian researcher, Professor Cesare Maltoni of Bologna University, OSHA reduced the exposure level to 50 parts per one million of air—one-tenth of what was previously allowed.

The level was reduced after hearings in which labor representatives warned that even the proposed 50 ppm level was unsafe for workers. But OSHA acceded to management representatives who contended it would be impractical to further reduce concentrations in vinyl chloride plants.

The AFL-CIO Industrial Union Department, backed by findings of its medical consultants, continued to press for a standard that would ban any worker exposure to vinyl chloride. Additional studies by scientists in the United States and other countries reinforced the IUD warnings that any measurable level of vinyl chloride could be a serious health threat.

The Labor Department is now prepared to reduce worker exposure to the cancer-causing chemical to "no detectable level," which could come in a permanent standard to replace the emergency standard issued April 5.

But for the estimated 6,500 U.S. workers handling vinyl chloride, the reduction may come too late. Medical examinations conducted in cooperation with unions showed that hundreds of workers are suffering from abnormal liver functions and other serious disorders.

The hazard may also extend to nearly one million other workers involved in the secondary use of PVC where concentrations of the vinyl chloride fumes are known to exceed 200 ppm. Had NIOSH been able to operate with adequate funding for the needed research functions, the vinyl chloride threat might have been detected earlier.

NIOSH almost ceased to function effectively recently because the lack of funds threatened the cutback of key positions, phaseout of manpower training programs, a further downgrading in the HEW hierarchy, and the proposed transfer of the agency to the Commerce Department under the Administration's executive reorganization plan. Many of these problems could be overcome by transferring NIOSH to the Labor Department so it can work more closely with OSHA in developing occupational health standards.

Only three of the 550 projected OSHA health standards were issued in the past three years. This lag is traced not only to the cumbersome methods of converting NIOSH criteria documents into OSHA standards, but also to the agency's lack of information about the thousands of new chemicals flooding workplaces.

NIOSH has 15,000 chemicals on its toxic substances list, which at the present rate of chemical development should double by next year, said Edward J. Baier, deputy director of NIOSH.

"But when it comes to knowing how dangerous each chemical is—let alone how carcinogenic—we just don't have the data. If these products were tested prior to their introduction to the worksite, we might not be surprised by any more vinyl chloride incidents," Baier noted.

Toxic substances control legislation is temporarily stalled in a Senate-House conference committee. That measure would require company testing of new chemicals under Environmental Protection Agency rules.

On the other hand, labor is supporting efforts to increase appropriations for NIOSH and the National Institute of Environmental Health Sciences for further research in petrochemical health hazards.

With a NIOSH budget of $23.5 million and a staff of 611 spread across the country and dealing in all aspects of occupational health, the agency has little resources left for definitive research into vinyl chloride hazards or any other toxic substance. Thus far, most of the research on harmful chemicals has been conducted by industry. But much of what industry did uncover on vinyl chloride, for instance, has been held under tight wraps. Many of these closely held secrets were not revealed until Labor Department hearings in February that led to the temporary emergency standard.

As early as 1964, workers at the Goodrich plant in Louisville who clipped away residue and cleaned the insides of polyvinyl chloride reactor vessels were found to have a serious "hand problem" that was identified as acoosteolysis—a disease of finger bone joints.

Tests of 271 Goodrich plant workers conducted last year showed that 55 were suffering from abnormal liver functions. As suspicions grew, medical records of several deceased employees were reviewed. One died of an unknown type of liver cancer in 1968. Two died of angiosarcoma of the liver, one in 1971, the other in 1973. Another died of what was diagnosed as cirrhosis of the liver.

At the Labor Department hearings, Professor Maltoni reported that laboratory animals developed liver cancer at 250 ppm. In additional limited experimentations, Maltoni reported that none of his animals developed liver cancer at 50 ppm. Although scientists and medical experts considered this phase of the Maltoni study inconclusive because of the few animals involved, the Secretary of Labor established the 50 ppm standard.

The standard was issued over the warnings of Dr. Marcus M. Key, director of NIOSH, who said NIOSH had been unable to determine any safe level of exposure to vinyl chloride. He urged a strict ban on workplace exposures.

Only after the results of studies for the Manufacturing Chemists Association disclosed that laboratory animals developed liver cancer and other diseases at 50 ppm did the Labor Department propose the permanent standard that would restrict any worker exposure to vinyl chloride.

But even if the "no detectable level" standard is established, there is serious concern whether it can be effectively enforced. Presently neither NIOSH nor OSHA is adequately equipped or staffed to do the job. The myriad enforcement problems for millions of other workers magnify the government's enforcement dilemma.

Another problem complicating effective enforcement of OSHA is the Occupational Safety and Health Review Commission, a three member, presidentially-appointed adjudication agency which was opposed by organized labor when the act was before Congress.

The Review Commission passes final judgment on contested citations for violations of OSHA standards, rules and orders. In 106 important cases before the Commission last year, the employer was given relief in 93 against only 13 in which the employer was dealt with more severely. Nearly 90 percent of all employer requests for longer abatement periods were approved and less than one percent rejected.

Delay is another problem. More than 2,200 contested citations are currently awaiting action, and decisions on a number of important cases have been inordinately delayed by the commission itself. For example, the commission held up its final decision on an Omaha smelter case for more than two years after the judge had submitted the record for review.

The overall federal safety and health program needs to be upgraded if the government is expected to comply with the intent of Congress in the passage of the act. However, Congress must also provide the funds that would meet its goal, starting with the addition of at least 1,400 OSHA compliance officers in the next fiscal year.

Coverage should also be extended to all American workers, including government and public employees and those who are under other federal safety and health statutes, including most miners and railroad workers.

To achieve uniform nationwide protection, the state plans should be phased out. During the transition, qualified state compliance officers should be trained by OSHA to catch up on the lag in federal inspections.

The figures on work related injuries or illnesses—one of every 10 workers—are for 1972, the latest year for which the Bureau of Labor Statistics has complete data. The BLS report shows that of the 58.8 million workers under OSHA in 1972, 5.8 million were affected by occupational accidents and diseases. One-third of those workers lost time because of their disabilities, totaling 25 million workdays.

The construction industry traditionally has the highest injury-illness rate, with 19 of every 100 workers affected while construction workers make up on 5.9 percent of the OSHA-covered workforce. Manufacturing comes next with 15.5 of every 100.

Despite the high toll in job-related injuries and illness and the estimated 14,500 workers killed every year on the job, employers often accuse OSHA of harsh enforcement policies and excessive penalties.

However, the tally of fines proposed by the safety agency are averaging less than $30 per citation—about the same cost as running a red light. Fines for serious violations, particularly those involving fatal accidents, are higher but not excessive.

For example, when 14 construction workers were killed and 34 injured in the collapse of a high-rise apartment complex at Baileys Crossroads, Virginia, the total penalty amounted to $13,000.

A concrete subcontractor for the project was found in willful violation of three federal standards, including the premature removal of concrete forms from the 23rd floor after the 24th floor was poured. OSHA also charged the company with using damaged timber for shoring on two lower floors and failing to provide guard railings.

The company contested the case to the Occupational Safety and Health Review Commission. After a series of conferences, the firm agreed to pay the $13,000 penalty, but made no admission to the charges. At the rate, the company paid a fine of about $30 per injured worker and less than $800 for each of the workers killed in the disaster. This lack of teeth in enforcement is part of the continuing problem affecting millions of U.S. workers.

Because of the meager funding and thin compliance force—well under 1,000 officers to cover the more than 4 million workplaces—the chances of an OSHA inspection at a worksite are slim. With the present staff, even if an inspector would visit one plant every day, the odds against an annual inspection are no better than 17 to 1. Only when a serious danger exists can workers expect a prompt and thorough inspection of their workplace.

Most of the routine safety and health problems still must be resolved at the local level by workers and their union representatives. An effective approach to meeting these goals is bargaining safety and health clauses into collective bargaining agreements or developing joint labor-management committees that operate in a manner similar to the grievance procedure.

One new aspect in job safety agreements is the move toward studies of job perils negotiated by the Rubber Workers. The United Rubber Workers has an agreement with the top five U.S. rubber companies calling for one-half cent per hour worked to be contributed to the on-the-job environmental health fund to finance the studies.

The General Objectives of Workmen's Compensation

National Commission on State Workmen's Compensation Laws

A. The Basic Nature of Workmen's Compensation

There is a workmen's compensation act for each of the 50 states. . . . No two acts are exactly alike, but many have similar basic features.

Workmen's compensation provides cash benefits, medical care, and rehabilitation services for workers who suffer work-related injuries and diseases. To be eligible for benefits, normally an employee must experience a "personal injury by accident arising out of and in the course of employment." All states provide benefits for workers with occupational diseases, although not all cover every form of occupational disease.

Chapter 2 considers in some detail the phrase "personal injury by accident arising out of and in the course of employment." In general, its effect is to exclude some injuries and diseases from the scope of the program. But the distinguishing feature of workmen's compensation is that it assures benefits for many who could not win suits for damages under the common law, which usually requires that an injured party prove the defendant was at fault. Workmen's compensation benefits are paid even when the employer is free of negligence or other fault. These benefits are the employer's exclusive liability for work-related injuries and diseases. As the next section indicates, this decision to hold the employer liable without fault, while limiting his liability, was a deliberate choice.

When an injury or disease falls within the scope of the workmen's compensation programs, the employer must furnish medical care, usually unlimited in time or amount. Most states also provide vocational and medical rehabilitation services, or supervise these services as furnished by the employer.

Cash benefits usually are classified as temporary total, temporary partial, permanent total, permanent partial and death benefits. Temporary total benefits are paid to employees unable to work after a specified waiting period. Temporary partial benefits are paid during a period of reduced earnings. These temporary benefits cease when the worker returns to full wages or is found eligible for permanent total or permanent partial benefits. Permanent total benefits are paid to those disabled completely for an indefinite time. Permanent partial benefits are paid if the employee

Reprinted from the *Report of the National Commission on State Workmen's Laws* (Washington, D.C.: U.S. Government Printing Office, 1972), pp. 31–40.

incurs an injury or disease which causes a permanent impairment or experiences a permanent but partial loss of wages or of wage earning capacity. If the worker is fatally injured, the employer is required to provide burial expenses and to pay benefits to specified dependent survivors. For each category of benefits, all States prescribe a maximum weekly benefit and usually a minimum weekly benefit. Some States prescribe limits on duration or total amount or both for certain classes of benefits.

The primary purpose of these benefits is to replace some proportion of wage loss, actual or potential. Many States also provide benefits because of impairment, whether or not this results in lost wages. Most laws prescribe a schedule of permanent partial impairments which specifies the number of weeks benefits paid for the loss (including loss of use) of particular parts of the body.

In all but one State, an administrative agency supervises workmen's compensation claims; in 45 States, the agency also adjudicates disputes concerning eligibility for benefits and extent of disability. Decisions of these agencies may be appealed for review by the courts. In five States, the courts decide all disputed claims.

Despite the State role in workmen's compensation, it is largely a privately administered and funded program. The workmen's compensation statutes provide that each employer shall compensate disabled workmen by a certain formula of benefits, and that the employer must pay for these benefits. The employer usually makes private insurance arrangements to meet his statutory obligations. In all but four States, the employer may self-insure the risks of work-related injuries and diseases if he can meet the State financial standards. In 44 States, the employer may purchase workmen's compensation insurance from private insurance carriers. There are 18 States which operate insurance funds, but 12 of these compete with private carriers. Of the States which bar private carriers, three allow eligible employers to self-insure. Private insurance carriers are responsible for about 63 percent of all benefits paid, self-insurers for 14 percent, and State funds for 23 percent.

Workmen's compensation benefits are financed by charges in the form of insurance premiums at rates related to the benefits paid. The relationship between benefits paid and the employer's cost is most direct for self-insuring employers. Other employers are rated on the experience of their class by State insurance funds or private carriers. Typically, several hundred insurance classifications are used in each State. The individual employer usually pays a rate related to the benefits paid by all employers in his class, but employers with sufficiently large premiums can have their rates modified to reflect their own record of benefit payments relative to other firms in their class. Some employers pay three times as much per $100 of payroll as others in their classification. These differences provide a powerful incentive to reduce the frequency of compensable injuries and diseases.

B. The Origin of Workmen's Compensation in America

In the first decade of the twentieth century, U.S. industrial injury rates reached their all-time peak. In 1907, in two industries alone, railroading and bituminous coal mining, the toll was 7,000 dead. Despite these tragedies, the remedies available to recompense disabled workers or their families were inadequate and inequitable, consisting mainly of appeals to charity or lawsuits based either on the common law or, in many jurisdictions, on employers' liability statutes.

The common law for work injuries originally developed when most employers had few employees. Often a firm was like a large family that settled disputes without appeal to the courts. With this tradition, courts tended generally to lack sympathy for complaints by employees. In an economic and political climate favoring industrial growth, the courts were reluctant to burden entrepreneurs with the care of those disabled in their employment.

Most observers were critical of the common law handling of work-related injuries. As plaintiff, the workman had to prove the employer's negligence. Given the complexity of the work situation and the reluctance of fellow workers to testify against the employer, the worker often could not prove his claim. Even more obstructive to the employee's chance for recovery were three defenses available to the employer: (1) contributory negligence: the worker whose own negligence had contributed in any degree to his injury could not recover; (2) the fellow-servant doctrine: the employee could not recover if the injury resulted from the negligence of a fellow worker; and (3) assumption of risk: the injured man could not recover if the injury was due to an inherent hazard of which he had, or should have had, advance knowledge.

By the middle of the 19th century, protests against the grossest deficiencies and inequities of the common law led to employers' liability laws, which restricted the employer's legal defenses. However, these laws still obliged the employee to prove the employer's negligence, and their contribution to the ability of an injured workman to win a claim against his employer was minimal.

At the opening of the 20th century, the shortcomings of the legal remedies for work-related injuries were common knowledge. The compensation system which based liability on negligence was an anachronism in a time when work was recognized to involve certain inherent and often unpredictable hazards. Awards for injuries generally were inadequate, inconsistent, and uncertain. The system was wasteful, partially because of high legal costs. Settlements were delayed by court procedures. Society was disturbed by the burden of charity for uncompensated injured workmen. As Arthur Larson has observed, "the coincidence of increasing industrial accidents and decreasing remedies had produced in the United States a situation ripe for radical change. . . . "

Workmen's compensation statutes, as an alternative to the common law and employers' liability acts, had many objectives, most of them designed to remedy past deficiencies. The statutes aimed to provide adequate benefits, while limiting the employer's liability strictly to workmen's compensation payments. These payments were to be prompt and predetermined, to relieve both employees and employers of uncertainty and to eliminate wasteful litigation. Appropriate medical care was to be provided. Most radical of all these objectives was the establishment of a legal principle alien to the common law: liability without fault. The costs of work-related injuries were to be allocated to the employer, not because of any presumption that he was to blame for every individual tragedy, but because of the inherent hazards of industrial employment. Compensation for work-related accidents was therefore accepted as a cost of production.

These objectives were widely applauded. The workmen's compensation program eventually was supported by both the National Association of Manufacturers and the American Federation of Labor.

The no-fault approach spread rapidly: between 1911 and 1920, all but six States passed workmen's compensation statutes. These laws were influenced by the contemporary interpretations of constitutional law. The Supreme Court reading of the interstate commerce clause precluded the possibility of a Federal law on workmen's compensation for most private industry, although the Federal Employers' Liability

Act, applicable to railroad employees engaged in interstate commerce, and a compensation act covering certain Federal employees were both enacted in 1908. A New York State study commission, whose 1910 report was the basis for the New York Compensation Act, would have adopted the German compensation plan's feature of employee contributions had this been deemed constitutional. Of even greater impact was the 1911 decision by the Court of Appeals of New York that compulsory coverage was unconstitutional because the imposition of liability without fault was taking of property without due process of law. Consequently, these early laws made coverage elective and applied mainly to specified hazardous industries.

Although most of these consitutional views no longer hold, their imprint on today's workmen's compensation statutes is unmistakable. The present system is basically State operated and almost exclusively employer financed. Moreover, in some States, the tradition of elective coverage and the application to only certain occupations continues: only about 85 percent of all employed wage and salary workers are covered by workmen's compensation.

A description of the origins of workmen's compensation, including the vestigial constitutional inhibitions, serves a larger purpose than homage to history. The basic principles of the present program are largely those established 50 or 60 years ago; they can be completely understood only in the context of forces present at their creation.

Since then, the task of workmen's compensation has grown more difficult. Technological advances have produced unfamiliar and often indeterminable physical and toxic hazards. Occupational diseases associated with prolonged exposures to unsuspected agents or to fortuitous combinations of stresses have undermined the usefulness of the "accident" concept. While advances in medical knowledge have facilitated the treatment of many injuries and diseases, they have also enlarged the list of diseases that may be work-related. Simple cause/effect concepts of the past have yielded to an appreciation of the many interacting forces that may result in impairment or death. In addition to genetic, environmental, cultural, and psychological influences, physicians must consider predisposing, precipitating, aggravating, and perpetuating factors in disease. Etiologic analysis, estimates of the relationship to work, and evaluation of the extent of impairment have become accordingly complex for many illnesses.

Workmen's compensation has failed, meanwhile, to achieve certain of its original objectives. The program has not been self-administering but has seemingly spurred litigation. Benefits have increased but in most States have not kept pace with rising wage levels. The failure to adapt to changing conditions has led to many criticisms, but constructive criticism requires a restatement of the objectives for the modern era.

C. Five Objectives for a Modern Workmen's Compensation Program

Many of the traditional attributes of the workmen's compensation program, such as liability without fault, have continuing validity. Other attributes which persist, such as elective coverage, are no longer warranted in the light of the objectives of a modern workmen's compensation program. These are stated in general terms below. . . .

The four basic objectives are:

broad coverage of employees and work-related injuries and diseases;

substantial protection against interruption of income;

provision of sufficient medical care and rehabilitation services; and

encouragement of safety.

The achievement of these basic objectives is dependent on an equally important fifth objective:

an effective system for delivery of the benefits and services.

After discussing these five objectives in turn, we shall examine a distinctive attribute of workmen's compensation: the program is designed to assure that the objectives reinforce each other.

1. Workmen's Compensation Should Provide Broad Coverage of Employees and Work-Related Injuries and Diseases

Workmen's compensation protection should be extended to as many workers as feasible, and all work-related injuries and diseases should be covered.

Coverage of employees. Among the many reasons given for the lack of universal coverage of employees is that many of the currently excluded firms are small or have poor safety records and are reluctant to bear the cost of workmen's compensation. This argument is not convincing. Many States have been able to extend their laws to virtually all employers without undue financial distress. An economic advantage of coverage is that employers are relieved of possible liability in damage suits. Moreover, if the costs of newly covered employers are high, this means that employees and society were previously absorbing the costs of work-related impairments and deaths through enforced poverty or welfare payments. We believe these costs should be assessed against employers, not against the disabled or the ordinary taxpayer.

Another factor in the exclusion of certain occupations from workmen's compensation is that these groups, such as household workers, lack political influence. We believe that this explanation, while historically accurate, is unacceptable as a basis for a modern workmen's compensation program. Another historic reason for excluding certain workers was the constitutional requirement of due process. At one time, the due process standard forced States to make their laws elective, so that the laws embraced primarily work that was especially dangerous. Today, the constitutional limitations of due process have little or no relevance to workmen's compensation.

More cogent arguments against extending workmen's compensation to certain classes of employees are based on administrative feasibility. If certain employers, such as homeowners or owners of small farms, were required to cover all of their employees, many of whom are casual, the administrative burden on employers, insurance carriers, and State workmen's compensation agencies would be substantial. A related argument is that it is difficult to inform homeowners and other employers of casual labor of the coverage requirement. Because these arguments have some merit, our recommendations will reflect our concern for these conditions, while manifesting our primary interest in protecting workers, regardless of who are their employers.

A final argument against universal mandated coverage is that it limits the ability of employees and employers to decide freely how much protection against work-related injuries and diseases is desirable. In the absense of workmen's compensation, the parties would be free to negotiate contracts concerning the risks of industrial disabilities, or each party could individually purchase insurance.

For several reasons we do not find the freedom-to-contract plea convincing. A classic point against that plea is that employees do not have equal bargaining power with their employers, particularly when employees are not unionized. An even more compelling reason for mandatory insurance is that the task of selecting a job is complex. Most workers are unlikely to assess properly the probabilities of being exposed to work-related impairments. Often employees and employers are contemptuous of the risks they assume. We believe that society can appropriately mandate workmen's compensation coverage as a way of insuring that those injured at work do not become destitute.

Coverage of injuries and diseases. All work-related injuries and diseases should be covered by workmen's compensation. Of necessity, the meaning of "work-related" must be defined by statute and interpreted judicially, but injuries and diseases which are in fact work-related should not be excluded from coverage because of legal technicalities. On this basis, statutes which restrict coverage to a list of specified occupational diseases are incompatible with the objective of complete protection.

Arguments against broad coverage of injuries and diseases are sometimes similar to those against broad coverage of employees, e.g., the expense of full coverage. Experience refutes these theories: many States have succeeded with broad coverage of work-related injuries and diseases.

2. Workmen's Compensation Should Provide Substantial Protection Against Interruption of Income

Workmen's compensation must be an insurance program, not a welfare program. The availability and extent of cash benefits should not depend primarily on a beneficiary's economic needs, as in public assistance programs. Rather, the cash benefits for the disabled worker should be closely tied to his loss of income. The benefit formulas should also be carefully predetermined in order to reduce uncertainties of employees and employers about the possible consequences of injuries and diseases.

Disability benefits. The basic measure of the worker's economic loss is the life-time diminution in remuneration attributable to the work-related injury or disease. This can roughly be described as wage loss, although renumeration is composed of earnings plus supplements. Supplements include fringe benefits, such as health insurance, and legally mandated expenditures, such as employers' contributions for Social Security.

The appropriate measure of lost remuneration is not the difference between total remuneration before and after the disability. Rather, the difference in net remuneration before and after the disability should be considered. This comparison reflects factors that are affected by disability such as taxes, work-related expenses, some fringe benefits which lapse, and the worker's uncompensated expenses resulting from the work-related impairment.

Workmen's compensation should replace a substantial proportion of the worker's lost remuneration. From the standpoint of the worker, insurance against the full possible loss of remuneration is desirable. Replacement of a substantial proportion is justified by a feature of workmen's compensation which distinguishes the program from other forms of social insurance. In exchange for the benefits of workmen's compensation, workers renounced their right to seek redress for economic damages and pain and suffering under the common law. In no other social insurance program, such as Social Security or unemployment compensation, did workers surrender any right of value in exchange for benefits.

As discussed below, other objectives of workmen's compensation have implications for the proportion of lost remuneration that should be replaced, but the general conclusion stands: a substantial proportion of the disabled worker's lost remuneration should be replaced by workmen's compensation.

While workmen's compensation benefits should be a substantial proportion of the worker's lost remuneration, there are reasons to set minimum and maximum weekly cash benefits. A low-wage worker, if totally disabled, may be unable to live on the same proportion of lost remuneration that is appropriate for most workers. To avoid committing such a worker to dependence on welfare, a minimum weekly payment may be needed. Of course, if another program, such as a family income maintenance program, were to guarantee a basic level of income for all workers, there might be no need for minimum benefits under workmen's compensation.

The arguments for maximum benefit are more troublesome. As long as benefits are linked to the losses in net remuneration caused by the work-related impairment, the task of providing incentives for return to work should be no more difficult for a worker with high earnings than for others. To argue that maximum benefits will reduce the costs of the program for employers is to ask disabled high-wage workers to bear a high proportion of their own lost remuneration. A somewhat more appealing argument for maximums is that highly paid workers presumably are able to provide their own insurance and to make decisions about risks. A maximum limit on benefits would provide high-income workers an opportunity to design their own insurance programs: if, for example, the maximum benefits would replace only half of a high-wage worker's lost remuneration, he may choose to increase his private insurance. Another possible argument for maximums is that if one conceives of workmen's compensation benefits being paid out of a fixed fund, then other uses for the fund, such as an extended duration for permanent total benefits, may have a greater priority than the replacement of a high proportion of lost remuneration for well paid workers. A final argument is that if workmen's compensation engages in some income distribution to the low-wage workers through the device of minimum benefits, then the same philosophy justifies income redistribution at the expense of high-wage workers. We are not totally unsympathetic to this philosophy, but we emphasize again that the primary purpose of workmen's compensation is to provide insurance against interruption of income, not welfare or income redistribution. We conclude that there is an uneasy case for maximum and minimum benefits as long as they do not distort the primary insurance function of workmen's compensation.

Impairment benefits. In the preceding paragraphs, we argue that the primary basis for determining workmen's compensation income benefits should be the remuneration lost by the worker because of disability. As noted in Section A, many States also provide cash benefits because of work-related impairment, even if this does not result in lost remuneration. We believe that, within carefully designed limits, impairment benefits are appropriate, but they should be of secondary importance in a modern workmen's compensation program and the amount of such benefits should be limited.

The argument for impairment benefits is that many workers with work-related injuries or diseases experience losses which are not reflected in lost remuneration. Permanent impairment involves lifetime effects on the personality and on normal activity. This factor suggests that workmen's compensation benefits should not be tied solely to lost remuneration.

There are several reasons, however, why impairment benefits should be of limited number and amount. One is the historical exchange, or quid pro quo, which we believe is of continuing validity insofar as impairment benefits are concerned. The quid is the principle of liability without fault, which means that many workers qualify for workmen's compensation benefits who could not qualify for damages under negligence suits. The quo is that an employer's liability is limited. The employer's liability is less in some workmen's compensation cases than it would be under negligence suits, where awards can include payments for full economic loss, pain, and suffering concurrent with an accident, and the non-financial burdens of permanent impairment.

The objective of an effective delivery system also requires limits on impairment benefits. The determination of the degree of impairment is inherently complicated and expensive. If benefits linked to the degree of impairment play a secondary role in workmen's compensation, there will be far less time consumed in evaluating such claims.

For these reasons, we believe that the primary basis for determining workmen's compensation benefits should be lost remuneration, and that cash benefits for impairment should be limited.

3. Workmen's Compensation Should Provide Sufficient Medical Care and Rehabilitation Services

Too often workmen's compensation is viewed simply as a cash indemnity to pay the disabled worker for loss of earnings or impairment or both. The cash benefits are important, but equally so are medical care and rehabilitation services. The objectives of workmen's compensation include repair of the damage both to earning capacity and the physical condition of the worker.

A proper medical care and rehabilitation program is a triad of functions. First, high quality medical care must be provided to restore promptly the patient's abilities or functions. Medical care includes not only hospitalization and medical and surgical services but also a wide variety of treatment and supplies furnished by health professionals such as physical therapists. Second, vocational counselling, guidance, or retraining may become necessary if the worker suffers a job-related loss of endurance or skills needed to perform accustomed duties. The third step of rehabilitation is restoration to continuing productive employment.

These three functions can be achieved only if disabled employees receive prompt and sufficient medical care with continuous physical and vocational rehabilitation as long as restorative efforts are justifiable. Positive incentives that encourage disabled workers, employers, insurance carriers, and administrative agencies to provide and utilize appropriate rehabilitation services should be built into a modern workmen's compensation program.

Rehabilitation is not a mere gesture of social responsibility: it is economic wisdom. With a relatively small investment of resources, many disabled workers can be returned to productive jobs where they are again self-sufficient and where their efforts increase the total yield of goods and services. At the same time, restoration relieves others of the burden of supporting the disabled.

There is economic wisdom in efforts to improve the worker's physical condition even when the expenditures cannot be justified by the gain in earning capacity. The worker's feeling of worth and well-being is a legitimate concern. Nevertheless, it is reasonable to place some limits on the employer's liability for rehabilitation benefits which do not increase the worker's earning capacity. Expenditures for rehabilitation that will not enhance a worker's earning capacity do not deserve priority over other uses for those rehabilitation resources outside of the workmen's compensation system.

A further function of rehabilitation is to offer incentives to employers to put the beneficiaries of rehabilitation services on the payroll. Some employers feel that should such workers again suffer from a work-related injury or disease after being hired, the rise in their insurance costs will be substantial. In order to remove that barrier to employment of the rehabilitated, statutes should provide for procedures to limit the employer's liability for pre-existing impairments.

4. Workmen's Compensation Should Encourage Safety

Workmen's compensation should encourage safety directly by providing economic incentives for each firm and employee, and indirectly by providing incentives for increased output in firms and industries having fewer work-related injuries and diseases.

First, workmen's compensation should encourage each employer to utilize safety devices and methods and to stimulate employees to observe safe practices. Proper allocation of the costs of work-related injuries or disease, including lost wages and production and accidental damages to property, can provide a powerful economic incentive for safety programs. Because the employer's control over working conditions far exceeds that of the employee, we believe that assigning to the employer the largest portion of the costs of work-related injuries and diseases will best serve the objective of safety.

It might be argued that the appropriate way to assess the cost of work-related impairments is on a case-by-case basis, with the burden assigned in proportion to each party's negligence. This scheme, however, would be inherently litigious and would clearly violate the objective of an effective delivery system, discussed below.

In order to provide the most powerful direct incentives to safety, we believe in strengthening the concept of relating each employer's workmen's compensation costs to the benefits paid to his employees.

Second, workmen's compensation can indirectly encourage safety by strengthening the competitive position of firms and industries which have superior safety records. It does this by allocating the costs of work-related injuries and diseases to the appropriate firms and industries. An industry with high workmen's compensation costs owing to a poor safety record may have to increase its prices. Consumers will then tend to patronize industries with low rates of injury and disease. Within an industry, the firm with an inferior safety record will tend to have higher costs and lower profits than its direct competitors, who consequently are more likely to prosper and grow.

5. There Should Be an Effective Delivery System for Workmen's Compensation

An effective system for the delivery of benefits and services, as relevant for workmen's compensation as for any other program, is needed to insure that other program objectives are met efficiently and comprehensively.

Comprehensive performance means that the participating personnel and services are of sufficient number and quality to serve the program's objectives. The personnel and institutions contributing to a comprehensive performance include employers, insurance carriers, attorneys, physicians, and State courts and workmen's compensation agencies.

Efficient performance means that a given quality of service, such as the treatment necessary to restore the functions of an injured hand, is provided promptly, simply, and economically. The efficiency of a program may be judged by comparing its performance with similar activities inside and outside the system. To justify itself, workmen's compensation should meet its objectives more economically than any other system of delivering such benefits. Within the system, functions should be designed and performed with the least expense for a given quality of service.

The Interrelationship of the Objectives of Workmen's Compensation

Although in the preceding parts of this section we discuss the objectives of workmen's compensation separately, the program is designed to serve its several objectives simultaneously and automatically. The degree to which workmen's compensation serves multiple objectives simultaneously is a feature which distinguishes it from other social insurance programs.

To the extent that the objectives of workmen's compensation are complementary, the interrelationship or linkages built into the program are desirable. For example, the replacement of a high proportion of lost remuneration by income benefits provides a spur to safety efforts by employers, since the benefits are charged against the employer via experience rating. Conversely, if an inadequate proportion of lost remuneration is replaced by income benefits, then the stimulus to safety will be inadequate. In this way the objectives of safety and replacement of lost remuneration reinforce each other.

On the other hand, to the extent that the objectives of workmen's compensation are in conflict, the linkages compel compromises or trade-offs. For example, the rehabilitation objective suggests that the portion of the disabled worker's lost remuneration replaced by cash benefits should be low enough to provide the worker with an incentive to return to work. This reduction, however, conflicts with income protection and safety objectives. In the abstract, there is no "correct" balance between conflicting objectives.

The
Quality
of
Work

The quality of working life, a subject long debated in academic journals, emerged as a public issue in the early 1970s after a Special Task Force to the Secretary of Health, Education and Welfare released its report entitled *Work in America.* The general conclusion of the report is that the work ethic is alive but not well. The major cause of this condition is identified as the boring, repetitive, and unpleasant nature of so many of the jobs in the present-day economy. The contemporary labor force, better educated than earlier generations of workers, is described as alienated and vulnerable to a variety of economic and social disabilities due to the lack of challenge at the workplace. Various recommendations are presented but the most prominent is for a redesign of jobs so as to make work a meaningful and significant experience for American workers.

The data, logic, and conclusions of the Report have been subjected to severe criticism and the debate as to whether there is a "quality of work" problem and what should be done about it if there is has continued to the present time. The following selections include excerpts from *Work in America* and reactions to the Report, with the last two addressing the problems of job redesign directly.

Work in America

*Special Task Force to the Secretary of
Health, Education and Welfare*

Our nation is being challenged by a set of new issues having to do, in one way or another, with the quality of life. This theme emerges from the alienation and disenchantment of blue-collar workers, from the demands of minorities for equitable par-

Reprinted from *Work in America,* the MIT Press Edition (Cambridge, Mass., 1973), with the permission of the publisher.

ticipation in "the system," from the search by women for a new identity and by the quest of the aged for a respected and useful social role, from the youth who seek a voice in their society, and from almost everyone who suffers from the frustrations of life in a mass society. Rhetorical, ideological, and partisan responses to these issues abound. But truly effective responses are far more likely to be made if the obscure and complex sources of discontent are sorted out and the lever of public policy is appropriately placed. . . .

Significant numbers of American workers are dissatisfied with the quality of their working lives. Dull, repetitive, seemingly meaningless tasks, offering little challenge or autonomy, are causing discontent among workers at all occupational levels. This is not so much because work itself has greatly changed. Indeed, one of the main problems is that work has not changed fast enough to keep up with the rapid and widescale changes in worker attitudes, aspirations, and values. A general increase in their educational and economic status has placed many American workers in a position where having an interesting job is now as important as having a job that pays well. Pay is still important: it must support an "adequate" standard of living and be perceived as equitable—but high pay alone will not lead to job (or life) satisfaction.

There have been some responses to the changes in the workforce, but they have been small and slow. As a result, the productivity of the worker is low—as measured by absenteeism, turnover rates, wildcat strikes, sabotage, poor-quality products, and a reluctance by workers to commit themselves to their work tasks. Moreoever, a growing body of research indicates that, as work problems increase, there may be a consequent decline in physical and mental health, family stability, community participation and cohesiveness, and balanced sociopolitical attitudes, while there is an increase in drug and alcohol addiction, aggression, and delinquency. . . .

Many workers at all occupational levels feel locked-in, their mobility blocked, the opportunity to grow lacking in their jobs, challenge missing from their tasks. Young workers appear to be as committed to the institution of work as their elders have been, but many are rebelling against the anachronistic authoritarianism of the workplace. Minority workers similarly see authoritarian work-settings as evidence that society is falling short of its democratic ideals. Women, who are looking for work as an additional source of identity, are being frustrated by an opportunity structure that confines them to jobs damaging to their self-esteem. Older Americans suffer the ultimate in job dissatisfaction: they are denied meaningful jobs even when they have demonstrable skills and are physically capable of being productive. . . .

Several dozen well-documented experiments show that productivity increases and social problems decrease when workers participate in the work decisions affecting their lives, and when their responsibility for their work is buttressed by participation in profits. The redesign of jobs to permit participation must go well beyond what has been called "job enrichment" or "job enlargement," and there are specifiable roles for management, trade unions, and the government in the redesign of work. For all, and particularly for government, it is necessary to recognize that if workers were responsible for their work decisions, each workplace would be an "experiment in redesign." And through experimentation of this type in a fundamental institution, we might gain the enthusiasm of living in an experimenting society.

The redesign of jobs is the keystone of this report. Not only does it hold out some promise to decrease mental and physical health costs, increase productivity, and improve the quality of life for millions of Americans at all occupational levels, it would give, for the first time, a voice to many workers in an important decision-making process. Citizen participation in the arena where the individual's voice directly affects his immediate environment may do much to reduce political alienation in America. . . .

The Economic purposes of work are obvious and require little comment. Work is the means by which we provide the goods and services needed and desired by ourselves and our society. Through the economic rewards of work, we obtain immediate gratification of transient wants, physical assets for enduring satisfactions, and liquid assets for deferrable gratifications For most of the history of mankind, and for a large part of humanity today, the economic meaning of work is paramount.

Work also serves a number of other social purposes. The workplace has always been a place to meet people, converse, and form friendships. In traditional societies, where children are wont to follow in their parents' footsteps, the assumption of responsibility by the children of one task and then another prepares them for their economic and social roles as adults. Finally, the type of work performed has always conferred a social status on the worker and the worker's family. In industrial America, the father's occupation has been the major determinant of status, which in turn has determined the family's class standing, where they lived, where the children went to school, and with whom the family associated—in short, the life style and life chances of all the family members. (The emerging new role of women in our society may cause class standing to be codetermined by the husband's *and* wife's occupations.)

The economic and societal importance of work has dominated thought about its meaning, and justifiably so: a function of work for any *society* is to produce and distribute goods and services, to transform "raw nature" into that which serves our needs and desires. Far less attention has been paid to the *personal* meaning of work, yet it is clear from recent research that work plays a crucial and perhaps unparalleled psychological role in the formation of self-esteem, identity, and a sense of order.

Work contributes to self-esteem in two ways. The first is that through the inescapable awareness of one's efficacy and competence in dealing with the objects of work, a person acquires a sense of mastery over both himself and his environment. The second derives from the view, stated earlier, that an individual is working when he is engaging in activities that produce something valued by other people. That is, the job tells the worker day in and day out that he has something to offer. Not to have a job is not to have something that is valued by one's fellow human beings. Alternatively, to be working is to have evidence that one is needed by others. One of these components of self-esteem (mastery) is, therefore, internally derived through the presence or absence of challenge in work. The other component (how others value one's contribution) is externally derived. The person with high self-esteem may be defined as one who has a high estimate of his value and finds that the social estimate agrees.

The workplace generally, then, is one of the major foci of personal evaluation. It is where one finds out whether he is "making the grade"; it is where one's esteem is constantly on the line, and where every effort will be made to avoid reduction in self-evaluation and its attending sense of failure. If an individual cannot live up to the expectations he has of himself, and if his personal goals are not reasonably obtainable, then his self-esteem, and with it his relations with others, are likely to be imparied. . . .

When it is said that work should be meaningful, what is meant is that it should contribute to self-esteem, to the sense of fulfillment through the mastering of one's self and one's environment, and to the sense of what is valued by society. The fundamental question the individual worker asks is "What am I doing that *really* matters?"

When work becomes merely automatic behavior, instead of being *homo faber,* the worker is *animal laborens.* Among workers who describe themselves as "just laborers," self-esteem is so deflated that the distinction between the human as worker and the animal as laborer is blurred. The relationship between work and self-esteem is well summarized by Elliot Jacques:

> . . . working for a living is one of the basic activities in a man's life. By forcing him to come to grips with his environment, with his livelihood at stake, it confronts him with the actuality of his personal capacity—to exercise judgment, to achieve concrete and specific results. It gives him a continuous account of his correspondence between outside reality and the inner perception of that reality, as well as an account of the accuracy of his appraisal of himself. . . . In short, a man's work does not satisfy his material needs alone. In a very deep sense, it gives him a measure of his sanity.

Work is a powerful force in shaping a person's sense of identity. We find that most, if not all, working people tend to describe themselves in terms of the work groups or organizations to which they belong. The question, "Who are you?" often solicits an organizationally related response such as "I work for IBM," or "I'm a Stanford professor." Occupational role is usually a part of the response for all classes: "I'm a steelworker," or "I'm a lawyer." In short, "People tend to become what they do."

Several highly significant effects result from work-related identification: welfare recipients become nobodies; the retired suffer a crucial loss of identity; and people in low-status jobs cannot find anything in their work from which to derive an identity or they reject the identity forced on them. Even those who voluntarily leave an organization for self-employment experience difficulties with identity—compounded by the confusion of others—as the following quote from an article entitled "Striking Out on Your Own," illustrates:

> No less dramatic . . . are those questions of identity which present themselves to the self-employed. These identity crises and situations usually come packaged in little episodes which occur when others find that they have encountered a wierdo without a boss. . . . You are stopped by a traffic policeman to be given a ticket and he asks the name of your employer and you say that you work for yourself. Next he asks, "Come on, where do you work? Are you employed or not?" You say, "Self employed." . . . He, among others you meet, knows that self-employment is a tired euphemism for being out of work. . . . You become extremely nervous about meeting new people because of the ever-present question, "Who are you with?" When your answer fails to attach to a recognized organization . . . both parties to the conversation often become embarrassed by your obscurity.

Basic to all work appears to be the human desire to impose order or structure on the world. The opposite of work is not leisure or free time; it is being victimized by some kind of disorder which, at its extreme, is chaos. It means being unable to plan or predict. And it is precisely in the relation between the desire for order and its achievement that work provides the sense of mastery so important to self-esteem. The closer one's piece of the world conforms with one's structural plans, the greater the satisfaction of work. And it follows that one of the greatest sources of dissatisfaction in work results from the inability to make one's own sense of order prevail—the assembly line is the best (or worst) example of an imposed, and, for most workers, unacceptable structure. . . .

Although social scientists have long disputed the precise contribution of the Protestant ethic to the genesis of capitalism, they generally agree that thrift, hard work, and a capacity for deferring gratification historically were traits widely distributed among Americans. Moreover, as part of the legitimacy of the economic system, individual members of our society were to be credited or blamed for their own circumstances, according to the degree of their prosperity.

But the ethic, or what has passed for it, appears to be under attack. Some futurists tell us that automation will make work unnecessary for most people, and that we may as well ignore work and look to other matters such as "creative leisure." More immediately, our attention is drawn to these alleged signs of work's obsolescence:

The growth in the number of communes

Numerous adolescents panhandling in such meccas as Georgetown, North Beach, and the Sunset Strip

Various enterprises shifting to 4-day workweeks

Welfare caseloads increasing

Retirement occurring at earlier ages.

All of these are relatively benign signs; more malignant signs are found in reduced productivity and in the doubling of mandays per year lost from work through strikes. In some industries there is apparently a rise in absenteeism, sabotage, and turnover rates.

Ironically, many of these symptoms have increased despite the general improvements in physical conditions and monetary rewards for work. In comparison with the dreary lot of most workers during the industrial revolution and, indeed, until quite recently, the workplace today is an Elysian field. Sweatshop conditions have all but disappeared. The extreme dangers of work appear to have declined in most industries. Women and children are seldom engaged in back-breaking drudgery. Arbitrary wage cuts and dismissals are relatively rare, and enlightened laws, personnel policies, and labor unions protect the worker in a variety of ways.

Quantitatively, the lives of workers away from work similarly have improved. Real income, standard of living, health status, and life expectancy have all risen markedly. Among most classes of workers, homes and cars are owned in abundance, and bank accounts continually grow. For those without work, there is social security, unemployment compensation, workmen's compensation, and an income floor will very likely be established under welfare compensation. On the average, then, no workers have ever been as materially well-off as American workers are today. What, then, is wrong?

Social scientists are suggesting that the root of the problem is to be found in the changing needs, aspirations, and values of workers. For example, Abraham Maslow has suggested that the needs of human beings are hierarchical and as each level is filled, the subsequent level becomes salient. This order of needs is:

1. Physiological requirements (food, habitat, etc.)
2. Safety and security
3. Companionship and affection
4. Self-esteem and the esteem of others
5. Self-actualization (being able to realize one's potential to the full).

It may be argued that the very success of industry and organized labor in meeting the basic needs of workers has unintentionally spurred demands for esteemable and fulfilling jobs.

Frederick Herzberg suggests an alternative way of looking at the needs of workers —in terms of intrinsic and extrinsic factors. Under this rubric, job satisfaction and dissatisfaction are not opposites but two separate dimensions. Extrinsic factors, such as inadequate pay, incompetent supervision, or dirty working conditions, may lead to dissatisfaction, which may be reduced in turn by such "hygienic" measures as higher pay and "human relations" training for foremen. But such actions will not make workers satisfied. Satisfaction depends on the provision of intrinsic factors, such as achievement, accomplishment, responsibility, and challenging work. Satisfaction, then, is a function of the content of work; dissatisfaction, of the environment of work. Increases in productivity have been found to correlate in certain industries and occupations with increases in satisfaction but not with decreases in dissatisfaction. Hence, hygienic improvements may make work tolerable, but will not necessarily raise motivation or productivity. The latter depends on making jobs more interesting and important. . . .

What the workers want most, as more than 100 studies in the past 20 years show, is to become masters of their immediate environments and to feel that their work and they themselves are important—the twin ingredients of self-esteem. Workers recognize that some of the dirty jobs can be transformed only into the merely tolerable, but the most oppressive features of work are felt to be avoidable: constant supervision and coercion, lack of variety, monotony, meaningless tasks, and isolation. An increasing number of workers want more autonomy in tackling their tasks, greater opportunity for increasing their skills, rewards that are directly connected to the intrinsic aspects of work, and greater participation in the design of work and the formulation of their tasks. . . .

Based on what we know about the attitudes of workers toward their jobs, we can identify the following two factors as being major sources of job dissatisfaction: the anachronism of Taylorism and diminishing opportunities to be one's own boss.

The Anachronism of Taylor

Frederick Winslow Taylor, father of time and motion studies and author of *Principles of Scientific Management*, propagated a view of efficiency which, until recently, was markedly successful—so long as "success" was measured in terms of unit costs and output. Under his tutelage, work tasks were greatly simplified, fragmented, compartmentalized, and placed under continuous supervision. The worker's rewards depended on doing as he was told and increasing his output. Taylor's advice resulted in major, sometimes spectacular, increases in productivity.

Several events have occurred to make Taylorism anachronistic. Primarily, the workforce has changed considerably since his principles were instituted in the first quarter of this century. From a workforce with an average educational attainment of less than junior high school, containing a large contingent of immigrants of rural and peasant origin and resigned to cyclical unemployment, the workforce is now largely native-born, with more than a high school education on the average, and affluence-minded. And traditional values that depended on authoritarian assertion alone for their survival have been challenged.

Simplified tasks for those who are not simple-minded, close supervision by those whose legitimacy rests only on a hierarchical structure, and jobs that have nothing but money to offer in an affluent age are simply rejected. For many of the new workers, the monotony of work and scale of organization and their inability to control the pace and style of work are cause for a resentment which they, unlike older workers, do not repress.

Attempts to reduce the harmful effects of Taylorism over the last two generations have not got at the nub of the problem. For example, the "human relations" school attempts to offset Taylor's primacy of the machine with "tender, loving care" for workers. This school (which has many adherents in personnel offices today) ignores the technological and production factors involved in a business. This approach concentrates on the enterprise as a social system—the workers are to be treated better, but their jobs remain the same. Neither the satisfaction of workers nor their productivity is likely to improve greatly from the human relations approach. Alternatives to Taylorism, therefore, must arise from the assumption that it is insufficient to adjust either people to technology or technology to people. It is necessary to consider both the social needs of the workers and the task to be performed. This viewpoint challenges much of what passes as efficiency in our industrial society.

Many industrial engineers feel that gains in productivity will come about mainly through the introduction of new technology. They feel that tapping the latent productivity of workers is a relatively unimportant part of the whole question of productivity. This was the attitude that was behind the construction of the General Motors auto plant in Lordstown, Ohio, the newest and most "efficient" auto plant in America. Early in 1972, workers there went out on strike over the pace of the line and the robot-like tasks that they were asked to perform. This event highlights the role of the human element in productivity: What does the employer gain by having a "perfectly efficient" assembly line if his workers are out on strike because of the oppressive and dehumanized experience of workers on the "perfect" line? As the costs of absenteeism, wildcat strikes, turnover, and industrial sabotage become an increasingly significant part of doing business, it is becoming clear that the current concept of industrial efficiency conveniently but mistakenly ignores the social half of the equation.

It should be noted that Taylorism and a misplaced conception of efficiency is not restricted to assembly lines or, for that matter, to the manufacturing sector of the economy. The service sector is not exempt. For example, in the medical care industry, the phenomenal growth in employment over the past decade or so has occurred largely in lower-level occupations. This growth has been accompanied by an attempt to increase the efficiency of the upper-level occupations through the delegation of tasks down the ladder of skills. This undoubtedly results in a greater efficiency in the utilization of manpower, but it rigidifies tasks, reduces the range of skills utilized by most of the occupations, increases routinization, and opens the door to job dissatisfaction for a new generation of highly educated workers.

As we have seen, satisfying jobs are most often those that incorporate factors found in high-status jobs—autonomy, working on a "whole" problem, participation in decision making. But as Ivar Berg and others have noted, as a result of countless public and private policies and decisions that determine our occupational structure, growth in occupational opportunities has occurred largely in middle and lower levels. The automation revolution that was to increase the demand for skilled workers (while decreasing the need for humans to do the worst jobs in society) has not occurred. What we *have* been able to do is to create such jobs as teacher aides, medical technicians, and computer keypunch operators—not jobs with professional characteristics. Undoubtedly, these jobs have opened opportunities for many who would otherwise have had no chance to advance beyond much lower-skilled positions. But it is illusory to believe that technology is opening new high-level jobs that are replacing low-level jobs. Most new jobs offer little in the way of "career" mobility—lab technicians do not advance along a path and become doctors.

This problem of a fairly static occupational structure presents society with a formidable barrier to providing greater job satisfaction to those below the pinnacle of the job pyramid. Without a technological revolution there is little hope of flattening out this structure in order to give more workers higher status jobs. It then becomes crucial to infuse middle- and lower-level jobs with professional characteristics, particularly if we plan to continue offering higher and higher degrees of education to young people on the assumption that their increased expectations can be met by the world of work.

Diminishing Opportunities to Be One's Own Boss

Our economic, political, and cultural system has fostered the notion of independence and autonomy, a part of which is the belief that a hardworking person, even if he has little capital, can always make a go of it in business for himself. Or, to put it another way, if things get too bad in a dependent work situation, it has been felt that the individual worker could always strike out on his own.

This element of the American dream is rapidly becoming myth, and disappearing with it is the possibility of realizing the character traits of independence and autonomy by going into business for oneself. The trend of the past 70 years or more, and particularly in recent years, has been a decrease in small independent enterprises and self-employment, and an increase in the domination of large corporations and government in the workforce. . . .

Social scientists identify four ingredients of alienation: (1) powerlessness (regarding ownership of the enterprise, general management policies, employment conditions, and the immediate work process), (2) meaninglessness (with respect to the character of the product worked on as well as the scope of the product or the production process), (3) isolation (the social aspect of work), and (4) self-estrangement ("depersonalized detachment," including boredom which can lead to "absence of personal growth"). As thus broken down, alienation is inherent in pyramidal, bureaucratic management patterns and in advanced, Taylorized technology, which divides and subdivides work into minute, monotonous elements. The result of alienation is often the withdrawal of the worker from community or political activity or the displacement of his frustrations through participation in radical social or political movements.

It seems fair to conclude that the combination of the changing social character of American workers, declining opportunities to establish independence through self-employment, and an anachronistic organization of work can create an explosive and pathogenic mix. . . .

The Redesign of Jobs

. . . inherent in our analysis of current work-related national programs and policies is the suggestion that there *is* a better way to do things. Of course, there are many "better ways," and the choice between these alternatives is, as it should be in a democratic society, a political choice. It would be presumptuous of us, then, to suggest that any one route to change is the right route, or that any one alternative *must* be pursued. Consequently, we shall limit our discussion here to a few alternative responses to national problems in order to indicate (1) the range of options that are open to policy makers, and (2) the promise of a work-oriented policy analysis.

Recapitulation of the Problem

To recapitulate, the following factors are, with high probability, determinants of satisfaction and dissatisfaction at work:

Occupation and status: The higher the status of an occupation, the more satisfied are the people who engage in it. Researchers reason that the major variables are prestige, control over conditions of one's own work, cohesiveness of one's work group, and ego gratification from the challenge and variety of the work itself.

Job content: Intrinsic factors such as challenge appear to affect satisfaction and dissatisfaction most substantially. The aspects of job content that appear most consistent in their negative effects are fractionation, repetition, and lack of control, or, in positive ways, variety and autonomy. Workers in all occupations rate self-determination highest among the elements that define an ideal job. Content of work is generally more important than being promoted.

Supervision: High worker satisfaction is associated with considerate and thoughtful behavior among employers. Satisfaction is also associated with supervisory behavior that shares decision making with subordinates. The delegation of authority (participative management) has positive effects.

Peer relationships: Most people are more satisfied to work as members of a group than in isolation. Workers prefer jobs that permit interaction and are more likely to quit jobs that prevent congenial peer relationships.

Wages: High pay and high satisfaction with work tend to go together. However, it is difficult to ascertain the extent to which high wages in themselves produce sustained high levels of satisfaction, and the extent to which the higher levels of satisfaction that are typical of higher paid jobs reflect the variety, substantive interest, and autonomy that are also typical of such jobs. Moreover, even among high-paid workers, variations in job control make a difference in the degree of job satisfaction. But in a culture in which wages constitute the major source of income for most workers, wages undoubtedly determine a portion of job satisfaction. Certainly, a level of wages that will support an adequate standard of living is of primary importance. Beyond that point, workers tend to measure their wages in terms of "equity"—i.e., in relationship to the contribution that their fellow workers are making to the enterprise, and the salaries they are receiving.

Mobility: More than three-quarters of all workers queried by the Survey of Working Conditions said that it was important or somewhat important to them that their chances for promotion should be good. Also, large percentages of workers strongly resent being trapped in a job.

Working conditions: Bad physical conditions (long hours, temperature, ventilation, noise, etc.) can make any job unbearable. Involuntary night shift work also causes low job satisfaction—probably because it interferes with other valued activities such as marriage, child rearing, and friendships.

Job security: Older workers, in particular, find that security of employment is a prerequisite for other sources of satisfaction.

It follows that if autonomy, participation, challenge, security, pay, mobility, comfort, and the opportunity for interaction with co-workers are increased, the satisfaction of workers with their jobs should increase. . . .

Solutions: Reforms and Innovations in the Workplace

Most of the work redesign effort has confined itself to small work groups. Little of it has embraced the wider implications of the system's viewpoint and involved a plant or a corporation as a whole. The major exception to this trend is a General Foods manufacturing plant that was designed to incorporate features that would provide a high quality of working life, enlist unusual human involvement, and achieve high productivity. Management built this plant because the employees in an existing plant manifested many severe symptoms of alienation. Because of their indifference and inattention, the continuous process type of technology used in the plant was susceptible to frequent shutdowns, to product waste, and to costly recycling. There were serious acts of sabotage and violence. Employees worked effectively for only a few hours a day and strongly resisted changes that would have resulted in a fuller utilization of manpower.

Management enlisted the advice and cooperation of workers and consultants from business schools and together they designed a plant along the following lines:

Autonomous work groups: Self-management work teams were formed and given collective responsibility for larger segments of the production process. The teams are composed of from eight to twelve members—large enough to cover a full set of tasks, and small enough to allow effective face-to-face meetings for decision making and coordination. The teams decide who will do what tasks, and most members learn to do each other's jobs, both for the sake of variety and to be able to cover for a sick or absent co-worker.

Integrated support functions: Activities typically performed by maintenance, quality control, custodial, industrial engineering, and personnel units were built into the operating team's responsibilities. The teams accepted both first and final responsibility for performing quality tests and ensuring that they maintained quality standards.

Challenging job assignments: An attempt was made to design every set of tasks in a way that would include functions requiring higher human abilities and responsibilities. The basic technology employed in the plant has been designed to eliminate dull or routine jobs insofar as possible. Still, some nonchallenging but basic tasks remained. The team member responsible for these operations is given other tasks that are mentally more demanding . . . .

Job mobility and rewards for learning: The aim was to make all sets of tasks equally challenging although each set would comprise unique skill demands. Consistent with this aim was a single job classification for all operators, with pay increases geared to mastering an increasing proportion of jobs, first within the team and then in the total plant. . . .

Facilitative leadership: In lieu of supervisors whose responsibilities are to plan, direct, and control the work of subordinates, a "team leader" position was created with the responsiblity to facilitate team development and decision making. It is envisioned that in time the team leader position might not be required.

Managerial decision information for operators: The design of the new plant called for providing operators with economic information and managerial decision rules. This enables production decisions ordinarily made at the second level of supervision to be made at the operator level.

Congruent physical and social context: Differential status symbols that characterize traditional work organizations were minimized in the new plant—for example, by a parking lot open to all regardless of position, single plant-office entrance, and common decor throughout office, cafeteria, and locker room. . . .

Using standard principles, industrial engineers had indicated that 110 workers would be needed to man the plant. But when the team concept was applied, and when support activities were integrated into team responsibilities, the result was a manning level of less than 70 workers. . . .

What is particularly encouraging is the impact of this unique worksetting on employees' extra-plant activities. For example, many workers have been unusually active in civic affairs—apparently, significantly more so than is typical of the workers in other plants in the same corporation or in the same community. It has long been observed that workers in dull, isolated or routine jobs seldom participate in community affairs, but this is the first instance where it has been shown that the redesign of work can have positive effects on community participation.

This General Foods plant is not a unique example, although the extent of the redesign in unusual. . . .

Participative Management

In the redesigned worksettings . . . one finds the workers participating in decisions on:

Their own production methods
The internal distribution of tasks
Questions of recruitment
Questions regarding internal leadership
What additional tasks to take on
When they will work.

Not all of the work groups make all of these decisions, but the list provides the range within which the workers are participating in the management of the business or industry. Participative management does *not* mean participation through representatives, for, as experience has shown, that kind of participation may foster alienation through the inevitable gap between expected and actual responsiveness of the representatives. . . .

Participative management means . . . that workers are enabled to control the aspects of work intimately affecting their lives. It permits the worker to achieve and maintain a sense of personal worth and importance, to grow, to motivate himself, and to receive recognition and approval for what he does. It gives the worker a meaningful voice in decisions in one place where the effects of his voice can be immediately experienced. In a broader sense, it resolves a contradiction in our Nation—between democracy in society and authoritarianism in the workplace. . . .

The Role of the Government in Job Redesign

Management, unions, and workers, in the final analysis, are the only ones who know the right way to build their product or perform their service. However, government does have a legitimate role to play in encouraging these parties to redesign work tasks —especially since the failure to do so is adding to the tax burden of Americans through increased social costs. . . .

International experience in Scandinavia suggests that government can act as a catalyst to encourage and aid union and management efforts to redesign work. In Norway, the government, employers, and labor unions jointly sponsor an organization . . . that encourages experimentation in the design of work. . . . Similar efforts have taken place in Sweden and have helped to create the climate that led to changes on the automobile assembly line at the SAAB and Volvo corporations. . . .

Research and Training

A variety of training, demonstration, research, and experimentation options exist. For example, the government might consider funding programs to retrain the tens of thousands of managers and industrial engineers who were taught the "efficiency expert" concepts of Frederick Taylor and the inadequate approaches of the "human relations" school. While this is a project primarily for our business and engineering schools to undertake in conjunction with employers and employer associations, the government might consider financial incentives to encourage the process.

Demonstration grants might also be awarded to address the considerable technical problems involved in redesigning some of the worst jobs in the economy—e.g., those on the assembly line. . . .

Experimentation

. . . A general experimental goal for America might be to incorporate those functions of variety and autonomy that make for job satisfaction among independent professionals into the jobs of lower-level workers. For example, professionals can work at home if it is convenient. But a great deal of other work can be done this way—for example, product design and planning, market research, or computer programming.

Robert Kahn has suggested an experiment to suffuse even lower-level jobs with the flexibility of professional jobs. He would break down the work day into units (modules) that represent the smallest allocation of time on a given task that is sufficient to be economically and psychologically meaningful. Workers could allocate their time as they saw fit—working on a two-hour module on one task, the next two hours on another task, etc. The modules would provide variety and a chance to learn other tasks. They would also facilitate the scheduling of one's work to meet personal needs (child care, schooling) and would open up needed part-time employment. One could also accumulate work credits in order to earn a sabbatical. Kahn posits that the benefits from the experiment might be the improved self-esteem, self-development, and mental and physical health of the worker, and higher productivity for the organization. To what extent the costs of the experiment would reduce or offset gains could only be determined by trial and evaluation.

The major issue, however, is not the work module or any other single idea, but the problem of society to which it is an attempted response—dissatisfying work. That problem can be solved by the process of innovation, trial, and evaluation—in other words, by action—and by no other means.

We have had too much of assumption and stereotype. Management has accepted too long, for example, the assumption that every fractionation in a job represented a potential increment of production. Unions have assumed too long that they could prevent workers from being exposed to unreasonable hazards or physical strains, but not from being bored to death. And the larger society has assumed too long that there was no such thing as social-psychological pollution—that the effects of monotonous or meaningless jobs could be sloughed off as the workers went through the plant gates to home and community.

An experimenting society would approach the humanization of work by replacing such assumptions with facts, and by learning such facts through the familiar and unavoidable process of trial and evaluation. In this process, industry, unions, and government could collaborate to the benefit of all.

The options for governmental action, then, are numerous. They range from establishing trade-offs between medical expenditures and funding work redesign experiments, to establishing a public corporation to encourage work redesign, to a major commitment to become an experimenting society. Large-scale experimentation in the redesign of work could well begin within the Federal Government itself. The range of options and the opportunities for trade-offs are clearly great. . . .

What's Wrong with Work in America?

Harold Wool

The rash of rank-and-file contract rejections and wildcat strikes during the late 1960s and early 1970s, particularly the well publicized strike by workers at the General Motors facility in Lordstown, Ohio, highlight what some are interpreting as a sort of gut revolt against work as it is organized in the American economy.

Reports of apathy, absenteeism, and even industrial sabotage among blue collar workers, of poor morale among some white collar workers (particularly those in repetitive dead-end jobs), of college youth's disdain of bureaucratic jobs in government or industry, and even of executives forsaking promising careers to head out to fields unknown—all these have caused some observers, notably commentators from the print and broadcast media, to question the future of work in American society. Is our commitment to the work ethic fading?

Since all of these symptoms appeared to imply some weakening of this commitment, it is not surprising that the search for a culprit has turned its spotlight on the institution of work itself—the way it is organized, its adequacy in meeting human needs, and the effects of work upon other dimensions of human welfare. A special focus of concern has been the "blue collar worker" with the automobile assembly line as the inevitable archtype. The "blue collar blues" has become part of the media lexicon, together with knowing references to more esoteric psychological terms such as "work satisfiers and dissatisfiers," "alienation," and "anomie."

The media, moreover, have simply reflected a growing concern on the part of key officials in industry, labor, and the Government—a concern that "all is not well" among important segments of our nation's work force. An initial official effort to place these concerns in broader perspective was contained in a paper on the "Problems of the Blue Collar Workers," prepared in early 1970 by U.S. Department of Labor staff for an ad hoc White House Task Group. The paper pointed to symptoms of growing disaffection among lower-middle-income workers (those in the $5,000–$10,000 family income range), and suggested that this was due to a combination of pressures: an economic squeeze resulting from inflationary pressures and limited advancement opportunities; a social squeeze, reflected especially in deterioration of

Reprinted from the *Monthly Labor Review*, March 1973, pp. 38–44.

their communities and in racial ethnic conflicts; and a workplace squeeze associated with a variety of depressing working conditions, ranging from grinding monotony to unpleasant or unsafe work environments.

Further evidence that job satisfaction had become a matter of top-policy interest was provided by this reference in President Nixon's 1971 Labor Day Message: "In our quest for a better environment, we must always remember that the most important part of the quality of life is the quality of work, and the need for job satisfaction is the key to the quality of work."

Against this backdrop, Elliot Richardson, then Secretary of Health, Education and Welfare, approved initiation in December 1971 of a broadgaged study of the "institution of work" and of its implications for health, education, and welfare.

The study was conducted by a 10-member Task Force, chaired by James O'Toole, a social anthropologist serving as a staff assistant in Secretary Richardson's office. Patterned after an earlier HEW study group on higher education policies, the members of the task force were apparently given full rein to develop their own thinking on the issues, independent of the usual bureaucratic constraints. The resulting report, *Work in America*, was released in December 1972, together with a cautious foreword by Secretary Richardson, which praised the report for "the breadth of its perspective and its freshness of outlook," but clearly disassociated himself and the administration from many of its recommendations.

The Task Force View

The study takes as its point of departure the premise that "work"—broadly defined as socially useful activity—is central to the lives of most adults. In addition to the obvious economic functions of work, work performs an essential psychological and social role in providing individuals with a status, a sense of identity, and an opportunity for social interaction. Referring to recent surveys as evidence, it concludes that individuals on welfare and the poor generally have the same needs and compulsions for work as do those in the economic mainstream.

But, though the work ethic is still "alive" in America, the report finds that it is not "well"—and it ascribes this condition to the institution of work itself. Citing a variety of psychological studies and survey findings, the task force concludes that large numbers of American workers at all occupational levels are pervasively dissatisfied with the quality of their working lives. Significant numbers of employed workers are locked into "dull, repetitive seemingly meaningless tasks, offering little challenge or autonomy." And many others, including large numbers of older workers, "suffer the ultimate in job dissatisfaction" in being completely deprived of an opportunity to work at "meaningful" jobs.

The principal sources of worker discontent as seen by the authors are to be found in the confines of the individual workplace itself. The central villains of the piece are (1) the process of work breakdown and specialization associated with the pernicious influence of Frederick W. Taylor and his industrial engineer disciples, and (2) the diminished opportunity for work autonomy resulting from the shift in locus of jobs from self-employment or small scale enterprises to large impersonal corporate and government bureaucracies. Although these trends are recognized as having been underway for many decades, what is new in the current climate, the study contends, is a revolutionary change in attitudes and values among many members of the work force—youth, minority members, and women. With higher expectations generated by increased educational achievement, these groups in particular are placing greater emphasis on the intrinsic aspects of work, its inherent challenge and interest, and less on strictly material rewards. In the case of minority workers, the study recognizes that large numbers are still concerned with the elemental needs for a job—any job—that pays a living wage, but it notes relatively high rates of discontent among black workers in many better paying jobs as well. The relegation of women to poor paying, low status jobs, and the plight of older workers, both in and out of the labor force, are also discussed.

This complex of discontents is, in turn, identified as the root cause of various ills besetting the American economy—"reduced productivity," "the doubling of man-days per year lost through strikes," and increases in absenteeism, sabotage, and turn-over rates. In addition, a variety of other ills are attributed to work-related problems, including problems of physical and mental health, family instability, and drug and alcohol addiction.

Since the central diagnosis for this wide array of economic and social problems is found in the faulty organization of work, the principal remedy presented by the task force is the reorganization of work. Although "work redesign" is never explicitly defined by the authors, a number of recent experiments are cited—both here and abroad—which have had in common an extensive restructuring of jobs designed to broaden and vary the scope of workers' duties and to provide increased worker autonomy and participation in work related decisions, often accompanied by some form of profit sharing. Collaborative efforts by labor, management, and government in Norway and Sweden, resulting in a number of pilot job redesign projects are cited as a model for emulation.

Although work redesign is identified as the "keystone" of the report, the authors concede that this is not a sufficient solution to the problem of work—and of workers—in America. The final two chapters therefore address themselves, more generally, to a range of other work-related problems and possible solutions. Since some jobs can never be made satisfying, an alternative approach is to facilitate movement of workers out of these jobs, through a massive midcareer retraining option or "self-renewal program" for workers.

In a concluding chapter, the report addresses itself broadly to a variety of other manpower and welfare policy issues. It endorses a "total employment" strategy, designed to produce "reasonably satisfying" jobs not only for the 5 million workers currently reported as unemployed but for an estimated 10 to 30 million additional persons who are underemployed, on welfare, or out of the labor market but who—the authors contend—would take meaningful jobs, if available. This is to be accomplished through a combination of large-scale manpower training and public employment programs and through appropriate fiscal and monetary policies. With respect to welfare reform, it is strongly critical of mandatory work provisions, as applied to welfare mothers, as reflecting a lack of appreciation of the social value of the mother's role in housekeeping and childbearing activities. The report suggests that policy emphasis be shifted to obtain suitable employment for the fathers, while upgrading the status of housework—in part, by including housewives in the statistical count of the labor force.

Evaluating the Report

From this summary, the coolness of official response to this study will not be difficult to understand.

For somewhat different reasons, this reviewer also has mixed feelings about the value of the study as a basis for broad social policy. Its strength—and its weaknesses —lie in its advocacy of a humanistic approach to assessment of work as a social institution. Its perspective is primarily that of the behavioral scientist, who appraises the "value" of work in terms of its total impact upon the individual—in contradistinction to the market oriented perspective of many economists, who view work primarily as another factor contributing to the GNP and measure its value solely in terms of financial rewards. The task force offers insightful—if still framentary—documentation concerning the ways in which many jobs (both blue collar and white collar) are proving dissatisfying, particularly to some members of the new generation. And scattered through its chapters are a number of provocative recommendations which deserve further study and follow-through. However, in its zeal to advance the cause of "humanization of work" the report suffers from overgeneralization concerning the extent and nature of work dissatisfaction and from overstatement of the potentials of work redesign as a primary solution to work-related ills.

A central theme of the study is that "a general increase in their educational and economic status has placed many workers in a position where having an interesting job is now as important as having a job that pays well" and that the organization of work "has not changed fast enough to keep up with rapid and widescale changes in worker attitudes, aspirations, and values." From this premise it is reasonable to infer that the level of work discontent has significantly increased in recent years.

A Look at Available Data

Yet a review of available research and statistical evidence offers very limited support for this hypothesis. For this purpose we have explored two types of data: (1) job satisfaction survey findings, and (2) those statistical indicators which have frequently been cited as manifestations of worker discontent, such as quit rates, strikes, absenteeism, and productivity.

Job Satisfaction Surveys.

In a recent review of the extensive literature on job satisfaction, Robert Kahn reports that some 2,000 surveys of job satisfaction were conducted in the United States over a period of several decades. These surveys have varied greatly in scope and design, from intensive studies of workers in a particular plant, occupation, or industry to much more general polls covering a national cross-section of the work force. In spite of these differences, Kahn—as well as earlier observers—has noted a certain consistency in the response patterns. "Few people call themselves extremely satisfied with their jobs, but still fewer report extreme dissatisfaction. The modal response is on the positive side of neutrality—'pretty satisfied.' The proportion dissatisfied ranges from 10 to 21 percent. . . . Commercial polls, especially those of the Roper organization, asked direct questions about job satisfaction in hundreds of samples and seldom found the proportion of dissatisfied response exceeding 20 percent." Neither Kahn nor other scholars could detect a consistent trend in job satisfaction from available data.

Statistical Indicators

It is not unreasonable to infer, as does the task force report, that job dissatisfaction will be reflected in a variety of cost-increasing worker behaviors, such as low productivity, high voluntary turnover, high absenteeism, and increased strike activity. Research evidence based mainly on specific plant or industry studies is available to support at least some of these direct relationships, notably in the case of turnover and absenteeism. If worker discontent has been significantly increasing, some indication of this might be reflected in the overall trends of the relevant statistical indicators. Yet the evidence in this respect is inconclusive:

1. *Labor turnover.* A detailed multivariate analysis of quit rates of manufacturing workers recently completed by the Bureau of Labor Statistics indicates that year-to-year fluctuations in these rates over a 20-year period are largely explained by cyclical variations in job opportunities, as measured by the rate of new hires, and that there has been *no* discernible trend in the quit rate over the period.

2. *Absenteeism.* In the absence of any direct program for statistical reporting of absenteeism trends, the Bureau of Labor Statistics has analyzed data from the Current Population Survey on trends in the proportion of workers who have been absent from their jobs for all or part of a week due to illness or other personal reasons. This initial analysis does point to a small increase in worker absence rates since 1966. The average daily rate of unscheduled absences rose from 3.3 percent in 1967 to 3.6 percent in 1972, an increase of about 10 percent. The data are, however, far from conclusive and do not provide a basis for generalization of longer term trends or their causes.

3. *Strikes.* A sharp increase in the level of strike activity was recorded in the second half of the 1960s and in the early 1970s. Man-days of idleness due to strikes rose from 0.13 percent of estimated working time in 1961–65 to 0.26 percent in 1966–71. However, the incidence of strikes normally tends to increase during inflationary periods. Strike idleness as a percentage of working time was actually considerably higher during the years immediately following the end of World War II (1946–50) and following the outbreak of the Korean War (1952–53) than during the more recent period of rapid price increases. Moreover, "bread and butter" issues such as pay, benefits, job security, and union organization or security issues, have continued to account for all but a modest percentage of all strikes. In 1971, only 5.5 percent of strike idleness was attributed to plant administration or other working condition issues.

4. *Productivity.* Productivity growth, as measured by output per man-hour in the private economy, which had experienced a longer term growth trend of about 3–3.5 percent a year, slackened appreciably following the mid-1960s and dropped to less than one percent a year in 1969 and 1970. Declines in productivity growth have occurred in the past during or immediately after periods of high economic activity. The productivity growth rate rebounded sharply, moreover, in 1971–72, thus suggesting that cyclical factors rather than any deep-seated worker unrest, were mainly responsible for the previous decline.

5. *Labor force participation.* Abstention from work or work-seeking activity is the ultimate form of rejection of work as an institution. Yet there has been no evidence of a downward trend in the overall proportion of the population, 16 years and over, reported as in the labor force. In fact, this percentage has increased over the past two decades from 59.9 percent in 1950 to 61.3 percent in 1970. . . .

From this necessarily brief review, it will be evident that there is little objective evidence to support an inference of a rising wave of discontent among workers, associated directly with the nature of their jobs. Fluctuations in the indicators, which appeared at first blush to support this hypothesis (such as labor turnover rates, strike activity, and productivity growth rates) can, on closer inspection, be attributed to the tight labor market and inflationary trends prevailing in the late 1960s and to associated labor market forces. The overall labor force participation trends—such as the sharp and sustained inflow of married women into gainful employment—simply cannot be reconciled with any hypothesis of an extensive rejection of "low quality" work. The available absenteeism data, which suggest some increase since the mid-1960s, are still too incomplete to support any broad generalizations—although they tend to reinforce more specific reports concerning the special frustrations of the automobile assembly-line workers. Even the mass of survey data designed to elicit direct measures of job dissatisfaction have failed to show any consistent trend.

Why Are Supposed Trends Not Visible?

If this trend has not in fact developed in visible and measurable dimensions, we may well ask "Why not?" Is it because the statistical barometers for measuring emerging social trends are too incomplete, too gross, and too insensitive for this purpose? Or is it because the theoretical constructs which lead to certain expectations as to worker behaviors and attitudes simply do not conform to reality?

Most of the available statistical indicators are clearly much too aggregative to serve as reliable indexes of worker discontent. Statistical series such as productivity and labor turnover were designed for quite different purposes. Much more disaggregation of the data, and supplementary research, is needed before we can reliably isolate the influence of specific causal factors. And we are still in the early stages of development of meaningful indexes of job satisfaction and absenteeism. It is quite possible, therefore, that the available measures—separately and in combination—are too crude and insensitive to detect any new emerging social force.

In part, however, the explanation lies in the model of worker aspirations and behavior postulated by the social psychologists. Their point of departure is a heirarchical ordering of human needs, which, as outlined by Abraham Maslow, begins with satisfaction of basic material wants, such as food and shelter, and ascends to higher order needs, such as "self-esteem" and "self-actualization." An alternative formulation by Herzberg is couched in terms of "extrinsic" and "intrinsic" job factors. Extrinsic factors, such as poor pay, inadequate benefits, or poor physical working conditions, may lead to job dissatisfaction, while true satisfaction depends upon the intrinsic nature of the job, its work content, and its inherent challenge and interest. But both models lead to the inference that, as the general wage level increases and physical working conditions improve, the emphasis shifts from strictly economic issues to demands for improvement in the nature of work itself.

It is difficult to challenge this scale of aspirations in the abstract. In fact, numerous surveys indicate that when workers are asked what aspects of work are most important to them, "interesting work" often heads the list, particularly among the more educated or more affluent segments of the population. Given this apparent scale of values and the rising "affluence" of American workers, why then have most workers not overtly attempted to change the contents of their work? For example, has the continued concentration of organized labor on "bread and butter" issues, rather than quality of work, simply reflected a lack of sensitivity on the part of union leaders to the real needs of their members—or has it in fact reflected the priorities of their rank-and-file members.

As a broad generalization, we believe that the latter assumption corresponds much closer to reality. One fallacy in the Maslow-Herzberg model of worker aspirations, as a guide to behavior, lies in its inherently static premises. Even though individual earnings and family incomes have increased steadily over the decades, the great majority of American workers certainly do not consider themselves as "affluent" when they relate their spendable income to their spending needs, for what they now consider an acceptable standard of living. As Christopher Jencks has recently pointed out, this escalation of living standards "is not just a matter of rising expectations or of people's needing to 'keep up with the Joneses' " but is due in part to the fact that with changes in our mode of life, such goods as an automobile, a telephone, or packaged foods have become an integral part of our cost of living—of participating in our social system. Thus, when hard choices have to be made between a monotonous job in a regimented environment, which pays relatively well and which offers job security, and a poorer paying, less secure but more "satisfying" job, most workers—and particularly those with family commitments—are still not in a position to make the trade-off in favor of meeting their "intrinsic" needs.

Moreover, most workers and most union leaders tend to be highly skeptical of the real potential of "job enrichment" as a practicable means of improving their work environments. This skepticism results from earlier experiences when worker participation, profit sharing, and similar approaches were instituted by some firms as an alternative to pay increases or as a means of staving off unionization. . . .

The Quest for Autonomy

One of the more questionable premises made by the authors concerning the nature and sources of worker discontent is the assumption that large numbers of workers have an urge for "autonomy" at the work place and are chafing at the disciplines and controls imposed by large bureaucratic organizations—whether big business or big government. Is this in fact a major preoccupation of most workers in our society today—or is it an image created by popular emphasis on extremes; the extreme of the real frustrations of the automobile assembly-line worker, on the one hand, and of the revolt of some (probably small) fraction of upper-middle-class youth on the other?

Certainly, one of the most "bureaucratic" organizations in modern society is the military; no other large organization imposes equal constraints upon both the personal lives and the working lives of its labor force. Yet in 1972, while the Vietnam War was still underway, over 330,000 young men, about one-fourth of the militarily eligible manpower pool, elected to voluntarily enlist in military service. . . . Between 1970 and 1972, voluntary (not draft motivated) enlistments into the army had risen by fully 80 percent, largely in response to major increases in compensation and other special inducements offered as part of the effort to move to an all-volunteer military force. Numerous surveys have shown that few young men have any great illusions about the "intrinsic" aspects of most enlisted jobs. By large majorities, young high school graduates (who account for a large majority of enlistees) have recognized that civilian jobs are preferable to military service in terms of such criteria as "freedom," "interesting work," and "highly respected job." Yet, when faced with the limited range of choices open to them, large numbers of young men have been willing to accept the constraints and risks of military service in exchange for some of its visible benefits—its training and educational opportunities, its opportunity for travel and new experiences, and its material rewards.

In a similar vein, prestige rankings of various civilian occupations, based on a number of surveys, have failed to reveal any consistent preference for autonomous, self-directed employment, in comparison with more regimented, but better paying and more secure occupations. Office machine operators and bookkeepers rate higher than small independent farmers in these rankings. Assembly-line workers outrank taxi drivers in popular esteem. And as we have previously noted, many millions of women have moved from household work, which, though unpaid, has the virtue of being self-directed, into the more regimented world of gainful employment.

The foregoing comments are clearly not designed to imply that "all is well" with the quality of work in America or that, as a nation, we can afford to be complacent about some of the danger signals which have been brought to our attention. The fact that over 10 percent of employed workers express general dissatisfaction with their jobs, that many more are dissatisfied with specific aspects of their work situation, and that these proportions are much higher for youth, for women, and for minorities, is a challenge to management, unions, and the government to pursue corrective actions.

However, if our interpretation of the recent labor market behavior of American workers is valid, it does imply a different set of criteria for measuring quality of jobs and a different set of priorities for improvement of the quality of work. Our premise is that workers have no difficulty in distinguishing between the "good" and "bad" jobs in our economy. The least desirable jobs, typically, are inferior *both* in terms of pay and related benefits and in terms of the intrinsic nature of the work itself. Included in this category are most domestic and hired farm labor jobs and a large proportion of the 20 million jobs in the private nonfarm economy which . . . paid less than $2.50 per hour in April 1970. Numerous unskilled or semiskilled jobs paying somewhat higher wages can also be included in this category because of the oppressive nature of the work and the lack of advancement opportunities.

It has been possible for employers to recruit an adequate supply of workers for most of these low level jobs because of the continued existence of a large pool of workers who have had no effective labor market choices. Included in this pool are a disproportionate number of minority members, teen-aged youth, women, and recent immigrants who share common handicaps of limited skill, limited work experience, restricted mobility, and various forms of institutionalized discrimination. These categories of workers constitute a relatively large share of the 5 million visibly unemployed workers and probably represent an even larger proportion of the "invisible" unemployed not included in our statistics of active job-seekers. So long as this reservoir of low-wage labor is available, employers have little incentive to increase the pay or enhance the quality of these jobs.

The most potent strategy for improving the quality of these jobs and/or reducing their relative numbers is by reducing the size of this reserve pool of workers. It is no coincidence that the most significant progress in improving the relative status of low-wage workers in this country has been made during periods of acute wartime labor shortages, such as during World War II. It is no coincidence, either, that employer initiatives for experimentation with work redesign abroad have been most evident in countries such as Sweden and West Germany, which have managed their economies with much lower ratios of peacetime unemployment than in the United States—and have been initiated in precisely those industries, such as the automobile industry, which have most acutely felt a labor shortage situation.

The most important single set of measures which can contribute to improvements of *quality* of work in America are, thus, those designed to increase the *quantity* of work in America. This requires a much more positive national commitment to a maximum employment policy—even, if need be, at the cost of a somewhat higher level of acceptable inflation. In turn, a climate of sustained high employment can make possible more effective implementation of specific manpower and labor market policies designed to upgrade the status of workers in low level jobs and to promote equality of employment opportunity. It may, in fact, bring us closer to the era of the "post-subsistence" economy when those jobs which do not meet minimum economic *and* psychological standards will·be effectively ruled out from the labor market competition.

There should be no illusion that these goals are easily attainable—either through the recommendations scattered through *Work in America* or through those proposed in the numerous other recent studies concerned with national manpower and economic policies. . . .

Job Satisfaction: A Union Response

William W. Winpisinger

After some years of seeking legislative alternatives to collective bargaining, plus even more years of academic debate on the pros and cons of union responsibilities in relation to public rights, it now appears that labor's good friends in government, intellectual, and academic circles have discovered an interesting new malady. They've already provided it with a name, a diagnosis and even a cure.

The name is the "blue-collar blues." The diagnosis is that because younger workers are brighter and better educated than their fathers they refuse to accept working conditions that past generations took for granted. The cure consists of a shot of psychic penicillin known as job enrichment.

There can be little doubt as to the existence of a rising tide of dissatisfaction, or alienation, among those who are increasingly and even sneeringly referred to as the Archie Bunkers of America.

Employers feel it in more absenteeism, more turnover, and more strikes over working conditions. Politicians feel it in the perceptible shift of blue-collar workers from the principles of the New Deal to the philosophy of George Wallace. Unions feel it in the rising level of contract rejections and the growing number of defeats suffered by long established business representatives and officers in union elections.

Just a couple of months ago, *Time* magazine, in an essay on the work ethic, noted that according to a Gallup poll taken in 1971, 19 percent of all workers expressed dissatisfaction with their jobs. This was viewed with some pessimism by the learned editors of that magazine. If they had chosen to be optimistic they could just as validly have noted that 81 percent of all workers seemed to be satisfied with their jobs.

There is, of course, no way to prove it but I feel reasonably certain that at no time in the entire history of man would Gallup have found 100 percent happiness and job satisfaction in the labor force. I doubt if 100 percent of the ancient Egyptians who

Reprinted from the *American Federationist,* February 1973, pp. 11–13, with the permission of the AFL-CIO.

built the pyramids, or 100 percent of the medieval craftsmen who constructed the great cathedrals, or 100 percent of the 19th century Irishmen who laid the tracks for the American railroads were so filled with job satisfaction that they consistently whistled while they worked.

The right to bitch about the job, or the boss, or the system, or even the Union, is one of the inalienable rights of a free workforce. Whether workers today are generally happier today than those in the so-called good old days is not provable one way or the other. Some claim that increasing automization of work processes and the mind-deadening monotony of the modern assembly line cannot help but lead to anything except increasing alienation in the workforce. And yet the assembly line has been with us for a long time. The concept of the robotized worker, endlessly repeating one function, tightening the same bolt over and over, was already well established before Charlie Chaplin satirized it in the movie *Modern Times* more than 40 years ago.

Strangely enough, Gallup's polls on worker dissatisfaction, which were started in 1949, consistently registered slow but steady increases in the level of worker satisfaction right up to 1969. Though workers throughout the 1950s and 1960s were never really affluent in the Galbraithian sense, they were making progress. On the whole, jobs were plentiful and the gap between what the average production worker earned and what the Bureau of Labor Statistics said he needed for a "modest but adequate" standard of living was narrowing. But then between 1969 and 1971 the overall rate of job satisfaction, according to Gallup, fell 6 percent. If this decrease were due to some substantial change in the nature of the jobs that people did I would have to agree with those who prescribe job enrichment as the answer to worker dissatisfaction.

Don't get me wrong. I am not opposed to efforts by management or industrial psychologists to make assembly-line jobs less monotonous and more fulfilling. But the point is—and it may not be too palatable to some in management or government or academic circles—that just as job dissatisfaction in the workplace yielded to trade union solutions in the past, such dissatisfaction can be decreased to the extent that trade union solutions are applied today.

One of the reasons that worker satisfaction declined in the late 1960s and early 1970s is that worker income, in relation to inflation and taxation and the purchasing power of the dollar that was earned by labor, also declined.

Because of government policies leading to rising unemployment, establishing one-sided controls on wages and permitting multinational companies to export thousands of American jobs to Hong Kong, Taiwan, and other low-wage areas, the gap between what the average family earns and what this family needs for a decent standard of living has been growing. So it should come as no surprise to anyone that worker dissatisfaction is also growing.

The recent rash of strikes and other labor problems at the General Motors plant in Lordstown, Ohio, has been seized upon by those who write articles for learned journals as proof that even if the nature of the assembly line hasn't changed, the workforce has. As every student of industrial relations knows, the overwhelming majority of the workforce at Lordstown is young. On the basis of management's unhappy experiences with these kids, the experts have solemnly proclaimed the discovery of a new kind of workforce. They inform us that here is a generation that has never known a depression and thus has no interest in security; that grew up in a time of crass materialism and thus rejects the work ethic; that has been infected by the rebellion of youth and thus has no respect for authority. I have seen one scholarly analysis, in fact, that compares the "rebellion" at Lordstown in the early 1970s with the free speech movement at Berkeley in the early 1960s. And the conclusion was drawn that the nation's factories, like her colleges, would never be the same again.

Quite frankly, I submit that that kind of analysis overlooks one salient fact. The young workers at Lordstown were reacting against the same kind of grievances, in the same kind of way, as did generations of workers before them. They were rebelling against an obvious speed-up; protesting safety violations; and reacting against working conditions that have been unilaterally imposed by a management that was determined to get tough in the name of efficiency. Anyone who thinks wildcats or slow-downs or even sabotage started at Lordstown doesn't know very much about the history of the labor movement.

An almost identical series of incidents took place over much the same issues at Norwood, Ohio, at almost the same time but very few inferences were drawn about the changing nature of the workforce because, in this case, it was older workers who were involved.

Many people . . . are viewing the decline of the work ethic in the United States with alarm. On the basis of my experience, which includes many day-to-day contacts with Machinists, I can assure you that the work ethic is alive and well and living in a lot of good work places.

But what the aerospace workers and auto mechanics and production workers we represent want, in the way of job satisfaction, is a wage that is commensurate with their skill.

If you want to enrich the job, enrich the pay check. The better the wage, the greater the job satisfaction. There is no better cure for the "blue-collar blues."

If you want to enrich the job, begin to decrease the number of hours a worker has to labor in order to earn a decent standard of living. Just as the increased productivity of mechanized assembly lines made it possible to decrease the workweek from 60 to 40 hours a couple of generations ago, the time has come to translate the increased productivity of automated processes into the kind of enrichment that comes from shorter workweeks, longer vacations, and earlier retirements.

If you want to enrich the job, do something about the nerve shattering noise, the heat, and the fumes that are deafening, poisoning, and destroying the health of American workers. Thousands of chemicals whose effects on humans have never been tested are being used in workplaces. Companies are willing to spend millions advertising quieter refrigerators or washing machines but are reluctant to spend one penny to provide a reasonably safe level of noise in their plants. And though we are now supposed to have a law that protects people against some of the more obvious occupational hazards, industry is already fighting to undermine enforcement. . . .

If you want to enrich the jobs of the men and women who manufacture the goods that are needed for the functioning of our industrialized society, the time has come to re-evaluate the snobbery that makes it noble to possess a college degree and shameful to learn skills that involve a little bit of grease under the fingernails. The best way to undermine a worker's morale and decrease his satisfaction with himself and his job is to make him feel that society looks down on him because he wears blue coveralls instead of a white collar. I think it is ironic that because of the prevailing attitudes many kinds of skilled craftsmen are in short supply while thousands of college graduates are tripping over one another in search of jobs.

Some of the most dissatisfied people I know are those who got a college degree and then couldn't find a position that lived up to their expectations. And that has been especially true the last few years. A lot of college trained people are driving cabs today; they would have had a lot more job satisfaction and made a lot more money if they had apprenticed as auto mechanics.

If you want to enrich the job, give working people a greater sense of control over their working conditions. That's what they and their unions were seeking in the early 1960s when management was automating and retooling on a large scale. That's why we asked for advance consultation when employers intended to make major job changes. That's why we negotiated for clauses providing retraining and transfer rights and a fair share of the increased productivity that resulted from automation.

What workers resent—and what really causes alienation—are management decisions that rearrange job assignments or upset existing work schedules without reference to the rights of the workforce.

If you want to enrich the job, you must realize that no matter how dull or boring or dirty it may be, an individual worker must feel that he has not reached the end of the line. If a worker is to be reasonably satisfied with the job he has today he must have hope for something better tomorrow.

You know this is true in universities, in government, and in management. Even an assembly line must have some chance of movement, even if it's only from a job that requires stooping down to one that involves standing erect. But here again, we are talking about a job problem for which unionism provides an answer. And the name of that answer is the negotiated seniority clause. Perhaps when workers first negotiated the right to bid on better shifts, overtime, or promotions on the basis of length of service, they weren't thinking in terms of "job enrichment" but were only trying to restrict management's right to allocate jobs and shifts and overtime on the basis of favoritism. But even if they weren't thinking in terms of "job enrichment," in actual practice that's what they got.

It's true that many young workers in their 20s resent the fact that while they have to tighten the same old bolt in the same old spot a thousand times a day, the guys in their 40s are walking up and down the line with inspection sheets or running around the factory on forklifts.

They may resent and bitch about it now—but they also know they are accumulating seniority which they can trade for a better job of their own some day.

These many ways in which jobs can be enriched may not be what management has in mind when it talks about job enrichment. On the basis of a fairly extensive experience as a union representative, I find it hard to picture management enriching jobs at the expense of profits. In fact, I have a sneaking suspicion that "job enrichment" may be just another name for "time and motion" study. As labor historian Thomas Brooks said in a recent *Federationist* article, "Substituting the sociologist's questionnaire for the stopwatch is likely to be no gain for the workers. While workers have a stake in productivity, it is not always identical with that of management. Job enrichment programs have cut jobs just as effectively as automation and stopwatches. And the rewards of productivity are not always equitably shared."

What some companies call job enrichment is really little more than the introduction of gimmicks such as doing away with time clocks or developing "work teams" or designing jobs to "maximize personal involvement"—whatever that means.

In conclusion let me say that I know there are those who worry about what the younger generation is coming to and wonder whether the rebellious young workers of today will be willing to fill their fathers' shoes in the factory jobs of tomorrow. We can't generalize from isolated examples, but I was very interested in an NBC television documentary recently that studied the dissatisfaction of young workers. The part that interested me most was the transformation in an assembly-line "hippie" who followed his electrician father's footsteps by becoming an apprentice and cutting his hair.

All the studies tend to prove that worker dissatisfaction diminishes with age. That's because older workers have accrued more of the kinds of job enrichment that unions have fought for—better wages, shorter hours, vested pensions, a right to have a say in their working conditions, and the right to be promoted on the basis of seniority and all the rest. That's the kind of job enrichment that unions believe in.

The Tensions of Work

Jack Barbash

The oppressiveness of much of the work performed by blue-collar workers is imbedded in the structure of industrialism. My objective here is to identify these structural features and suggest their effects on the organization of work. For if we wish to ease the oppressiveness of work, we must find ways to change these structural features which persist under both capitalism and socialism.

The structural requirements of industrialism are, in shorthand form: *technology; scale; cost discipline; a disciplined labor force; organization; uncertainty;* and *the state.*

Technology consists of production hardware, skills, science, and technique.

Scale means large concentrations of workers and capital investment.

Cost discipline is the technique for economizing on scarce resources in order to achieve a favorable net return.

A disciplined labor force means men and women workers who by education, culture, and motivation will be responsive to cost discipline techniques.

Organization is the structured association of people and procedures that is necessary for administering the technology, scale, cost discipline, and labor force.

Uncertainty refers to the unpredictability of economic events, given the forward nature of economic transactions.

The state signifies the overhead facilitative, regulatory, public-procurement, and planning functions usually provided by government.

These structural features generate tensions of a peculiar force among manual workers, tensions that can be categorized as: *subordination; competitiveness; monotony and drudgery; exploitation;* and *economic instability.*

Tensions of subordination derive from the vertical or hierarchical division of labor. The relatively large labor force at the enterprise level demanded by industrialism requires a vertical or hierarchical division of labor, for there is a limit to the span of control any one supervisor can efficiently exercise—especially if one assumes, as industrial management does, that the "lower order" or workers will malinger if left

Reprinted from *Dissent,* Winter 1972, pp. 240–48, with the permission of the author.

unsupervised. Many employees in the hierarchical division of labor are both order-givers and order-takers, but the largest group at the lowest level is invariably composed of permanent order-takers. In his later years Engels understood this very well; he wrote: "Wanting to abolish authority in large scale industry is tantamount to wanting to abolish industry itself, destroy the power loom in order to return to the spinning wheel."[1]

It is in the nature of hierarchical organizations that "leaders can shift rewards to themselves and deprivations to non-leaders. . . . Extensive hierarchy is likely . . . to produce great inequalities in dignity, respect, and opportunity. . . ."[2] Hierarchy expressed in "the employer's power to exercise arbitrary control over his workers" contributes "one of the chief sources of unrest."[3] In the hierarchical industrial system, "management is constantly originating activity for" the workers "at the bottom of the industrial pyramid" with little opportunity for the workers "to originate back. . . . (the) people in the bottom positions develop some resentment against the people who are always originating for them."[4]

Competitive tension follows from the horizontal division of labor because no one can know operationally more than a small segment of the range of specializations which the technology and organization of industrialism thrust up. Moreover, industrialism manifests a powerful tendency to proliferate specializations, which then become professionalized and jurisdiction-minded:

Work groups compete among themselves for the available economic rewards.[5]

The organization of the plant provides incentives for the banding together of individual workers into *interest* groups. These incentives are not only the desire to protect the status quo, work standards, degree of rule enforcement and discipline meted out by supervision, relative earnings and seniority position, but also include the opportunity to improve their relative position. Improvement can take the form of looser standards, a preferred seniority position, more overtime, more sympathetic supervision, correction of inequities, and better equipment.[6]

Competition for improvements in working conditions and benefits appears to be most frequent among groups that are more than half-way up the status ladder. Their position is somewhat ambiguous. They are almost the best but not quite. Members of these groups seem to be carrying a chip on their shoulders.[7]

Relative scarcity of employment, earnings opportunity, and status concerns pit one work group against another—the classic divisions being those between production workers and skilled craftsmen, manual and white-collar workers. In addition, divisions within the work force get tied in with differences in color, ethnic origin, and sex, which tend to sharpen existing differences.

Tensions of exploitation—a feeling on the part of the worker that the monetary return for his labor is less than he is worth or deserves—stem from the clash between the employer's cost imperative and the worker's wage consciousness, or between the former's production orientation and the latter's consumption orientation. To the employer, the worker's wage is a cost; to the worker, the wage is income and a standard of life, which he tries to insulate as much as possible from the uncertainty that besets the employer's product market.

The basic peculiarity of the purchase and sale of labor is that here we have an exchange in which the exchangeables appear very differently to the two parties. . . . For the employer the transaction is significant insofar as it is an exchange of money or liquid assets for the product of the work. . . . The worker is exchanging life for income; the transaction involves him in status, prestige, his standing in the eyes of his family and of the community and his whole position as a man.[8]

Ordinarily, the worker perceives himself at a considerable disadvantage in bargaining for his income and other objectives against the employer. Among these disadvantages are: the worker's total dependence on a wage income; the short-term character of his employment (ordinarily a week) and its instability; his inability to withhold his effort for a better price because of lack of reserves and the perishability of his labor as a commodity; the relatively large number of sellers of labor compared to the relatively small number of buyers; his lack of knowledge of alternative opportunities in the market and of his actual worth to the employer, and his low occupational and geographical mobility.[9]

To all these factors must be added the employer's resistance against wage bargaining, because for him the wage transaction represents not only a traditional kind of price contract. By now, as a joint determination of the conditions under which the labor is to be performed, the wage bargain also represents a sharing of power in an area over which he previously exercised unilateral control.

The labor transaction represents not only the differences in industrial rank—that between the managers and workers—but these differences in industrial rank also are closely related to those in social rank. And participants in the labor transaction meet one another as adversaries, which deepens the feeling of difference. This is unlike the manager's experience when bargaining for other factors of production, since in those transactions the adversary confrontation is likely to be mediated by common interests and associations in the noneconomic relationships of church, political party, and neighborhood.

As for "deprivation," let us use Baldamus's concept of it as the tension which arises directly out of the effort of work. The "three main elements, defined as different aspects of the deprivation inherent in industrial work (are) . . . impairment, tedium and weariness."[10] Impairment "is the state of mind of a person aware of his physical discomfort caused by strenuous work."[11] Tedium is a feeling experienced by manual workers, and it stems from the repetitiveness of light work—as distinguished from the boredom experienced in professional occupations.[12] Weariness is not always easy to distinguish from tedium, but "analytically" it is the distinction between the work realities of repetitiveness (i.e., tedium) on the one hand, and the coercion of prolonged routine work on the other. By comparison, "office routines . . . are less coercive than factory routines."[13]

As defined here, the feeling of deprivation stems mainly from the minute specialization in the horizontal division of labor that makes the worker literally "an appendage of the machine," to use Marx's well-known phrase. "Management pays a price for the work simplification, routinization, and ease of supervision inherent in mass production work," a modern commentary observes. "The cost is largely in terms of apathy and boredom, as positive satisfactions are engineered out of jobs."[14] How high the cost is a matter of speculation, just as the degree to which workers are affected by boredom and monotony. On the one side are those who say that monotony in work is by now one of the lower-order discontents. A survey sponsored by the U.S. Department of Labor reported that only 5 percent of the sample singled out the boredom and routinization of work as the "single biggest problem they faced on their jobs."[15] Blauner reported that "there is remarkable consistency in the findings that the vast majority of workers in virtually all occupations and industries are highly or moderately satisfied rather than dissatisfied with their jobs." There are, however, differences in the degree of satisfaction.[16] The Goldthorpe research group in Britain found that in their affluent worker group "the performance of work tasks was accompanied by various, and in some groups fairly generalized psychological work stresses."[17]

The tension of uncertainty derives from the general economic uncertainty that, as we know, is a pervasive feature of modern society. It works with special force on the worker for whom stability of expectations is a major concern. Uncertainty has stemmed historically from the worker's dependence, as Frank Tannenbaum has observed, on a money wage. "As long as men had the greater part of their living in real income produced by themselves, the uncertainties of the money wage could be tolerated."[18]

While change is literally a way of life for management, the worker often sees it as a threat.

> The appearance of something new whether in the form of a new labor saving-device, a new incentive system, a new kind of supervision, or a new process, seems to sound an alert among men at work; they mount guard, as it were, suspicious in advance that the change bodes them no good. The problem that emerges becomes particularly baffling when time and again it appears immaterial whether an innovation affects the workers adversely or not. Indeed, even when it promises them substantial benefit, they may still pull, haul, and balk.[19]

The method of payment, a product of the cost discipline, in which "a man's income can be paid to him an hour's worth at a time"[20] is an immediate source of instability, considering the infinite variety of exigencies to which it is subject.

All of these tensions of work induce a strong protective cast in the worker's outlook. His protectivism consists, first, of a short-run time horizon, if only because he works under a relatively short-duration contract of employment.

> "Working class life (a generalization from the British experience which probably holds just as well for the American) puts a premium on the taking of pleasures now, discourages planning for some future good." This emphasis on the present and the lack of concern for planning ahead are . . . encouraged by the view that there is in fact little to be done about the future, that it is not to any major extent under the individual's control.[21]

Robert Hoxie, generalizing from the American worker's experience, observes, "There is no long run but immediate needs."[22]

Protectivism also takes the form of a kind of sectionalism that constrains the worker's scope of interest to where he happens to be located in the division of labor. "In industry . . . it is what occurs at the lowest level, on the factory floor, that matters most to the worker."[23]

Selig Perlman formulated the central interests of workers as "job control," "job consciousness," and "shop rights which to the working men at the bench are identical with 'liberty' itself."[24] This protectivism is further expressed in the worker's characteristic pessimism, in what Selig Perlman called "scarcity-consciousness." "The manual worker is convinced by experience that he is living in a world of limited opportunity."[25] So the worker acquires a kind of job-fund theory, that there is only a limited supply of work that needs to be prudently rationed. Managers and higher-rated workers, by contrast, are likely to take a broader, longer-run, more optimistic view—because they are higher up in the organization, exercise a larger degree of autonomy, and usually do not feel that economic security is for them the immediate problem that it is for the worker.

The extent of this protectivism varies directly with the worker's place in the job hierarchy, the level of economic activity, and the society's stage of industrial development. A salaried employee is likely to be more confident than the wage worker, because his fundamental economic needs are already met and he exercises more control over his job circumstances. An expanding economy, with its brighter future, encourages relaxation of protective attitudes—and a highly developed industrial economy, i.e., "the affluent society," upgrades the worker's level of need as compared to, say, a subsistence agricultural economy.

Most workers put up with tensions of work because:

Wage or salary employment is the only available method of financing a desired standard of living and a respected place in the community; they have found ways of warding off the full impact of work tensions; a few with high professional or craft motivation find their work intrinsically satisfying and perceive the tensions as a challenge and the necessary cost of producing a product or service in which they can take pride.

In the long run, the development of industrialism has probably brought about a lessening of the tensions incident to work. The sources of these alleviating influences are technology, trade unionism, the welfare state, management philosophy, and full employment.

Technology has done much to ease the drudgery and physical demands of work, although in the worker's mind its beneficial results have frequently been overshadowed by the tension-inducing effects of displacement and skill obsolescence. The relatively modern concern with the human consequences of technological change, including full-employment policies, has also somewhat eased these tensions.

Trade unionism has eased the harshness of the hierarchical division of labor by introducing through collective bargaining a system of bilateral industrial government, which has established some rights and orderly procedures in the hierarchical relationship between management and workers. Trade unionism also performs the function of mediating the competitive claims among workers. It has also moderated the abrasiveness of the income-cost interaction, thereby compensating to a degree for the worker's bargaining inferiority. Trade unionism's protective activities have been complemented, with broader scope, by the welfare state's lightening of disabilities that arise from unemployment, old age, ill health, and inadequate education.

Besides the pressures of trade unionism there is a growing perception in management, derived from both experience and research, that the labor input differs from all other factor inputs in being inseparable from the human being who sells it, and that therefore the management of labor needs to deal not only with labor's characteristics as a commodity but also with at least some of its human needs.

The gradual incorporation of this perception into personnel policy has had its effects: it has sensitized the manager to the needs of the managed through techniques of "human relations"; it has professionalized "human relations" expertise; it has made "human relations" compatible to a degree with cost consciousness; it has provided in many instances a substitute for unionism.

Yet the main purpose of "human relations"—with all its concern for conserving human values at work—is the harnessing of these values in the interests of management efficiency. But the pressure of trade unionism often has forced management to acknowledge the legitimacy of other interests and to recognize that "the firm is a plural society containing many related but separate interests and objectives which must be maintained in some kind of equilibrium."[26] The most important implication of what amounts to a pluralistic management philosophy is that it views the union or a similar assertion of worker interests as integral to the labor process of the enterprise and not an alien influence.

There is also a socialist management theory of work humanization that begins with the utopians—Owen and Fourier—and Marx's ideas about alienation. As part of this tradition and also of trade unionism, movements have arisen for "cooperativism," workers' control, "industrial democracy," and workers' councils. But with the exception of Fourier, radical ideologists have largely focused on the question of *who* makes the work decisions rather than on the organization and mechanics of the work process itself.

Marx was extraordinarily perceptive in identifying the division of labor, and particularly the division between intellectual and manual labor, as a source of alienation. He was wrong, as it turned out, in associating alienation only with capitalist industrialism.

The "socialist" systems, whose ideologies are based upon the destructiveness of the labor process under capitalism, have hardly addressed themselves to its reform. The Soviet Union has yet to emerge from the commodity stage of the labor process. Lenin was, in fact, an admirer of Taylorism, which was, of course, the ultimate rationalization of labor as a commodity.

While the "socialist" systems produced a "new class" to make the work decisions, they have not found it possible to reconstruct the logic of subordination and cost discipline by which the decisions are made; nor is there any indication that, with the possible exception of the Yugoslavs, a serious effort has been made in this direction. Only the anarchists diagnosed correctly that a boss is a boss is a boss—but to this day they have not been able to make their antibossism work in an industrial environment. Their sovereign remedy (which has not worked either) has been withdrawal from industrial society. The evidence is plain, then, that the transfer of power from the capitalists to "the people" is by itself simply not capable of sustaining an idealism powerful enough to overthrow the traditional logic of industrialism. As Fidel Castro instructs us:

> Perhaps our greatest idealism lies in having believed that a society that had barely begun to live in a world that for thousands of years had lived under the law of an "eye for an eye and a tooth for a tooth," the law of the survival of the fittest, of egoism and defeat, the law of exploitation could, all of a sudden be turned into a society in which everybody believed in an ethical, moral way.[27]

Each era gives its own imprint to the labor problem. Trade unionism and management philosophy imprinted the dominant mark on the labor problems for the period from the New Deal to World War II. Full employment and the welfare state have been the paramount influences in shaping the labor problems of the post-1950s. Not only has full employment helped blunt the edge of the cost problem to make it more compatible with "human relations" and a more tolerant view of trade unionism, it also has abated the competitive struggle within the working class by increasing the volume of jobs and earnings opportunities.

But full employment, paradoxically, is also an influence in generating new tensions, for it has raised to prominence a new order of problems as earlier ones have receded. First of all, full employment is associated with inflation. Inflation aggravates workers' discontent with their inability to keep their wages in line with rising prices and with the wages of other workers to whom they compare themselves. Inflation forces union leaders, under pain of rank-and-file reprisal to defy the inevitable public pressures aimed at wage repression; and inflation may be the fundamental force at work in the eruptive discontents among young workers who are likely to suffer disproportionately from its effects.

Full employment makes all the more intolerable the existence of a special, disadvantaged class barred by structural handicaps from sharing in the general affluence. The attempt of this disadvantaged class to achieve a measure of social justice has thrust up a new interest group demanding recognition of its claims from both employers and the established working class under pain of disruption, litigation, and withdrawal of federal procurement. Militancy by and on behalf of black workers has stimulated militancy in other ethnic groups, notably the Mexican-Americans. In both situations we see how a growing ethnic awareness cements an atomized mass of low-wage workers into unions, to deal on their own power with the problem of wage exploitation.

By making job security more general, full employment has also narrowed the job-security advantage public employees enjoyed but had to pay for with salaries lower than those of their private counterparts. This relative worsening of the public employees' position, plus the inflexibility of their wages vis-a-vis changes in consumer prices, has turned firemen, police, teachers, and postal employees to the tactics of militant unionism.

The increasing recourse to wildcats, quitting, and absenteeism may be interpreted as the workers' willingness to accept reduced earnings for some relief from oppressive job monotony and discipline. Full employment makes such trade-off possible, for it frees workers from the fear of immediate deprivation if they don't work.

The militant temper of the times—what some have called the authority crisis—has shaped the modes in which workers' tensions have been expressed. What is tantamount to civil disobedience by public employees may reasonably be interpreted as a demonstration effect of campus and civil-rights activism. But student and civil-rights activism can also be read as having set in motion a backlash reaction among workers. In this view the conspicuous antipatriotism and special "life-style" of campus dissent have aroused the blue-collar worker to a militant defense of the system, suggesting that even with all the tensions he must endure, the American worker still feels a sufficient stake in the system to be outraged by broadside attacks on it and even, on occasions, to be moved to violence in its defense.

Workers' tensions, as located here, derive from the organization of the work processes and the economic environment. Such tensions are related in large part to the subordination and specialization systems imposed by industrialism. Although progress has been made in "humanizing" the effects of subordination and specialization, both research and experience suggest that more can be done to develop autonomous "responsible job behavior"[28] without impairing, and perhaps even increasing, cost efficiency. Yet if we truly value the lessening of work tensions and their social consequences, we must be aware that, as in ecology, the price to be paid may be in sacrifices of cost efficiency—if we consider the human cost.

Neither socialism nor workers' participation guarantees the lessening of work tensions, if the underlying systems of subordination, specialization, and cost calculation are left intact in the organization of the work process. Work organization, as a variable, apparently needs to be dealt with independently. One or another form of society might facilitate or be more concerned with the solution of this problem; but the mere establishment of any society—capitalist, socialist, or some amalgam of the two—would not guarantee a solution.

The extent to which the work process may be humanized seems to be most closely related to the stage of economic development. An industrial society that has surpassed the subsistence stage is likely to be freer in experiments with work-easing methods, and in advanced societies the utilization of labor is less of a problem. The humanization of work has reached its greatest development under capitalism—but this reflects only Western capitalism's advanced stage of development, not the tendency of private enterprise as such to humanize work. Both capitalism's and socialism's industrial revolutions have, in fact, been monuments to the inefficient and inhumane uses of labor.

It is not generally understood that freedom on the job will provide not only autonomy at work but also the freedom to change jobs. This, normally, is possible only under full employment and in a relatively free labor market, which is the special problem of socialist systems. Modern postwar capitalist economies, however, have been able to achieve full employment only at the cost of inflation, which carries with it its own tension inducing effects. Viable solutions will have to permit sustained full employment at a considerably lower level of inflation than is now possible. Since inflationary impulses at full-employment level are generated to an important degree by labor scarcities and a poor use of the existing labor supply, the remedies offered by modern manpower measures seem more compatible with free work choices than the new standard anti-inflation remedies of deflation and unemployment.

Concretely, the methods of manpower policy—education, training and retraining, financial inducements to mobility, job counseling, job creation in underemployed areas, and effective institutions in the labor market to facilitate these processes— seem indispensable to a condition of free work choices in modern industrial society. Here again, as in the design of work, there is a body of knowledge and analysis that, though far from constituting a science, can provide a foundation on which to build.

For the unions, the task ahead is to focus more directly on how the worker can be liberated from the tyrannies of the work process without impairing his income and thereby his living standard. Having introduced a semblance of due process in work relationships, the union now ought to explore more systematically how work and work organization as such can be reformed to make them more humanly tolerable.

The alleviation of work tensions has to be achieved at two levels. On the shop floor, the hierarchical organization and division of labor and the design of work have to be altered to permit greater autonomy and satisfaction in the work itself. And at the level of the economy, full employment without inflation and greater efficiency in the labor market have to be realized in order to give the worker his ultimate sanction: the effective opportunity to leave an oppressive job and get a better one.

Still, a caveat must be entered against utopianism in thinking about work freedom. We still cannot foresee a time when the tyranny of necessity and scarcity, which underlies the essential oppressiveness of work for most people, will fade away. There are no total remedies for necessity and scarcity, and their abatement will most effectively yield to step-by-step methods which take time. We must remember, too, that a substantial part of our population still has to conquer subsistence or the quantity of work before it can move on to the problem of the quality of work. For the impatient it should be of some comfort to know that this era is possibly the first in history when the question of personal freedom at work has become both relevant and practical.

NOTES

1. Friedrich Engels, "On Authority," in Karl Marx and Friedrich Engels, *Basic Writings on Politics and Philosophy*, Lewis S. Feuer, ed. (New York: Doubleday Anchor, 1959), p. 483.

2. Robert A. Dahl and Charles E. Lindblom, *Politics, Economics, and Welfare* (New York: Harper, 1953), p. 256.

3. A.E.C. Hare, *The First Principles of Industrial Relations* (New York: St. Martin's Press, 1965), p. 27.

4. W. Whyte, *Money and Motivation* (New York: Harper, 1955), p. 234.

5. Leonard R. Sayles, *Behavior of Industrial Work Groups* (New York: Wiley, 1958), p. 155.

6. Ibid., p. 55.

7. George Strauss and Leonard Sayles, *Personnel*, 2nd ed. (Englewood Cliffs, N.J.: Prentice-Hall, 1967), p. 93.

8. Kenneth Boulding, *Conflict and Defense: A General Theory* (New York: Harper and Row, Harper Torchbooks, 1962), pp. 210–12 *passim*.

9. Hare, *The First Principles*, pp. 34–48.

10. W. Baldamus, *Efficiency and Effort* (London: Social Science Paperbacks, in assoc. with Tavistock Publications, 1967), p. 124.

11. Ibid., p. 53.

12. Ibid., pp. 57–58.

13. Ibid., pp. 68–69, *passim*.

14. Strauss and Sayles, *Personnel*, p. 43.

15. Neal Herrick and Robert Quinn, "The Working Conditions Survey as a Source of Social Indicators," *Monthly Labor Review*, April 1971, p. 16.

16. Robert Blauner, "Work Satisfaction and Trends in Modern Industrial Society," in Walter Galenson and Seymour Lipset, eds., *Labor and Trade Unionism* (New York: Wiley, 1960), p. 353.

17. John H. Goldthorpe et al., *The Affluent Worker: Industrial Attitudes and Behaviour* (Cambridge: The University Press, 1968), p. 20.

18. Frank Tannenbaum, *A Philosophy of Labor* (New York: Knopf, 1951), p. 147.

19. Benjamin M. Selekman, *Labor Relations and Human Relations* (New York: McGraw-Hill, 1947), p. 111.

20. Neil W. Chamberlain, "Unions and the Managerial Process," in C.R. Walker, *Technology, Industry and Man* (New York: McGraw-Hill, 1968), p. 262.

21. John H. Goldthorpe, et al., *The Affluent Worker in the Class Structure* (Cambridge: The University Press, 1969), p. 119.

22. Robert F. Hoxie, *Trade Unionism in the United States* (New York: Appleton, 1923), p. 262.

23. Paul Blumberg, *Industrial Democracy: The Sociology of Participation* (New York: Schocken, 1969), p. 3.

24. Selig Perlman, *A Theory of the Labor Movement* (New York: Augustus Kelley, reprint of 1928 ed., 1949), pp. 275, 278.

25. Ibid., p. 239.

26. N. Ross in *Human Relations and Modern Management* (The Hague: North-Holland Publishing Co., n.d.), p. 121.

27. Maxine and Nelson Valdes, "Cuban Workers and the Revolution," *New Politics* 8, no. 4 (1971):43.

28. Louis E. Davis, "The Design of Jobs," *Industrial Relations*, October 1966, p. 42.

Job Design and Employee Motivation

Edward E. Lawler III

The psychological literature on employee motivation contains many claims that changes in job design can be expected to produce better employee job performance. Very few of these claims, however, are supported by an explanation of why changes in job design should be expected to affect performance except to indicate that they can affect employee motivation. Thus, I would like to begin by considering the *why* question with respect to job design and employee performance. That is, I want to focus on the reasons for expecting changes in job design to affect employee motivation and performance. Once the question is answered, predictions will be made about the effects on performance of specific changes in job design (e.g., job enlargement and job rotation).

A Theory of Motivation

Basic to any explanation of why people behave in a certain manner is a theory of motivation. As Jones (1959) has pointed out, motivation theory attempts to explain "how behavior gets started, is energized, is sustained, is directed, is stopped and what kind of subjective reaction is present in the organism." The theory of motivation that will be used to understand the effects of job design is "expectancy theory." Georgopoulos, Mahoney, and Jones (1957), Vroom (1964), and others have recently stated expectancy theories of job performance. The particular expectancy theory to be used in this paper is based upon this earlier work and has been more completely described elsewhere (e.g., Lawler and Porter, 1967; Porter and Lawler, 1968). According to this theory, an employee's motivation is determined by two variables. The first of these is contained in the concept of an effort-reward probability. This is the individual's subjective probability that directing a given amount of effort toward performing effectively will result in his obtaining a given reward or positively valued outcome. This effort-reward probability is determined by two subsidiary subjective probabilities: the probability that effort will result in performance and the probability that performance will result in the reward. Vroom refers to the first of these subjective probabilities as an expectancy and to the second as an instrumentality.

The second variable that is relevant here is the concept of reward value or valence. This refers to the individual's perception of the value of the reward or outcome that might be obtained by performing effectively. Although most expectancy theories do not specify why certain outcomes have reward value, for the purpose of this paper I would like to argue that the reward value of outcomes stems from their perceived ability to satisfy one or more needs. Specifically relevant here is the list of needs suggested by Maslow that includes security needs, social needs, esteem needs, and self-actualization needs.

The evidence indicates that, for a given reward, reward value and the effort-reward probability combine multiplicatively in order to determine an individual's motivation. This means that if either is low or nonexistent then no motivation will be present. As an illustration of this point, consider the case of a manager who very much values

---

Reprinted from *Personnel Psychology* 22, no. 4 (Winter 1969), pp. 426–34, with the permission of the publisher.

getting promoted but who sees no relationship between working hard and getting promoted. For him, promotion is not serving as a motivator, just as it is not for a manager who sees a close connection between working hard and being promoted but who doesn't want to be promoted. In order for motivation to be present, the manager must both value promotion and see the relationship between his efforts and promotion. Thus, for an individual reward or outcome the argument is that a multiplicative combination of its value and the appropriate effort-reward probability is necessary. However, an individual's motivation in influenced by more than one outcome. Thus, in order to determine an individual's motivation it is necessary to combine data concerned with a number of different outcomes. This can be done for an individual worker by considering all the outcomes he values and then summing the products obtained from multiplying the value of these outcomes to him by their respective effort-reward probabilities.

According to this theory, if changes in job design are going to affect an individual's motivation they must either change the value of the outcomes that are seen to depend upon effort, or positively affect the individual's belief about the probability that certain outcomes are dependent upon effort. The argument in this paper is that job design changes can have a positive effect on motivation, because they change an individual's belief about the probability that certain rewards will result from putting forth high levels of effort. They can do this because they have the power to influence the probability that certain results will be seen to result from good performance, not because they can influence the perceived probability that effort will result in good performance. Stated in Vroom's language, the argument is that job design changes are more likely to affect the instrumentality of good performance than to affect the expectancy that effort will lead to performance.

Before elaborating on this point, it is important to distinguish between two kinds of rewards. The first type are those that are extrinsic to the individual. These rewards are part of the job situation and are given by others. Hence they are externally mediated and are rewards that can best be thought of as satisfying lower order needs. The second type of rewards are intrinsic to the individual and stem directly from the performance itself. These rewards can be thought of as satisfying higher order needs such as self-esteem and self-actualization. They involve such outcomes as feelings of accomplishment, feelings of achievement, and feelings of using and developing one's skills and abilities. The fact that these rewards are internally mediated sets them apart from the extrinsic rewards in an important way. It means that the connection between their reception and performance is more direct than is the connection between the reception of externally-mediated rewards and performance. Hence, potentially they can be excellent motivators because higher effort-reward probabilities can be established for them than can be established for extrinsic rewards. They also have the advantage that for many people rewards of this nature have a high positive value.

Job content is the critical determinant of whether employees believe that good performance on the job leads to feelings of accomplishment, growth, and self-esteem; that is, whether individuals will find jobs to be intrinsically motivating. Job content is important here because it serves a motive arousal function where higher order needs are concerned and because it influences what rewards will be seen to stem from good performance. Certain tasks are more likely to arouse motives like achievement and self-actualization, and to generate among individuals who have these motives aroused, the belief that successful performance will result in outcomes that involve feelings of achievement and growth. It is precisely because changes in job content can affect the relationship between performance and the reception of intrinsically rewarding outcomes that it can have a strong influence on motivation and performance.

There appear to be three characteristics which jobs must possess if they are to arouse higher order needs and to create conditions such that people who perform them will come to expect that good performance will lead to intrinsic rewards. The first is that the individual must receive meaningful feedback about his performance. This may well mean that the individual must himself evaluate his own performance and define the kind of feedback that he is to receive. It may also mean that the person may have to work on a whole product or a meaningful part of it. The second is that the job must be perceived by the individual as requiring him to use abilities that he values in order for him to perform the job effectively. Only if an individual feels that his significant abilities are being tested by a job can feelings of accomplishment and growth be expected to result from good performance. Several laboratory studies have in fact shown that, when people are given tasks that they see as testing their valued abilities, greater motivation does appear (e.g., Alper, 1946; French, 1955). Finally the individual must feel he has a high degree of self-control over setting his own goals and over defining the paths to these goals. As Argyris (1964) points out, only if this condition exists will people experience psychological "success" as a result of good performance.

Thus, it appears that the answer to the *why* question can be found in the ability of job design factors to influence employees' perceptions of the probability that good performance will be intrinsically rewarding. Certain job designs apparently encourage the perception that it will, while others do not. Because of this, job design factors can determine how motivating a job will be.

Job Design Changes

Everyone seems to agree that the typical assembly line job is not likely to fit any of the characteristics of the intrinsically-motivating job. That is, it is not likely to provide meaningful knowledge of result, test valued abilities, or allow self-control. Realizing this, much attention has been focused recently on attempts to enlarge assembly line jobs, and there is good reason to believe that enlarging assembly line jobs can lead to a situation where jobs are more intrinsically motivating. However, many proponents of job enlargement have failed to distinguish between two different kinds of job enlargement. Jobs can be enlarged on both the horizontal dimension and the vertical dimension. The horizontal dimension refers to the number and variety of the operations that an individual performs on the job. The vertical dimension refers to the degree to which the job holder controls the planning and execution of his job and participates in the setting of organization policies. The utility man on the assembly line has a job that is horizontally but not vertically enlarged, while the worker who Argyris (1964) suggests can participate in decision making about his job while he continues to work on the assembly line, has a vertically but not a horizontally-enlarged job.

The question that arises is, what kind of job enlargement is necessary if the job is going to provide intrinsic motivation? The answer, that is suggested by the three factors that are necessary for a task to be motivating, is that the jobs must be enlarged both vertically and horizontally. It is hard to see, in terms of the theory, why the utility man will see more connection between performing well and intrinsic rewards than will the assembly line worker. The utility man typically has no more self-control, only slightly more knowledge of results, and only a slightly greater chance to test his valued abilities. Hence, for him, good performance should be only slightly more rewarding than it will be for the individual who works in one location on the line. In fact, it would seem that jobs can be over-enlarged on the horizontal dimension so that they will be less motivating than they were originally. Excessive horizontal enlargement may well lead to a situation where meaningful feedback is impossible, and where the job involves using many additional abilities that the worker does not value. The worker who is allowed to participate in some decisions about his work on the assembly line can hardly be expected to perceive that intrinsic rewards will stem from performing well on the line. His work on the line is still not under his control, he is not likely to get very meaningful feedback about it, and his valued abilities still are not being tested by it. Thus, for him it is hard to see why he should feel that intrinsic rewards will result from good performance.

On the other hand, we should expect that a job which is both horizontally and vertically enlarged will be a job that motivates people to perform well. For example, the workers Kuriloff (1966) has described, who make a whole electronic instrument, check, and ship it, should be motivated by their jobs. This kind of job does provide meaningful feedback, it does allow for self-control, and there is a good chance that it will be seen as testing valued abilities. It does not, however, guarantee that the person will see it as testing his valued abilities since we don't know what the person's valued abilities are. In summary, then, the argument is that if job enlargement is to be successful in increasing motivation, it must be enlargement that affects both the horizontal and vertical dimensions of the job. In addition, individual differences must be taken into consideration in two respects. First and most obviously, it must only be tried with people who possess higher order needs that can be aroused by the job design and who, therefore, will value intrinsic rewards. Second, individuals must be placed on jobs that test their valued abilities.

Let me now address myself to the question of how the increased motivation, that can be generated by an enlarged job, will manifest itself in terms of behavior. Obviously, the primary change that can be expected is that the individual will devote more effort to performing well. But will this increased effort result in a higher quality work, higher productivity, or both? I think this question can be answered by looking at the reasons we gave for the job content being able to affect motivation. The argument was that it does this by affecting whether intrinsic rewards will be seen as coming from successful performance. It would seem that high quality work is indispensable if most individuals are to feel they have performed well and are to experience feelings of accomplishment, achievement, and self-actualization. The situation is much less clear with respect to productivity. It does not seem at all certain that an individual must produce great quantities of a product in order to feel that he has performed well. In fact, many individuals probably obtain more satisfaction from producing one very high quality product than they do from producing a number of lower quality products.

There is a second factor which may cause job enlargement to be more likely to lead to higher work quality than to higher productivity. This has to do with the advantages of division of labor and mechanization. Many job enlargement changes create a situation in which, because of the losses in terms of machine assistance and optimal human movements, people actually have to put forth more energy in order to produce at the same prejob enlargement rate. Thus, people may be working harder but producing less. It seems less likely that the same dilemma would arise in terms of work quality and job enlargement. That is, if extra effort is devoted to quality after job enlargement takes place, the effort is likely to be translated into improved quality. This would come about because the machine assistance and other features of the assembly line jobs are more of an aid in bringing about high productivity than they are in bringing about high quality.

The Research Evidence

There have been a number of studies that have attempted to measure the effects of job enlargement programs. These were examined to determine if the evidence supports the contention stated previously that both horizontal and vertical job enlargement are necessary if intrinsic motivation is to be increased. Also sought was an indication of whether the effect of any increased motivation was more likely to result in higher quality work than in high productivity.

In the literature search, reports of ten studies where jobs had been enlarged on both the horizontal and vertical dimensions were found. . . . Every study shows that job enlargement did have some positive effect since every study reports that job enlargement resulted in higher quality work. However, only four out of ten studies report that job enlargement led to higher productivity. This provides support for the view that the motivational effects produced by job enlargement are more likely to result in higher quality work than in higher productivity.

There are relatively few studies of jobs enlarged only on either the horizontal or vertical dimensions so that it is difficult to test the prediction that both kinds of enlargement are necessary if motivation is to be increased. There are a few studies which have been concerned with the effects of horizontal job enlargement (e.g., Walker & Guest, 1952), while others have stressed its advantages. However, most of these studies have been concerned with its effects on job satisfaction rather than its effects on motivation. None of these studies appears to show that horizontal enlargement tends to increase either productivity or work quality. Walker and Guest, for example, talk about the higher satisfaction of the utility men but they do not report that they work harder. Thus, with respect to horizontal job enlargement, the evidence does not lead to rejecting the view that it must be combined with vertical in order to increase production.

The evidence with respect to whether vertical job enlargement alone can increase motivation is less clear. As Argyris (1964) has pointed out, the Scanlon plan has stressed this kind of job enlargement with some success. However, it is hard to tell if this success stems from people actually becoming more motivated to perform their own job better. It is quite possible that improvements under the plan are due to better overall decision making rather than to increased motivation. Vroom (1964) has analyzed the evidence with respect to the degree to which participation in decision making *per se* leads to increased motivation. This evidence suggests that vertical job enlargement can lead to increased motivation when it leads to the employees committing themselves to higher production goals.

Perhaps the crucial distinction here is whether the participation involves matters of company policy or whether it involves matters directly related to the employees' work process. Participation of the former type would seem much less likely to lead to increased motivation than would participation of the latter type. Thus, it seems to be crucial to distinquish between two quite different types of vertical job enlargement, only one of which leads to increased motivation. Considered together, the evidence suggests that, of the two types of job enlargement, vertical is more important than horizontal. Perhaps this is because it can lead to a situation in which subjects feel their abilities are being tested and where they can exercise self-control even though horizontal enlargement does not take place. Still, the evidence, with respect to situations where both types of enlargement have been jointly installed, shows that much more consistent improvements in motivation can be produced by both than can be produced by vertical alone.

Summary

It has been argued that, when a job is structured in a way that makes intrinsic rewards appear to result from good performance, then the job itself can be a very effective motivator. In addition, the point was made that, if job content is to be a source of motivation, the job must allow for meaningful feedback, test the individual's valued abilities, and allow a great amount of self-control by the job holder. In order for this to happen, jobs must be enlarged on both the vertical and horizontal dimensions. Further, it was predicted that job enlargement is more likely to lead to increased product quality than to increased productivity. A review of the literature on job enlargement generally tended to confirm these predictions.

REFERENCES

Alper, Thelma G. "Task-orientation vs. Ego-orientation in Learning and Retention." *American Journal of Psychology* 38 (1946):224–38.

Argyris, C. *Integrating the Individual and the Organization.* New York: John Wiley & Sons, 1964.

Biggane, J.F. and Stewart, P.A. *Job Enlargement: A Case Study.* Research Series no. 25, Bureau of Labor and Management, State University of Iowa, 1963.

Conant, E.H. and Kilbridge, M.D. "An Interdisciplinary Analysis of Job Enlargement: Technology, Costs and Behavioral Implications." *Industrial and Labor Relations Review* 18 (1965):377–95.

Davis, L.E. and Valfer, E.S. "Intervening Responses to Changes in Supervisor Job Designs." *Occupational Psychology* 39 (1965):171–89.

Davis, L.E. and Werling, R. "Job Design Factors." *Occupational Psychology* 34 (1960): 109–32.

Elliot, J.D. "Increasing Office Productivity through Job Enlargement." *The Human Side of the Office Manager's Job.* A.M.A. Office Management Series, no. 134, New York, 1953, pp. 5–15.

French, Elizabeth G. "Some Characteristics of Achievement Motivation." *Journal of Experimental Psychology* 50 (1955):232–36.

Georgopoulos, B.S., Mahoney, G.M., and Jones, M.N. "A Path-goal Approach to Productivity." *Journal of Applied Psychology* 41 (1957):345–53.

Guest, R.H. "Job Enlargement: A Revolution in Job Design." *Personnel Administration* 20 (1957):9–16.

Jones, M.R., ed. *Nebraska Symposium on Motivation.* Lincoln: Nebraska University Press, 1959.

Kilbridge, M.D. "Reduced Costs through Job Enlargement: A Case." *Journal of Business* 33 (1960):357–62.

Kuriloff, A.H. *Reality in Management.* New York: McGraw-Hill, 1966.

Lawler, E.E. and Porter, L.W. "Antecedent Attitudes of Effective Managerial Performance." *Organizational Behavior and Human Performance* 2 (1967):122–42.

Marks, A.R. "An Investigation of Modifications of Job Design in an Industrial Situation and Their Effects on Some Measures of Economic Productivity." Unpublished Ph.D. dissertation. University of California, Berkeley, 1954.

Porter, L.W. and Lawler, E.E. *Managerial Attitudes and Performance.* Homewood, Ill.: Irwin-Dorsey, 1968.

Rice, A.K. "Productivity and Social Organization in an Indian Weaving Shed." *Human Relations* 6 (1953):267–329.

Vroom, V.H. *Work and Motivation.* New York: John Wiley & Sons, 1964.

Walker, C.R. "The Problem of the Repetitive Job." *Harvard Business Review* 38 (1950): 54–59.

Walker, C.R. and Guest, R.H. *The Man on the Assembly Line.* Cambridge, Mass.: Harvard University Press, 1952.

Job Redesign, Reform, Enrichment—Exploring the Limitations

Sar A. Levitan   *William B. Johnston*

American industry has long been committed to redesign of executive and professional jobs with a view to improving the quality of work. Recently this interest in the quality of managerial, professional, and high-level sales jobs has been extended to other white-collar workers. Sometimes reports on these experiments (as well as those involving blue-collar workers) imply and occasionally state that sweeping, even radical, job reform is in the offing and can be undertaken once inertia in the workplace is overcome. But is widespread job reform possible? Is it necessary? This article considers some of the limitations on job reform. But first a few examples of the type and scope of experiments in job redesign should be considered.

In 1965, American Telephone and Telegraph Co. began experimenting with new job designs for clerical workers in an attempt to cut turnover and improve productivity. Analyzing the work of the office staffs, the job designers found most departments had compartmentalized and divided the work into essentially a paperpushing assembly line. Few workers appreciated their work or took pride in their accomplishments. The results were high rates of turnover, low productivity, and low quality output.

To improve things, the planners analyzed the task to be performed, for example, service order processing, telephone book assembly, or customer billing. They reevaluated the division of labor based upon ideas of the overall job to be performed. Instead of having order-form clerks, typists, and bill verifiers, they assigned entire modules of work to individuals. Telephone book assemblers were given the entire job of processing and verifying a book or sections of a book. Billing clerks were given complete responsibility for certain accounts, rather than a single operation on each account. In many cases, typists took over tasks once routinely assigned to "higher ups." Along with job enlargement, the designers initiated changes in office layout and grouping of personnel, to facilitate communication among employees with related jobs.

Almost all these changes had positive results. In many instances productivity rose and output was more prompt and error-free. The improvement in employee morale was often spectacular. Employees seemed to take pride in their new jobs and began to learn the jobs of those around them. Absenteeism fell sharply and turnover decreased in most cases.

The AT & T methods have been duplicated in a variety of companies and situations. For example, at Bankers Trust and Merrill Lynch, Pierce, Fenner, and Smith in New York, the fractionated, time-consuming tasks of processing new stock certificates were consolidated into jobs for one worker. In both cases, significant money savings were realized, in terms of increased productivity, and in freed supervisory time. . . .

Blue-Collar Experiments

Work restructuring also has been tried in factories. The redesigners of blue-collar work have utilized two basic approaches—"participative management" and task reassignment—along with improvements in working conditions designed to minimize

Reprinted from the *Monthly Labor Review*, July 1973, pp. 35–41.

differences in status. In most cases participative management has been favored because production technology allows little leeway in the delegation of tasks. On the assumption that even a dirty, dull, or unpleasant task can be made more acceptable if the worker has the responsibility for deciding where, when, and how fast it will be done, these plans have concentrated on developing a spirit of cooperation and teamwork on the job.

One of the oldest and most widely noted attempts at improving productivity through worker participation has been carried out at the Donnelly Mirrors Corp. of Holland, Mich. Nearly a decade ago, the Company, which makes auto mirrors, dramatically expanded its concepts of incentive plans and open-line communication, instituting democratic reforms which sought to humanize assembly line production. The employees were divided into task-oriented teams who set production goals. The workers had the authority to control the pace of product assembly and the assignment of jobs along the assembly line. In addition, all employees received salaries, rather than hourly wages, and they collectively set the rates at which they would be paid. In return for this, the employees also had the responsibility for implementing productivity increases to support pay raises. In essence, the production function was delegated to the men on the line.

Reported results were impressive. The quality of production jumped sharply, even though inspectors were cut two-thirds. Scrap losses dropped by 75 percent from their former level and goods returned amounted to less than a tenth of the previous volume. Productivity gains have resulted in an average salary bonus of 12 percent since the changes were instituted. . . .

Donnelly's history is the most successful but not the only model of delegating responsibility to workers to increase satisfaction, productivity, and company profits. At Texas Instruments, full responsibility for janitorial service was delegated to the workers involved. The men met to decide how the work would be divided, and to set up schedules and establish standards for jobs. The sense of personal involvement made possible a reduction of manpower from 120 to 71, a rise in cleanliness evaluations from 65 to 85 percent, and a remarkable alleviation of the problem of worker turnover from 100 to 10 percent quarterly. . . .

Gaps in the Advocates' Case

These experiments with job redesign are all success stories. Indeed, most of the literature on work reform is the product of advocates reporting positive results. But there are major gaps in the case for job reform. Companies which find authoritarian controls and unchanged job rewards to be as successful as ever are not included in the surveys. Companies whose enrichment and participation plans turn sour rarely trumpet the news.

The productivity gains from these projects are seldom controlled against gains from alternative innovations, and have not been followed over long enough periods to be considered permanent. Some studies have reported a "Hawthorne effect" in which productivity can be improved by either autocratic or democratic changes in management style. Thus, the experimenters may have concluded, more on faith than hard facts, that democratic techniques will eventually prove superior because of investment in "human assets." But the history of varied schemes to develop workers' sense of participation and support for corporate goals makes it clear that reforms which rely on the morale or attitudes of the work force cannot be guaranteed to last.

Just as today's young union members have little appreciation for the wages and working conditions won by earlier generations, so new workers in "humanized" plants may fail to find their work upgraded or more enjoyable. Those who were present when assembly lines were changed to benchwork, or those who remember the authoritarian supervision before the introduction of participative management, may appreciate the better quality of their work. But positive reactions resulting from innovations inevitably fade as novel systems become routines. Moreover, new arrivals will be likely to see only jobs with certain tasks, wages, and bosses. This is, of course, no argument against making changes, but they should be made because of intrinsic merit and not because they will lead to everlasting rises in productivity.

Cogent reasons suggest that the possibilities for reforming work may be limited. The projections of assembly lines abolished, jobs humanized, and productivity spiralling in the industrial world of the future are highly tentative. Neither the alternative of improving the work itself through job enrichment, nor the correlative approach of molding more satisfied employees by allowing them greater control of their work lives, is certain to have sweeping results.

Limits of Participative Management

Participative decision making, profit sharing, and autonomous work arrangements all seek to unite the individual's goals and the firm's. It is easy to see, however, that the goals of any sizable corporation and those of its employees are not easily harmonized. The ideal of communal effort in which a group of individuals are united by common beliefs to achieve a common aim is foreign to large corporate enterprises. The firm is interested in profits, with most other goals being measured by how they affect this single variable. The firm's employees, especially the production workers, are concerned with improving their lives, a goal only incidentally connected with the corporation's success and in part opposed to it because there is only one corporate revenue pie to be divided. By its nature, the corporation is not primarily concerned with workers' lives. Unless corporate enterprise were to radically alter its functions to make the welfare of its employees its first reason for being, it is hypothetical to talk of "internalizing" the firm's goals.

It has been suggested that the key to participative management is profit sharing. But profit sharing and even outright ownership by workers would, for any large organization, be hopelessly diffused and diluted. It is doubtful that the marginal increase in income generated by full distribution of profits could do much to change workers' attitudes towards their jobs, or that a few shares of stock could do much to transform employees into members of the corporate "family." Overall, the total of all corporate after-tax profits would add less than 10 percent to employee compensation.

The idea of profit sharing based on small production units highlights the basic goal of participative management. At bottom, all such changes seek to repartition industry into organizations of smaller size, where the individual does not get "lost." Autonomous work groups who make their own decisions and pocket their own profits would actually be tiny companies who have become subcontractors to the larger organizations. The breaking up of the corporation into small units may indeed be desirable from the standpoint of improving the quality of work, but it runs counter to the established principles of industrial organization and is not conducive to optimizing profits.

Rhetoric about a community of interest cannot obliterate elemental conflicts between employees and employers. Many workers in subservient jobs continue to perceive their work as unstimulating activity in the service of others. They see themselves neither as supporters of the free enterprise system nor as contributors to their enterprise's profits. With unflinching realism, they see themselves as bolt tighteners and machine tenders, occupations which they do not find exciting or meaningful. Inevitably, they are dissatisfied with their work and seek to change it or escape it. The kind of worker control or independence which could relieve this kind of alienation is not likely to be granted without an upheaval in corporate structures. Even then it is not clear that the new order would lead to greater work satisfaction.

Enriching Jobs

Paralleling the challenge to traditional ideas of work organization and supervision are challenges to accepted rules for designing jobs and dividing tasks. Theorists of work reform emphasize that work roles are not inalterably defined by the technology of production. Underlying work redesign proposals is the argument that within any technological framework there are equally productive alternatives.

Recognition that technology is not an absolute determinant of jobs does not negate its decisive influence. Without question, technology, especially its hardware, is far and away the most important factor in job design. Milling machines, computers, forklifts, and arc welders determine what tasks will be performed, dwarfing in importance work arrangements or task assignments.

The capital investment required to significantly alter methods of production is awesome. If manufacturing jobs have hardened in molds cast generations ago, much of the reason lies in the physical plants and machinery accumulated over the years. Plants manufacturing durable goods average over $25,000 of fixed capital per worker. In the oil industry, this rises to over $125,000. Because product cost in capital-intensive industries is less affected by variations in employee productivity, employers may be more willing to experiment with innovations to improve working conditions because failure would entail little risk. But changes which would require replacement of expensive capital are less appealing, particularly if managers cannot be assured the changes will lead to greater profits as well as better quality work. If changes in technology and hardware to improve the quality of work are to be made, they must also promise higher profits.

Champions of job enrichment have, of course, pitched their appeals to the profit motive. They urge that eliminating high turnover rates, raising product quality, decreasing waste, tapping firsthand knowledge for design innovations, and cutting manpower requirements are productive and profitable improvements. But even when changes in techniques and processes appear financially sound, there are other limitations to their adoption. For example, changes which are feasible in the production of small items may not apply to larger products. The inescapable problem of storing and moving large components means that assembling cars or refrigerators or engines probably can be accomplished most efficiently on a moving line. The widely heralded "benchwork" assembly methods involved products with small components, fairly lengthy assembly times, and few tools.

At some point, suggestions for enlarging jobs, increasing skills, lengthening job cycles, or rotating tasks bump into the logic which dictated division of labor in the first place. Essentially, job enrichers counsel more complex jobs with longer training times. But the present system favoring simple jobs originated as part of a long trend to greater specialization, which may be psychically expensive, but it is economically cheap. It is possible that in many industries jobs have become too specialized and that workers could produce more if they had more interest in their work. Specialization may go too far and become counterproductive, but it cannot be denied that division of labor, as Adam Smith argued two centuries ago, is an essential ingredient of efficient mass production. The return to craft production may be humanly desirable, but it is impractical. Every addition to jobs which requires workers to spend more time learning the job, or alternating tools, or which entails greater inventories or duplication of tools, is likely to raise unit labor costs. The reactions of managers to suggestions which involve new production techniques or job realignments are therefore understandably cautious. Production methods have been developed not from the arbitrary decisions of engineers, or even as a result of the inevitable progression of technology, but in a rational search for efficiency. Industrial survival of the fittest has produced a species not easily changed for the better.

Can efficient mass production ever provide challenging or creative work? A surgeon doomed to perform appendectomies for his entire career would likely come to envy a butcher who at least could carve different cuts of meat. Repetition, the foundation of mass production, slays interest. Although job rotation may hold some hope for relieving monotony, it is wishful thinking to ignore the inherent limitations of job design imposed by repeated identical operations.

It is understandable, then, that many production workers and some union leaders have tended to view workplace reforms and enriched jobs with distrust. From the vantage point of the dissatisfied worker, management, as the instigator of work redesign, is suspected of perpetrating another elaborate ploy to convince the skeptical that a lousy job is after all important or challenging or likeable. Without fundamental changes in the kinds of jobs industrial workers do, can job enrichment and motivating workers with "challenging work" be more than subtle con games? In this regard, reports of increased absenteeism, turnover, sabotage, and other visible signs of discontent do not forecast the death of the work ethic, but rather logical and long-delayed reactions by workers to jobs that are not worth doing well, or perhaps worth doing at all.

The kinds of changes which could relieve these suspicions are not likely to occur as rapidly as supporters of job enrichment hope. Personnel psychologists may sweep through factories putting glass windows in the manager's office, unlocking executive toilets, taking out time clocks, and having the workers meet on company time to set their daily schedules. But when they finish, the same machines and hands will go back to cranking out coffee pots or card tables or cookie jars. As long as processes remain the same, and machines are unable to perform all the tasks of production, job improvement for manufacturing workers will be partly just a new cosmetic on the same old crone.

Social Efficiency Model

Recognizing the costs involved in meaningful job reform, some reformers have argued that job enrichment should control the design of production processes, even if productivity is reduced. They suggest that "social efficiency" should be given priority over considerations of purely economic efficiency. The argument is that unrewarding, inhuman work has high costs in terms of social alienation, poor health, violent aggression, and other social ills. Enriching the work experience, even if it were economically costly, would be socially beneficial.

Conceptually appealing though they are, these arguments are hardly practical. Faced with a choice between satisfying its workers and maintaining its profits, a corporation could be expected to resist job humanization. Nor is there evidence of any social ground swell of sacrificial spirit, or willingness of industrial workers to lower their standards of living in order to have more satisfying jobs. Any retreat to more primitive, costly, and "human" methods of manufacturing would require governmental intervention likely to be rejected by owners and workers.

Is it not more reasonable to assume that increased specialization and large hierarchical organizations are not accidents, but logical developments in a complex society seeking to support its growing population at an ever-rising standard of living? Whatever the price that society is paying in terms of "dehumanized" jobs in monolithic, faceless organizations, it is unrealistic to hark back to a simpler world in which organizations were small and jobs were large, as though the paradise lost could be regained. Specialized roles and specialized knowledge are essential to large organizations, and large organizations appear unavoidable in an advanced society.

To some extent, hierarchies can be leveled and the roles of individuals interchanged and broadened; but the constraints on such developments cannot be overcome by planned social change or even by violent social upheaval. Improved social efficiency cannot proceed along opposite paths to industrial efficiency, but must parallel it. Without the tremendous affluence generated in part by efficient mass production, there would be no alternative life styles or occupations for workers to envy, and no time to invest in the education which has contributed to some workers' dissatisfaction with their jobs.

Despite all this, improvements *can* be made by rotating workers among jobs, by enlarging jobs, by expanding responsibility. Generally, managements (and unions) have done too little to change working conditions which could be improved. But there can be no gainsaying that meaningful work and maximum productivity are at odds in important ways. Until the machine entirely replaces man in the performance of routine tasks, man as adjunct to machines will likely be restless.

Fallacy of Radical Work Reform

The limitations imposed by the imperatives of efficiency suggest that job designers face stubborn obstacles to the humanist reformation of work. The evidence that productivity will necessarily increase if jobs are humanized is far from conclusive, and an argument can be made that the technology of efficient production leaves little room for extensive job reform. Neither can a "social efficiency" model be used to justify a reduction of economic efficiency in order to improve jobs. Moreover, are workers that interested in job redesign? Is the quality of worklife the main standard by which they judge the quality of their lives? It appears that for most workers the quality of work is less important than the standard of living.

In making their case, job redesigners often use examples of workers on assembly lines in steel and textile mills, oil refineries, and machine tool factories. However, occupational data indicate the collective importance of these workers is declining. Though they have serious job problems, these workers constitute a relatively small fraction of the expanding labor force. Moreover, the advance of technology allows more production with fewer men. For example, the entire oil industry requires but 200,000 production workers, and a handful of supervisors manage to run the refineries during strikes. Thus, the most important effect of technical advance is that it shifts employment away from mechanized manufacturing processes to the jobs which are difficult if not impossible to automate—services and the professions.

Moreover, in discussing workers "trapped" in routine factory jobs, some workplace analysts often seem to see reflections of themselves: the descriptions of work sound as though the factories were filled with restless inquisitive consultants chained to assembly lines. There seem to be no placid TV watchers, none who may be pleased with simple, repetitive tasks or high wages or long weekends. From such assumptions it is not difficult for these analysts to discover great reservoirs of alienation and to claim that profound changes must be made in work. A generation too late, they are suggesting dubious solutions to problems which were gradually being solved by the elimination of such work.

One view is that the jobs of the future will demand workers who can cope with rapidly evolving technology and constantly changing environments. But a glance at the seven largest expanding occupational groups—secretaries (3.8 million); retail sales clerks (3.1 million); precollege teachers (2.7 million); restaurant workers (2.5 million); drivers and deliverymen (2.4 million); bookkeepers and cashiers (2.4 million); and cleaning workers (2.2 million)—reveals that none of these jobs is undergoing rapid change. The last great technological change in the jobs of retail sales workers was the invention of the cash register in 1879. Secretarial typing tasks have not been altered basically since the introduction of the shift register almost a century ago. Despite the proliferation of educational theories, teachers still explain concepts, assign homework, and grade tests much as they did in Abraham Lincoln's day. Janitors have witnessed the sweeping change from brooms to vacuum cleaners, and waitresses now serve bottled rather than draft beer, but few would argue that these jobs have been revolutionized by technology. (This is not to say that significant changes have not occurred, such as greater use of self-service, assignment of administrative tasks to secretaries, and greater specialization of teaching functions.)

Another school predicts crisis in the industrial workplace as workers will increasingly reject meaningless jobs. But this prophecy ignores society's method for matching workers to jobs. The economic system determines whether a job is worth doing. Industry may find that it will have to pay higher wages for some jobs, or that the most onerous jobs will price themselves out of the market. If workers make themselves unavailable for certain jobs at any reasonable wage, then it may be expected that few employers will be willing to hire them. In return for dollar rewards, workers will either accept or reject employment. In return for tasks performed, employers will either hire or fire.

While the foregoing points up some weaknesses in the arguments for job reform, the critics of current work arrangements are far from wrong in their central thrust. In general they hold a kernel of the truth. But repeatedly in making their arguments, the trees blind them to the forest. There *is* a problem with the design of work but not a massive problem. There *are* specific solutions but no one solution of utopian finality. Like social critics in other areas, some job reformers have become oversold on the need for change and in their ability to bring it about.

The way in which work is created is often ignored in reformers' analysis. Jobs are established by aggregate demand coupled with technological possibility. Society currently supports 828,000 janitors, 430,000 gas station attendants, and 125,000 librarians. The work these people do can be eliminated either by reducing demand for it, or by building machines to perform it. A host of factors can influence the demand for certain types of work, notably government priorities, advertising, education and income levels. But jobs are created by the willingness of some part of society to pay for the performance of them.

Moreover, once tasks are determined they cannot be changed much. Basically, janitors sweep floors, gas station attendants pump gas, and librarians keep books on shelves, no matter what surroundings or supervision they have. More than anything else, the job itself will determine how a person will react to it. Society's requirements have already preempted much of the leeway for designing jobs. Once the tasks to be performed have been determined, work designers may shuffle the tasks among people, or put white collars on them, but work can only truly be reformed by shifts in the aggregate demand for labor. All the shuffling of assignments, rotation of duties, recombinations of tasks, or restructuring of organizations and supervisory methods cannot change the basic nature of the work to be performed.

As employment shifts further away from production for survival, society should be freer to determine what work will be done based upon what people want to do. Man tends to attack the unpleasant or bothersome aspects of life first; thus the worst work will steadily be eliminated or changed. In some future, perhaps, machines will allow everyone to work at meaningful jobs. Until then, however, work will probably continue to be organized in a way that makes it simple, easily learned, and which promotes greatest efficiency and maximum production. As yet, society continues to pay for a great variety of jobs the tasks of which some people find undesirable.

The obvious limitations of job enrichment should not be taken as mandates to maintain the status quo in the workplace. Though the experimental evidence on job reform is incomplete and the problem may not be as serious as some have claimed, job reformers are addressing issues of importance. Further research may determine that the improvements are temporary and the productivity gains disappointingly small when compared with other methods of improving productivity. But the job reform results thus far indicate that substantial improvements can be made within the framework of efficient, profitable enterprises. The upgrading of work which can be realized from redesigned jobs may not promise nirvana for workers, but it is clearly a change for the better. The various strategies for reinvolving alienated workers deserve to be tried, not because they can be expected to solve *the* problem of the workplace but because they are likely to raise in some measure the quality of work and of life. When these innovations come to represent the wishes of workers (rather than those of productivity-minded managers or well-intentioned consultants) they should be instituted. The egalitarian ideal of enjoyable work for all may be unattainable, but a just society should aspire to no less.

III

Industrial Relations Issues

Industrial Relations in the Public Sector

The rapid growth of public employee unionism, which has occurred within the past ten years, has created many questions for public policy, some similar to those in the private sector and others novel with no precise counterparts in the experience of private sector industrial relations. The problem of how to address the strike actions of public servants has tended to dominate discussions of industrial relations in the public sector but other significant questions exist and, as yet, have not been fully answered. The first set of selections in this section is concerned primarily with these "other" questions. The lead-off article presents a history and discussion of the growth of public employee unions at the federal, state, and local levels, and the following three deal with a variety of problems, including those resulting from the need to mesh collective-bargaining processes with local government management structures and budget-making procedures in public institutions. A second group of articles deals with the problem of work stoppages in both the private and public sectors and includes a range of opinions and suggestions for moderating the impact of industrial conflict. The final three selections identify and discuss emerging industrial relations which, though not yet fully defined and whose full ramifications remain conjectural, promise to be troublesome in the years ahead.

Labour Relations in the Public Sector in the United States

Charles M. Rehmus

The Scope of Public Employment

Public service is the most rapidly growing major sector of employment in the United States. In the last 30 years, public employment has tripled, growing from 4.2 million

Reprinted from the *International Labour Review* 109, no. 3 (March 1974): 199–216, with the permission of the author.

to 13.1 million employees. Today nearly one out of five workers in the United States is on a government payroll.

Part of this dramatic increase in public employment can be attributed simply to population growth, necessitating a proportional increase in publicly provided services. More fundamental to growth than simple demographic change, however, have been increases in the demand for new services, shifts from private to public provision of certain kinds of service, and advances in technology which have intensified the need for new levels of existing government services. Ever since the Great Depression of the 1930s, United States citizens have expected government to provide more and more services for more and more people. As an example, provision for social welfare services to the poor and those too young or too old to work has created many new public jobs. At state and local levels of government, education, health care, the public highway system, and police and fire protection are the largest sources of employment. At the federal level, the government's role in the international arena has steadily increased as the United States has become more and more involved in military assistance and economic aid throughout the world.

This growth of government service has not been steady or equal at all levels of government in the United States federal system. Any consideration of public employment and public employee labour relations must distinguish between three primary levels of government—federal, state and local—as well as the large postal and educational subsections of federal and local government. Each level of government has specific areas of administrative authority and service responsibility which are in turn affected by specific constituency demands. Each of these levels of government has its own laws regulating public employer-employee labour relations.

Federal government. Federal government employment has increased the least of the three primary levels of government, expanding by only 40 percent between 1950 and 1970. This represents a decline in the proportion of all public employment from 33 to 23 percent during the same period. It should be noted that the federal government's share of total government expenditures has not declined proportionately, but this is because nearly half of all federal expenditures go into national defense. If defense were discounted, the federal expenditure share would be approximately the same as the federal employment share, about 23 percent. In the United States the federal government's income is derived primarily from individual and corporate income taxes and, in addition to defense and military expenditures, is spent on social welfare insurance, veterans' benefits, agricultural and natural resource programs, international gifts and loans, space research, and a multitude of general welfare programs.

State government. State employment represents 27 percent of total government employment in the United States. State governments derive their income primarily from sales and excise taxes, and increasingly from individual and corporate income taxes as well. Primary state expenditures go towards public education, maintenance of highways and waterways, and administration of public welfare and health programs.

Local government. Local government accounts for 50 percent of all public employment in the United States. Local governments derive their income primarily from taxes on real property and from subventions out of state and federal revenue-sharing funds. They carry out the police, public safety and sanitation functions, and have more recently been expending a large share of the moneys that are devoted to urban renewal programs.

Education. Education ranks second only to national defense in terms of public economic expenditures in the United States. Twenty-nine percent of all government expenditures are directed to national defense and related purposes, and approximately 16 percent to education. Education accounts for 32 percent of all public employment and represents slightly over half of all state and local employment. Although state governments bear the responsibility for establishing and maintaining the system of public schools, the actual operation of the schools is ordinarily delegated to local school districts. Over 90 percent of these districts are administratively independent of any other local government unit. Moreover, most school districts are atypical of the United States governmental structures in that their local governing bodies—school boards or their equivalents—have both executive and legislative authority. School boards both make and administer educational policy, and most school boards have been given the authority to levy property taxes, subject to voter approval.

Postal service. The fifth substantial sector of public employment in the United States is unusual: the United States Postal Service is by far the largest and the only major public corporation in the United States. Until 1970 the Post Office Department had been one of the component agencies of the federal government. Its employees were federal civil servants whose conditions of employment were legislated by Congress. Its workforce was also unusual in having been overwhelmingly union-organized since the nineteenth century, and was restless and militant. An unprecedented major strike by postal workers, beginning on the eastern seaboard and extending to many other parts of the nation, created pressure for the immediate realization of a long-discussed idea; the transformation of the Post Office Department into a public corporation. Postal service employees are now in general subject to the labor relations rules and regulations that pertain to the private sector. The main remnant of the postal employees' former civil servant status is the retention of the ban on the right to strike in the event of bargaining impasses and the substitution for it of compulsory binding arbitration.

This notable modification in the status of postal employment in only one of the fundamental changes that overcame public service in the United States in the 1960s—a period that has been called by some—"the decade of the public employee revolution."

The Background to Public Employee Labour Relations

Workers in the industrial private sector in the United States were given the statutory right to organize and bargain collectively in the 1930s. By 1960, approximately 30 percent of all non-agricultural private sector employees were represented by unions. Yet by this date there was practically no unionization in the public sector other than in the traditionally organized postal service and in a few other isolated situations.

The reasons for this delay are complex. In part they stem from certain philosophical ideas long prevalent in the nation. Traditional concepts of sovereignty asserted that government is and should be supreme, hence immune from contravening forces and pressures such as collective bargaining. Related to this concept was that of the illegality of delegation of sovereign power. This asserted that public decision making could only be done by elected or appointed public officials, whose exclusive and complete discretion was therefore unchallengeable.

More practical considerations also delayed the advent of public employee unionism in the United States. The private sector unions and their international (i.e., North American) federations were fully occupied in trying to increase the extent of organization in the private sector. They had neither the money nor the energy to turn to the public sector until the 1960s. Equally or more important, public employees were not generally dissatisfied with their terms or conditions of employment and therefore, except in isolated cases, did not press for collective bargaining rights. Though the wages and salaries of public employees in the United States had traditionally lagged slightly behind comparable private sector salaries, the greater fringe benefits and job security associated with public employment were usually thought to be adequate compensation.

By the late 1950s and early 1960s, several of these practical considerations which had delayed public employee unionism had disappeared. Moreover, new factors came into play whose sequence or relative importance is difficult to assess but which added up to a new militancy. Change increasingly became endemic in American society as more and more groups, including public employees, found it commonplace to challenge the established order. Some public employees were made less secure by organizational and technological changes as government came under pressure to reduce the rate of tax increases and therefore sought out ways to increase efficiency and lower unit labour costs. Public employee wages and salaries began to lag further behind those in the unionized private sector as the postwar inflationary spiral continued. The private sector international unions saw the large and growing employment in the non-union public sector as a fertile field which might compensate for their failure after 1956 to increase membership steadily in the private sector. Finally, many observers of public employment both in and out of government began strongly and publicly to question the logic by which government at various levels protected collective bargaining in the private sector while refusing to grant similar privileges and protections in the public sector.

By the 1960s, these practical challenges to the traditional arguments of sovereignty and illegal delegations of powers had won the day in a number of government jurisdictions. The city of New York, the school board of that same city, and the state of Wisconsin gave modified collective bargaining rights to their public employees. Most importantly, in 1962 President Kennedy by executive order gave federal employees a limited version of the rights that private employees had received 30 years before. These seminal breakthroughs led increasingly to similar kinds of state legislation, particularly in the more industrialized states. Today over 30 American states have granted some form of collective bargaining rights to some or all of their public employees. President Nixon in two subsequent executive orders expanded and clarified the bargaining rights of federal employees. Fifty-five percent of civilian federal employees are now represented for collective bargaining purposes, and this figure excludes the organized postal service. Though precise figures are not available, probably one-third of all state, municipal and educational employees are similarly represented and this fraction is steadily growing.

As a matter of general law in the United States, the federal courts have held that an individual's right to form and join a union is a protected right under the First Amendment to the Constitution. Federal courts have also held, however, that there is no constitutional right to bargain collectively in either the public or private sector. Hence, so far as the public sector specifically is concerned, an enforceable duty on an employer to bargain collectively in the public service can only be imposed by statute or executive order. Recent state court decisions suggest similarly that state authorities are under no legally enforceable duty to bargain in the absence of a statutory requirement, but are free to do so if they choose. In short, public and private employees alike in the United States have the constitutional right to form and join unions, and thus attempt to gain collective bargaining rights. But their employers, even today, are under no legal obligation to bargain collectively unless this duty is imposed upon them.

The reticence of about 20 states to allow collective bargaining in the public sector is largely based upon the fear of increased strike action. In reality, however, many public employee strikes have taken place in jurisdictions where collective bargaining was regarded as unlawful, and demands for recognition and bargaining rights constitute the second highest cause of strikes in the public sector. Many public employee strikes could have been averted had the employer been required by statute to recognize and bargain with the employee organization. Furthermore, the acceptance of collective bargaining in the public sector does not necessarily call for the acceptance of strikes in support of bargaining demands. Experience in various jurisdictions of United States government shows that the issues of public employee bargaining and public employee strikes are separate and distinct. This subject will be further discussed below.

The Federal Experience

As one of his first official acts in 1961, President Kennedy appointed a task force of high administration officials to review and advise him on labor-management relations in the federal service. The task force report served as the basis of Executive Order 10988 which gave all federal employees the right to join (or not to join) organizations of their choice. In effect, this original federal executive order was designed to encourage union representation throughout the federal service. It did so by means of a device unique in labour-management experience in the United States: the creation of three levels of recognition. An employee organization having any members at all within a federal department or agency could be granted *informal* recognition which gave it the right to speak to management on behalf of its members. An organization representing as many as 10 percent but fewer than 50 percent of the employees within an appropriate bargaining unit in the federal structure was entitled to consult and be consulted by federal managers on personnel policies broadly affecting its members (*formal recognition*). An organization which represented a majority of employees within an appropriate bargaining unit was entitled to *exclusive* recognition, the characteristic form of recognition in North America, which gives the right to negotiate a written bargaining agreement.

Under this original federal executive order the scope of bargaining was limited to basic working conditions; wages and fringe benefits continued then as now to be set by Congress. Moreover, a very strong management rights clause had to be included in every federal agreement recognizing management's right: to direct employees; to hire, promote, transfer, assign, suspend, demote, discharge and discipline them; to relieve them from duty because of lack of work; and to determine the methods, means and personnel by which operations are to be conducted.

Despite these limitations on the scope of bargaining, which have been retained in all subsequent executive orders, union representation expanded rapidly in the federal civilian service. Excluding the postal service, only 19,000 federal employees were in exclusive bargaining units at the end of 1962. By the end of 1972, 1,083,000 federal employees were covered by 3,400 exclusive units. This represented 55 percent of the federal civilian workforce, which no longer included the postal service. Though approximately 200 different employee organizations represent federal employees, the major employee organizations in the federal service are of three basic kinds:

1. Unions with all or a major proportion of their membership in the federal service. Typical of such organizations is the American Federation of Government Employees, with some 325,000 federal members. It is an affiliate of the AFL-CIO, the large, predominantly private sector union federation.

2. Unions with a major proportion of membership in the private sector but with a substantial federal membership. Typical of such organizations is the Service Employees International Union, an AFL-CIO affiliate with nearly 450,000 members, over 30 percent of whom are in government service.

3. Independent associations of unions whose membership is often professional in orientation and is limited to a specific employee craft or agency. Typical of such organizations in the federal service are the National Treasury Employees Union or the Professional Air Traffic Controllers Association. The latter association has recently affiliated with a private sector AFL-CIO affiliate.

Executive Order 10988 was followed in 1969 by a second labour relations executive order issued by President Nixon. This new order, EO 11491, came out in favor of the single form of union recognition characteristic in the private sector, majority exclusive recognition. It also removed from the individual federal agencies and departments much of the authority they had retained for labour-management affairs during the seven years of EO 10988, vesting this authority instead in a co-ordinated federal labour relations system. Under EO 11491, the Assistant Secretary of Labor for Labor Management Relations has the authority to determine appropriate bargaining units, to supervise elections, and to rule on alleged unfair labour practices. Thus the Department of Labor now plays much the same role in the federal labour-management program as does the National Labor Relations Board in the private sector. EO 11491 also broadened the scope of negotiability in several areas of working conditions. Perhaps the most important of these was permission for agencies to negotiate agreements providing for binding neutral arbitration of employee grievances. This replaced the former system wherein arbitral decisions were only advisory.

The foregoing is not intended to suggest that labour relations in the federal services are now, or are becoming, identical with those in the private sector. A number of obvious differences remain. Bargaining unit determinations have resulted in less fragmentation and fewer specific craft units than in the private sector. Professional employees, who are prevalent in government, are treated in special ways that are not characteristic of organized professionals in the private sector. The continuous reorganization of government agencies and activities brings constant change in unit structure and federal bargaining relationships, which are far less common in private industry.

Allegations of unfair labour practices in the Federal Government must be processed and carried forward by the protesting unions themselves, rather than by an independent government agency like the National Labor Relations Board or the equivalent. Quite unlike the private sector, the federal programs still forbid "union security" clauses which require union membership or financial support from members of a bargaining unit. The Federal Government maintains its "no strike" ban and has taken punitive action against employees who engage in coercive job actions such as that by the air traffic controllers several years ago. (The one significant exception to this generalization regarding punishment was the postal employees' strike. As noted previously, this strike was one of the factors leading to the creation of a new public corporation for postal services in which postal employees acquired a largely private sector status. Ironically, however, they are still under a "no strike" ban.)

In general, progress and change in the federal labour-management relations thus far have not been as great as the growth of unionism *per se*. The most important reason for this is the continuing limitation on the scope of negotiable issues. Unions of federal employees are maintaining their pressure to broaden the scope of bargaining, however, primarily through increasing the coverage and size of bargaining units. Any subject is negotiable that falls within the discretionary authority of the highest level of management directly supervising employees in the unit. As unit sizes gradually increase over time, it is believed that the scope of negotiable issues will ultimately reach practically all personnel matters which are within the discretion and control of each individual federal agency.

State and Local Experience

Although the Federal Government's power to regulate inter-state commerce has been construed by the Supreme Court as giving Congress the authority to regulate relations between local governments and their employees, no federal statute has been enacted in this area. This has meant in practice that the structuring of labour-management relationships and of collective bargaining mechanisms in the states has been left to individual states, no doubt wisely since the myriad of state and local government fiscal policies, tax structures, and budgetary and personnel practices make federal determinations of labour-management policies and enforcement mechanisms for local governments virtually impossible. The result, however, has been that the individual states and municipalities have come up with widely differing structures and mechanisms of labour relations. Prior to the example set by the 1962 federal executive order, only the state of Wisconsin had enacted legislation establishing bargaining mechanisms for its public employees. Since then, 30 of the 50 states have enacted some kind of legislation concerning all or some groups of their public employees. Twenty-one states have enacted comprehensive statutes in this area. A comprehensive statute is one which: (1) guarantees public employees the right to bargain collectively; (2) establishes procedures for selection of employee representatives; (3) prescribes remedies for unfair labour practices committed by employers or employee organizations; and (4) provides dispute resolution mechanisms.

The coverage and scope of state statutes are extremely varied. Some states cover all state and local government employees, including teachers, under one statute. Other states have excluded state civil servants from statutes that cover all local government and educational employees. Fifteen states have enacted separate statutes covering teachers and ten have statutes covering only firemen and/or policemen.

To determine representation rights and appropriate bargaining units in the public sector, most states use the same agencies as serve the private sector. This tends to promote a uniform approach to labour-management relationships in the two sectors. Other states have set up new and separate agencies to administer public sector labour relations, while yet a third group of states has left the creation of administrative and enforcement machinery to local initiative. Finally, though most importantly, the scope of collective bargaining under most state statutes is broader than that in the federal government usually covering wages, hours, and fringe benefits as well as working conditions.

A few examples will illustrate the variety of state experience. The state of New York and its local units of government have over one million public employees, 90 percent of whom are now covered by collective bargaining. Some 12,000 labour agreements exist with 1,100 different units of local and municipal government throughout the state. On the other hand, several hundred thousand state civil servants have been placed in only six bargaining units on a state-wide basis. This broad collective bargaining coverage has been achieved in New York State despite the fact that its law has been largely effective in preventing strikes over collective bargaining impasses in all but New York City itself.

In Michigan, state civil servants have no right to bargain collectively but employees of local government and educational units do. In less than 10 years, over 90 percent of Michigan teachers and over one-third of all employees of counties, municipalities and townships in the state have come to be represented for collective bargaining purposes.

The union that represents most local government employees in Michigan, as well as throughout the nation, is the American Federation of State, County, and Municipal Employees. The AFSCME has more than doubled in size in the last ten years and has over half a million members nationally. It is potentially the largest union in the United States, simply because its jurisdiction gives it an organizing potential of over 8 million employees. Other unions, some with their primary base in the private sector such as the Teamsters and the Steelworkers, are also organizing and bargaining for tens of thousands of local and municipal government employees.

Returning to Michigan, this state like almost all others has maintained its ban on public employee strikes. In practice, however, such strikes are fairly frequent and employees engaging in them are seldom punished. In recognition of this growing *de facto* right to strike, four states have legalized strikes for some or all public employees. Hawaii and Pennsylvania have totally eliminated their strike bans. But even these two states have provided for special safeguards in the case of strikes endangering the public health or safety. The one group of public employees who by general consensus cannot be allowed to strike are the uniformed services—police and firefighters. As an alternative to the strike for these uniformed services, eight states, including Michigan, Pennsylvania and Wisconsin, are experimenting with varieties of compulsory arbitration systems.

At the other extreme to states with comprehensive public employee statutes are those with no legislation in the field, except perhaps for a blanket strike prohibition. Yet even in these states organization of municipal employees is growing rapidly. In the major cities of Ohio, local recognition and bargaining rights are being granted as a matter of course, but without statutory authority or control. Even in some southern states, where regulatory laws are least common, recognition strikes are being won by sanitation and hospital workers, and by the AFSCME on behalf of many categories of municipal workers.

As a gross generalization and with important exceptions, collective bargaining for public employees at the state and municipal level appears to be shifting authority for personnel issues to the executive branch of local government at the expense of the legislative branch and of traditional civil service systems. It has been suggested that certain elements of these existing systems seem doomed to be replaced by collective bargaining structures. In addition, authority for collective bargaining increasingly appears to be centralized within the executive branch of many cities with primary bargaining responsibility for all departments of the city assigned to an individual or office directly responsible to the chief executive. As yet, however, multi-employer bargaining units covering more than one governmental unit are almost unknown in local government in the United States.

Again as a major generalization, the growth of a *de facto* right to strike in some states is creating some severe problems for their local governments. Because municipal unions are only slightly subject to the discipline of the product market and because their membership is relatively immune from the threat of technological displacement, their collective bargaining demands have often been high and inflexible. Because the services of some municipal unions' members are deemed essential, major cities such as Detroit, Philadelphia and New York, have found it difficult or impossible to muster counter-pressure to employee strikes. Local bargaining impasses tend to induce a crisis atmosphere in which public decisions are often made in the hope of remedying immediate crisis situations. In some cities this has meant that carefully evaluated wage policies developed over the years have been jettisoned because garbage is piling up in the streets, the buses are not running, or police officers are threatening some sort of protest action. In sum, the unions with the greatest leverage on the public appear for the moment at least to be advantaging themselves at the expense of other categories of public employees who work in less critical areas. In other cases these powerful groups have advantaged themselves at the level of public services provided. At this point in time, no other group of claimants on the public tax funds seems in a position to exercise the same amount of influence on public resource allocation as the powerful and cohesive municipal unions.

The Experience in Education

Teachers are perhaps as widely organized and are engaging in as many forms of bargaining as any group of public employees in the United States. As previously noted, some states which have not passed general statutes affecting public employees have specifically granted teachers the right to organize and bargain. Other states, while not granting complete collective bargaining rights to teachers, have granted them the right to "meet and confer" with local school boards. In theory, the "meet and confer" right implies that management must listen to employee suggestions but retains a more or less free hand in making decisions. Where teacher organizations are strong, however, the limited right has had results largely indistinguishable from collective bargaining. Finally, in some major cities of the United States such as Chicago and Cleveland, collective bargaining between teacher organizations and local boards of education has taken place for a number of years without specific authorization of law.

One of the main reasons for the substantial extent of organization among public school teachers has been the competition between the two major federations of teachers, the American Federation of Teachers (AFT) and the National Education Association (NEA). The AFT is affiliated with the AFL-CIO and its leadership generally feels a fairly close identity with the trade union movement. The NEA, on the other hand, is a long time professional organization of approximately one million classroom teachers and their supervisors. In the past decade, the NEA has given up its traditional reluctance to engage in collective bargaining and has competed aggressively for bargaining rights with the AFT. The competition between these two groups is analogous to that which existed between the AFL and the CIO during the 1930s and 1940s, and just as employees in private industry were better served because of the competition that occurred in those decades, so it appears that teachers have benefited by the competition between their two federations. As organized teacher relationships have matured, however, local organizations of the NEA and the AFT have begun to merge in a few cities in the United States. . . . If the NEA and the AFT ever merge nationally, the combined membership would make it the largest union of professional employees in the world.

Collective bargaining has made a significant impact on the financial circumstances of teacher employment. Salaries and compensation levels have improved markedly. In the state of Michigan, for example, teacher salaries have risen by nearly 50 percent in the past five years and this experience is by no means unusual. While only half of this increase can be attributed to the institution of collective bargaining—the other half reflects increases matching inflation that probably would have occurred in any event—it is nevertheless clear that, in the short run at least, the wage and fringe benefits of public employees increase more rapidly under conditions of collective bargaining than in its absence.

Problems concerning the scope of collective bargaining or the appropriate subject matter for bargaining which are common in the public sector are well characterized in teacher negotiations. In private sector negotiations, the quality of the product is considered to be the concern and the prerogative of management. In the provision of services in the public sector, particularly in education, the quality of the product is usually determined in great part by performance at the point of delivery. Professional employees such as teachers have a strong interest in the quality of service they provide. Hence they frequently challenge management on matters sometimes said to be questions of basic educational policy, for example, curricular reform, textbook selection and student discipline. Moreover, there are issues such as class size and the length of the school year which are matters of educational policy but are undeniably conditions of employment as well. As a result, teachers press strongly for collective agreements which either cover these matters or provide procedures whereby they will be jointly worked out by employers and employees during the life of the agreement. Some collective bargaining agreements now permit teachers to participate in evaluating probationary colleagues, require school boards to employ certain kinds of ancillary and support professionals, and envisage joint determination of curriculum changes.

Teacher pressure to expand negotiations to cover subjects such as these is viewed with alarm by many school administrators. They feel that union preoccupation with these matters of educational policy reflects little more than member self-interest. In addition, many of these subjects are of concern not only to school administrators and teachers but to parents and the community as well. Matters such as teacher transfer policies and student discipline in the United States today have racial and social implications far transcending the educational sphere.

Several states have tried to approach this problem legislatively. The state of Maine, for example, has enacted that "public employers of teachers shall be required to meet and consult but not negotiate with respect to educational policies" with representatives of organized teachers. Such statutes reflect increasing exploration of the concept that many public policies of legitimate concern to professional employees should nevertheless not be determined solely through collective bargaining but through some kind of joint determination by all affected groups. But in the public sector, to a much greater degree than in the private sector, the line between policy making, which should be the responsibility of officials, and working conditions, which should be set in negotiations, is extremely hard to draw.

Some Continuing Problems

A basic argument for the extension of collective bargaining rights to public sector employees in the United States is that rights which have been mandated by law in the private sector should in equity be given to the government's own employees. This is not to suggest that there are not important differences between private and public employment, however, and that these differences have not created some difficult problems as the private sector bargaining model increasingly pervades the public sector.

Probably the most fundamental of these problems lies in the different purposes of public and private undertakings. The public employer is an artificial creature of the electorate established to minister to the needs and desires of the public and to provide the mechanical and administrative structure to carry on these functions. In a democratic system of government it is elected officials who are normally charged with the control and determination of budget and tax rates, which is the primary way of setting goals and priorities. While extra-parliamentary influences are both inevitable and necessary elements of the democratic process, they should not be allowed to obscure the fact that elected legislative bodies are supposed to be essentially deliberative bodies. If democratic governments are to distinguish between public passions and public interests, legislatures have to be at least partially insulated from group pressures. In a number of major American cities, the crisis pressures that result from actual or threatened withdrawal of public services have at times usurped the legislature's deliberative process in this most fundamental government function of setting goals and priorities.

A second problem lies in the existence of civil service systems in the public sector in the United States. These systems are basically designed to ensure that the selection, retention and promotion of public employees are based on qualifications and meritorious performance alone. They are often considered to be the warp and woof of public employment. To employees, however, merit rating is sometimes considered a euphemism for favoritism. Public employee organizations therefore attempt to weave into this tight fabric somewhat coarser threads such as strict seniority, across-the-board wage adjustments, and the like. It is a yet unsettled question whether the civil service and merit systems can survive the assault of traditional collective bargaining practices. But it is clear that protection of the public employees' right to continued employment, assuming meritorious service, is increasingly being enforced through negotiated grievance procedures culminating in binding neutral arbitration rather than through statutory devices such as the tenure system.

A third problem is that of unions for supervisory staff. In private industry, the lines of authority and supervision are ordinarily clearly drawn, even in areas of white-collar employment. In the public sector, however, the lines between supervisor and employee are far more indistinct. There are several reasons for this. The appellation of supervisor tends to be pushed further down in the organizational hierarchy in public than in private bureaucracies. Where all are dedicated to serving the public, there is a greater community of interest among all employees. In the public service both supervisors and non-supervisors alike are often compensated within an identical and fairly rigid salary structure. As a reflection of these facts many existing state collective bargaining laws have not drawn the traditional distinctions between supervisors and employees. Hence labour relations boards that implement the state laws have permitted supervisory unionism. In some cases they have required the recognition of supervisory units as components of the same union that organizes those who are supervised. Whether conflict of interest is inevitable between the supervisory goals of the organization and the fraternal goals of the union is as yet uncertain. It is clearly a danger, however.

A fourth problem in public employee bargaining arises because of the diffusion of decision-making authority which frequently exists in the public sector. Parliamentary systems of government permit a greater unity of legislative and executive authority than is common in United States governmental systems, which are more often characterized by division of authority with checks and balances operating between the executive and legislative powers. In federal, state and local governments an agency head may have authority to negotiate only on a portion of the issues which are normally subjects of collective bargaining—other negotiable subjects may be retained within the control of the legislative body or an independent civil service board. Often a chief executive may not have final authority regarding the distribution of funds and can only submit recommendations to the appropriate legislature. May the legislative body repudiate his decisions? Does it have to provide funds to pay for the salary structure he has negotiated? Finally, where voter approval of increased millage is necessary to pay for the negotiated increases, local taxpayer revolts are increasingly common. Questions of this kind are extremely difficult to answer within many, though not all, governments. But the internal logic of collective bargaining is leading to considerable centralization of power and to increased executive power vis-a-vis both legislatures and civil service boards.

Related to but distinguishable from the previous problem in one characterized as "end-run" or "double-deck" bargaining. Some public employee unions attempt by lobbying to secure from the state legislature those items they have failed to attain or have traded away at the municipal bargaining table. In many states, civil service organizations have formed one of the strongest lobbies in the state legislature. These powers can hardly be taken away from such organizations. But from the municipal government's point of view, freedom to trade cost reductions in one area for contractually bargained new expenditures in another is an essential element of bargaining flexibility and bargaining equality. Where state legislatures mandate wage and fringe bargaining at the municipal level and yet continue to legislate on municipal employee benefits, they place local units of government in a Procrustean bed. Public employee bargaining may be desirable and inevitable, but public employees hardly seem entitled to the benefits both of collective bargaining and of traditional state protective laws.

A final problem of collective bargaining in the public sector, one which perhaps receives more attention than it deserves, is that of public employee strikes. Most contemporary discussions of this subject concern the issue of whether public employees have or should be given the legal right to strike. The fact is, of course, that despite the *de jure* absence of this right in almost all United States governmental jurisdictions, in practice they can and do strike, often with impunity. Moreover, though it is not commonly recognized, the public employee strike problem exists both in jurisdictions which permit collective bargaining and in those which have not yet done so.

The public employee strike problem is not overwhelming on a national basis. In the past decade such strikes have grown in frequency from approximately one per month to one per day in the whole nation, but strike activity in the public sector is still far below that in the private sector. Public employees involved in work stoppages in recent years represent about 1.5 percent of total employment, compared with nearly 4 percent in the private sector. In 1970, strike idleness represented 0.08 percent of man-days worked by government employees; for the economy as a whole this figure was 0.28 percent. The average duration of public employee strikes is less than five days for what might be termed "essential employees;" for those in less crucial occupations the average duration is over twice as much. . . .

Mediation and non-binding neutral recommendations by so-called fact finders are the most common governmental devices used to help resolve collective bargaining impasses. While they are effective in the large majority of disputes, they are obviously not a panacea. Where it is deemed that no strike can be permitted, as is almost invariably the decision with police and firemen, compulsory binding arbitration is the most frequently used alternative. Eight states are now experimenting with variants of this device. The newest, though largely untested, idea in compulsory arbitration is "final offer selection," in which the arbitrator is given no power to compromise issues in dispute, but must select one or the other of the parties' final offers.

Conclusion

The coming of collective bargaining to the public sector is the most significant development in the industrial field in the United States in the past 30 years. Its growth has been both rapid and extensive and appears to be continuing. Even now, however, bargaining does not occur in more than half of all government jurisdictions in the United States. In many areas where bargaining has begun, it is less than ten years old. Hence, one must be cautious in making generalizations about the future of public employee labour relations. A few may be put forward tentatively, however.

The coming of unionism to the public sector has provided enough new recruits to the labour movement to reverse the decline in trade union membership which took place during the later 1950s and early 1960s. Moreover, it is at least possible that as government employees join unions, or as their traditional professional associations begin to behave more like unions, this will change the general blue-collar image of the labour movement in the United States. Private sector trade unionism has never exceeded 30 percent of the non-agricultural workforce and has never had any strong appeal to white-collar workers. Organizing success among white-collar and professional employees in the public sector may make unionism acceptable and normal to private sector white-collar workers who will in the near future, if they do not already, represent a majority of employment in private industry. In summary, public employee unionism has halted the decline in trade union membership in the United States and may in fact contribute to substantial new growth in the private sector in the next decade or two.

Public employee unionism appears to have contributed to centralization of government decision-making power in the United States, though it is by no means the sole cause of such developments. At the municipal level it is clear that the exigencies of collective bargaining have forced decision-making authority towards the chief executive at the expense of municipal legislatures and civil service boards. In the educational field, pressures exerted by organized teachers along with a number of constitutional decisions are forcing a shift away from the local property tax towards the state-imposed income tax as the primary means of financing public education. Almost inevitably this will mean that many financial decisions will be removed from local school boards and centralized in intermediate or state-wide decision-making bodies. At the federal level, the movement towards nation-wide bargaining units of federal civil servants may slow or halt efforts at federal decentralization that were initiated in the 1960s. In short, public employee unionism appears in many areas to be leading to more centralized decision making in the United States, as it has in many other industrialized democracies.

The economic results of public employee bargaining are as yet unclear and controversial. Some authorities believe that public employees have driven their salary and benefit levels far higher than would have been the case in the absence of collective bargaining, and higher than can be justified on the basis of economic equity. Others challenge this assumption. They state that recent increases in public employee compensation are largely reflective of inflationary pressures in American society and the need for public employees to "catch up" with others whose wages and salaries should be comparable. Quantitative data that would support either argument are still scanty. Public employees in some occupations clearly have fared more favorably in recent years than has the average employee in the private sector. The differences are not large, however, and during 1971 and 1972 increases in both sectors were held down by government wage policies.

As yet, the impact of public employee unionism on governmental decision making has not been as great as the numerical increase in public union membership and bargaining unit growth might suggest. In the federal sector it is estimated that employees so far have the right to bargain on perhaps only 25 percent of the subjects that are negotiable in the private sector. Though the scope of bargaining is increasing at the federal level, and is already more extensive at the local and educational levels, it cannot be said with any certainty that the large majority of governmental and public policy decisions are fundamentally different from what they would have been in the absence of collective bargaining.

Finally, and most speculatively, it is possible that public employee unionism will bring changes to the whole of the labour relations environment in the United States. As previously noted, white-collar and professional organization in the public sector may bring a greater acceptability of white-collar unionization in the private sector. If devices such as compulsory arbitration become common and effective for resolving collective bargaining impasses in the public sector, their use may increasingly be urged in the private sector. In general, and with many obvious exceptions, public sector labour relations practices and laws in the United States have thus far been strongly modelled on the private sector structure which had evolved earlier. Over time, experience in the public sector may prove certain procedures and practices, now uncommon or unknown in the private sector, to be useful or effective. It is not at all unlikely that such practices might then become acceptable in the private sector. In sum, the future may well be one of simultaneous changes in both sectors, each tending generally to become more like the other.

Local Government Bargaining and Management Structure

John F. Burton, Jr.

This paper deals with the impact of bargaining on the administration of personnel relations. The primary focus is on the management side, and the discussion is directed at local governments which are just beginning or which recently have begun to bargain with trade unions. My comments catalogue the changes in management structure that can be expected as the bargaining relationship matures. Analysis of these long-run effects should help a city decide the short-run strategies and changes that are required.

The paper is based on field work in about 40 cities and other local government units for the Brookings Institution *Studies of Unionism in Government.* The article will primarily consist of generalizations based on this field work, although I will include some specific examples of the practices about which I am generalizing.

My discussion consists of three parts: (1) a brief overview of how cities decide personnel issues in the absence of unions; (2) the initial impact of collective bargaining on management structure; and (3) the impact of a mature bargaining relationship on management structure.

The central thesis of this paper is that bargaining forces a centralization of authority within management which overcomes the fragmentation of control over various issues typical in a nonunionized unit of local government.

Management Structure Before Collective Bargaining

By the term "management structure," I primarily mean the location within the local government of the authority to decide management's position on personnel issues. There are two primary types of personnel issues: budget issues and nonbudget issues.

Budget Issues

Authority over personnel issues which require budget appropriations, primarily wage rates and fringe benefits, is typically a joint responsibility of the chief executive and the local legislature. The city manager or mayor, in cooperation with his budget director, prepares wage and fringe recommendations for the city council as a part of his preparation of an annual city budget. However, the mayor's proposed executive budget is only a recommendation to the city council which can amend, reject, or accept the recommendation. Authority over budget issues, then, is shared by the chief executive and the local legislature. Which branch of government is the dominant partner varies from city to city. The dominance to some extent depends on whether the city has a mayor-council, council-manager, commission, or other form of government. Within each of these forms, variations in the relative power of the executive and legislature are also found. In Chicago, which has a mayor-council form of government, the mayor is in practice able to dominate the entire budgetary process, while in Los Angeles the city council has primary authority over employee wages and salaries, and the mayor has only a minimal role.

Reprinted from *Industrial Relations,* May 1972, pp. 123–39, with the permission of the publisher and the author.

The basic authority of the chief executive and legislature over budget issues is complicated by legal or charter restrictions and the existence of intermediate agencies which also participate in the setting of wage rates and fringe benefits. First, either the state or the local city charter may limit the discretion of local officials on appropriations for wages. Also, nonwage aspects of employee compensation may be set either by state law, as in the case of police and fire pensions in Wisconsin, or by city charter, as in the case of vacation and sick leave benefits in San Francisco. Municipalities may also be restricted as to source of revenue. Chicago, for example, may not increase its sales tax without the approval of the state legislature, and state law in Washington permits municipal budgets to increase by only 6 percent per year. In other municipalities, home rule charters impose limitations on local taxes which can be modified only by referendum. Fiscal authority is shared thus not only with the state legislature but also directly with the electorate.

Second, there can be intermediate agencies between the mayor and the council, and even semi-autonomous departments which are not dependent on the city for financing, which have an impact on budget issues. In numerous cities, such as San Francisco, the civil service commission is responsible for preparing salary recommendations for the city council and these recommendations need not be coordinated with the mayor's proposed budget. In much of New England, independent boards of finance, which are appointed by the major for fixed terms, have full legal responsibility for preparing municipal budgets for submission to the city council, leaving the elected mayor or appointed city manager with only an indirect control over his budget. The delegation of partial responsibility for salaries and wage rates to independent civil service commissions and boards of finance was intended to insulate the setting of public employee wages from undue political influence by providing an independent check on the authority of the elected officials.

Authority for budget issues is further fragmented by the existence of semi-independent departments which have considerable discretion on wage rates and fringe benefits. Such departments are most common in counties and in municipalities with the commission form of government, but are also found in other cities. These departments either have their own taxing power or are the beneficiaries of earmarked funds from the state or city. In either instance, they are often found under no legal compulsion to coordinate their wage strategies with other city departments or to take guidance from the mayor or city council. Los Angeles, which has six independent salary-setting authorities, exemplifies this point. The mayor and the council set salaries for less than 60 percent of the city employees. Clearly, there is no one central salary-setting authority in Los Angeles, and there is a similar diffusion of authority in many large cities.

Nonbudget Issues

The "standard" method for resolving issues relating to the selection of employees, the allocation or definition of jobs, and the resolution of job related disputes is to delegate authority for the issues to a civil service commission which makes decisions on the basis of the merit principle. Because many of the cities in our survey deviated from this standard method, an elaboration of the civil service merit system is necessary.

A merit system may be defined as "a personnel system in which comparative merit or achievement governs each individual's selection and progress in the service. . . ." As an alternative to the merit system, selection and progress can be based on factors such as seniority, party affiliation, union membership, race, and sex. The merit principle can be used for various personnel issues: (1) narrow scope—recruitment of new personnel; (2) intermediate scope—recruitment, retention, promotion, training, and classification of positions on the basis of objective analysis; or (3) broad scope—all previous issues, plus salary administration based on objective standards.

The scope of the merit principle can vary, and so can the role of the civil service commission. The commission can be: (1) independent—with full legal authority to make unilateral decisions without the approval of the mayor or council, and the legal authority is not infringed upon by other agents of the government; (2) dominated—where the ostensible autonomy of the commission is illusory because elected officials are able to appoint commissioners who are subject to political influence and manipulation; or (3) nonexistent.

When the term "civil service merit system" is used, or shorter terms such as "civil service system," the reference is usually to an independent civil service commission which applies the merit principle to a broad or intermediate scope of issues and which also serves as an appeals board for grievances filed by employees because of disciplinary actions taken by the city. This model of a civil service system was found in many cities in our sample, including Milwaukee and St. Louis, but several cities did not fit the model. For example, in Chicago, the civil service commission is neither independent nor a defender of the merit principle, but is just one component of a flourishing patronage system. And in Bloomington, Illinois, there is no civil service commission, but the city manager uses the merit principle for all nonwage personnel issues such as recruitment and promotion. These examples demonstrate that any discussion of the civil service merit system must carefully distinguish between the civil service commission as an institution and the merit principle as a basis for resolving personnel issues.

Other Sources of Control over Personnel Issues

In addition to the primary split between budget issues normally handled by the legislative and executive branches, and nonbudget issues, usually handled by an independent civil service commission, other patterns of influence were observed in the precollective bargaining status cities in our sample. For example, authority over personnel issues may be shared with a political organization through a patronage system. Although the elected mayor and city council retain full legal control over such issues, in practice, authority is fragmented by the involvement of party chairmen, ward committeemen, and other nonelected political leaders.

Conclusion

Prior to the emergence of collective bargaining, the major characteristic of management structure is the bewildering fragmentation of authority for personnel issues among numerous management officials. Depending on the issue being considered, a newly formed union might be required to negotiate with the chief executive officer, the finance committee of the legislative body, the civil service commission, the personnel director, the city attorney, and others. I stress this fragmentation, not only because it is a necessary background for understanding the balance of this paper, but because it is one of the factors which distinguish public and private sector bargaining. In the private sector, authority for personnel issues is more likely to be concentrated at a particular point within the management structure, and that point is more likely to be obvious to a new union.

The Initial Impact of Bargaining on Management Structure

How does management at the local government level alter its structure in response to the emergence of bargaining? This section discusses the early stages of bargaining, which could be either informal bargaining or rudimentary formal bargaining. In informal bargaining, the end result of the negotiations is not a written contract, but some other evidence of union influence such as an amended city ordinance, a revised personnel manual, or an oral agreement. In formal bargaining, the parties negotiate a written contract.

Initial Patterns

A common initial response of local governments is to impose a system of collective bargaining on the existing structure of authority with little or no modification. Primary responsibility for negotiations can be assigned to either the executive or legislative branch, but no pre-existing center of authority is subordinated or greatly diminished in influence.

In municipalities with executive budgets, the chief executive or his fiscal officer (budget director) will normally meet informally with employee organizations prior to the formulation of a final budget. Employee organizations are permitted to petition or to meet and confer with city officials and make proposals on pending wage and fringe benefit increases. Since the employee organizations are primarily interested in economic issues, the budget director represents the city in these informal discussions. The same individual may initially attempt to retain this responsibility after the establishment of formal collective bargaining.

In Chicago, which is still largely characterized by informal bargaining, the employee organizations submit all requests to the budget director, and after conferring with him may meet directly with the mayor on any outstanding problems. A similar procedure was used in Seattle until 1967 when a transition to formal bargaining was made. Since Seattle has an executive budget, the mayor assumed initial responsibility for negotiations and appointed his budget director, along with the budget consultant to the city council, to represent the city in negotiations. In other cities, the personnel director or solicitor may be part of a negotiating committee which assists the budget director on issues not related to the budget. For example, the mayor of Wilmington, Delaware, appointed a negotiating committee comprised of the city solicitor, the director of finance, and the personnel director. A similar negotiating committee was appointed by New York City's Mayor Wagner in 1958. The budget director and personnel director were given primary responsibility for representing the city in labor negotiations because both individuals had previously represented the mayor in administering the Civil Service Career and Salary Plan and had been responsible for granting and approving wage increases for employees before collective bargaining.

Shortcomings of the Typical Initial Model

There are two reasons why the normal response of local government to the emergence of bargaining is to attempt not to disturb the existing management structure: (1) to utilize existing experience or expertise, and (2) to not disturb established authority relationships. Nevertheless, the initial delegation of bargaining authority to the budget director, the personnel director, or other staff officials is usually unstable. One reason is that such staff officials are not professional labor negotiators and often are unable to match the expertise of professional union negotiators who have considerable experience in negotiating labor contracts. A budget director will often be at a disadvantage on issues relating to union security, management prerogatives, formal grievance procedures and workloads. A second reason is that labor relations, especially in large cities, is time consuming and requires the attention of a full-time official. A budget director or personnel director, each of whom has primary responsibilities elsewhere, will not be able to devote sufficient attention or time to the negotiation and administration of contracts. This consideration is especially important in the administration of contracts, whether through a grievance procedure or through the supervision of the contract to insure that negotiated standards are observed.

The most serious problem, however, with this delegation of authority is that it leaves unresolved the problem of fragmented authority for labor relations. The budget director or personnel director, or even the chief executive authority if he chooses to negotiate personally, will not be able to transcend existing authority relationships in the city. Semi-independent departments which are not under the budgetary control of the mayor and city council will be untouched; the authority of line managers to negotiate on issues within their discretion will be undefined; and the ability of the legislative body to overrule negotiators on contract provisions will be undiminished. The result is that the multiple centers of power will continue to exist, forcing the labor organization to negotiate with numerous city officials on various issues. For example, the Teamsters Union in Detroit wanted to negotiate over the reassignment of motor vehicles to specific size classifications. The city's labor negotiator claimed a lack of authority and refused to negotiate, a position also adopted by the major city departments. Eventually the union was able to convince the civil service to use its authority over job classifications to establish size classes for motor vehicles.

At the same time, the lack of clear lines of authority for labor relations permits the unions great flexibility in choosing which representatives of management it will negotiate with on each issue. Generally, the various city officials are anxious to negotiate with the union in the belief that by doing so they will strengthen their own autonomy and authority over their traditional jurisdictions. The city is, however, subject to whipsawing under this arrangement with favorable terms granted by one part of the city used to justify similar terms for other employees. Even when the unions are not strong enough to force the favorable terms granted by one part of the city on the whole city, the nonstandard terms complicate the city's administrative tasks and invite employee dissatisfaction. Cities which have had even a moderate amount of experience with bargaining through decentralized authority have almost invariably reacted by attempting to reduce the decentralization.

The next section discusses the emerging patterns in the shifts in bargaining structure that are evident in cities with reasonably well developed bargaining relationships.

The Ultimate Impact of Bargaining on Management Structure

Collective bargaining superimposed on the prebargaining management structure is unstable. Stability only emerges as tensions within the management structure are reduced, and this appears to require new organizational forms and often a restructuring of the previous authority relationships. Several trends in the structure of management are clear. These I will discuss in terms of the executive and legislative branches, and the civil service system.

Executive Branch

There are three general tendencies concerning the executive branch which will be documented and explained. The executive branch is increasingly gaining effective authority for labor relations, with corresponding losses of influence for the legislative branch and for such independent agencies as civil service commissions and pension boards. Within the executive branch, authority for labor relations is becoming centralized. Also, bargaining authority is being removed from staff officers and transferred to full-time labor relations specialists. These three tendencies are examined in turn.

1. The executive branch has several clear advantages at the bargaining table. First, management is best able to adopt an integrated position in preparing for negotiations and in implementing the resulting agreements. The executive can, for example, coordinate bargaining with the preparation of the budget, which is usually its responsibility, and with the overall legislative program. Similarly, the executive will inevitably be responsible for implementing negotiated agreements which can best be discharged by the officials who negotiate the basic agreement. Second, the executive will usually be more capable of devising appropriate negotiating strategies. The executive is able to formulate a unified policy and confront the union with a single management position. The divisions and uncertainties characteristic of legislative negotiating committees (where each participant has an independent political power base) are dissolved when management is able to negotiate within guidelines set by the chief executive officer.

2. The most important factor which has led to the centralization of authority within the executive is the need to coordinate management's position on all issues. As indicated in the previous section, when various officials represent management, the union has more than one opportunity to obtain a concession, and it is difficult for management to view the negotiating process as an integrated whole in which concessions in one area are seen as having effects elsewhere. Another advantage of centralization is that it permits negotiations to be delegated to full-time personnel who can develop expertise in bargaining. Formal collective bargaining requires the attention of full-time negotiators who must negotiate the original contract. In large cities with a multiplicity of bargaining units, this may involve bargaining on a year-round basis. The management negotiators must also administer the contract, and are likely to be involved in representation elections and in grievances, fact finding and arbitration procedures.

3. Assuming that the executive branch will become the dominant factor within the management structure, and that the authority will be centralized within the executive branch, the next question is: where within the executive should negotiating responsibility be located? Two interrelated trends are evident. Bargaining authority is increasingly being removed from staff officers, such as the budget director or personnel director. The complementary trend is that full-time labor relations specialists are emerging who have responsibility for negotiating and administering labor contracts. In some cities, this second trend has manifested itself in new organizational forms, such as the Office of Labor Relations in New York City.

Why have the old time staff officers, such as budget directors, lost authority as bargaining matures? (The disadvantages of delegating bargaining authority were previously discussed and will only be highlighted here.) First, bargaining requires a sophisticated negotiator who is aware of the forms and rituals of the bargaining process. Also, placement of primary responsibility for labor in an existing staff position creates conflicts of loyalty which can impair the bargaining process. For example, the personnel director may willingly trade off higher wage increases in exchange for less union encroachment into areas of importance to personnel.

As a result of these disadvantages, there is a tendency under mature formal bargaining to assign responsibility for all personnel issues to full-time labor relations specialists. In some cities, this may require one management negotiator or, in large cities, a central labor relations agency may be needed. In such large cities, the staff officials participate in the negotiations in an advisory capacity, but all decision-making authority is centralized in the one agency. For example, in Detroit, Mayor Cavanaugh created a labor relations office by reassigning all staff officials who had previously bargained with the unions to the one central agency. The rate setting division of the Budget Bureau and part of the Personnel Department were merged, along with appropriate legal advisors, to form the Labor Relations Office. The Office of Labor Relations in New York City has pre-empted the former labor responsibilities of the Budget Bureau and the Personnel Department. In addition, a new central agency may also reassert its authority over semi-autonomous departments which had previously represented themselves in labor negotiations. OLR in New York has reached an agreement with most independent authorities in the city whereby it represents them in wage negotiations in city-wide titles and on other issues which have a city-wide impact. In Cuyahoga County (Cleveland) the director of labor relations, who was appointed in 1969, is now beginning to represent all county departments in negotiations, including even semi-autonomous departments such as the Cuyahoga County hospitals, the county sheriff, and the county engineeer, which had previously negotiated their own contracts. The county is in the process of centralizing its authority structure to respond to the challenge of a single union which has organized most county departments and is in a position to whipsaw the county's agencies if they negotiate independently.

Legislative Branch

Several cities visited in our field work were represented in labor relations by their legislative bodies, at least in the early stages of the bargaining relationship. The reliance on the legislature to represent the government in labor relations primarily occurs in counties which do not have chief executive officers and in municipalities which do not have executive budgets.

The main advantage of having the city council or one of its standing committees represent management in collective bargaining is that the councilmen have the ultimate legal authority to make binding commitments, which avoids the delegation of authority problem. Direct control over labor relations enhances a legislature's influence on the outcome of bargaining and insures the legislators that they will share in any political benefit which accrues to the public officials responsible for granting wage increases to a significant part of their constituency.

Usually, however, the participation of the elected legislative officials in labor negotiations is short-lived and bargaining responsibility is soon transferred to the executive branch. The main reason is the inability of the legislators to be effective negotiators. City councilmen and county commissioners are usually inexperienced in labor negotiations. They do not have detailed knowledge of most items which are subject to negotiations, such as work rules and job security, grievance procedures, union security and other personnel issues. Furthermore, partially because most local legislators are part-time officials, they do not usually have sufficient time to become experts in these areas or even sufficient time to personally participate in time-consuming negotiations. Especially in larger cities, where there are numerous bargaining units, legislators do not have sufficient time to devote to negotiations.

An illustration of the difficulties encountered by legislators who seek to negotiate is provided by the experiences of Multnomah County (Portland), Oregon, where AFSCME was certified as the exclusive bargaining representative of most county employees in 1967. At first, the county commissioners insisted upon handling all negotiations themselves. They did not think it would be appropriate to delegate any authority for expending public funds to nonelected officials. They feared that the public would react adversely if it were thought that staff personnel were deciding how much to pay county employees and if taxes had to be increased as a result of negotiations. The commissioners wanted their constituency to know that they took budget matters seriously and were personally involved in all negotiations that could possibly affect the expenditure of county funds. Nevertheless, the county commissioners withdrew from direct negotiations after several weeks when they became convinced that they did not have the background or the knowledge to effectively represent the county. At almost every meeting, the commissioners had to delay the negotiations while they consulted on the various items submitted by the union.

Exceptions to the Rule

Perhaps the extreme case of an exception to the rule that authority for labor relations is being shifted from the legislative to the executive branch is Milwaukee. The key there, however, quite probably is that the city has a weak mayor form of government, and the city council has never lost control of labor relations. The finance committee of the council also serves as the labor relations committee, which in turn sets policy for the labor negotiator. The city of Milwaukee has strengthened the position of its labor negotiator by requiring a three-fourths vote of the city council to amend any agreement reached by the negotiator. This institutional requirement has significantly enhanced the ability of the city negotiator to speak effectively on behalf of the city and to make binding commitments in the negotiations. Another part of the explanation for the Milwaukee schema is that the city negotiator is a former councilman who is trusted by the current council members. While Milwaukee does not fit the normal pattern of cities with emerging bargaining, it is still typical in the sense that the enhancement of the position of the labor negotiator has resulted in a centralization of authority for labor relations.

The General Rule

The tendency of legislators to abandon rapidly any substantial participation in negotiations is occurring in most cities, and is probably desirable. Legislators, as elected officials, are often subject to political pressures from employee organizations and may be tempted to secure union support through the bargaining process. The "hero syndrome" is most serious in cities where organized labor is particularly strong. Legislators may vie with each other in an effort to be first with concessions to their labor friends: it is difficult to maintain a united front of legislators with diverse political interests. A legislator dependent upon labor support may actively support a union position at the bargaining table or may even divulge management's bargaining strategy to the union. It is unrealistic to expect that management will be able to speak with one voice when numerous independent legislators participate directly in these negotiations.

Another reason, previously mentioned, why it is generally desirable to assign responsibility to the executive branch is that even if the council could successfully negotiate a labor agreement, the executive branch would in all likelihood still be responsible for administering these agreements. There is some efficiency in having the contracts negotiated by the agency which will ultimately be responsible for administering them.

Delegation of Legislative Authority

In most cities, the executive branch is assuming the primary responsibility for both the negotiation and administration of labor contracts. But institutional or informal arrangements must be developed to ensure the effective delegation of authority from the legislative branch, which in pre-collective bargaining situations generally has legal authority to decide most personnel issues, to the chief negotiator, who is usually in the executive branch. The delegation problem has not been solved in most cities, but two mechanisms are worth noting: prior commitment of legislators through consultations, and the Connecticut solution, which eliminates the role of the legislature on some nonwage issues and imposes restrictions on its ratification powers in the balance of the nonwage issues and on budget issues.

The Philadelphia Solution

At a minimum, a labor negotiator will attempt to secure the commitment of legislators to a proposed contract by consulting with them in advance, perhaps even to the extent of accepting guidelines established by the legislators. The strategy improves communications between the executive and legislative branches and allows the legislators to participate in the determination of policy. In Philadelphia the management negotiators, all of whom were in the executive branch, conferred with representatives of the city council before each set of negotiations.

The attempt to involve the legislature in the negotiating process was not successful in Philadelphia, and most other cities in our sample have not attempted to institutionalize communication channels between the executive and legislative branches. In no large city in our sample, other than Philadelphia, have councilmen participated in the formulation of bargaining strategy. Chief executives, especially in strong mayor cities, are reluctant to share their negotiating authority with legislators, even if the latter participate only as advisors in policy formulation. Moreover, legislators are unwilling to bind themselves in advance in negotiations which they cannot control and the outcome of which may become a political liability. Therefore, legislators generally have not participated in the negotiating process when the primary responsibility for bargaining has been assigned to the executive branch, but rather have reserved the right to amend or reject agreements when they are submitted for ratification. This insures that the final outcome of negotiations will not be totally repugnant to the legislature, while granting the executive considerable latitude in the actual negotiations.

The Connecticut Solution

Connecticut state law vigorously supports executive authority and responsibility for labor relations. The ability of the local legislature to reverse decisions made by the chief executive has been greatly diminished. The 1965 state labor relations law assigns all responsibility for labor negotiations to the chief executive or his designee in every unit of local government. Additional provisions of law enhance the executive authority. For example, negotiated agreements ratified by the legislative body are binding, even if they modify existing rules or regulations of other governmental agencies, such as civil service commissions and police or fire commissions. Also, the legislative body can only review those provisions of a negotiated agreement which require funds for implementation or which conflict with an existing charter, ordinance, or regulation of the municipality or one of its agents or subsidiaries. Purely administrative items, such as union security, grievance procedures, and work rules, are not subject to a legislative veto. Furthermore, even if the legislature does reject a provision negotiated by the executive, it may only return the rejected agreement to the executive for further negotiations. The legislative body is prohibited from amending agreements or from participating directly in any negotiations. Management is assured that it will have only one spokesman. Finally, agreements submitted to the legislative body for approval are considered approved if the legislative body fails to approve or reject the agreement within 14 days.

No other state has yet followed the Connecticut precedent. In other areas, legislatures still actively participate in labor negotiations. The local legislatures in Detroit and Boston, for example, have not accepted any limitations on their authority to revise agreements negotiated under the auspices of their mayors. The problem of coordinating the roles of the executive and legislative branches, as the executive assumes primary responsibility for labor relations, has not yet been adequately resolved in most cities we surveyed.

Civil Service

As discussed in the first section, the theory of the civil service merit system is that public employees will be hired, fired, promoted, and paid on the basis of merit, and that this merit principle will be protected by a commission that is independent of the public employer.

Both the existence of the commission and the use of the merit principle are threatened by the emergence of collective bargaining. One reason for the attack on the commissions is that often they are not autonomous agencies, but agents of the employer. As Jerry Wurf, the President of AFSCME, has stated: "The role of the Civil Service Commission is not regarded by the workers as that of a third impartial party: to most of them, the Commission is felt to represent the employer." In varying degrees, most of the cities in our sample have civil service commissions dominated by management, and this lends credence to Wurf's charge. But truly independent civil service commissions are also under union assault, partially because, as discussed below, they are likely to protect the merit principle and also because their existence as a source of authority over personnel issues complicates the union's role. A theme of this paper has been the diffusion of authority for personnel issues in a typical city, and if the civil service commission can be eliminated as one source of authority, the union's negotiating task is simplified.

Union Attacks on the Merit Principle

The use of the merit principle is also under attack by unions. According to AFSCME:

> Unions of public employees see the Civil Service agency as a recruiting organ . . . Wages, hours, working conditions, rates of pay, fringe benefits, pensions—procedures for layoffs

where necessary, classifications, reclassifications, appeals in the discharges or disciplinary actions and on all other work matters—all must be handled as part of the contractual relationship between the employer and the union.

The AFSCME view would limit the merit principle to a narrow scope—the recruitment of new personnel—and for other personnel issues would replace the merit principle with other considerations, such as union membership or seniority. It would also end the adjudicative function of the civil service commission in grievances.

The potential impact of collective bargaining on the civil service merit system is best illustrated by recounting an example from our field work. The prerogatives of the Detroit Civil Service Commission have been largely eroded by collective bargaining. The authority of the commission is derived from the city's charter, and neither the mayor nor the common council has power to commit or bind the commission on issues within its jurisdiction. The charter, for example, establishes a civil service classification system and gives full authority to make changes in the classifications to the commission. The crucial issues in Detroit became whether the state labor relations act takes precedence over sections of the charter or whether the charter vests in the Detroit Civil Service Commission the exclusive authority to make unilateral determinations of some conditions of employment, such as classification and position allocations in the classified service. The commission maintained that authority over classification and position allocation determinations is within its exclusive jurisdiction. However, the Circuit Court of Wayne County ruled:

> The charter of the City of Detroit does no longer vest in the Detroit Civil Service Commission the exclusive authority to make classification and position allocations in the classified service of the City in view of PERA and the Master Labor Agreement of October 1967.
>
> . . . the mayor and the Common Council have the power and authority on matters of classification or position allocation to bind the Civil Service Commission through the orderly process of approving the results of collective bargaining and as such collective bargaining is finally reduced into written collective bargaining agreements.

As a result of this decision, the Detroit labor relations office is now able to negotiate on issues which previously were the sole responsibility of the Civil Service Commission. For example, most of the bargaining agreements in Detroit now specify lines of promotion and require competitive examinations limited to the departmental bargaining unit, or a smaller subdivision, before considering city-wide applicants.

The Eventual Status of Civil Service

In most political subdivisions, civil service has been delegated legal responsibility for many personnel issues and has administered a system of industrial jurisprudence which overlaps the potential jurisdiction of collective bargaining. But, as suggested above, the merit principle, administered by an independent civil service commission, is basically incompatible with collective bargaining. The possible consequences for management structure are: (1) collective bargaining will totally replace civil service commissions and the merit principle; (2) civil service commissions will become the bargaining agent for management in negotiations on issues under its control, thus clearly ending the notion that civil service is "neutral" and largely ending the use of the merit principle; or (3) civil service will retain its traditional unilateral authority, but over a limited scope of issues such as recruiting. Under the third option, civil service and collective bargaining are not totally incompatible. Yet, if civil service is to survive as an independent system, even in a truncated form, it probably will have to be given explicit protection in public policy not under the direct control of local collective bargaining. This will probably require that state legislatures define in stringent terms the authority of municipal and county civil service commissions and their relationship to management's collective bargaining agencies. Without such legal protection, civil service and the merit principle will probably not be able to survive the collective bargaining onslaught.

Summary and Conclusions

This paper undoubtedly overgeneralizes at several points and ignores important exceptions. But at the risk of being compared to the artisans who can write the Lord's Prayer on the head of a pin, let me attempt the ultimate distillation of my views. First, collective bargaining will shift authority for personnel issues to the executive branch at the expense of the legislative branch and the civil service system. Indeed, the civil service system seems doomed. Second, within the executive branch, authority for bargaining will be centralized and primary responsibility assigned to an individual or office directly responsible to the chief executive.

I have made clear my sympathy with the increasing responsibility of the executive branch, and for the centralization of authority within the executive branch. I find normative judgments about the loss of authority for the civil service merit system more troublesome. Writing a brief for the continued existence of a civil service commission dominated by city management would stretch my competence and conscience. Truly autonomous commissions, though rare, may be worth preserving as an independent check on management, employees, unions, et al. But this independence has now been criticized as a hindrance to "sound administrative practices," and for most public jurisdictions the delegation of personnel issues to "a personnel director appointed by, and accountable to, the chief executive" has been recommended by the National Civil Service League, the very organization that helped start the independent civil service commission movement in the nineteenth century.

The case for the merit principle is also debatable. In the private sector, collective bargaining has tempered merit (or ability) with such factors as seniority for many personnel decisions, including promotions and layoffs, and the dilution of the merit principle often has some advantages, such as providing greater job security to workers. Even now, the use of the merit principle for recruitment purposes is harder to embrace, now that the Supreme Court has discovered the vehicle for implementing merit recruitment in many firms as unvalidated personnel tests. Perhaps the most severe test of the continued wisdom of the merit principle is provided in the *Model Public Personnel Administration Law* recently released by the National Civil Service League. Section 1 stipulates that all appointments "shall be based on merit and fitness" without regard to "sex, race, religion or political affiliation." Section 3(9) urges preferential treatment for "members of disadvantaged groups, handicapped persons, and returning veterans." Even a lax constructionist is likely to have trouble reconciling these provisions, and yet the underlying sentiments are simultaneously endorsed by many in addition to the League. It is little wonder that the merit principle is plainly on the wane.

Bargaining and Budget Making in Illinois Public Institutions

Milton Derber   Ken Jennings
Ian McAndrew   Martin Wagner

The rapid rise of employee organization and collective bargaining in the public sector has raised a number of important new issues for public policy makers. One that has received little systematic study is the relationship between collective bargaining and the budget-making process. Existing rules and procedures on raising, allocating, and spending public funds were developed when public administrators, for the most part, exercised unilateral control over the terms and conditions of public employment. Collective bargaining introduces considerations that may not be entirely compatible with traditional budget-making practices.

Concern about the relationship between bargaining and budget making is reflected in a number of state laws on public employee collective bargaining. New York's Taylor Act, for example, initially provided that an impasse in bargaining would be deemed to exist if no agreement had been reached at least sixty days prior to the budget submission date. In Massachusetts, the parties must meet at reasonable times, "including meetings appropriately related to the budget-making process." With respect to municipalities, if no agreement has been reached by sixty days prior to the final date for setting the municipal budget, either party may initiate fact-finding procedures.

In Rhode Island, whenever negotiations involve money, the employee organization must give written notice requesting collective bargaining at least 120 days before the last day on which money can be appropriated by the municipal employer. In Nebraska, the law provides that any agreement with the state or one of its agencies shall cover a biennial period coinciding with the biennial budgeting period of the state. Similarly, in Wisconsin, although the municipal law is silent on the budget question, the 1972 statute governing state employee bargaining requires all agreements to coincide with the fiscal year or biennium. The relevant laws in Pennsylvania and Minnesota also tie together the bargaining and budget-making process.

These varied approaches suggest that research on the subject is desirable for both policy and theoretical considerations. Such research would have particular relevance for states, like Illinois, that have not yet adopted public employee bargaining legislation. A survey of the limited literature, study of the legal budgetary and revenue framework in Illinois, discussions with public administration specialists, and the experiences and observations of the authors identified the following pertinent questions:

1. Do statutory requirements for the submission and approval of budgets create timing problems for the bargaining process? What are the critical target dates for public-sector bargaining, and how do they correspond with budget or other fiscal dates? If the legal budget deadline date is reached without agreement, does the budgeting process allow for effective bargaining to a conclusion?

2. How much attention do public negotiators pay to the budget-making process? Are they adequately informed concerning the budget situation? Conversely,

Reprinted with permission from the *Industrial and Labor Relations Review*, Vol. 27, No. 1, October 1973.

to what extent are those responsible for budget making involved in negotiations? How much attention do budget makers pay to the bargaining process?
3. Does the requirement of public disclosure of budget items complicate or impair the collective-bargaining process? Does collective bargaining lead to overbudgeting or result in concealment techniques?
4. To what extent do employee organizations go outside the collective bargaining system to bring political pressures to bear on the bargaining-budget-making processes?
5. Do external agencies that provide funds affect or intervene in the bargaining process?

To obtain some answers to these and related questions, a field survey was undertaken of perceptions, norms, and opinions of practice in Illinois. The study was made through personal interviews and the collection of relevant documents, of a sample of thirty public institutions, chosen purposely (not on a random basis) to represent the major categories of public service, the various geographical sections of the state, and the main employee organizations. Six government entities (such as a department, agency, or school system) were selected in each of five categories—elementary and secondary schools, institutions of higher education (four junior colleges and two universities), municipalities, counties, and special districts. The size and composition of the employee units varied considerably. In the schools and junior colleges, the focus of the study was on academic personnel. In the universities, academic employee organizations did not have collective bargaining rights; therefore, inquiry was limited to those nonacademic personnel who were covered by bargaining agreements. In the municipalities, counties, and special districts, the coverage ranged from fairly comprehensive "industrial type" units of employees, to narrower occupational categories like nurses, fire fighters, police, and social workers. Management and union officials were interviewed at each entity. If more than one union existed in a category, an attempt was made to cover different types (e.g., within a municipality, both a "broad" union, such as that often found representing street department employees, and a "craft" union, such as those representing police or firemen). A total of fifty-five management and forty-one employee representatives were interviewed.

In many of the governmental entities studied, negotiations had a rather short history; some, however, went back over twenty years. This time difference may have affected practices and opinions. The situation was further complicated by the introduction of the national wage stabilization program while the study was being conducted. This factor was confusing to the parties but quite significant in negotiations. The data were gathered over a fifteen-month period from March 1971 through June 1972.

Budget and Fiscal Dates

The major concern of this study was to determine the relationship between the bargaining process and legal requirements for establishing fiscal years, the submission and adoption of budgets, and the raising of money by taxes, borrowing, and intergovernmental transfers. The legal requirements concerning these items are highly diversified. The Illinois School Code, for example, provides that the board of education in each district (other than Chicago) shall fix its own fiscal year. The tax levy must be filed by the fourth Tuesday of September, with an advertisement of the levy to be placed in the local newspaper no later than thirty days prior to this date. The annual budget must be adopted prior to the tax deadline.

In Chicago, at the time of this study, the fiscal year was fixed by statute on a calendar year basis. In 1972, after the study had been completed, the state legislature shifted the fiscal year to a September 1 starting date. The board of education must adopt a budget within the first sixty days of each fiscal year and make a tentative budget public at least ten days before final action is taken. The board is currently authorized to levy taxes in January of each fiscal year to support appropriations for the January through August period and in September to cover the remainder of the year.

The state universities have no statutory requirement regarding the submission of their budgets to the state Board of Higher Education or to the Bureau of the Budget. Schedules for the submission of budgetary data are determined by the agencies involved. They are guided, however, by a statutory provision that requires the governor to submit the state budget to the general assembly no later than the first Wednesday in March. The general assembly normally attempts to adopt legislation, including appropriation bills, before July 1 to take effect by October 1. A three-fifths vote of each house is necessary for a law to become effective on an earlier date. The university fiscal year starts on July 1; this coincides with the state fiscal year.

Municipalities are not required by law to fix budget submission or adoption dates, but they have the authority to adopt a budget ordinance if they so desire. The Illinois Municipal Code for cities under 500,000 (this includes all cities except Chicago) requires an appropriation ordinance to be adopted in the first quarter of the fiscal year. There is no requirement for a public hearing. Each municipality determines the beginning of its fiscal year.

The collective bargaining process may also be influenced by legal requirements for levying taxes, raising revenue by other forms (i.e., tuition and licensing fees), and borrowing. Any general relationship between these requirements and the bargaining process, however, is difficult to trace because of the complexities of revenue-raising laws, procedures, and practices.

Budget Making by Schools

Elementary and secondary schools, for example, depend on a mixture of local, state, and federal revenue. Each source of revenue is governed by separate legal rules and time schedules. About half of a school district's operating budget comes from local property taxes (the exact percentage varies because of such factors as federal aid programs that do not have a uniform impact). State law specifies that the school board must issue an annual property tax levy on or before the last Tuesday in September. The law also sets maximum rates for such local taxes, and if an increase in the existing rates beyond certain levels is necessary, a referendum must be held in the district to secure the approval of the local taxpayers. The timing of the referendum is at the discretion of the school board.

School district administrators generally have a fairly good idea of how much local property tax money will be available at existing rates when they are negotiating a new contract with the teachers. Occasionally, the legality of a tax may be challenged in the courts (as in the case of the personal property tax in 1972). This creates a situation of uncertainty. Uncertainty may also develop because of unexpected assessment and collection losses, such as the shutdown of some major businesses. More seriously, uncertainty may exist if the budget is dependent on the outcome of a referendum, since voters frequently turn down tax increase proposals. By and large, however, the fact that local tax increases must be approved by a certain date does not pose a bargaining problem in terms of timing. Funds are available from taxes spread over two years, and tax anticipation warrants are used to provide the necessary income flow throughout the year.

State allocations to the schools through the Common School Fund are administered by the Office of the State Superintendent of Public Instruction. They pose a greater element of uncertainty for the bargainers than property tax income, because they are outside the control of the school district. As noted previously, the fiscal year in Illinois starts on July 1. The legislature in regular session normally attempts to pass all appropriation bills by that date. Appropriations for education generally come late in the legislative term. The governor then has sixty days in which to veto or reduce a bill; the legislature in turn has thirty days to override any negative action by the governor. Even if the appropriation bill is accepted by the governor, the implementation of the law by the computation of a complex pupil attendance and equalization formula may take from two to six weeks. Since state funds average almost half of a district's budget, serious negotiations ordinarily cannot occur prior to the July 15 through August 15 period, unless the parties are prepared to act on the basis of the previous year's appropriation and equalization formula.

Federal funds for the schools may pose a further element of uncertainty, since congressional bills need not be adopted by any given time, and federal administrators may use varying schedules in formulating, changing, or applying distribution policies. With a few exceptions, however, school districts receive relatively small amounts of federal funds for operating purposes.

Budget Making by Municipalities

With the adoption of the 1970 state constitution, home rule came to most Illinois municipalities. At the time of this study, however, the communities had had little experience with home rule. The new constitution contains a variety of constraints on taxation and borrowing. It forbids home rule units to license for revenue, impose an income tax, or tax occupations without prior authorization. The general assembly may, by a three-fifths vote of each house, deny or limit the unit's power to tax; it may also limit the amount of debt that can be incurred and may require referendum approval of a debt to be financed from *ad valorem* property receipts in excess of specified percentages of assessed valuations. This study found no evidence that these constraints affected the collective bargaining process.

The allocations of state and federal funds to the municipalities, as in the case of the school districts, may affect the bargaining process because of the timing of legislative action and uncertainties about the amounts to be approved. Revenue sharing by the federal government was not in effect at the time of the study. This, however, may be a complicating factor in the future.

A somewhat more serious element of uncertainty for municipalities is the amount of money various taxes (particularly property and sales) will yield. The sales tax revenues, for example, depend upon unpredictable business conditions. To counteract this uncertainty, the municipality has the authority to amend the budget and make supplemental appropriations or raise additional taxes.

The interviews seemed to indicate that the parties had learned to live with the uncertainties described above since very few respondents expressed serious concern about the effect of these conditions on the bargaining process. In the case of the two universities, for example, it was understood that negotiations could not be completed until the struggle between the governor and the legislature over university appropriations had been resolved. School negotiations in Chicago were similarly perceived as contingent on the success of the mayor in raising additional revenues from local taxes and from state allocations.

Budget Making and Bargaining Time Schedules

Budget making and bargaining, therefore, follow many different time schedules in the public sector in Illinois. The schedules followed in each of the five governmental sectors investigated in this study will be summarized in this section.

Elementary and Secondary Schools

School districts (except for those in Chicago) followed a common budgetary schedule in 1971–72, the period of this study. The fiscal year started July 1; budget formulation began during the period of December-February; a tentative budget was made public in August; and the budget was formally adopted and taxes levied by the last Tuesday in September, in accordance with state law. In other words, the budget was formally adopted nearly three months after the start of the fiscal year. In Chicago, at the time of the survey, the budget was on a calendar rather than a school year basis. Budget formulation began in August; a tentative "planning budget" based on program categories rather than funds, was published in mid-October; a tentative annual budget was made public in early December; and the budget was adopted in January.

In a formal sense, the bargaining process was tied to one of the three target dates: the end of the fiscal year; the opening of the school; or the budget adoption–tax levy date. In four of the six districts investigated, contracts expired at the end of the fiscal year (June 30 for the "downstate" schools, December 31 for Chicago). In the other two school districts, the contract expiration dates were September 1 and September 30, respectively.

Bargaining settlements often deviated, however, from the contract expiration dates. Of the four contracts tied to the fiscal year, only one was renegotiated prior to its expiration date during the period of this study. One of the late downstate settlements came in mid-August (as the opening day of school approached); a second case occurred in November (after dismissal of the school superintendent); and the hard fought Chicago settlement did not come until February 17—six weeks after contract expiration. Budget adoption in Chicago was postponed by adjourning the budget adoption meeting until after contract settlement.

In negotiations involving the two non-fiscal year contracts, one settlement was achieved several months before the contract expiration date (in June, just before the new fiscal year and the beginning of summer vacation), and the second settlement was made in mid-September, shortly before budget adoption.

Higher Education

In the four junior or community colleges surveyed, the relationship between budgets and bargaining schedules was even more varied than in the elementary and secondary schools. Budget formulation began in September, November, and (in two cases) February; and final adoption occurred at the end of February, in early July, and in late September, respectively. The fiscal year in all four colleges began on July 1.

The contract expiration dates for these colleges were much more varied than they were for the schools. In one case, this date was linked to the fiscal year (June 30); in two cases to the start of the academic year (August 31); and in one case to the budget adoption date (February 28).

Contract settlement dates were equally varied. During the period of this study, two settlements were reached near the fiscal year date. A third settlement was reached two weeks after the fiscal year began but just before the date of budget adoption. The fourth was reached several weeks after the beginning of classes and after the budget had been adopted, but without any particular sense of pressure because funds on hand were adequate to cover the increases allowable under the wage stabilization program.

The two universities in the sample differed from the junior colleges in two respects: (1) bargaining in the universities was limited to certain nonacademic groups and therefore affected a relatively small portion of the budget, and (2) the bulk of the budget came from the state and depended on legislative and gubernatorial action instead of local property taxes. The universities began formulating their budgets in April, fifteen months before the beginning of the fiscal year (July 1). The budgets were adopted by the boards of trustees in October and formally submitted to the state board of higher education and to the state budget bureau in November. The state board of higher education submitted its recommendations to the governor early in January, the governor presented his budget to the legislature by early March, and the legislature completed action on appropriation bills late in June for gubernatorial approval, reduction, or veto. Contract negotiations with the numerous nonacademic unions typically began between April 1 and May 1, after the budget had been published and about three months prior to the expiration dates of the contracts which coincided with the end of the fiscal year. The final settlements were usually held up until after legislative action, and, if necessary, were made retroactive to July 1. In 1971, the settlements did not come until November, because the governor reduced the salary appropriation and a strong effort was made in the legislature to override his action.

Municipalities

Illinois municipalities are free to adopt their own fiscal years and budget submission and approval dates. As a result, a wide range of schedules was found. Fiscal years ended on December 31 in two cases, on April 30 in two cases, and on February 28 and March 31 in the remaining two cases. Budget adoption dates tended to be two or three months after the start of the respective fiscal years.

Contract expiration dates were tied to the fiscal year in four cases and to the budget adoption dates in two. In the first group, contract settlements preceded the fiscal year in three cases; in the fourth case, the settlement came just before budget adoption date. In the other two cases, the settlement was reached before the budget adoption date.

Counties

With one exception, the county fiscal years ended on November 30, and budget adoption was December 1 in four cases and January 1 in the fifth. The sixth county ended its fiscal year on August 31 and adopted its budget on September 15. Budget formulation started from two to five months before the adoption dates.

The contract expiration date coincided with the end of the fiscal year in four cases. In the other two, efforts to achieve a first agreement failed. Of the four contract cases, one settlement was reached shortly before the expiration date, and two were settled after both the fiscal year and budget adoption dates. Negotiations in the fourth case broke down and were not renewed after a strike and the jailing of a union leader. In one of the two post-budget settlements, the first contract was tied to the time of union recognition, and both sides agreed that later negotiations would be closely related to the fiscal year.

Special Districts

The six special districts in the sample (park, transit (two), sanitary, zoo, and hospital) ended their fiscal years on either December 31 or April 30. Budget adoption dates varied because, in some cases, the decision rested with a board of trustees and, in others, with a higher level of government such as the city or county. Typically, however, the budget was adopted by the special district either shortly before the end of the fiscal year or shortly thereafter; in one case, the budget adoption followed the beginning of the fiscal year by three months.

Contracts expired at the end of the fiscal year in three cases; in two cases, there were no formal contracts (merely an exchange of letters or a memorandum); the sixth case (a transit company) was complicated because of the transfer of ownership from the private to the public sector. In the first five cases, settlements came before the end of the fiscal year. In the sixth case, the settlement was concluded about three weeks after the arrival of the new transit manager and was unrelated to either the budget or fiscal year.

Conclusions on the Relations between Bargaining and Fiscal Dates

Three major conclusions may be drawn from this complex body of evidence;

1. Among the thirty bargaining relationships studied, by far the most common practice was to tie the contract starting and expiration dates to the fiscal year. This practice was found in twenty cases, which were distributed almost equally among the five agency categories. Of the remaining cases, three apparently tied the contract dates to the budget adoption date and three to the opening of school. In the four other cases, a total breakdown in negotiations or some other exceptional circumstances occurred.

2. Settlement dates frequently deviated from the contract expiration dates. Of the twenty cases in which the contract was tied to the fiscal year, only nine had settlements reached prior to or on the expiration dates. In the other eleven cases, ten settlements came after the contract expiration date, typically several weeks thereafter, and in the remaining case the relationship broke down after a strike and the jailing of the union leader, and no agreement was reached. Of the six cases in which contracts were apparently tied to either the budget or school opening dates, two were settled prior to the expiration date and four settlements came later.

3. The relationship of bargaining to fiscal law was highly flexible. In general, the legal dates designated for fiscal years, budget adoption, and tax levies did not serve as critical pressure points, although they often did offer target dates for the bargainers.

This looseness of the relationship between bargaining and budget making can be attributed to a variety of factors—the widespread use of the retroactivity principle, flexibility in the way public funds are raised, and the inevitable looseness of the budget-making process itself.

There seemed to be agreement among those interviewed that making settlements retroactive to the beginning of a new contract year was legally permissible, although it was not approved as a bargaining device by all of the management spokesmen. Of the fourteen cases in which agreements were not reached before contract expiration date, the retroactivity principle was used in eleven. Four of these situations occurred in higher education and three in the public schools.

Budget making, and in some respects the budgets themselves, also contained sufficient flexibility so that a settlement could be reached after the budget adoption date without creating a financial crisis. One device used to accomplish this was the adoption of the budget with an estimate of wage and salary increases. If the estimate proved to be too low, the additional money was provided by transfers within the budget's several "funds" (allowed in all but one case); by transfers between funds (allowed in sixteen cases—often with a requirement of subsequent repayment); by supplemental appropriations based on borrowing, higher taxes, or fees, or by external grants. Except for within-fund transfers, however, post-budget adoption transfers or appropriations required the approval of some legislative body, such as a municipal council, a county board, or the state legislature.

The question of overbudgeting or "padding" as a budget safeguard was raised. Whereas union representatives in nine cases and management representatives in twelve cases acknowledged that their agencies sometimes or regularly overbudgeted or kept special reserve accounts, only four unionists and two management officials asserted that it was done for bargaining purposes and only five management officials felt that it was a useful bargaining tactic. The general view was that "padding" could be readily detected by skillful negotiators and that if it did succeed on one occasion it would be less likely to succeed on the next.

Although this study has been mainly concerned with the relation of the budget-making process to the bargaining process, the impact of bargaining on budgeting also received attention. In a number of cases, for example, we were told that bargaining caused a delay or adjournment in budget adoption. This was notably the case in the large Chicago school and junior college negotiations. In a small number of other cases, the outcome of bargaining was so uncertain that it hampered the budget-making process. These incidents were, however, exceptions. In most cases, the cost of the bargaining package was relatively so small or could be estimated within such a narrow range that it posed no serious problems for the budget makers.

The Negotiators' Concern with the Budget

The second major area of concern in this study was the relationship of bargaining to the availability of funds projected in the budget. Did negotiators pay serious attention to the budget when they formulated economic demands and counterdemands, or did they ignore the budget on the assumption that bargaining takes priority, and the budget would be adjusted to the outcome of the bargaining?

The survey revealed that attitudes toward the budget varied strikingly between the union and management representatives. Virtually none of the union representatives gave serious consideration to the budget when formulating their initial demands. Their position was typically that the union's task was to press for fair and appropriate wages and conditions and that it was up to the management to find the necessary funds. In other words, they argued that public employees should not be expected to subsidize public activities by substandard or inferior terms. As one union official commented, "The budget does not mean too much to me—if we based our bargaining demands on the budget, we would never get any money. The union is never cognizant as to the amount (in the budget) because there is never enough money. We are aware of the dire need for money and campaign politically (to obtain additional funds), but when we go into negotiations we don't discuss the budgetary problems." In contrast, the management representatives at about half the agencies reported that they based their initial responses to union demands on budgetary or financial grounds. They contended that only so much money was available and that the public would not support additional taxes or charges. In nine of the remaining cases, it appeared as if the budget determined the outside limits of management's position, but their bargaining position was actually based on other grounds such as the rise in consumer prices, prevailing rates, or practice in comparable occupations. Increases for these items could often be covered within the budget boundaries, but sometimes the inability-to-pay argument was also introduced.

Attitudes toward the importance of the budget as a bargaining factor were partially reflected in the composition of the agency bargaining team. In fifteen cases, the team included an officer who had a major responsibility for the preparation of the budget, such as the city controller, the business manager for a school, the budget director, the finance committee chairman, the vice chancellor for financial affairs, the auditor, or the general accountant. In most of the other cases, these officers were not at the bargaining table but were consulted by the bargainers informally. In some of the smaller units, elected officials handled both bargaining and budget making.

The elected (or in some cases appointed) officials who comprised the local legislative units, such as school boards, city councils, county boards, and the governing boards of special districts, and who were therefore responsible for budget adoption, participated on bargaining teams more frequently than expected. In five cases (a junior college, two municipalities, and two counties), they constituted the entire management bargaining team. In thirteen other cases, one or more legislators were on the bargaining team, notably in all six of the public schools, in the municipalities, and in the counties. In the last category, the finance or personnel committee often negotiated for the governmental unit. In six other cases, a mayor or board chairman was chief negotiator.

Views on the desirability of legislative representation in the bargaining process were mixed. About half of the union respondents favored having legislative representatives on the management team at the bargaining table. Union representatives holding this opinion were rather evenly distributed among the five governmental categories. An equal proportion of the management respondents agreed with this view. They came mainly from the public schools (four), the municipalities (three), and the counties (five). Only seven of the unionists thought legislative representation was undesirable —these were scattered throughout the governmental categories. On the other hand, fourteen of the management representatives were opposed to the presence of legislative officials. These management representatives came notably from higher education (five) and the special districts (four).

One school administrator indicated having some school board members at the bargaining table probably added credibility to the management team, increased the board's understanding of the negotiations, and alleviated an earlier problem in which the administrative negotiators found themselves "negotiating in two directions." The disadvantage which the administrator found somewhat more compelling was that the chief negotiator had trouble limiting board members to a secondary position on the negotiating team.

Another school administrator also saw advantages and disadvantages to having board members at the bargaining table but felt that, on balance, the advantages justified inclusion of board members. The disadvantages were (1) they tended to give away management prerogatives and (2) they were not familiar with the collective bargaining process and did not really understand the impact on the educational process of the issues being negotiated.

One city manager indicated that the city council did not have the time or knowledge to participate in negotiations. On the other hand, the mayor and budget director of another city felt that the chairman of the finance committee served as an important liaison to the rest of the council and made the chief negotiator's role easier.

From the union standpoint, the chief advantage of having legislative representatives at the bargaining table was their responsibility for final decision making. Those who were opposed to or dubious of the idea based their feelings on a preference for dealing with full time professional negotiators.

Availability of Fiscal Information

Union sensitivities to the budget were reflected at least in part in the amount of budgetary information that unions sought and obtained. When the question was asked whether employee representatives requested budgetary information, both sides responded affirmatively in fourteen cases and negatively in ten cases. In the remaining six cases, there was either a division of opinion (four cases) or only one side offered a view (two cases); in all six cases, management maintained that union representatives did not request such information. Of the fourteen affirmative cases, six involved the public schools and three involved higher education, whereas in the negative response group, there was less concentration of cases in any single category. The explanation for this pattern seems to lie in the fact that in public schools the bargaining unit accounts for a large segment of the budget, whereas in most of the other cases, bargaining covers only small or fragmented units and has relatively little impact on the total budget.

Union officials almost always obtained the budgetary information they requested for bargaining purposes. In only four cases did they express any dissatisfaction on this point. In all of the cases, they received the desired information from management, although in ten cases, the same information was available to the general public as well. In a few cases, notably in schools or junior colleges, some union representatives were involved in the budget making process and therefore had direct access to budget information. In five cases, budget information was also obtained through legislative channels. In providing information, management usually distinguished between official data and materials informally assembled for the preparation of proposals. The latter were not ordinarily given to the unions.

How carefully was the budget information scrutinized? Only one union reported an examination in detail, sixteen stated that they made only a general examination, eleven ignored the budget data and two did not respond to the question. A large majority of union officials were skeptical about both the validity of the budget statistics and the tactic of using budget statistics to make a case for their demands. One union representative summarized these reservations in the following statement: "We don't like to get into the box of proving they (management representatives) don't have money. It is a waste of time to go digging into budget figures. Sometimes when we proved they had the money they said it was being used for something else; or they would simply say 'you're wrong.' "

External Political Pressures

One of the main differences between private sector and public sector bargaining is that in the private sector the bargainers usually have clear and direct ties to their principals and one group can rarely appeal around or over the heads of the other group's negotiators to their principals with any expectation of success. In the public sector, the possibility of an "end run" is much greater, because the principals on management's side are often elected officials who are susceptible to political pressure or persuasion. Sometimes they have been elected through the support of the employee organization; on occasion they may even be members of the organization. The "end run" may be particularly important when the bargaining significantly affects the budget. One teacher representative rated extra-bargaining procedures as more important than table talk. He characterized school board members as "very political" people for whom the board is often a stepping stone to further political office and who therefore will often support the union's position in return for future political support from organized labor.

When those interviewed were asked whether employee organizations went outside of the collective bargaining relationship during negotiations to influence the bargain and possibly the budget, the answer from both management and union was "yes" in fifteen of the thirty cases. In ten cases both said "no," although in two of these cases, exceptions were noted. In four of the remaining five cases, the union said that it had gone outside the negotiations, but management did not confirm this contention. One union spokesman frankly observed that most members of a county board were sympathetic to the union and that the union "lobbied" with board members even prior to negotiations. Another unionist reported that his organization tried to persuade individual council members to influence the mayor who was conducting negotiations. A third considered lobbying "essential" because of the political nature of the employer. Clearly political pressure is an important ingredient of the bargaining process.

Sometimes the appeal was to the general public rather than directly to the politicians. Informational picketing by firemen is an example. On the other hand, few of either the union or management respondents wanted to open their bargaining sessions to the public. The general belief was that the public would represent an "outside interference" that would only "complicate and disrupt collective bargaining procedures." Only three union and three management respondents (in five cases) favored open sessions, hoping to influence public opinion and to expose the weakness of the other side's position; only two groups (not among the five) had tried open negotiations.

The use of political pressures *after* negotiations were concluded was apparently much less common. Five management and two union representatives (in six cases) reported such actions, but in two of these cases the union denied the allegation. Post-negotiation pressure was sometimes attempted in order to obtain more funds from higher-level government agencies in order to finance the new agreement.

Finally, external pressure might arise from the fact that most local units of government depend upon external sources of revenue to help meet budgetary needs. These external funds come particularly from state and federal agencies and often amount to 20 to 50 percent of the total budget. Generally, they are restricted to specific types of expenditures. In no case, however, did the respondents indicate the conditions attached to these funds had any significant impact on the bargaining process, although, on five occasions, the mayor of Chicago was asked to use his influence by "mediating" a dispute.

Policy Implications

The Illinois experiences described in this article occurred without any legislative guidelines. They suggest, however, that guidelines on the relation between bargaining and budgeting need consideration.

Bargaining and budget making have their own dynamics as instruments of decision making, yet neither can ignore the other, since each is influenced by and has an effect on the other. Fortunately, they are both highly flexible processes that can be adjusted if they do not initially mesh. Retroactivity and supplemental negotiations provide flexibility for the bargaining process; transfer of funds, short-term borrowing, and supplemental appropriations do the same for the budget-making process.

It can be argued that bargaining and budget-making patterns are so variable that no single legislative rule is desirable or feasible and that "nature should take its course," as it appears to be doing in Illinois. On the other hand, there is much to be said for a general system of order—not one that is too rigid or constraining, but one that will assist the parties in planning and conducting their affairs in an efficient and harmonious manner. Budget making was developed to improve fiscal management and accountability in public enterprise. Bargaining is justified not only as a device to promote the interests of public employees but also as a basis for the improvement of the public service. To the degree that legislation would reduce uncertainties, both processes would be facilitated.

If collective bargaining agreements are tied to the fiscal year of a governmental unit (as the predominant practice appears to be in Illinois), bargaining and budget making schedules have a common target date. It will not always be possible to meet this date because of the many sources of conflict in both the bargaining and political processes, but the flexibility devices mentioned earlier can cope with deviations from the rule. Impasse procedures can then be related to the contract expiration date as is the customary practice in the private sector under the Taft-Hartley Act. In those situations in which the pressure point in bargaining has tended to differ from the fiscal year (most notably in some of the school and community colleges in which the school starting date often is the cutting edge in negotiations), consideration should be given to shifting the date of the beginning of the fiscal year so that it coincides with the pressure point date.

Finally, it should be emphasized that collective bargaining was a relatively new process in most of the cases studied. It will be interesting to see whether close ties develop between bargaining and critical budgeting dates as these new relationships become stabilized.

Reflections on the Future of Bargaining in the Public Sector

E. Wight Bakke

The appropriateness of collective bargaining in the public sector of the sort and style developed in the private sector has been both asserted and denied thoughtfully, eloquently, and even passionately by knowledgeable partisans and presumably unbiased neutrals.

Today, as a result, it can be said that the basis for the right of public employees to negotiate collectively their terms of work through representatives of their own choosing has been thoroughly explored, and on the whole that right has been accepted although not by all public employers and even some public employees.

But we are a long way from being certain about how to handle the following problems in the public sector: the appropriate bargaining unit; the practicality of exclusive bargaining representation; compulsory union membership; the need for a Public Employee Relations Board to judge and enforce sanctions on either public employers or unions which refuse to bargain in good faith or commit unfair labor practices; the determination of the scope of bargainable, in relation to mandated, issues; the integration of the use and applicability of political and economic power simultaneously; the relation of the bargaining timetable to budget submission dates; the kinds of impasse-breaking procedures that have a chance to succeed; the right of public employees to strike; the rights of the public to uninterrupted essential services; and the possibility of coupling coercive practices with professional ethics. All these have been subject to research and lively debate.

Based upon the consensus that is developing in some areas and the uncertainties remaining in others, it seems to me that seven trends can be identified in the evolution of collective bargaining in the public sector. In brief, here is what appears to lie ahead.

Unionization in the public sector is going to increase rapidly and extensively.

Union action in the foreseeable future is going to be militant.

The achievement of collective power is going to become the major objective of union leaders for a considerable time.

The combination of political and economic bargaining strategies and tactics will disturb for some time the pattern of collective bargaining between public management and public employee unions and associations.

The civil service concept of personnel policy and arrangements is going to suffer and be severely modified.

The public is going to pay a big price for what the public employees gain.

Despite this, nothing is going to stop the introduction and spread of collective bargaining in the public sector.

Growth of Unionism

The first prediction is probably the least controversial: Unionization in the public sector will increase rapidly and extensively.

All the conditions and circumstances that have made employees ready for collective bargaining in sectors where it has been established are present in the employment

Reprinted from the *Monthly Labor Review,* July 1970, pp. 21–25.

relations of a critical mass of public employees. The predisposition to organization and collective bargaining becomes manifest under the following conditions:

Common Standards. When a group of individual employees work under, and must be provided with, approximately the same pay, benefits, hours, and conditions of work, it is impossible for the individual employee, or employer for that matter, to make any substantial modifications for individuals which departs from the common rule. This is not the result of a demand for equality or of bureaucratic rigidity, but of operating necessity. The implication is that standards and rules applicable to the whole group should be negotiated by the group rather than by the individual.

Absence of Individual Bargaining Power. Where an individual's unique or outstanding skill or individual worth to the employer is difficult for the employer to replace, that individual normally will rely on his own personal bargaining power. When the group of employees have (or have the opportunity to demonstrate) few unique qualities, where within reasonable limits one is replaceable by others, this individual bargaining power does not exist to the same degree. The implication is that a lack of individual bargaining power can be compensated for by group bargaining power maintaining a solid and united front.

Social Products. Where the goods or service produced are social products in the sense that no one employee's contribution produces the whole, it is difficult to disentangle for personal evaluation the value of any employee's contribution to the total process.

Impersonality of Relations. When the organization is large enough so that there are several strata of supervision between the employee and the decision-making employer, the problem is to find and get to the employer. The implication is that many persons cannot do this individually, but it can be done by collectively forcusing their search and dealings in an organizational representative.

Employers as an Organized Group. When the employer is in reality another group of organized employees (or agents) called "management," the implication is that an organized group is needed to deal with them. In the case of a school system, the school superintendent and the school board constitute an organized group of employees of the public.

Group Concerns and Personal Complaints. When an effort is made to present effectively the human and professional interests shared by the whole group, some person has to speak up. Lacking the support of an organized group, that person is likely to be a trouble maker, an agitator, disloyal, and other terms scarcely designed to increase that person's job security. The implication is that organized group support for a group spokesman is essential to provide that spokesman with a regularized role that does not damage his personal security.

Performance Results Dependent on Management. When the product of the individuals in the group is greatly dependent on the policies, decisions, resource supplies, and so on, controlled by management, such common dependency can best be dealt with through collective representation designed to make managerial action advantageous to good performance results by the group.

Community of Interest. There is a basis for a community of interest among teachers and many other public employees. Identification arises through common skills and standards of performance, similarity in type and extent of training and in status in the eyes of the community, and the dependence of individual status on the status of the group as a whole. Where there is this community of interest, the other bases for collectively organized representation are reinforced. If the community of interest is exaggerated by the commonly experienced sense of being left behind by more privileged groups, or being as a group taken for granted, the predisposition is increased.

All of these factors apply to large numbers of public employees; not to all of them, but enough to provide large numbers who are ready to listen to the appeal of the union organizer.

Increased Militancy

My second prediction, that unionism in the public sector in the foreseeable future is going to be militant, is based on the following observations:

1. In spite of the Federal and State executive orders and laws nominally giving the right to organize and bargain and providing mechanisms for recognition, half of the States have not taken that step and three absolutely forbid it. Even where the right to bargain is recognized, many public managers have not wholeheartedly accepted their responsibility to recognize those rights and to engage in realistic collective bargaining leading to mutual consent. Even where they have done so, they are often babes in the woods when it comes to dealing with unions and sharing their decision-making power with union leaders supported by mass solidarity. Union leaders are also going to be inept for some time in adapting the only pattern of bargaining they are familiar with—that which has been developed in the private sector—to the peculiarities and necessities of industrial relations in the public sector. Ineptness and inexperience are certain to produce militant attitudes on both sides. Even as they gain experience, the confusion over how far public employers can go and still meet their governing obligations and their ultimate responsibility to the public is going to produce puzzling uncertainties as stubbornness, arbitrariness, and buckpassing that can only be met by a show of strength.

2. Added to these volatile factors is the situation of jurisdictional conflict between different unions, and between the traditional trade unions and so-called professional associations, particularly in the educational field where nearly one-half of the public employees are concentrated. The impact of this factor will be less if election procedures are quickly established. Even so, the competition for acceptance of one union or association over another is likely to cause the leaders of those organizations to demonstrate their militancy as proof to prospective members that they have most to gain by expressing their preference for the union that will really stand up to management. Associations like the National Education Association and civil service associations have already begun to adopt coercive tactics to prove themselves as they compete for members with the more traditional type of unions.

3. Direct action and coercive mass pressure, once thought to be a tactic used only by laboring people and communists, is becoming an acceptable approach to upper middle-class people who cannot realize their desires by the use of orthodox methods. Following the civil rights movement and welfare clients, taxpayers, landlords, students, teachers, and even priests are learning the utility of mass pressure as a way of getting action on demands that formerly got lost in bureaucratic buckpassing and red tape. The social atmosphere is charged with militancy. If the revolt of women gains momentum, it will be another important factor. Over half of public servants are women.

4. The use of the strike by public servants is not going to be legitimized, but the strike or some other form of reduction or withdrawal of services having the same impact is going to be used extensively nevertheless. Declarations of union leaders

equating collective bargaining with negotiations against a strike deadline make that clear. The record of successes by public employees who have resorted to strikes encourages confidence that, notwithstanding its illegality, it is a method that gets results.

I happen to believe that impasse procedures and mechanisms, once they are perfected and generally available, will reduce that development. The adoption by all states of a guarantee of the right to organize and provisions for employee participation through collective bargaining in setting the terms of public employment will reduce the chances of strikes. If we were to have public enforcement on both public employee unions and public employers of a duty to bargain in good faith on a mutually predetermined set of bargainable issues, there would be fewer occasions when public employees would have some justification for their perception that strikes are the only way to get action.

Achieving Collective Power

The third prediction is that the dominant objective of union leaders for some time will be the achievement of collective power. That objective will compete successfully with their efforts to adapt the private sector pattern of union activities to the requirements of effective public administration and to improve the professional status of their members. For example, union leaders' proposals for the determination of the appropriate unit for collective bargaining will be the one that is most strategically favorable to the immediate opportunity to organize rather than one that is geared to meeting the requirements of effective public administration. Groups of employees that appear ready for organization will be defended as an appropriate unit. The result may well be a fractionalization of bargaining units without reference to their community of interest with other public employees or without reference to efficient administration of public services and equitable allocation of public resources.

The definition of the appropriate bargaining unit of employees with respect to whose terms of employment a government executive is expected to negotiate affects his administrative tasks in many ways: the number of employee organizations with which he must deal; the problem of giving equitable treatment to all the employees under his management; and the variety of negotiating results that must be integrated into a pattern of employment terms so that they make budgetary sense for the whole unit of government. It also affects the scope of bargainable issues, for some of the terms of employment must necessarily be the same for all employees in the political unit rather than peculiar to a particular group. It contributes to chances that negotiated terms for one group will result in a sense of injustice or inequity in another.

This is not to criticize unions for pushing for a definition of the appropriate unit that is most likely to facilitate organizing. I am only indicating that the immediate problem in accumulating power for public employee unions is to increase the number of groups they can get organized; that *this* power objective at this time, and for some time in the future, is going to be most immediately satisfied by defining as an appropriate unit any group apparently amenable to organization, regardless of whether the resulting pattern of bargaining units makes sense in the effective administration of public industrial relations. One strategy for the accumulation of union power is the development of group solidarity by means of substituting the common rule for the merit system of rewards. The merit system is intended to result in the professional advancement and transfer and the maintenance of professional standards among those public employees to which the term professional accurately applies. This expected result may be more fancy than fact, and the system may not be perceived by employees as worthy of preservation or even improvement so as to achieve the result. Public employee unions to date have shown very little inclination to modify their approach to solidarity via the common rule approach so that an improved merit system would have a chance of success.

Another example is rooted in the previous prediction that militant direct action including the strike will be a continuing instrument of power for public employee unions. Those who participate in such direct action are not going to improve their public image as dedicated professionals. Their experience and perception of the degree to which their public employers accord them this status now may be such that this result may appear to be no loss. Unions' efforts to improve professional status will have to be great to overcome the loss of status in the public mind by those who gain personally by withholding essential services from the public.

Combined Strategies

The fourth prediction was that the combination of political and economic bargaining strategies by unions in the public sector will produce a confusing pattern of collective bargaining interactions. It will be similar to a situation in private industry in which the union could go around management and make deals with the board of directors representing the stockholders, and union members had an important voice in electing the board of directors.

There will be an uneasy relationship between the administrative managers of public agencies and the elected legislative and executive officials to whom they are responsible and upon whom they depend for support in the pursuit of their professional interests. The labor movement, particularly in local and State situations, can and often does play an important part in the election process. The working class vote can make a difference in elections. When the union, which is ostensibly bargaining with the management and administrators, bypasses them in the hope of getting a better deal directly with city hall or the statehouse, a serious modification of collective bargaining as developed in the private sector occurs. The management administrators can find their efforts at reaching a settlement shortcircuited.

Collective bargaining as it is defined by practice in the private sector does not involve back-door deals with the board of directors, and directors are not elected either by union members and their allies in the labor movement or by the ultimate consumers of their services or goods. Collective bargaining in the private sector assumes the existence of two relatively independent parties, the management and the workers represented by their union, trying to accommodate their differences and satisfy their respective interests through negotiation and administration of a contract.

Civil Service Changes

The fifth prediction dealt with modification of the civil service concept. It may be adjustable to collective bargaining, but it could also be destroyed. The question of what will happen to the civil service system is a serious one. The divergence between ordering industrial relations by a civil service commission administering legislative mandates and by collective bargaining is clear. We are already seeing signs of incompatibility. The civil service approach assumes a uniform set of terms of employment for a large number of functional groups of classified employees. Selection, performance standards, salary grades, tenure, promotion and transfer arrangements, grievance procedures, and so on, now apply across the board to employees of numerous agencies. Under collective bargaining, each organized group bargains for and in the interest of its own members. It cannot be expected that any uniformity in terms will be achieved. Leapfrogging would become a serious possibility.

The civil service approach, however, has been unilaterally determined ultimately by legislative mandates and detailed commission regulations. It conflicts, therefore, with the principle represented by collective bargaining, involving authoritative participation by employees in determining the conditions of and payment for their work. There will be an uneasy effort to maintain both approaches for a time by eliminating mandated items from bargaining, and by making the bargaining units as comprehensive as possible.

The Price to Pay

The sixth prediction is that the public will pay a big price for what the public employees gain through collective bargaining. This is not to say that the price is unjust or that the results are not worth it. But the public interest is going to play second fiddle for a time to serving partisan and sectoral interests.

The most obvious price is that tax burdens will increase. No one is going to be able to argue, as some economists have concerning unionism in the private sector, that the unions only negotiate costly improvements in the economic welfare of their members, which workers would have received anyway due to increasing productivity and competition for workers in a free market. And the price for administering a system of industrial relations that includes collective bargaining is not likely to decrease government costs per unit of service unless unions promote some form of union-management cooperation which does not yet appear on the horizon.

Another cost is rooted in the predisposition to militancy. The interruption in the flow of public goods and services is going to be costly not only in public inconvenience, but in the cost of substitute services and goods. When the latter cannot be had, as will usually be the case, the disturbance to the normal operations of income-producing enterprise for individuals and organizations will add costs that are far from hidden.

Collective bargaining is coming into the public sector before it has developed an adequate concern for the public interest in the private sector save as that interest is served by improvement in the conditions of life and work of union members directly and all workers indirectly.

My seventh prediction is an outgrowth of the others. Nothing is likely to be able to stop the spread of collective bargaining in the public sector. There can be no doubt that, should the foregoing predictions materialize, the task of devising a bargaining system which protects and advances the interests of public employees and makes possible the effective administration of public services will be difficult. It will challenge the best efforts of employee organizations, of public employers, of legislators, of judges, and of those who from time to time are called on to serve as mediators, fact-finders, and arbitrators. But individually or collectively, the developments named cannot prevent the extension of employee organization in the public sector to the point where collective bargaining replaces unilateralism as the pattern of industrial relations.

It is always possible that in the light of the obvious and inescapable impact of industrial relations in public employment on the whole public that a pattern of collective bargaining in the public sector will be developed by public employers, public union leaders, and public employees, which reveals a higher standard of public responsibility than that previously attained by any section of the labor movement.

Work
Stoppages

Is the Strike Outmoded?

Theodore W. Kheel

When a major strike threatens to disrupt an important service, a sense of hopelessness often pervades the public. Publicity about the impasse sometimes tends also to make our entire system of industrial relations appear chaotic. The public wants to know, why can't these disputes be prevented? If the parties themselves cannot agree, why shouldn't they be told what to do? Why can't we have a law that prevents these disruptions?

Well, we have a law. Indeed we have many laws. Labor-management relations in this country are subject to a system of laws, regulating what can and cannot be done, as extensive as any in the free world. This body of laws has developed over a course of two centuries. It is built to some extent on English common and statutory law, but it is uniquely American. It has developed mainly into its present form during the past 40 years.

The strike that annoys the public is not a quixotic uprising. Almost invariably it has been preceded by months of intensive negotiation under ground rules set by the National Labor Relations Act. Under the act, the company and the union are directed to bargain in good faith. They are told to file their demands in advance of the onset of negotiations. They are required to invoke the assistance of Federal or State mediators when needed.

We like to stress that collective bargaining is a free process. It *is* a form of self-government, but it is no more free in the sense that the parties can do as they please than the process we call "free" private enterprise. But within the parameters set by law it is a process of voluntary decision making that has evolved over many years. The dividing line between management prerogatives and union concerns is still evolving. It is an effective process because it encourages companies and unions to govern themselves. It is sometimes viewed superficially as the means by which one side or the other strives to get the most possible from the other side. But it is a process of shared decision making by the parties most directly affected by the decisions. The alternatives

Reprinted from the *Monthly Labor Review,* September 1973, pp. 35–37.

are decision making by one side alone or decisions imposed by a third party, both unsatisfactory alternatives.

Collective bargaining is a group relationship conducted through representatives. The latter, in turn, must report to their principals. Because unions usually report to a larger group than employers, their reporting problems frequently are more difficult. Union rules generally provide that strikes be authorized in advance. Settlements almost invariably must be submitted to the rank and file for ratification. This sometimes bogs down the decision-making process.

Despite the difficulties that flow from the lapses that flesh is heir to, collective bargaining is a highly disciplined process, conducted against a background of rules that generally are honored. The strike itself is part of the discipline. It makes collective bargaining work by inducing decisions on differences that otherwise might drag on interminably.

Although labor always has claimed the right to strike as its most precious possession, it is not an absolute right. With the development of rules and practices for collective bargaining have come important restrictions on the strike, and these generally affect the bargaining process, sometimes adversely. Strikes or lockouts threatening railroad or airline disputes that the President believes might create emergencies can be enjoined pending study by a board to make findings and issue recommendations. Major strikes in any other industry threatening public health or safety can be enjoined for 80 days. Strikes by public workers are generally prohibited, although some modifications are being introduced by State legislatures as the interrelationship of the strike and collective bargaining becomes better understood and the States decide to encourage bargaining. There are other restrictions, but these do not seriously affect the main arena of collective bargaining. (For example, secondary boycotts are prohibited. Jurisdictional strikes can be prevented and the competing claims decided by the National Labor Relations Board. Arbitrators can enjoin strikes in violation of an agreement.)

At first, the right to strike was essential to labor and it was claimed as its most treasured possession in the battle for recognition, fought from the onset of the industrial revolution through the passage of the Wagner Act, which guaranteed workers the right to organize and to be represented by a union of their own choice. As a product of this history, the right to strike for recognition has now been relegated to a minor role.

But with procedures enabling unions to win recognition came the right to bargain collectively, and the right to strike was then viewed as essential to the bargaining process. The National Labor Relations Board can command an employer to bargain collectively but cannot order him to accept specific terms. Without the right to strike, labor could not, in its judgment, secure a fair settlement.

One of the most interesting things about collective bargaining—even if not fully recognized—is that the employer has as much a right to bargain collectively as the union. Collective bargaining is a two-way street. It's just as much a right of management as it is of labor. One important point frequently overlooked is that the Taft-Hartley law (Labor Management Relations Law of 1947) provided specifically that employers have a right to bargain with unions and that unions have an obligation to bargain with employers, just as the earlier National Labor Relations Act gave unions—employees through unions—the right to bargain collectively with their employers. From this derives, I believe, a corollary right of employers to the union's right to strike: the right to take a strike. Absent that right, the employer can be denied the right to disagree.

When people write about their labor relations, they often bracket the strike with the lockout. In one instance the work relationships are terminated by the action of the employees, in the other by the employer. I don't believe they are correctly put in juxtaposition to each other. If there is an impasse in the decision-making process, what then? If the one side is satisfied with the status quo, that side obviously is not going to precipitate an end to the working relationship. Consequently, if the union wants to change the status quo, it is the one that may, in the absense of agreement, disrupt the relationship through a strike. That is the usual though not the invariable situation. There are instances—many during the depression years—where the employer wishes to change the working relationship and the union won't go along. To do this he imposes a lockout. Where the initiative for a change in the status quo comes from the union, the employer's right in balance is the right to *take* a strike. On the other side, it is the union's right to take a lockout.

So, from its origin in the battle for recognition, the strike (and lockout) have now assumed indispensable roles in the bargaining process. In my judgment, the prospect of a strike in the vast majority of bargaining situations can never be outmoded, unaccepted, outlawed, or rendered obsolete without doing more damage to collective bargaining than the relief the public would supposedly get. The strike and collective bargaining are Siamese twins. They cannot be severed. But that does not mean that strikes cannot be avoided. It does not mean that the bargaining process cannot be improved. It does not mean that the parties cannot voluntarily accept arbitration with carefully designed limitations as an alternative to the prospect of a strike. But the essential point of departure is a proper understanding of the role of the strike in collective bargaining and the importance of the bargaining process in a democratic society.

When we think of alternatives, we tend only to think of them in terms of how the union will react to compulsory arbitration, to fact finding with recommendations, to labor courts or what have you, when in fact the employer is equally affected by the consequences. If you deny the employer the right to take a strike, you are likewise taking away from him his power of decision making in the bargaining process.

This leads me to a conclusion. It is a philosophy expressed in a poster promulgated by the International Association of Machinists some years ago, that there is no alternative to collective bargaining in a free society. When we think of the problems, particularly of strikes that inconvenience the public (and the parties!), we know that strikes are not a right that gives satisfaction in the way that the right to free speech does. It is a right to preserve a right, and the right to be preserved is the right to bargain collectively.

Thus we come to what I think is the essential challenge faced in private and public employment: How can we make the bargaining process better? It is a difficult question. You cannot answer it by saying, "People should be more decent toward each other and do the right thing." But there are many things that can be done. Some have been done by law. The bargaining process which is free in most industries in connection with decisions on wages, hours, and working conditions is far from free in its structuring or even in its execution in all industries. So as alternatives to the strike are considered, I think most of us would answer "no" to our main question: "Is the strike outmoded?" Our focus, instead, must be on "How do we make the bargaining process work better?"

Basic Steel's Experimental Negotiating Agreement

I. W. Abel

The Steelworker's and the 10 major steel companies have agreed to an unprecedented experiment in collective bargaining. The new bargaining procedure is officially known as the Experimental Negotiating Agreement.

We are excited about it. We regard it as a historic breakthrough on the collective bargaining front. It's called an experimental agreement because we are going to test the usefulness of this approach in our bargaining talks in 1974 when the present 3-year agreement expires. Both sides are committed to the procedure only for the 1974 negotiations. If it works to the satisfaction of both sides—and we hope it does—we will continue to utilize it. If it proves unsuccessful, then it's back to the drawing boards. But I am convinced it will work.

This is what the new negotiating plan does: it provides certain guaranteed preliminary benefits for our members in the Basic Steel Industry; it protects certain existing employee benefits and rights; it allows the parties to negotiate freely in almost all economic fringe benefit areas; it safeguards certain management rights; it eliminates the possibility of a nationwide strike or lockout in the steel industry; and it provides for voluntary arbitration of any unresolved bargaining issues.

This new approach did not come about with any suddenness. In fact, it is something that the founder and first president of our union envisioned about 33 years ago. At that time, Philip Murray co-authored a book on the evolution of relations between management and unions called *Organized Labor and Production.* As both sides become more nearly equal in bargaining power, he predicted, they will "either wage war to gain the spoils of production restriction and scarcity prices, or they will together devise improved production practices that increase social income."

There's no doubt that we've done our share of waging war with the Basic Steel Industry over the years. Those of us still around have the scars to prove it. Sometimes the fighting amounted to little skirmishes, but at other times the future of the union and the industry was on the line. But after our shoot-outs and bargaining hassles down through the years, conditions began to change and problems of mutual concern began to emerge.

In the late 1950s, foreign steel producers started to make inroads on the U.S. domestic market. The 116-day strike in 1959—the last one incidentally—provided foreign steelmakers an initial opportunity to acquire and cultivate American customers. That was when our problems started to build up each time we went to the bargaining table. During our negotiating periods, the market was being glutted with more and more imported steel, while the industry kept stepping up production to satisfy the stockpiling steel customers undertook as a hedge against a possible strike.

The stockpiling had its impact not only on our bargaining and on our successes at the bargaining table, but it also had a tremendous impact on the ups and downs of production and employment.

This resulted in a "feast and famine" or "boom-bust" treadmill for our members in the Basic Steel Industry. Most steelworkers enjoyed steady work and many worked

Reprinted from the *Monthly Labor Review,* September 1973, pp. 39–42. The 1974 negotiations in the steel industry were concluded without resort to the procedures described in this article. The bargaining parties, however, have expressed interest in the Experimental Negotiating Agreement for future negotiations.

overtime just prior to the negotiating periods and during the negotiating period. But then came the peaceful settlements, the working off of stockpiles, partial plant shutdowns, and prolonged layoffs.

The Experimental Negotiating Agreement was approved overwhelmingly by the Union's 600-member Basic Steel Industry Conference on March 29 of this year (1973) and was signed a few days later by officials of the 10 major steel firms. In a joint union-industry statement following installation of the new procedure, we made this comment:

> Both parties feel sure that the action taken today will assure the Nation and steel customers a constant supply of steel and an end to the "boom-bust" cycles associated with past labor contract negotiations. . . . The new agreement not only provides for additional wages and benefits for employees, but it also provides an opportunity for the companies to increase production through stability of operations and enhance the steel industry's competitive position.

The new agreement applies only to the 10 companies that bargain together as the Coordinating Committee Steel Companies: Allegheny Ludlum, Armco, Bethlehem, Inland, Jones & Laughlin, National, Republic, U.S. Steel, Wheeling-Pittsburgh, and Youngstown Sheet and Tube.

Here are the major elements of our Experimental Negotiating Agreement:

Our members employed by the 10 companies—some 350,000 workers—will be guaranteed wage increases of at least 3 percent each year of the 3-year agreement; on August 1 in each of the years 1974, 1975, and 1976. I want to emphasize that these are guaranteed minimums that do not prevent us from seeking greater pay increases in the negotiations. The wage increases of 3 percent in each of the three years of the agreement will also be included in the incentive wage calculation scales.

Also, each of our members having employee status as of August 1, 1974, will receive a one-time bonus of $150. The companies agreed to pay this amount in recognition of the production savings they anticipate from avoiding the effects of stockpiling. This one item will mean a payout by the 10 companies to our members in excess of $50 million.

The Experimental Negotiating Agreement assures that the cost-of-living clause we won in 1971 will continue to operate through 1977. There will be no floor and no ceiling on the amount of cost-of-living adjustments that can become payable through the life of the new agreement.

Also, there are certain fundamental safeguards in our existing collective bargaining agreements that each side wants to protect and preserve. These pertain to local working conditions or past practices, the union shop and checkoff provisions, the no-strike and no-lockout provisions, and the management rights provision.

Under the new procedure there will be one bargaining procedure to resolve national issues and another to resolve local issues. On the national level, both sides will start talks no later than February 1 of next year. If an agreement is not reached by April 15, either party can submit their unresolved bargaining issues to an Impartial Arbitration Panel which will have authority to render a final and binding decision on such issues. This arbitration panel will be made up of one union representative, one representative of the companies, and three impartial arbitrators selected by both sides. At least two of the three arbitrators to be chosen by both sides will be persons thoroughly familiar with collective bargaining agreements in the steel industry. This panel will hear any disputes during May 1974 and must render its decision no later than July 10,

1974. The balance of July will be available for implementation of the Panel's award. The renewal date for the Basic Steel Agreement is August 1 of next year.

On local issues, for the first time in the union's history, we have established a separate right to strike over such issues. At the same time, the companies will have the right to decide upon a lockout on local issues at the plant level. We believe—and so does the industry—that if such local plant strikes or lockouts do materialize, there will be little likelihood of any significant disruption of domestic steel production.

Support among our Basic Steel members for the new procedure has not been unanimous. It has been overwhelming, but not unanimous. Some of our opposition is based on a sincere concern over third party influence and impact on our negotiations. And some is based on an unwarranted fear that the union will be powerless to negotiate effectively without a big club.

A review of early union experience and an examination of our bargaining disputes with the steel industry will show that our collective bargaining historically has been subject to third-party influence and impact, as far back as 1937, in the days of the Steel Workers Organizing Committee, the forerunner of the United Steelworkers of America. Inland Steel and the Steel Workers Organizing Committee, for example, reached agreement that year in the office of the Governor of Indiana, after the company recognized the Committee as the workers' collective bargaining agent.

During the years of World War II, the Steelworkers received a number of beneficial awards from the National War Labor Board, including wage increases, union security, improved vacations, and rate adjustments. In 1949, after negotiations based on recommendations of a Presidential fact-finding board, we won a trailblazing noncontributory pension plan with a minimum payment of $100 a month, plus social security, for employees with 25 years of service, also hospital and surgical care benefits. In 1959, the date of our last strike in Basic Steel, intervention by third parties in that rather bitter 116-day strike was credited with convincing the industry to soften its hard-headed position and settle with the union. The third parties at that time were the then Vice President, Richard M. Nixon, and Secretary of Labor, James P. Mitchell. In 1965, when our negotiations were completely deadlocked, President Johnson invited—if that is the correct word—both sides to Washington. And just to make sure that we came, he sent his own plane to get us there. He then put both sides under virtual house arrest in the Executive Office Building next to the White House, saw that meals were not too appetizing, and engaged in some arm twisting as only he could do. As a result, we wound up with an excellent settlement, including the first general pay increase in many years, and with major benefit gains on pensions and in other areas.

And in 1968, we got hung up over incentive pay coverage and finally turned the matter over to a voluntary arbitration panel for final and binding disposition. The end result, in 1969, was a decision directing the major steel companies to provide incentive pay opportunities to at least 85 percent of their total production and maintenance work force and to at least 65 percent at each plant. The decision extended incentive pay coverage to almost an additional 50,000 of our members employed by the 11 largest steel firms.

I am convinced that the agreement will work. First, the industry and the union have agreed to try this experimental approach on a one-time basis. The parties know that if the experiment fails, there may never be another chance to establish a long period of industrial peace in the industry. We realize that failure this time could lead to a long, disastrous strike 3 years later. I believe that these realities will be uppermost in the minds of both company and union negotiators as they meet next year. And it will put on all of us a degree of pressure that we may never have felt before—if the parties sincerely seek a long-range, stabilized labor-management relationship, and I think we do.

Also, it is only natural for both sides to prefer a settlement shaped by themselves, and not by a third party. The parties themselves know the problems best and they also know what solutions will work best. A third party dictating the terms of a settlement might not be aware of technical problems that may, unwittingly, stem from an imposed settlement.

The need to formulate contract conditions that are workable and acceptable to both sides will serve as additional pressure to resolve issues independent of the arbitration machinery that has been established. In fact, I predict that chances are reasonably good that an entire agreement on national issues could be negotiated without submitting anything to the arbitration panel. This, certainly, will be the objective of the union.

Another positive factor in the 1974 negotiations is the fact that local unions will have the right to strike over local issues, which have always been a festering sore in our negotiations, and which often produced demoralizing reactions from our members—even when we negotiated good national economic terms. Since local unions, in 1974, will for the first time have the right to strike over local issues, we expect speedier resolution of major issues and more effective bargaining on local issues. Faced with the genuine possibility of a strike locally—however limited—the companies will have reason to bargain out such issues promptly in negotiations. This should help produce a more satisfactory settlement. The right to strike over local issues is an essential ingredient of the experimental procedure, and the plan could not succeed without it.

The preliminary "sacred cow" concessions are also a vital part of the new procedure that will help insure its success. The initial wage increases of 3 percent in each year of the 3-year contract, the $150 bonus, and retention of the union security, cost-of-living, and local working conditions clauses demonstrate to our members that the companies are acting in good faith.

They also demonstrate to our members that the companies really want a settlement based on equity and are willing to back up that desire with a down payment, so to speak, even before contract negotiations begin. This will help put at ease any fears that management is out to weaken or undermine the union, or that the industry is seeking a cheap, cut-rate settlement, and it creates the type of climate for bargaining that will lead to success. The preliminary concessions are, of course, another integral part of the experimental agreement and no approach to strikeless bargaining could have taken place without them.

There is an additional factor motivating both sides to reach a prompt, peaceful, and trouble-free settlement: the import threat. The experimental procedure was designed to mitigate crisis bargaining and reduce steel imports that always thrive during steel negotiations. Since the union and the industry acknowledged the import threat by agreeing to the new procedure, it is only logical that both sides will want to protect themselves further against steel imports by making the new bargaining approach work.

We believe this unprecedented experiment will prove that there is a better way for labor and management to negotiate contracts. The new procedure will not only relieve both sides of the pressures of a potential shutdown, but also offers us a genuine opportunity to achieve results equal to those obtainable when the threat of a strike exists. We have carefully preserved the nature and role of our bargaining relationship. What we have done is to extend and refine the tools of collective bargaining to solve a special and highly vexing problem afflicting our industry. Fourteen years of uninterrupted industrial peace in the steel industry have gradually established the maturity and respect for each other that justified this sort of an advanced step in our collective bargaining relationship.

Public Sector Strikes—Legislative and Court Treatment

Jerome T. Barrett   *Ira B. Lobel*

Historically, public policy toward public sector work stoppages was typified by Franklin D. Roosevelt's feeling that they were "unthinkable" and Calvin Coolidge's thought that they were a form of "anarchy." That attitude persisted into the 1960s despite the number of public sector collective bargaining relationships which had been established and the occurrence of some work stoppages. In the mid-1960s, it would be accurate to say that public policy in all States clearly prohibited work stoppages of public employees by statute, court decision, or attorney's general opinion.

The Federal Government's policy toward work stoppages by its employees has been spelled out in section 19(b)(4) of Executive Order 11491, which makes it an unfair labor practice for a public employee labor organization to "call" or engage in a strike, work stoppage, or slowdown, to picket an agency in a labor-management dispute, or to condone any such activity by failing to take affirmative action to stop it. Just as explicit is 5 USC section 7311(3) which provides, "An individual may not . . . hold a position in the Government of the United States . . . if he . . . participates in a strike . . . against the Government of the United States. . . ."

Some Federal courts have enjoined U.S. employees from striking, and in *Postal Clerks* v. *Blount,* [1] a Federal district court rejected the union's argument that an absolute prohibition of strikes by such employees was a denial of their First Amendment rights and equal protection of the law. These rights could not be denied, simply because they do not exist, the court said.

With a few highly publicized exceptions in the last several years, the absolute ban on work stoppages of Federal employees has been respected by employee organizations. The same condition does not prevail in State and local governments today. In 1960, 36 public sector strikes resulted in 58,400 man-days lost, compared with 412 work stoppages in 1970 involving a man-day loss of 2,023,000. [2]

Because of the growing unwillingness of public employees to continue the tradition of respecting the public policy prohibiting work stoppages, some State legislatures and courts have begun to adjust public policy regarding such stoppages. This article summarizes these changes.

Reprinted from the *Monthly Labor Review,* September 1974, pp. 19–22.

Legislative Actions

Most of the States have established public policy through legislation which prohibits work stoppages. In 1967, the Vermont legislature became the first to give public employees a limited right to engage in a legal strike. Since that action, Montana, Pennsylvania, Hawaii, Alaska, Minnesota, and Oregon have enacted legislation allowing a limited opportunity for legal strikes by certain types of public employees.

The Vermont enactment of 1967 gave all municipal employees, except teachers, the right to strike so long as there was no danger to health, safety, or welfare. Not even policemen or firemen were denied this right. A 1973 amendment to the law established three conditions for a legal strike: 30 days must elapse after the delivery of a fact-finding report to the parties; the dispute must not be one subject to final and binding arbitration or must not have been ruled upon by an arbitrator; and the strike must not endanger the public health, safety, or welfare. [3] In 1969, the State's legislature extended the right to strike to teachers, provided the stoppage does not present a clear and present danger to a "sound program of school education." The law instructs courts considering a strike injunction to enjoin only those specific acts expressly found to impose a clear and present danger. [4] That same year, the Montana legislature passed a law giving nurses in public and private health care facilities a limited right to strike when two conditions are met: the union has given the employer a 30-day written notice of its intention to strike, and no other work stoppage is in effect in another health care facility within a 150-mile radius. [5]

The two most highly publicized laws allowing public employees work stoppages were passed in 1970 in Hawaii and Pennsylvania. The Hawaii law, covering all public employees, provides a limited right to strike when these conditions are met: there must be no danger to the public health or safety; the employees involved must be in a unit certified by the Public Employment Relations Board; the unit must not be one where arbitration is required to resolve interest disputes; the parties must have exhausted in good faith mediation and fact-finding efforts to resolve the dispute; if an unfair practice exists, the parties must have exhausted all proceedings under the statute; 60 days must have elapsed since the fact-finding report was made public; and the union must file a 10-day written notice of its intent to engage in a work stoppage. [6] The statute authorizes the Hawaii Public Employment Relations Board to decide whether these prerequisites have been met. The Board is also authorized to set requirements to avoid or remove imminent or present dangers found in a situation which may lead to a work stoppage.

The Pennsylvania statute covers all public employees except policemen, firemen, prison and mental hospital guards, and court employees. [7] The statute establishes two principal requirements which must be met if the work stoppage is to be legal: the parties must have exhausted all mediation and fact-finding requirements, and the stoppage must not endanger public health, safety, or welfare. [8] The law also provides that an unfair labor practice does not constitute a defense for an otherwise illegal strike, and that strikers may not be paid for the period of their strike.

The Alaska statute, passed in 1972, allows strikes but makes them contingent on the essentiality of the employees' functions. Employees are divided into three groups. [9] The first group, which includes police and fire protection employees, guards in prisons and other correctional institutions, and hospital employees, are absolutely prohibited from engaging in a work stoppage. Bargaining impasses for these employees must be submitted to arbitration. For the second group of employees, which includes employees of public utilities and those engaged in sanitation, snow removal, and public school teaching, a work stoppage is legal if it does not threaten health, safety, or welfare, the parties have utilized mediation, and a majority vote of the employees has supported the stoppage. In applying the law, the court must consider "total equities"—the effect of the strike and the extent to which the parties met statutory obligations—and, if it enjoins such a strike, it may direct arbitration of the issues in dispute.

All other employees may engage in work stoppages, provided a secret ballot election has been conducted. The statute refers to this category as "those services in which work stoppages may be sustained for extended periods without serious effect on the public."

In 1973, the legislatures of Minnesota and Oregon passed laws which dealt with the right to strike. The Minnesota statute, covering all public employees, does not legalize strikes but provides that the failure of a public employer to utilize arbitration in an interest dispute with "nonessential" employees may result in the court's refusal to enjoin their strike if it does not create a clear and present danger to the public health or safety. An employer's refusal to use arbitration may either be a refusal to request arbitration or a failure to comply with an arbitration award. In either case, the union representing nonessential employees may use the employer's refusal as a defense against enjoinment of a strike. [10]

The new Oregon law allows strikes by all employees in the State except policemen, firemen, and guards at the correctional or mental institutions. Impasses for the employees denied the right to strike are resolved by binding arbitration. [11] For all other employees, the statute provides certain criteria which must be met before a strike would be legal: a 30-day period must elapse after the fact-finder's report has been made public; a 10-day strike notice must be given by the union stating the reasons for a strike; and there must be an absence of a threat of a clear and present danger to the public health, safety, or welfare. An unfair labor practice does not constitute a defense against an otherwise illegal work stoppage. If a work stoppage is enjoined by the court, arbitration of the dispute is required to begin within 10 days.

In addition to the above studies with statutes clearly allowing strikes in certain situations, there are several states whose laws may be interpreted as granting their employees a limited right to strike. Massachusetts, for example, prohibits strikes by public employees, but its Labor Relations Commission has the authority to determine "whether a strike occurs." It may institute appropriate proceedings in court when a violation of the strike prohibition takes place. It seems clear that the initiative for enforcement of the strike ban rests with the Commission, not the courts, and that the Commission has discretion in seeking injunctions against an illegal strike. [12]

Montana's statute, covering all employees other than nurses and teachers, makes no mention of strikes. However, the rights section of that statute, in a language similar to that found in the Taft-Hartley Act, gives employees the right to engage in concerted activity. A State district court has recently interpreted the act as granting employees the right to strike. [14] In Idaho, the statute for firefighters provides that "upon consummation and during the term of the written contract or agreement, no firefighter shall strike. . . . " [15] It is not certain what the rights of firefighters are after the agreement has expired.

Judicial Action

Despite this legislative process in the matter of strikes, it is still clear that public employee work stoppages are prohibited in the vast majority of states. Typically, the courts in those states are asked to enjoin the work stoppage and impose the penalties where the statute provides for penalties. Of course, it is interesting to note that one of the major reasons for the enactment of the New York State Taylor Law in 1967[16] was that the severe strike penalties of the Condon-Walden Act had proved both unenforceable and unworkable. At least one state, South Dakota, has recently decreased strike penalties, while the laws of several others, such as Massachusetts and Wisconsin, simply do not mention strike penalties.

Several court decisions in recent years have indicated that, in the future, the availability of injunctive relief during a public employee strike may be reduced.[17]

One possible approach of State courts to this question is to apply anti-injunction statutes to public employees. These laws, which are similar to the Federal Norris-LaGuardia Act, are found in 26 States. In 1973, an appellate court of Illinois, in *City of Pana* v. *Crowe,*[18] held that the State's anti-injunction statute prohibited the issuance of an injunction against a strike of municipal workers despite an allegation of interference with the operation of the city's water, sewer, street, and police departments. The court found that the concern for public health, safety, and welfare was insufficient to override the mandate of the anti-injunction statute. Although the case was overturned by the Illinois Supreme Court in May 1974, this interpretation may be applied in other States.

Another approach was used by the Supreme Court of Michigan in *Holland School District* v. *Holland Education Association.*[19] The court found that the State's Hutchison Act, which prohibits public employee strikes, was constitutional, but the mere illegality of the stoppage could not compel a court of equity to issue an injunction in "every instance." The criteria for the court to enjoin a strike is "a showing of violence, irreparable injury, or breach of peace." The court also reasoned that public employer, to obtain an injunction, would have to enter the court with "clean hands," i.e., having bargained in good faith, free of having committed unfair labor practices, having exhausted impasse procedures, and not being viewed as having unduly provoked the strike. The result is that in Michigan, in spite of a clear statutory prohibition against strikes, the actual practice differs little from those of the States which grant a limited right to strike.

In 1973, the Supreme Court of Rhode Island[20] became the first State court to apply the principles enunciated in the *Holland* case. The court reasoned that while the statutory ban on public employee strikes was valid and constitutional, "every time there is a concerted work stoppage by employees, it should not be subject to an automatic restraining order." Relying on the reasoning in *Holland,* the court embraced the irreparable harm standard and held, "we must concede that the mere failure of a public school system to begin its school year on the appointed day cannot be classified as a catastrophic event. We are also aware that there has been no public furor when schools are closed for inclement weather, or on the day a presidential candidate comes to town, or when the basketball team wins a championship."

The New Hampshire Supreme Court[21] recently used a similar rationale in denying an injunction against an illegal strike of teachers in the absence of a showing of irreparable harm. The Court noted that the parties had not exhausted the possibilities of finding compromise in the collective bargaining process. . . .

In several other States, it is clear that there has been a reluctance to apply vigorously the letter of the law in imposing penalties. . . .

Thus, in the last 5 years, a number of States have become receptive to the concept of legalized public employee strikes, as indicated by their legislative actions or the decisions of their courts. Whether legislatures will continue to move toward eliminating prohibitions against work stoppages, and whether the courts will continue to limit injunctions of strikes is anyone's guess. However, one recent decision created doubt about the effectiveness of legislative liberalization on the strike question. In the *Ross* v. *Sullivan* case,[24] involving the 1973 Philadelphia teachers' strike, the court found that the increased threat of gang warfare, the additional cost of beefing up police patrols, and the threat to continued State funding of education were, in fact, a sufficient threat to health, safety, and welfare of the public to justify an injunction against the strike despite the presence of the legal right to strike. The decision has caused concern as to whether a legislative thrust toward relaxing the strike prohibition will really make any difference.

NOTES

1. 325 F Supp 879 (D–DC 1971). See *Monthly Labor Review,* July 1971, pp. 60–61; aff. 404 US 802 (1971).

2. See *Work Stoppages, 1958–68,* Report 348 (Bureau of Labor Statistics, 1970); and BLS Report 1727, 1972.

3. Vermont Municipal Labor Relations Act, U.S.A., Title 21, Chap. 20, L. 1973, Act III, eff. 7/1/73, Sec. 1370.

4. Labor Relations for Teachers, U.S.A., Title 16, Chap. 57, L. 1969, No. 127, Sec. 2010.

5. Revised Codes of Montana, Secs. 41–2201, L. 1969.

6. Hawaii Revised Statutes, Chap. 89, Laws of 1970, Chap. 171.

7. Police and Firemen are covered by Penn. Stat. Annot., Title 43, L. 1968, No. 111, which provides for final and binding arbitration of disputes. Chap. 19, No. 195 (footnote 9) prohibits strikes for guards and court employees.

8. Pennsylvania Stat. Annot., Chap. 19, L. 1970, No. 195, Sec. 1101.1103.

9. Alaska Statutes, Title 23, Chap. 40, L. 1972, Chap. 94.

10. Minnesota Statutes, Secs. 179.61–179.76. L. 1971, Chap. 33.

11. Oregon Revised Statutes, Secs. 243.711–243.795 as last amended, L. 1973, Chap. 536, Sec. 17–18.

12. Massachusetts Statutes, L. 1973, Chap. 1078, Secs. 2–2–B, 4–8, Sec. 9–A.

13. Montana Stat., L. 1973, Chap. 441.

14. 561 Government Employee Relations Report, July 1, 1974, B–2.

15. Idaho Code, Sec. 44–1801–1811, L. 1970, Chap. 138.

16. New York State Civil Service Law, Secs. 200–214, L. 1967, Chap. 392.

17. See *Peoria* v. *Benedict,* 47 Ill 2d 166 (1970).

18. 519 Government Employee Relations Reports B–4, 1973.

19. 151 NW 2d 206 (1966).

20. *Westerly* v. *Teachers Association,* 491 Government Employee Relations Report E–1, 1973.

21. 550 Government Employee Relations Report B–19, April 15, 1974.

22. 436 P 24273, C8 Cal 2d 137 (1968).

23. *City of Troy* v. *Uniformed Firefighters Association,* 2 NYS Public Employment Relations Board 3077 (1969).

24. 493 Government Employee Relations Report F–1, 1973.

Public Employee Strikes and the Political Process

Harry H. Wellington   *Ralph K. Winter, Jr.*

Although the market does not discipline the union in the public sector to the extent that it does in the private, the paradigm case, nevertheless, would seem to be consistent with what Robert A. Dahl has called the " 'normal' American political process," which is "one in which there is a high probability that an active and legitimate group in the population can make itself heard effectively at some crucial stage in the process of decision," for the union may be seen as little more than "an active and legitimate group in the population." With elections in the background to perform, as Mr. Dahl tells us, "the critical role . . . in maximizing political equality and popular sovereignty," all seems well, at least theoretically, with collective bargaining and public employment.

But there is trouble even in the house of theory if collective bargaining in the public sector means what it does in the private. The trouble is that if unions are able to withhold labor—to strike—as well as to employ the usual methods of political pressure, they may possess a disproportionate share of effective power in the process of decision. Collective bargaining would then be so effective a pressure as to skew the results of the " 'normal' American political process."

One should straightway make plain that the strike issue is not *simply* the essentiality of public services as contrasted with services or products produced in the private sector. This is only half the issue and in the past the half truth has beclouded analysis. The services performed by a private transit authority are neither more nor less essential to the public than those that would be performed if the transit authority were owned by a municipality. A railroad or a dock strike may be much more damaging to a community than "job action" by teachers. This is not to say that governmental services are not essential. They are, both because the demand for them is inelastic and because their disruption may seriously injure a city's economy and occasionally the physical welfare of its citizens. Nevertheless, essentiality of governmental services is only a necessary part of, rather than a complete answer to the question: What is wrong with strikes in public employment?

What is wrong with strikes in public employment is that because they disrupt essential services, a large part of the mayor's political constituency will press for a quick end to the strike with little concern for the cost of settlement. The problem is that because market restraints are attenuated and because public employee strikes cause inconvenience to voters, such strikes too often succeed. Since other interest groups with conflicting claims on municipal government do not, as a general proposition, have anything approaching the effectiveness of this union technique—or at least cannot maintain this relative degree of power over the long run—they are put at a significant competitive disadvantage in the political process. Where this is the case, it must be said that the political process has been radically altered. And because of the deceptive simplicity of the analogy to collective bargaining in the private sector, the alteration may take place without anyone realizing what has happened.

This selection is taken from the article, "The Limits of Collective Bargaining in Public Employment." Reprinted by permission of The Yale Law Journal Company and Fred B. Rothman & Company from *The Yale Law Journal,* Vo. 78, pp. 1123–27.

Therefore, while the purpose and effect of strikes by public employees may seem in the beginning merely designed to establish collective bargaining or to "catch up" with wages and fringe benefits in the private sector, in the long run strikes must be seen as a means to redistribute income, or, put another way, to gain a subsidy for union members, not through the employment of the usual types of political pressure, but through the employment of what might appropriately be called political force.

As is often the case when one generalizes, this picture may be thought to be over-drawn. In order to refine analysis, it will be helpful to distinguish between strikes that occur over monetary issues and strikes involving nonmonetary issues. The generalized picture sketched above is essentially valid as to the former. Because there is usually no substitute for governmental services, the citizen-consumer faced with a strike of teachers, or garbage men, or social workers is likely to be seriously inconvenienced. This in turn places enormous pressure on the mayor, who is apt to find it difficult to look at the long-run balance sheet of the municipality. Most citizens are directly affected by a strike of sanitation workers. Few, however, can decipher a municipal budget or trace the relationship between today's labor settlement and next year's increase in the mill rate. Thus, in the typical case the impact of a settlement is less visible—or can more often be concealed—than the impact of a disruption of services. Moreover, the cost of settlement may be borne by a constituency much larger—the whole state or nation—than that represented by the mayor. It follows that the mayor will look to the electorate which is clamoring for a settlement, and in these circum-stances, the union's fear of a long strike, a major check on its power in the private sector, is not a consideration. In the face of all these factors other interest groups with priorities different from the union's are apt to be much less successful in their pursuit of scarce tax dollars than is the union with power to withhold services.

With respect to strikes over non-monetary issues—decentralization of the gover-nance of schools might be an example—the intensity of concern on the part of well-organized interest groups opposed to the union's position would support the mayor in his resistance to union demands. But even here, if union rank-and-file back their leadership, the pressures for settlement from the general public, which may be largely indifferent as to the underlying issue, would in time become irresistible.

Sovereignty and Delegation Revisited

As applied to public employment, there is a concept of sovereignty entitled to count as a reason for making strikes by public employees illegal. For what sovereignty should mean in this field is not the location of ultimate authority—on that the critics are dead right—but the right of government, through its laws, to ensure the survival of the " 'normal' American political process." As hard as it may be for some to accept, strikes by public employees may, as a long run proposition, threaten that process.

Moreover, it is our view—although this would seem to be much less clear—that the public stake in some issues makes it appropriate for government either not to have to bargain with its employees on these issues at all or to follow bargaining procedures radically different from those of the private sector. It is in this respect that the judicial doctrine of illegal delegation of power should have relevance.

Consider, for example, the question of a public review board for police; or, for that matter, the question of school decentralization. These issues, viewed by the unions involved primarily as questions of job security, engage the interest of so many dis-parate groups in a relevant population, that it may be thought unfair to allow one group—the police, the teachers—to exert pressure through collective bargaining (quite apart from the strike) in which competing groups do not directly participate as well through the channels (e.g., lobbying) open to other interest groups.

Our hesitation in this area is caused by two factors. First, models of the political process have trouble with fine-grained distinctions about too much power. Given the vulnerability of most municipal employers, one can say with some confidence that the strike imparts too much power to an interest group only because the distinction addressed there is not fine-grained at all. Second, it is difficult indeed for any governmental institution to make judgments about the issues that should be included in the non-bargainable class. The courts are badly suited to this task; and the legislature is not well constituted to come in after the fact and effect a change. Nevertheless, limits will have to be set or bargaining procedures radically altered, and this will in a sense be giving content to the doctrine of delegation as it bears upon the subject of public employment.

While there is increasing advocacy for expanding the scope of bargaining in public employment and in favor of giving public employees the right to strike—advocacy not just by unionists but by disinterested experts as well—the law generally limits the scope of bargaining and forbids strikes. This is often done with little attention to supporting reasons. Ours has been an attempt to supply these reasons and thereby to give some legitimate content to sovereignty and delegation.

We do not, however, mean to suggest that legislatures should abdicate to the courts the task of constructing a new system of collective bargaining for the public sector through the elaboration of sovereignty and delegation. Legislation is needed, for the problems we have explored require solutions beyond the power of the courts to fashion. In the future, if strikes are to be barred, sophisticated impasse procedures must be established. If, on the other hand, some strikes are to be tolerated, changes in the political structure which will make the municipal employer less vulnerable to work stoppages must be developed. And, in any event, legislative action will be necessary either to separate out those non-monetary issues which might not be decided solely through collective bargaining, or to change bargaining procedures so that all interested groups may participate in the resolution of such issues.

Why Teachers Need the Right to Strike

Albert L. Shanker

Instead of talking about alternatives to strikes, we ought to be talking about *trying* to strike in the public sector. It has not been tried. In the private sector, we have paid a price for strikes. We have paid a price for the process of collective bargaining, because the only alternative is an unfree society—and the price that we pay for strikes is one that we are generally willing to pay.

Reprinted from the *Monthly Labor Review,* September 1973, pp. 48–51.

Collective bargaining has never been sold as an ideal answer to anything, but it is the lesser of a number of evils that exist in the private sector and, in a somewhat modified form, in the public sector. Management and labor have to go through some sort of messy process to find a way of agreeing with each other for a period of time, and the only alternatives are unilateral determination by management—which leads to exploitation—or arbitration which leads to the imposition by a third party of his views.

There are some differences in the public sector, but these are not adequate justification to abolish or modify the bargaining process. The notion, constantly stated, that in the public sector there is no profit motive is in a sense true. But in a sense it is irrelevant, because there is no question that the public employee bargains just as hard, if not harder, than the private employee.

The question of being reelected, the fear of being accused of throwing away public money—"giving it away" to public employees—and also the very fact that he is involved in a public activity in many ways makes it more difficult for public management to bargain than for private management. No one fought a tougher battle against labor unions than philanthropists who were involved in donating their own time as managers in hospitals in the City of New York. They spent many hours in getting many billions of dollars to see to it that these hospitals could be made viable. But when it comes to providing an effective union for employees earning $24 to $25 a week, they felt that those employees should donate their time too, since the philanthropists were. This happens frequently in public sector management.

Another issue in the public sector, somewhat more difficult to resolve, is that top public management is elected by the people, put there in order to effectuate public purposes. We do run into a conflict in the question of bargaining and it is just that—who is making these public decisions? Can public management make the decision on the basis of their platform, on the basis of their promises? Or will elections become relatively meaningless, because whatever the politician says he's going to do, eventually he's going to the bargaining table and be forced to do, not what the people or the general public want him to do, but what he is compelled to do. Who's really running the city, the Board of Education? the Department of Sanitation? Is it the people in a democracy, or is it the unions, here viewed as a greedy and private interest, compelling government to do for its purposes rather than those of the people. These are some of the issues in this sector.

As we look at alternatives, it is important to acknowledge that strikes originally were widespread in obtaining recognition for unions. No one has mentioned that the majority of states still do not recognize any form of collective bargaining for public employees. . . .

Instead of talking about alternatives to the strike in the public sector, I would say that the teachers and other public employees in the State of California, and the majority of other States in the United States, would be wise to follow the trends of teachers and other pubic workers in New York, Chicago, Philadelphia and elsewhere —because if they do not in fact exercise the right to strike, the government may never create the machinery that employees have in other States. It is not accidental that in States in which public employees have engaged in strikes the legislatures have found it possible to create mechanisms for collective bargaining.

Among the alternatives that have been offered, the State of New York has one of the most comprehensive. The process under the Taylor Law is essentially that there is a procedure for recognition and a time table based on the budgetary submission process of negotiations. There is a procedure for mediation and a procedure for fact-finding. Factfinding was expected to be the answer in the public sector, because the weight of the factfinder's opinion would be so strong in bringing public pressure to bear on public officials that the public officials would immediately just roll over, raise the white flag and say "Well, if the factfinder's report is printed in *The New York Times*, I have absolutely no choice but to see to it that the employees receive justice."

We might have realized some time ago that this would not happen. By and large, the general public believed for many years that teachers were underpaid and that other public employees were, but that belief didn't move the government toward providing adequate salaries and working conditions.

The terminal process in the Taylor Law is the legislative hearing. After the factfinder presents his report, the elected representatives of the people hold a hearing based upon this factfinding report and make the final decision. In any of 800 school districts in the State of New York, this means that the teachers first present their demands and then go through a process of negotiations; the mediator comes in and they go through that process; the factfinder issues his report, and 99 times out of 100 the board of education turns it down; then there is a hearing before the legislative body for the teachers in that district—which is the very same board of education that they have been negotiating with all along. The same is true of the Transit Authority in the City of New York. The same is true of State employees with respect to the State legislature. What we have is philosophically a very brilliant concept, that in a democracy ultimately those elected by the people will make these determinations on the basis of the facts given to them. But it turns out that the supposedly impartial legislative body representing the people is the very same government employer that the worker has been involved with all along. So we have a process of unilateral determination by the employer.

Laws like the Taylor Law provide very strict penalties—penalties like 2 days' fine to be paid by each employee for each day out on strike, unlimited financial penalties against the unions, unlimited suspension of dues check-off privileges, and jail sentences for all those found guilty of violating the injunction. Instead of preventing strikes, the existence of such legislation actually provokes strikes.

The public employer, knowing that this arsenal of weapons under the law must be used, sits back with the feeling that under no circumstances can the public employees go out on strike, because this battery of weapons is so strong. If they do go out on strike, facing this punishment once will solve the problem, and we won't have to worry about strikes next time, the time after that, or the time after that. Once the strike takes place, negotiations stop and government has to engage its entire machinery in the process of punishment.

Differences do exist with respect to strikes in the public sector and in the private sector. First, by and large, a strike in the public sector is not economic—it is political. In the private sector, both management and labor are losing money each day. At times we have suspected that teachers' strikes and other public strikes have been permitted to go on for a long time in order to help the city balance its budget.

One of the greatest reasons for the effectiveness of the public employees' strike is the fact that it is illegal. When the public sees a group of teachers—whom they tend to regard as rather docile human beings who have never done anything wrong and who chose to become teachers rather than meet the conflicts that exist in the rest of the world—when they see these teachers out on picket lines for 3 weeks, 5 weeks, or 7 weeks, when they see them being picked up by police and being sent to jail, frequently the public, instead of turning against the teachers, turns the other way. They say, "Now if those little old ladies . . . are willing to engage in this sort of thing, somebody must have done something wrong to them." We have that opinion in many strikes by teachers across the country. The teachers may not have majority support. But in the political sector, if you've got 25 percent of the public strongly on your side, any mayor would have to consider that the next time he runs (unless he won by a margin much bigger than that, and not too many mayors do that these days.)

Another problem of public employee bargaining is whether you negotiate salaries and working conditions, or whether you are really determining public policy. Take something in a school situation like class size. There is no question that keeping class size small is a working condition for the teacher, and yet the question of the desirable size of the classroom is also a question of public policy. Is reducing class size the most effective way of spending public funds? . . .

Finally, one other difference should be mentioned, that the argument of ability to pay doesn't really count in public sector negotiations. A private employer could pull out his books and show that he's going to go out of business if he pays more, but government can't.

There is no question that bargaining in the public sector is not a clear kind of issue. It's messy. If you try to push these arguments about sovereignty, if you try to push these arguments about who determines public policy, if you try to push arguments about how to get finality in this whole thing, we are going to end up with a whole mess of contradictions and we are going to try to impose solutions where solutions cannot be imposed.

In 1960, we had a very small teachers' union in New York City. We represented only 5 percent of the entire staff. We asked for a collective bargaining election, and at that time there was no collective bargaining for teachers anywhere in the United States. The Board of Education took the position that the Board was a governmental agency, government had sovereignty, and the sovereign could not sit down and treat his subjects as equals; therefore no collective bargaining. We had a 1-day strike on November 7, 1960, and the Board of Education changed its mind. Essentially, it said: We are the Board of Education, we are a government agency, government enjoys sovereignty, sovereignty is kind, and a king is all powerful; he is so powerful that if he *wants* to treat his subjects as equals (and bargain with them), no one can prevent him from doing so.

Some years ago, under the concepts of sovereignty, no subject could sue the government, but in a democratic society we found ways in which citizens can sue the government. In a democratic society we also ought to find ways in which public employees can engage in strikes against the government without raising the question of whether they are engaged in a revolution.

Mutual Anxiety: A California Proposal

Donald H. Wollett

What we are really talking about when we speak of alternatives to strikes is alternatives to strikes as the motive power for seeking agreements, or some other way to cause the parties to bargain in good faith in an effort to reach agreement. . . .

Our recommendation (of a committee reporting to the California State Assembly) with respect to the role of the strike was that it has a role, but not an exclusive role. What we were looking for was motive power for reaching agreement. And that in terms broader than the strike, the motive power for reaching agreement is the uncertainty, the fear on both sides of the bargaining table of possible consequences if agreement is not reached. If you want to put a tag on it, we would call it the "mutual anxiety system."

This is the way it would work: First, mediation. If that proved to be unsuccessful, then factfinding with recommendations—tripartite factfinding, with a timetable for the factfinders to issue their report and recommendations, with the parties to negotiate and consider those recommendations for 10 days or a longer period (if they mutually agreed to a longer period). At the end of the 10-day or extended period, the union, the employee organization, would put to its members this question as a condition precedent to permissible or lawful strike action: "Do you wish to accept the factfinders' recommendations?"

On the other side of the bargaining table, the public employer would put the same question to the members of the legislative body involved: "Do you now wish to accept the recommendations of the factfinder?" That, as a condition of the public employer's right to lock out. As far as I know, this is the only piece of public employment legislation that would legalize the lockout under some circumstances.

If both parties voted yes, obviously the strike would be settled on the terms recommended by the factfinders. If one of the parties voted no, the dispute would remain alive and either party might—they are not compelled to, but might—on 5 days' notice alert the other side and the public to the fact that they are either going to strike (the union) or lock out (the employer).

Within that 5-day period, or thereafter, any taxpayer or any affected consumer of the service interrupted could go into court. He could not get ex parte relief; there would have to be a hearing with witnesses, documentary evidence, exhibits, and so on. And on the basis of the evidence elicited in that hearing there would be two issues before the court. One, does the evidence support a finding that there is an imminent threat to public health or safety? Second, is there an alternative way in which the public employer can protect or safeguard against this imminent threat to public health or safety?

If the court made these two findings, the first answer affirmative, the second negative, then the court would do two additional things: one, issue an injunction against the strike or lockout, as the case may be, and two, convert the factfinders' recommendations into a binding arbitration award. If the court failed to make these findings, if the evidence did not support the finding of imminent threat to health or safety, then of course the strike or lockout would continue until the dispute was finally

Reprinted from the *Monthly Labor Review,* September 1973, pp. 51–52.

resolved. And of course they are all finally resolved, although some take longer than others.

Let me identify some of the points of fear in what I've described as the "mutual anxiety system." Take conventional mediation. In conventional mediation there is no fear of failure.

With our species of mediation under this bill, there is a fear, and that is if mediation fails the matter goes to factfinding, and factfinding becomes a risky process (which it is not ordinarily) because factfinding may, depending upon what happens down the road, ultimately become a binding arbitration award.

Let's compare conventional factfinding with the kind of factfinding we recommend in our report. In conventional factfinding there is no real fear—or shouldn't be—if it fails to produce a settlement. There certainly shouldn't be any fear on the part of the employer who can reject it with impunity. So can the employee organization, for that matter.

Factfinding, no matter how prestigious the factfinders, does not usually generate any significant public pressure on either side pushing them toward settlement. Studies show that the public really doesn't give a damn about the factfinders' report. Our factfinding—the kind we recommend—obviously does have the risk I've already alluded to, and that is that it may become a binding arbitration award. Rejection than becomes risky. The kind of risk depends upon whether there is going to be a strike, whether there is going to be a lockout, and, if one or the other, whether there will be an injunction.

Now let me deal with some more risks that are involved—some more anxieties and apprehensions that are created by this procedure. Suppose after receipt of the factfinders' recommendations, the parties begin to bargain but do not bargain to the point of settlement. They are making some progress, and both are satisfied that what they have tentatively agreed to is better than the factfinders' recommendation, although it's not something that they want to accept mutually and try to live with. Recall that the vote is on the factfinders' report—do you want to accept the factfinders' report, yes or no, *not* do you want to accept what the parties have now negotiated.

What if the vote on the acceptance of factfinding is "no" and one of the parties gives a "no" answer? Do you strike or lock out, thus risking the loss of progress in negotiations, and perhaps winding up with less than you now have if an injunction is issued and you are stuck with the factfinding recommendation which has been converted into a binding arbitrational award? Or do you want to continue negotiations and forgo the vote, or, having taken the vote, forgo the results? If you are a spokesman for one side or the other, what do you recommend to your constituents on the question of whether they should accept the factfinders' recommendation, if in fact you are making progress in negotiation?

And finally, looking at another point of anxiety and uncertainty, what would a judge do if you get to a certain point in a lockout or strike and some citizen—some taxpayer—goes into court seeking injunctive relief? It has been generally assumed that if the firefighters or police strike, for instance, an injunction would be issued—the evidence would support a threat of imminent threat to health or safety and an injunction would be issued almost automatically and you would have a species of compulsory arbitration. That's not true. There is an element of uncertainty there. I remember a firefighters' strike in San Diego back in 1970 that did not generate an imminent threat to public health or safety, because the city had planned for the strike. Fire stations in the central city were manned with supervisory personnel and with nonstrikers. On the perimeter of the city, they relied on mutual assistance pacts with voluntary fire companies and adjoining fire districts. So there is an element of doubt in a firefighters strike and might be an element of doubt in a police strike. Probably an injunction would be issued, but one cannot be sure, and it's the element of uncertainty that creates the anxiety or fear that we suggest makes this a viable mechanism.

How about a teachers' strike? Teachers probably assume that their strikes will not threaten health or safety, and therefore there would not be any injunction. Well, there is an element of doubt there too. Suppose a dispute arises in a little town in California, and suppose a petition for injunctive relief goes before a judge who looks at the decision of the Commonwealth Court of Pennsylvania in the Philadelphia strike during the current school year, and says, "I find that as a result of this strike, underachievers are on the street threatening the safety of the saintly natives, and I find a threat, an imminent threat to health and safety, and I'm going to issue an injunction to convert the factfinders' recommendations into a binding award." Again I suggest there is doubt. And it is the doubt and uncertainty that breeds the anxiety which in our judgment creates the motive to settle without running those risks. What we tried to do was to create a structural risk, so that rather than run the risk from nonagreement, the parties would prefer to settle.

Emerging
Issues
in
Industrial
Relations

Discriminatory Seniority Systems

Arthur B. Smith, Jr.

Rejecting the claim that the legislative history of Title VII (of the Civil Rights Act of 1964, as amended) requires that seniority practices not be subject to revision,[1] the courts have restructured job and departmental seniority systems where their operation has resulted in the continuation of past discriminatory hiring or assignment practices that confine employees of one race or sex to certain departments or jobs.[2] These seniority systems, which are neutral in application and have not expressly confined minorities or females to departments or jobs by prohibiting transfers elsewhere within a facility, nevertheless have been found not "bona fide" within the meaning of Title VII because they perpetuated the past effects of hiring and assigment discrimination in two distinct, but equally unlawful ways. These include:

(1) cases in which those persons formerly discriminated against in hiring and assignment are not willing to lose their accrued seniority and concomitant rights and privileges in transferring to a new job, and are effectively "locked in" to their present positions, which generally have been the least desirable jobs; and (2) cases in which those persons previously the victims of discrimination do transfer, but are forced to begin in the lowest-paying classification of a new department, although they would have had better positions in that department had not departmental or job seniority prevented them from carrying their seniority rights with them.

The task confronting the courts in restructuring seniority systems embodying years, even decades, of the conflict, accommodation, and experimentation, which is the essence of the collective bargaining process itself, would have taxed the wisdom of Solomon. On one side are victims of past discrimination—minorities and females locked into certain departments or job progression lines. On the other side are those employees—members of the majority group, as well as some minorities and females—who have not been disadvantaged by the operation of a seniority procedure but who will be affected by any remedy benefiting those previously discriminated against. In the middle is the institution of collective bargaining, used in the past by employers and unions as the vehicle for perpetuating hiring and assignment discrimination and apparently incapable of rectifying that misfortune.

The restructuring of discriminatory seniority systems has generally attempted to strike a balance between the rights of those employees adversely affected by past discrimination and the expectations of those not disadvantaged, ignoring, for the time being at least, the impact of any imposed remedy on the institution of free collective bargaining. Simply stated, the restructuring of these systems has generally been based on the so-called "rightful place" remedy first articulated in 1967.[3] Its goal is to provide those employees adversely affected by past discrimination the seniority rights they would have enjoyed but for the discrimination, a "rightful place" in seniority rosters and job progressions, without depriving other employees of their jobs or accumulated seniority rights or diluting the fundamental requirement that an employee must be qualified to perform the job that is sought.[4]

In practice, the rightful place remedy has not required the wholesale eradication of departmental or job progression bidding procedures or the merger of departments or job progression seniority lines, at least in cases in which the separation of departments or job progression lines is attributable to production efficiency and not solely to race or other unlawful characteristics.[5] Instead, a new seniority system providing special rights for those previously discriminated against is superimposed on an existing procedure that continues to govern when the job bidders consist of employees not adversely affected by past discrimination. The new procedure operates prospectively only and provides that junior employees in the group not previously discriminated against are not to be displaced by minority group or female employees with longer work histories. Future job vacancies are to be filled, pursuant to the existing job or departmental bidding procedures, by those persons with the greatest seniority on a plant- or company-wide basis. Thus, although the existing departmental or line seniority procedure continues to govern bidding involving only employees not previously discriminated against, plant- or company-wide seniority operates when the bidders include adversely affected employees in competition with those not discriminated against.

Transfer Rights and Seniority Carry-Over

The frequency with which the new interdepartmental transfer right may be exercised has been specifically considered in recent seniority cases. The remedies ordered in these cases have afforded those minority or female employees adversely affected by past discrimination perpetuated in a seniority system a right to exercise one interdepartmental transfer across bidding lines. The one transfer right is governed by an employee's plant- or company-wide seniority and includes a carryover of plant- or company-wide seniority to the new department for utilization in future job movements. In addition, the one-transfer-with carryover-seniority right is exercisable only during a specified period of time, after which the right expires; this procedure has been established for the purpose of encouraging those discriminated against to seek their "rightful places." At the same time, this special right preserves the fundamental interest in preventing the chaos that would result from the immediate imposition of complete plant- or company-wide seniority, which would permit widespread leapfrogging and bumping, as previously disadvantaged employees exercised their new rights to displace incumbent junior employees.[6]

The scope of seniority carryover to be given employees exercising an interdepartmental transfer has provoked some controversy. This has surfaced most extensively in the court decisions arising out of the trucking industry, where separate seniority progression lines existed for road and city drivers, often coupled with rules prohibiting transfers between the separate lines and where, with or without no-transfer rules, minorities have been locked into one of the two progression lines (usually the city driver progression line). There, seniority carryover equivalent to an employee's full company-wide seniority ("full seniority carryover") awarded uniformly in the industrial plant cases has not been accepted. Exploring the relationship between qualifications for performing a job and the scope of carryover seniority more extensively than have the courts in industrial plant cases, the courts in the trucking cases have concluded that full seniority carryover would provide a transferee with more than his "rightful place" on the seniority roster, if in fact the transferee would not have been qualified for the job to which he or she transferred until the employee had worked on another job with the company for a period of time after the date of full employment. Consequently, less than full seniority carryover has been ordered in these cases, with the scope of carryover dependent primarily on the date in the past on which the transferring employee first possessed the qualifications for the new job to which transfer is sought. [7]

The differences in the seniority carryover right ordered in the trucking and industrial plant cases probably do not represent a doctrinal conflict and can be explained in terms of the nature of the job progression structures involved. In both types of cases, the interdepartmental transfer right can only be utilized in bidding on a job for which the employee is presently qualified; however, the prevailing assumption in the industrial plant cases has been that employees transferring into new departments would be qualified for all entry level jobs, jobs for which they would have been "qualified" on the date of hire. Hence, full seniority carryover is consistent with the "rightful place" remedy. In the trucking industry case, the entry level job in the road service has required qualifications that an individual can only acquire after a specified period in city service or in road service for another company. Therefore, every employee is not necessarily qualified for all entry level jobs on the date of hire, and less than full seniority carryover is also consistent with the "rightful place" remedy. Less than full seniority carryover can be expected in future industrial plant cases to the extent that the courts permit skipping of entry level jobs and advancement of transferees to jobs in a progression line for which they are presently qualified but were not qualified on the date of hire.

Rate and Seniority Retention

As noted, the courts have been sensitive to the fact that an employee exercising the new one-transfer right might not be qualified to perform the skilled job in another department (to which he or she would be otherwise entitled by virtue of plant-wide seniority) because a job progression line in that department provides the necessary training for the skilled jobs. The seniority systems restructured under the "rightful place" remedy have, consequently, provided rate retention (red circling) for employees who are qualified only for transfer into entry-level jobs in new departments in which those jobs carry lower pay rates than the jobs transferring employees presently hold. Also, to encourage the exercise of the new interdepartmental transfer right, employees have been provided with retention of seniority in the department from which they transferred for a specified period. Therefore, if the new job cannot be performed by an employee or the employee wishes to return to the former department, he or she would not lose any seniority rights in that department. [8]

Residency and Job Skipping

In cases involving complex job progression structures wherein residence in lower-skilled jobs provides necessary training for higher-skilled jobs, restructuring pursuant to the "rightful place" remedy has recognized the function of on-the-job training provided by periods of residency in low-skilled jobs while, at the same time, scrutinizing existing residency requirements and eliminating those that do not serve as a training period. Thus, the restructuring has required employees exercising a transfer right to move into a new department to remain on the jobs they secure for specified residency periods before moving in the job progression but has also allowed employees to skip jobs in a progression ladder which do not provide training for future jobs in the progression. [9]

Layoff and Recall

With respect to layoff and recall procedures, the problem that has received the most attention under the "rightful place" remedy is recall after a layoff. If recalls are based on plant- or company-wide seniority alone, the result could be that an employee who had been a victim of past discrimination could be recalled to a job that he had not held prior to layoff in preference to the incumbent at the time of layoff. Because such a recall may displace an employee who had held a job at a time of layoff, it has not been deemed consistent with the "rightful place" remedy. [10] Hence, in the *Bethlehem Steel* decisions, [11] plant-wide seniority was not mandated for use in recall of employees after exercise of the one interdepartmental transfer right. In those situations, newly transferred employees were to be recalled, without regard to comparative seniority, to the same position, relative to other employees, held prior to the layoffs. Layoffs, however, were to be made in accordance with the conventional procedures specified in the bargaining agreement.

In the layoff and recall context, moreover, the "rightful place" remedy has not been uniformly applied. Thus, employees previously discriminated against have been successful in convincing at least one court to abandon the remedy when layoffs and recalls are involved. In that case, [12] the court ruled that plant-wide seniority was not to be used to govern layoffs and recalls and ordered that such job movements be governed instead by apportioning layoffs and recalls among whites and blacks on the basis of the proportion of each group in the total work force.

The extensive substantive restructuring of collectively bargained contract provisions exemplified by the court and agency seniority remedies appears to conflict with the conventional policy against court and agency interference with the terms of the collective bargaining agreement. Indeed, the debate and legislative history leading to the passage of Section 8(d) of the National Labor Relations Act [13] indicates a clear congressional intent to keep one arm of the government—the NLRB—from sitting in judgment on the substantive terms of collective bargaining agreements except in cases in which those terms violate an express statutory provision, [14] and the NLRB's attempt to employ its remedy power to impose a substantive contract term—a dues checkoff clause—as well as an entire contract on an employer has been conclusively rejected.[15] In stark contrast, however, the provisions of the Norris-LaGuardia Act expressing the policy against federal court interference in "labor disputes" were declared inapplicable by Congress in the formulation of Title VII remedies.

NOTES

1. *Congressional Record,* Vol. 110, pp. 7207, 7212–7215, and 7216–7217 (1964). The final version of Section 703 (h) of Title VII is pertinent in part:

(h) Notwithstanding any other provision of this title, it shall not be unlawful employment practice for an employer to apply different standards of compensation, or different terms, conditions, or privileges of employment pursuant to a bona fide seniority or merit system which measures earnings by quantity or quality of production or to employees who work in different locations, provided that such differences are not the result of an intention to discriminate because of race, color, religion, sex, or national origin; . . .

2. E.g., *Quarles v. Philip Morris Inc.,* 279 F Supp 505 (ED Va 1969); *Local 189 UPP v. United States,* 416 F 2d 980 (5th Cir 1969), cert. denied, 397 US 919 (1970); *Jones v. Lee Way Motor Freight Inc.,* 431 F 2d 245 (10th Cir 1970), cert. denied, 401 US 954 (1971); *United States v. Bethlehem Steel Corp.,* 446 F 2d 652 (2d Cir 1971); *United States v. Jacksonville Terminal Co.,* 451 F 2d 418 (5th Cir 1971), cert. denied, 406 US 906 (1972); *United States v. N.L. Industries,* 479 F 2d 354 (8th Cir 1973); *United States v. Allegheny-Ludlum Industries, Inc. et al.,* Consent Decree, Civil Action No. 74P339S, BNA FEP Manual 431:125 (ND Ala 1974). See also *In the Matter of Bethlehem Steel Corp.,* OFCC Docket No. 102–68 (1973).

3. Note, "Title VII Seniority Discrimination and the Incumbent Negro," *Harvard Law Review,* Vol. 80, pp. 1260–83 (1967).

4. The "freedom now" remedy which would have allowed those previously disadvantaged all rights to which they would have been entitled but for discrimination without regard to the rights and expectations of those not adversely affected, and the "status quo" remedy, which would not have disturbed the rights and expectations of those employees who had not suffered from past discrimination, have been rejected in favor of the "rightful place" remedy. For a discussion of these alternative remedies, see Note, "Title VII, Seniority Discrimination and the Incumbent Negro, pp. 1260–83; George Coopers and Richard B. Sobol, "Seniority and Testing Under Fair Employment Laws: A General Approach to Objective Criteria of Hiring and Promotion," *Harvard Law Review,* Vol. 82, pp. 1598–1636 (1969); and William F. Gardner, "The Development of the Substantive Principles of Title VII Law: The Defendant's View," *Alabama Law Review,* Vol. 26, pp. 1–42 (1973). Apparently for the first time, however, in *Patterson v. American Tobacco Co.,* 8 FEP Cases 778 (ED Va 1974), the court opted for the "freedom now" remedy and ordered immediate imposition of a company-wide seniority system that would result in displacement of incumbent employees by minorities and females.

5. *United States v. N.L. Industries,* 479 F 2d 354 (8th Cir 1973); *Sabala v. Western Gillette,* 362 F Supp 1142 (SD Tex 1973); but see, for circumstances requiring merger of seniority lines, *Rock v. Norfolk & W. Ry.,* 473 F 2d 1344 (4th Cir 1973); *Bush v. Lone Star Steel Co.,* 7 FEP Cases 1258 (ED Tex 1974); *United States v. U.S. Steel Corp.,* 5 FEP Cases 1253 (ND Ala 1973).

6. E.g., *United States v. Bethlehem Steel Co.,* 446 F 2d 652 (2nd Cir 1971); *In the Matter of Bethlehem Steel Co.,* OFCC Docket No. 102–68 (1973); *United States v. N.L. Industries,* 479 F 2d 354 (8th Cir 1973); *Stamps et al. v. Detroit Edison Co.,* 365 F Supp 87 (ED Mich 1973); *Bowe v. Colgate-Palmolive Co.,* 489 F 2d 896 (7th Cir 1973); *Pettway v. American Cast Iron Pipe Co.,* 494 F 2d 211 (5th Cir 1974).

7. *Bing v. Roadway Express Inc.,* 444 F 2d 687 (5th Cir 1971), on remand, 5 FEP Cases 1212 (ND Ga 1973), modified, 485 F 2d 441 (5th Cir 1973) (carryover right coextensive with date employee possessed experience necessary to qualify for road service); *Thorton v. East Texas Motor Freight Co.,* 7 FEP Cases 1245 (6th Cir 1974) (carryover right coextensive with date 6 months after employee requested transfer but was wrongfully denied it or filed an EEOC charge, but not earlier than January 2, 1966 or, in the case of an employee who did not request transfer or file, an EEOC charge, 18 months after the date on which employee became qualified for road service, but not earlier than July 1, 1970); *Sabala v. Western Gillette,* 362 F Supp (SD Tex 1974) (carryover coextensive with date an employee had the earliest opportunity to request transfer following his or her qualification for road service). See also *United States v. St. Louis-San Francisco Ry. Co.,* 464 F 2d 301 (8th Cir 1972), cert. denied, 409 US 1116 (1973) (carryover seniority equivalent to 50 percent of an employee's length of company-wide service.

8. See cases cited in footnote 6. In *Patterson v. American Tobacco Co.,* 8 FEP Cases 778 (ED Va 1974), where the "freedom now" remedy was ordered, incumbent employees displaced by minorities or females were provided "red circle" protection against rate reduction.

9. *United States* v. *H.K. Porter,* 7 FEP Cases 778 (ND Ala 1974), on remand from 491 F 2d 1105 (5th Cir 1974); *Pettway* v. *American Cast Iron Pipe Co.,* 494 F 2d 211 (5th Cir 1974).

10. See Gardner, "The Development of the Substantive Principles of Title VII Law: The Defendant's View," p. 27.

11. *United States* v. *Bethlehem Steel Co.,* 446 F 2d 652 (2d Cir. 1971); *In the Matter of Bethlehem Steel Co.,* OFCC Docket No. 102–68 (1973). See also *United States* v. *Allegheny-Ludlum Steel Co. et al.,* Consent Decree, Civil Action No. 74P–399S, BNA FEP Manual 431:125 (ND Ala 1974).

12. *Watkins* v. *Local 2369 Steelworkers et al.,* 369 F Supp 1221, Supplemented, 8 FEP Cases 729 (ED La 1974). Compare *Waters* v. *Wisconsin Steel Works,* 502 F 2d 1309 (7th Cir 1974), where "last on, first off" layoff and recall procedures pursuant to a seniority system were held not to violate Title VII or 42 USC 1981 and *Jersey Central Power & Light Co.* v. *Local 327, et al.,* IBEW, BNA Daily Labor Report, No. 22, p. E–1 (January 31, 1975).

13. 29 USC 158 (d) (1970).

14. See *NLRB* v. *American National Insurance Co.,* 343 US 395 (1952); *NLRB* v. *Insurance Agents' International Union,* 361 US 477 (1960).

15. *H.K. Porter Co.* v. *NLRB,* 397 US 99 (1970); *NLRB* v. *Burns International Security Services Inc.,* 406 US 272 (1972).

Group Cleavage: Declining and Rising Social Forces

Samuel P. Huntington

In any fundamental change in the nature of society, some social forces gain in social status, economic position, and numerical strength, absolutely and relatively, while others lose in status, position, and numbers, absolutely or relatively. As a result, the transition from one form of society to another often involves three major lines of cleavage: between rising and declining social forces; between declining social forces; and between rising social forces. The transition from agrarian to industrial society saw the decline of the landowning elite and peasantry and the rise of the urban bourgeoisie and industrial proletariat. This produced conflict of rural landowners versus peasants, of urban bourgeoisie and workers versus rural landowners and peasants, and of urban bourgeoisie versus industrial workers. The transition from industrial to postindustrial society involves a decline in the relative number and status of blue-collar workers and central city dwellers and an increase in the numbers and status of white-collar workers and suburbanites. This transition could involve three lines of cleavage comparable to those that characterized the earlier movement into industrial society.

In the first instance, the declining social forces conflict with each other, as blue-collar labor struggles with primarily black central city dwellers over segregation, schools, jobs, and welfare. This cleavage was, of course, a central focus of American politics in the late 1960s and early 1970s. In this process, history doubles back on itself so far as the blacks are concerned. In terms of the transition from agrarian to

This selection is an excerpt from the article, "Postindustrial Politics: How Benign Will It Be?" Reprinted from *Comparative Politics,* January 1974, pp. 177–82, with the permission of the publisher and the author.

industrial society, the blacks are a rising social force, their migration to the cities and improvement in socioeconomic status resembling simultaneous processes in Latin America and Asia. At the same time, however, the social-governmental unit to which they are moving is becoming less important in American society as the rest of that society begins the transit from the industrial to the post-industrial phase. The migration of farmers to the cities in the United States and other Western societies in the nineteenth century and the parallel contemporary migrations taking place in the Third World have been accompanied by the "rise of the city," with the principal locus of power and initiative shifting from rural to urban society. The migration of blacks into the cities of twentieth-century America, however, is accompanied by "the decline of the city" and its loss, relatively and absolutely, of numbers and influence to the suburbs. On the one hand, this dual transition reduces social conflict by substituting city-suburb segregation for rural-urban segregation; on the other hand, however, the longer term impact may be for one cleavage to reinforce another and to intensify the problems of those blacks who are better prepared for life in industrial than in post-industrial society. To be a rising social force in a declining sector of society could be a recipe for intense frustration.

A second line of cleavage finds city dwellers and blue-collar workers with parallel interests aligned against the expanding white-collar and suburban social forces. Insofar as numbers are important in politics, the power of the latter should be growing while that of the former declines; and American politics should be taking on more and more of the characteristics associated with the politics of well educated, white-collar suburbanites. In fact, however, numbers are not the only thing that counts, even in democratic politics and perhaps particularly in American politics. If the historical analogy with the shift from agrarian to industrial society means anything, a decline in the relative numbers, status, and position of a group does not necessarily lead to a decline in political power. The less important the farmers became in American society, the more powerful they became in American government. Declining social forces, indeed, are often galvanized into political action precisely because they are declining. Threatened by the apparent flow of events, they are stimulated to greater unity, better organization, and more vigorous action to protect their interests, entrenching themselves behind political and legal barricades, using the power of the state to preserve a privileged position. In the United States, the declining farmers first gave birth to populism, which failed precisely because the farmers were no longer a popular majority, and then turned to organization and interest group politics, particularly through the Farm Bureau Federation. As a result, the decrease in the number of farmers was accompanied by an increase in government benefits for those that remained. Somewhat similarly, the decline of the "old middle class" of independent professional men, shopkeepers, and small businessmen generated various right-wing movements in the United States and contributed to the rise of fascism in Europe.

In the transition from industrial to post-industrial society, the comparable declining groups are blue-collar workers and central city dwellers. In the past, the political activities of these groups have focused in large part on electoral politics. The big city machines were, of course, primarily concerned with the control of their own local governments, but they were often major factors in state politics and in the outcomes of presidential elections in the large industrial states as well. Similarly, the political activity of organized labor progressed from Samuel Gompers' efforts to reward friends and punish enemies through the CIO (Congress of Industrial Organizations)

Political Action Committee to the more recent important political role of COPE (AFL-CIO Committee on Political Education) both within the Democratic party and in supporting labor-endorsed Democratic candidates. The electoral power of the central cities and of union labor, symbolized dramatically in the aging personalities of Richard Daley and George Meany, is, however, clearly on the decline in comparison with that of other groups. Just as the farmers shifted from efforts to develop popular majorities, so the political spokesmen for the central cities and blue-collar labor will resort increasingly to interest group politics and to the effort to carve out semiautonomous arenas, governmental "whirlpools" as Ernest Griffiths once called them, within which they can play a dominant role and which will be protected by law, custom, and governmental organization from the impact of broader constituencies. They will thus maintain a toehold on the political system and a firm claim on resources distributed through the political system.

The efforts of the central cities and blue-collar labor to defend their interests against a population that is becoming increasingly suburban and white-collar could generate among the former a growing sense of group identity and class consciousness. In the European context in which social classes are generally more sharply articulated, class consciousness is often most intense when a group has begun to develop economically and socially and then attempts to establish itself firmly in the political sphere. Limitations on individual mobility lead to group consciousness among the members of the excluded group, with this consciousness reaching its most intense form in the final stages of the efforts by the group to win acceptance as a part of the established social, economic, and political order. In the United States, on the other hand, upward mobility has been an individual as well as a group phenomenon. Subjectively and objectively, rising social forces have been relatively easily absorbed into the great amorphous American middle class. As a result, the integration of a group into society has not been accompanied by the same levels of group consciousness as in Europe. On the other hand, a perceived threat to a group which does occupy a well-established and accepted position in the political, economic, and social system is likely to generate higher levels of group consciousness. Groups become most conscious of their common identity and interests not when they are making their way up in American society but rather when they are on the verge of being forced down. Consequently, the emergence of a post-industrial society is likely to increase the class consciousness and cohesion of blue-collar workers and central city dwellers. Since a majority of the population in many cities will belong to racial minorities, the "central city consciousness" which emerges as a result of the relative decline of the central city in social importance is likely to be reinforced by racial consciousness—the one area of American society where the European pattern of "consciousness when on the rise" tends to prevail, precisely because, of course, the barriers against the individual mobility of blacks have been comparable to those in Europe against the individual mobility of workers.

A third line of cleavage, comparable to that between capitalists and workers in industrial society, could be between white-collar workers in the public sector and those in the private sector. The former will want increases in wages and other economic benefits; the latter will not want to pay for these through higher taxes. The interaction between owners and workers in the private sector of industrial society could thus be reenacted in the interaction between while-collar bureaucrats and white-collar taxpayers in post-industrial society.

This conflict will place enormous strains on political leadership at all levels of government. Through unionization and threats of disruption in essential services, public sector employees can pressure, induce, or coerce political leaders to meet their demands. The trend toward white-collar unionism is perhaps strongest among governmental employees. In 1971, 52 percent of the civilians working for the Federal Government were members either of unions or of quasi-union associations. Indicative of this trend, in the fall of 1972 the American Foreign Service Association, previously a standard type of professional organization, won an election to become the bargaining agent for the foreign service officers of the State Department and the Agency for International Development (AID).

Increasing unionization has led to more strikes. In 1961, only 28 strikes involving governmental employees were reported; in 1966, there were 142 such strikes; and in 1970, 412. The benefits of unionization are real, however: the salaries of unionized teachers, for instance, average 4 percent to 15 percent more than those of non-unionized teachers in comparable positions.

Political leaders will also be subject to strong electoral pressure to avoid any increase in taxes if they wish to continue in office. The easy escape—perhaps the only escape—from this dilemma is to increase wages without increasing taxes, which will presumably mean high and increasing rates of inflation. Apart from this out, it is not clear than any industrial or post-industrial society has resolved the problem of how to reconcile the freedom of public employees to organize and to strike, on the one hand, with the selection of public officials through competitive elections, on the other.

The difficulty of keeping white-collar, public sector wages under control will be all the greater because of the absence of any clear criterion by which to judge when wage increases are justified. In most industrial work, wages can be tied to, or at least debated in terms of increases in productivity. In a post-industrial society, however, the concept of "productivity" is of dubious relevance. In the first place the transition from industrial to post-industrial society is marked by the decline of those industries in which productivity increases (as usually measured) are highest and the growth of those sectors of the economy in which productivity increases are lowest. The concept of "productivity" may in a sense be peculiarly appropriate only to industrial society. Secondly, even if the concept is relevant in post-industrial society, the problem of measuring it becomes increasingly difficult. The concept is useful enough when applied to a factory assembly line of blue-collar workers; it is generally difficult to apply to a bureaucratic office manned by white-collar workers, and it is particularly hard to apply to many service industries. As Peter Drucker has observed, "We have yet to learn what productivity really means" in nonmanual work. Yet the sales clerk and the college teacher, the nurse and the marketing manager, the policeman and the accountant all expect their incomes to rise as fast as that of the manual workers. In the absence of even a relatively "objective" standard such as productivity by which to evaluate wage claims, the competition between the bureaucrats who want more and political leaders who want reelection is likely to be determined not by any appeal to reason but primarily by the application of political muscle.

Trade Unions and the Challenge of the Multinational Corporation

David H. Blake

With the expansion of the multinational corporation and the emergence of giant firms adopting a worldwide perspective of business and management, there has developed an international side to employment with important consequences for the relationship between employer and employees. Unfortunately, complete and precise data are not available, but a few fragmentary figures may serve to illustrate the extent and pattern of international employment by multinational corporations.

In the first place, many of the multinational corporations have on a world-wide basis large numbers of employees. Data collected by the International Metalworkers' Federation indicate that twenty-seven major electrical and electronic companies employ 3,940,833 persons averaging about 109,000 employees per firm, and twelve major automobile manufacturers employ 2,401, 223 persons with a per-firm average of about 200,000. Another important dimension concerns the percentage of the total work force of various multinational corporations that is employed by the foreign affiliates. Procter and Gamble, International Telephone and Telegraph (IT&T), Philips, Nestle, Ford, Chrysler, Kodak, International Business Machines (IBM), and General Motors are just a few of the many companies that employ more than one-third of their worldwide work force outside of the headquarters country.

Numerous studies have shown that in various countries direct foreign investment tends to be concentrated in certain industrial sectors to the relative exclusion of others. The employment figures associated with such concentration have not been explored, but as an example, a report based on 1967 figures reveals that in the Belgian metal industry, 35 percent of all employment is provided by non-Belgian employers. The importance of this fact for the metalworking unions is obvious.

A final dimension of interest involves the patterns of employment in countries where multinational corporations operate. United States unions concerned about job exports claim that over a three-year period, five thousand jobs a month in the electrical industry were lost to foreign subsidiaries of U.S. multinational corporations, and the 1966 Census of Foreign Direct Investments indicates that majority owned affiliates of U.S. corporations employed 3,324,321 non-Americans abroad. A 1970 survey of seventy-four American-based multinationals reveals that the average annual domestic employment growth rate increased 3.3 percent in comparison to the 1.4 percent rate of non-international American firms. However, the average annual growth rate of foreign employment was 7.7 percent.

These incomplete figures merely suggest the significant impact that multinational corporations have had on patterns of employment. By expanding their operations in many different countries, these firms have created for themselves sizable international work forces whereby workers of several or many countries have in common the same employer but not the same nationality. Furthermore, for many firms, an important part of the worldwide work force is associated with the foreign subsidiaries thereby forcing industrial relations policies to take on a multinational orientation. Additionally, a large portion of the members of various national unions are employed by foreign enterprises and thus are confronted with special problems not faced by fellow unionists employed in domestic firms. Finally, the ability of multinational corporations to shift production from one country to another has affected trade unions in states that feel they have suffered a net job loss.

The Multinational Corporate Challenge

While an in-depth examination of the nature of the challenge posed by multinational corporations to trade unions is not necessary, a brief discussion of the problems created for host country, primarily European, and parent country unions will be useful for later discussion. One broad category of concern expressed by European trade union officials is that the international nature and resources of the multinational corporation make more difficult the task of influencing management and therefore representing union members effectively. There are many reasons for the feeling of decreased strength and comparative weakness, but the most important is the difficulty of identifying and then influencing the appropriate corporate decision-making center. European, regional, and international union officials are convinced that the crucial industrial relations and production decisions affecting their members are usually made outside of the country where the subsidiary is located or in the light of orders and standards established by the foreign headquarters. Compounding this problem is the feeling that management frequently masks the location of the decision center or engages in a strategy of "passing-the-buck" by denying responsibility for decisions on particular issues. As a result, union leaders find their efforts to be less effective simply because they are uncertain where they should concentrate their energies and power.

Of course, where decision-making responsibility is located in a regional office or corporate headquarters outside of the country where the subsidiary is located, union efforts to influence management are likely to be rather ineffective. Because of its single-state orientation and tradition, the union associated with a subsidiary does not have the legal, political, or customary basis to bargain with or pressure a foreign headquarters. Furthermore, union officials in one state are not likely to be familiar or to have had the opportunity to become familiar with the personal and organizational traits of the corporate headquarters which will make possible the development of a well-founded and successful strategy.

Contributing to the feelings of reduced effectiveness are the advantages accruing to the corporations as a result of their size and international nature. A large multinational corporation with many profit centers scattered around the world may well be able to hold out longer against the demands sought by one union associated with only one profit center. Also, because of its international orientation, multinational corporations may be and have been able to shift production among their subsidiaries in different countries in a way that minimizes disruptions in the overall production stream and maintains service to the market affected by the industrial dispute.

Additionally multinational corporations have an advantage over many national unions in that the latter often find it difficult to obtain the necessary financial data which will support their claims. Consolidated accounts, transfer pricing, and cost and profit allocations among subsidiaries mean that firms can structure financial data in such a way as to be most beneficial in industrial relations matters as well as in tax planning. Without adequate information and knowledge about corporate finances, the task of developing an effective union strategy based on financial data will be difficult indeed.

Labor officials are also concerned about the ultimate investment power of the multinational corporation which grants it the power, in some cases to restrict expansion, reduce investment and therefore employment, and totally shut down an operation in response to labor relations factors or other causes well beyond the control of unions. There are many anecdotes that circulate among European labor union leaders which testify to the number of times unions have felt threatened by the international mobility of the multinational corporation. For this and other reasons, labor union officials feel that their ability to represent effectively their membership is severely reduced when confronting a multinational corporation as opposed to a domestic one. The international nature of management gives it advantages not enjoyed by the national union whose experience and range of interest is limited to a single state.

There are other factors of concern to union officials, especially the annoyance of having to interact with a management that is unaware of or unwilling to accept established practices and customs with respect to such things as working conditions and union-management relations. There are frequent complaints that the multinational firm pursues policies that are contrary to well-established rules of the game. As a result, the range of predictability in the management-union relationship is reduced, and the problems of communication, suspicion, insecurity, and frustration are likely to ensue. Of course, there are many different problem areas of greater or lesser importance to various union leaders, but the most important issues involve job security, conditions of work, and consultation between management and unions prior to developments affecting job security.

In this brief consideration of the challenges posed by the multinational corporation to host state unions, it is worthwhile to note that union officials are also disturbed by the political, social, economic, and cultural threats of the multinational corporation to their particular nation-state. Both as a means of supporting a popular issue and out of deep conviction, trade union leaders are concerned about the failure of some international enterprises to advance various objectives of the host state.

While thus far the multinational corporate challenge has been presented from the point of view of host country unions, it is also apparent that parent country unions feel threatened by these firms. The AFL-CIO and numerous affiliated unions are conducting a vigorous campaign against the multinationals, accusing them of taking advantage of low wage rates in other countries at the expense of employment in the United States.

The unions charge that subsidiaries are frequently established in foreign countries for the major purpose of producing, more cheaply, goods which are then imported into the United States to serve the domestic market. Secondly, the unions feel that companies are producing abroad for distribution abroad as a substitute for the exportation of products manufactured in the United States. Thirdly, the unions claim that U.S.-based multinational firms are exporting too rapidly technological advances achieved in the United States to production facilities in lower-wage countries. The result of these actions, the unions suggest, is that American jobs are lost or exported, and balance of payments deficits and trade imbalances are heightened. Thus, parent country unions also have problems counteracting the international challenges posed by the multinational corporation.

In this connection it is important to note that recently the Trades Union Congress of the United Kingdom has expressed similar fears with respect to British-based multinational firms. More importantly, as the wage costs in European countries rise at a more rapid pace than wages in developing countries, it is quite possible that more and more unions in advanced industrial societies will begin to feel that multinational corporations, foreign-based or not, will be expanding operations in low-wage areas to the detriment of domestic employment. From their perspective, the greater mobility of capital and managerial skill works to the disadvantage of immobile national labor forces.

Union Responses

It was not really until the late 1960s that many labor union officials began to recognize and respond to the challenges posed by the multinational corporation. Since then, awareness of the threat has spread rapidly, particularly among industrialized countries, and each year sees the development and implementation of plans designed to increase the effectiveness of labor unions in their relations with multinational enterprises. However, a unified and coordinated strategy has not emerged because the union movement itself is not at all unified and coordinated. Instead, there are as many union systems as there are states, even within specific states, ideological splits and other areas of conflict serve to divide and separate. In addition, relevant union organizations exist at the state, regional, and international levels, and at each level there are some unions encompassing only a single trade or industry—metalworking for instance—and others that are comprehensive, embracing many types of industries and skills, such as the AFL-CIO. Given the complexity and diversity of the union movement, it is not at all surprising that, instead of a single union strategy, there are many. Consequently, the examination of the responses of unions to multinational corporations will focus first on the actions of national unions, then on efforts of regional institutions, and finally on the strategies pursued by international union organizations.

The State Level

National unions have developed a number of strategies to combat the advantages of the multinational corporation, but distinction must be made between the activities of unions associated with foreign subsidiaries and those established in the parent country of the firm. The efforts of parent country unions are motivated by their desire to protect themselves and their workers from loss of jobs to low-wage areas and by their intent to use their influence with management and within the political system to aid host country unions who are overwhelmed by the strength of the international enterprise. On the job export issue, the union movement in the United States has actively urged Congress to adopt the Burke-Hartke bill and others which would severely restrict the freedom of the multinational corporation to operate in other countries and generally to integrate operations on a worldwide basis. The main provisions of the Burke-Hartke bill would restructure the tax system applicable to multinational enterprises by repealing the foreign investment tax credit which has been such an incentive to direct foreign investment. In addition, the bill would give the President or an appointed commission the authority to regulate capital outflows and to control and in some cases prevent the transfer of technology from the United States to foreign countries either through direct investment or through licensing. Other provisions of the bill are also designed to protect jobs in the United States. Interestingly, in March 1972, the Trades Union Congress in the United Kingdom initiated efforts to get the

Labour Party to go on record supporting a similar program with respect to British-based multinationals.

Unions associated with the headquarters of multinational corporations have sometimes used their knowledge of and influence with top management to support the efforts of host country unions. Among a number of such examples, the United Auto Workers (UAW) interceded with Ford headquarters when union activists were fired by Ford's Venezuelan subsidiary, and British unions pressured British Leyland Motors Corporation management in behalf of employees of a Chilean subsidiary. A different type of parent country strategy has been implemented by the Swedish labor movement which has been able to have a social code adopted by the government's investment guarantee program which specifies standards of behavior with respect to workers and unions that must be accepted by Swedish firms covered by the insurance program.

Parent country unions may be helpful, but the host country unions see themselves as having the final responsibility for developing effective strategies to counteract the advantages of multinational corporations. One general strategic thrust involves the attempt to strengthen the host country union so that it is more capable of representing workers in the face of the multinational corporate challenge. Major efforts have been undertaken by various national unions to educate their members about the international nature of employers and the problems that result, for it is thought by many European labor officials that successful tactics cannot be adopted without the full support and understanding of the membership. Similarly, training programs with the objective of increasing the organizing, administrative, and negotiating skills of officials have also been initiated as have major organizing drives designed to increase the membership of the union. Additionally, conscious and partially successful efforts have been instituted in Japan, Mexico, and Italy to reduce competition and promote cooperation among competing unions in the same industry. Many of these union strengthening tactics benefit the union in relations with management regardless of the international or domestic nature of the firm, but anything that increases the ability of the union to confront management is thought to be helpful in the struggle with multinational corporations.

Cross-national Cooperation

A few national unions have attempted to seek rules and regulations from the host country government that are designed to protect unions from the problems presented by multinational corporations, but while much lip service is given to this tactic, few unions have undertaken, much less successfully completed, such campaigns. A more successful strategy that has developed largely on an ad hoc basis involves the establishment of cooperative linkages between host country unions on the one hand and parent country or other host country unions on the other. Cross-national cooperation among national unions takes a number of forms, but is important to note that the focus of cooperation is almost exclusively a specific multinational corporation or a multinational project, and the participants are industrial unions from several or more states representing employees at various facilities of the same international enterprise. Exchange of information—one form of cross-national cooperation—about working conditions, wage rates, fringe benefits, contract provisions, production and profit figures, and the nature of recent management actions may be most useful in planning strategy for negotiations with management or negating management moves designed to play off a union in one state against one in another state. Similarly, consultation among officials of several national unions facilitates the exchange of information, reduces barriers of distance, language, and difference among unions of different states, and often leads to the planning of joint actions with respect to the corporation. Whether a one-time activity or a more routinized and ongoing type of action, cross-national cooperation involving information exchange and consultation may somewhat reduce the advantages enjoyed by the multinational corporation solely because of its international nature.

Inter-union coordination is a third type of cross-national cooperation. In this case, plans are developed and implemented in such a way as to confront the multinational enterprise with the combined strength of two or more unions from at least two states. Solidarity actions, whereby unions in other states come to the aid of a union involved in a dispute with management in a particular state, are the most frequent type of inter-union coordination. Here are some recent examples: Norwegian and German employees of IT&T subsidiaries gathered contributions in support of Spanish unionists dismissed by IT&T's Spanish subsidiary; a French union associated with a subsidiary of Union Carbide refused to export to the United States during the duration of a strike against Union Carbide in America; and an official of the UAW testified before an Australian labor court in successful support of a wage increase for employees of a General Motors subsidiary. In the future, other efforts at inter-union coordination may consist of the development of harmonized (not equalized) demands with respect to fringe benefits and working conditions, or the establishment of a united front whereby a group of unions from different states insist upon settlement with all or settlement with none. Up to this point though, solidarity actions have been dominant.

While national unions have participated in information exchange, consultation, and inter-union coordination in about equal proportions, it is also apparent that most national unions much prefer to rely upon their own efforts to increase their strength vis-a-vis the multinational corporation. Many national union leaders in Europe and elsewhere would agree with the conclusion of the October 1970 meeting of the Trades Union Congress on multinational corporations which determined that British unions should concentrate on increasing their own abilities and strength rather than relying on cross-national cooperative efforts among unions.

The Regional Level

At the regional level—our discussions will be limited to developments in Europe—the growth of the European Economic Community (EEC) has stimulated the development of a number of European labor organizations among whose duties are the protection of unions against multinational corporations. The European Confederation of Free Trade Unions (ECFTU) is a comprehensive union organization composed of the noncommunist and nonconfessional unions in the EEC, which percieves itself essentially as a regional lobbying organization representing the interests of unions in the deliberations and decisions of the EEC Commission and the Council of Ministers. In the case of European cross-border mergers, the ECFTU has sought to obtain such things as: required preliminary consultation between union and management whenever employment stability is threatened; and the maintenance of existing collective agreements for the unions affected by a merger. With respect to the proposed European Company Law for new European firms, the ECFTU attempted unsuccessfully to have the *Comité de Surveillance* composed of workers, shareholders, and the public in equal proportions. However, it is still proposing that for each European company, there be established a permanent committee of trade union representatives from each plant of the company which would meet regularly with management. Of course, the ECFTU has other lines of activities, but the discussion serves to indicate the types of efforts being pursued. Mention should also be made of a November 1971 meeting of unions associated with the expanded EEC. The purpose of the initial meeting was to establish a European group to seek further cooperation and coordination among European trade unions, and while the form and policies of such a group have not been formulated, it is a development that may have important consequences for the nature of labor-management relations on a European basis.

There are a number of other European union organizations, but the most important for our purposes is the European Metalworkers' Federation (EMF) in the Community. Representing most noncommunist metalworking unions in the EEC, the EMF shares with the ECFTU an interest representation role towards the Common market, but the EMF is also an active promoter of cross-national cooperation among European metalworking unions with the objective of beginning discussions and negotiations with employers on an EEC level. Focusing on specific multinational firms, the EMF aids affiliated national unions in establishing mechanisms of information exchange and consultation, sometimes involving central union officials and other times factory-level shop stewards. Working groups corresponding to specific firms are formed to discuss problems, and at times the groups will indicate the types of information to be collected by each national union to facilitate forecasting with respect to employment stability, management tactics, and other matters. In addition, the EMF helps coordinate activities leading to solidarity actions among member unions.

However, the EMF is most noteworthy for the central role it has played in developing and instituting meetings between top management personnel of multinational corporations and union officials representing workers employed by various European installations of the firm. Four such meetings have already been held with Philips' management, and other conferences have been held or are scheduled with Brown-Boveri, VFW-Fokker, Honeywell, and AEG-Siemens. While these meetings are intended to be merely discussions of various matters, the general secretary hopes that they will evolve into collective bargaining sessions of a sort, and the history of the Philips meetings indicates a tendency in this direction.

The International Level

As at the state and regional levels, international union organizations are comprehensive in nature, like the International Confederation of Free Trade Unions (ICFTU), or industry-oriented, like the International Trade Secretariats (ITS). In addition, such organizations may be affiliated to or identified with the communist, the confessional, or the noncommunist labor movements, and while all three types are concerned with the problem of the multinational corporations, attention will be focused on the noncommunist ICFTU and ITS, as they have been most active in developing responses to the multinational corporate challenge.

As a broadly encompassing international labor organization, the ICFTU has concentrated on promoting the concept of internationally developed and enforced regulations which would establish standards of behavior with respect to workers, trade unions, and other matters to be followed by all multinational enterprises. In its own meetings, at the conventions and conferences of other union and nonunion organizations, and even before a joint committee of the United States Congress, the ICFTU has urged that GATT (General Agreement on Tariffs and Trade), the World Bank, the UN, the OECD (Organization for Economic Cooperation and Development), or some new organization take the lead in developing a mechanism to prevent multinational corporations from taking advantage of the limited influence of states and state labor movements. While success has not been achieved, the efforts have served to publicize the problems posed by the multinationals before a wide variety of prestigious organizations.

In contrast to the comprehensive and legalistic approach of the ICFTU, a number of the ITS have been particularly active in developing strategies to confront specific multinational firms. In the area of supporting union strengthening activities at the national union level, ITS, like the International Metalworkers' Federation (IMF) and the International Federation of Petroleum and Chemical Workers (IFPCW), have conducted seminars at headquarters and in the field to aid national officials in improving their ability to represent worker interests with international firms. Recently, a delegation from the IMF conducted a roving seminar in various Latin American states which focused on Philips and General Electric to provide local union officials with knowledge about the companies on a world-wide basis as well as to sharpen negotiating skills. In addition, ITS publications frequently highlight the multinational corporation problem hoping to increase the awareness, concern, and international orientation of workers and officials.

However, several of the ITS have designed strategies which have attempted to overcome the main advantage of the multinational firm—its international nature. Consequently, creative and persistent efforts to establish cross-national cooperation among unions to present international enterprises with an international union counterpart have been undertaken. Information exchange and consultation mechanisms have been established by the most active ITS, with approximately 90 percent of these efforts conducted on a routinized and continuing basis. The IMF has organized a number of World Autoworkers Councils corresponding to the major international automobile manufacturers, and it has also established similar councils for the giant electrical manufacturers. While these councils meet periodically and receive staff support from IMF headquarters, the IUF, FIET, and ICF have also formed corporate working groups with the objective of collecting and exchanging information about various corporate practices of relevance to trade unions. Periodic meetings of these groups supplement such efforts and sometimes lead to joint planning about contract negotiations or industrial disputes. Of course, ad hoc information exchanges and consultations are also pursued by the ITS as the occasion arises, but thus far primary emphasis has been put on developing continuing relationships focusing on a specific corporation.

The ITS have also exhibited a readiness to stimulate or coordinate inter-union coordination activities, especially of an ad hoc solidarity nature, implemented to aid a particular union or set of unions in disputes with a multinational corporation. Pressure at headquarters and facilities around the world, refusal of overtime work, collection of monetary contributions, foreign and international expert advice, and participation in bargaining have all been instituted by the more active of the ITS. In 1969 the ICF coordinated an effort among the unions of four different states with respect to the St. Gobain negotiations, and while the united front did break down, there was some uniformity of timing and tactics. Currently the IMF and the IUF are considering the possibility of common termination dates for contracts in a number of different companies. Unfortunately, there is not enough space to examine the many examples of ITS involvement in and stimulation of policies that are designed to make the union side more international and less fragmented in confrontations with multinational corporations, but while there are many obstacles to an immediate and complete achievement of this goal, it is clear that an action-oriented commitment does exist.

Projections about International Unionism

Assuming the continued growth and expansion of multinational corporations, it is appropriate to conclude by making some predictions about probable future developments and the roles various types of union organizations will play. National comprehensive unions will continue to assist national industrial unions in union-strengthening activities, but along with the regional and international comprehensive union organizations, another main function will be to seek the establishment of regulations and standards that will serve to control multinational corporations. However, this objective will not be easily achieved, for as long as the governments of states feel that foreign investment is desirable and necessary, it is unlikely that they individually will support restrictions that may drive away these firms. Thus, it will be difficult for a single state to adopt such a code except in isolated circumstances. On the international level, the task of getting a sufficient number of states to agree to such limitations is difficult indeed, particularly since established and trusted mechanisms for enforcement are lacking. On the regional level, though, there is a good possibility that some type of standards will evolve. With a centralized governmental structure in the EEC, trade unions have already formed regional interest representation organizations which are attempting to promote the concerns and objectives of their affiliated national union centers.

While there is some acceptance of the regulatory approach to the problem, a majority of the national, regional, and international industrial union leaders interviewed were quite skeptical of the possibilities of success, particularly on the international level. Instead, there was much greater support for the development of strategies that would directly confront the multinational corporation—not an industry or business in general, but specific international firms. The ITS are the most aware, most skilled, and most committed union organizations with respect to the multinational corporations, and while they are willing to aid national unions in their self-development efforts, the leaders of the ITS are convinced that cross-national cooperation is a necessity for effective response to the international challenge. Consequently, it is likely that the ITS will continue to play an initiatory role in developing activities designed to create an international labor counterpart to the international strength of the multinational corporation.

However, the ITS are frequently accused by national industrial union officials of being too far removed from the reality of practical situations existing at the national level. This cynicism is important because the national industrial unions provide the membership and finances upon which regional and international industrial unions are based. Furthermore, most of the crucial contacts with multinational corporations occur at the work place and national industrial union levels. Therefore, the ITS must have the active support and cooperation of the national industrial union leaders if any of their strategies are to be implemented successfully.

Thus, while much of the creativity, leadership, and skill with respect to union responses to multinational corporations will probably come from the ITS, the national industrial union leaders are in a powerful veto position. This situation becomes critical when it is recognized that, by their own admission, national union leaders and members tend to be highly nationalistic and rather suspicious of unions in other countries, and as a result they are somewhat reluctant to become committed to an international effort. In addition, at the national level, union members are generally unaware of the multinational corporate challenge, and their leaders, busy with everyday and immediate matters, tend to lack the time and necessary staff to develp long-term strategies involving cooperation.

It may be that regional European efforts at cross-national cooperation will meet with increasing success and support, for the EEC is developing an identity of its own, and the differences among unions and national industrial relations systems, while very large, are not as great as those existing between European unions and those from different regions of the world. Thus organizations like the EMF may grow in importance. It must be mentioned, though, that other areas of the world have not progressed very far towards regional integration, and while the European situation may be a forerunner of things to come, it is equally as likely that it may continue to be an exception for quite some time. As a result, where regional consciousness and organizations do not exist, the ITS will probably be instrumental in developing and implementing multinational efforts to confront the multinational corporation.

In conclusion, the response of labor unions to the multinational corporation will continue to be varied, although strategies and tactics will increase both in number and sophistication. The ITS and various regional industrial organizations will take the lead in developing cross-national cooperative efforts, focusing on particular multinational enterprises, which will involve unions from a number of different countries. Within five or six years, there will be a number of instances of European collective bargaining sessions and agreements involving specific corporations, and cooperation and coordination between U.S. and European unions will increase markedly. However, the single-state orientation of national industrial unions and their understandable concern with serving the interests of their members will produce situations in which various national unions will not perceive it to be in their best interests to enter into cooperative arrangements. This may become an especially serious problem where labor in advanced industrial states and workers in developing countries are seen to be competing for jobs. The job export complaints of U.S. unions are being repeated in the United Kingdom and most likely will become an issue in other European countries as their comparatively high wage costs lead to some production shifts to lower-wage areas. The labor union movement in general has failed to develop a satisfactory approach to this basic but largely ignored issue; yet the internationalism of the multinational corporation may force the issue upon labor shortly.

IV

Labor Market Issues

Labor
Force
Statistics

Is the rate of unemployment too high? If so, how can it be brought down in an economic context of upward price pressures? The answer to the first question depends, in part, upon how we go about counting the unemployed. Given the significance of the rate of unemployment as an economic indicator, it is not surprising that unemployment measurement methodology, always a sensitive issue, has been especially controversial during the 1970s. The first two selections in this section describe the problems involved in deriving a count of the unemployed and demonstrate the range of results produced by measurement methods which differ from the one currently used in the United States' monthly survey of the labor force. Succeeding selections describe, both generally and theoretically, the special characteristics of contemporary unemployment which pose unusual challenges for public policy. The third series of articles describes the unique problems of particular groups in the labor force, and the final piece is an extended analysis of the uses and limits of manpower policy for alleviating the problems of these and other groups which have fared poorly in the unsettled labor markets of recent years.

A Labor Market Primer

Steven P. Zell

After remaining at or below the 5.2 percent level for the first 6 months of 1974, the national unemployment rate began its long anticipated climb in the third quarter. In the coming months, it is reasonably certain that the economic slowdown will result in a continuing rise in the overall rate of unemployment. The furor and unease which have accompanied this increasing unemployment also are likely to continue to rise.

Reprinted from the *Monthly Review,* January 1975, pp.10–16, with the permission of the Federal Reserve Bank of Kansas City, Missouri.

While the national unemployment rate has long served as an important signal for policymakers, labor economists have repeatedly stressed that this composite unemployment rate has many component parts which must be examined separately. Changes in unemployment generally vary greatly among population groups when these groups are delineated by characteristics such as age, sex, race, and education. Therefore in assessing the impact of unemployment on the economy, it may be crucial to distinguish in which of these groups the major changes are taking place.

Beyond this, unemployment is not the only measure of the health of the U.S. labor market. Each month, the Bureau of Labor Statistics (BLS) of the U.S. Department of Labor collects and releases statistics on a broad range of labor market characteristics. As the economy continues its struggle with inflation and recession, we may expect increased public exposure to concepts such as the civilian labor force, rates of participation, duration of unemployment, and discouraged workers. Each of these statistics, along with other key data, plays an important role in the interpretation of labor market developments. The object of this article . . . is to provide a guide for interpreting these developments.

Where Do the Data Come From?

Each month the BLS publishes labor market data derived from two independent sources—the household series and the establishment series. Though tending to show the same underlying economic influences, these two series differ in many respects. The most crucial of these differences is that while the household series presents a picture of the work status of individuals, the payroll (or establishment) series is a count of jobs.

The household series data are compiled for the BLS by the Bureau of the Census through its monthly Current Population Survey (CPS). The CPS provides a unique source of detailed data on the economic status and activities of the U.S. population. In addition to providing information on the broad labor market concepts such as total unemployment, the CPS is designed to provide a large amount of detailed and supplementary data necessary for the interpretation of labor market phenomena. Thus, for example:

> It is the only source of monthly estimates of total employment, both farm and nonfarm; of nonfarm self-employed persons, domestics and unpaid family helpers in nonfarm family enterprises as well as wage and salaried employees; and of total employment, whether or not covered by unemployment insurance. It is the only comprehensive source of information on the personal characteristics of the total population (both in and out of the labor force) such as age and sex, race, marital and family status, veteran status, and educational background.

The CPS (also known as the household survey) is the only comprehensive source of data on the occupation of workers, providing statistics on their industrial distribution as well. Furthermore, detailed information is available on the characteristics of persons who are not currently in the labor force, including information on their past work experience, their reasons for nonparticipation, and their intentions to seek work in the future. Because of the wealth of information on individuals contained in the household survey and the sharply different emphasis of the establishment series, attention in this article shall be concentrated on the household series data.

Properties of the Sample

Once each month, in the calendar week containing the 19th of that month, the interview staff of the Bureau of the Census conducts the household survey on behalf of the

BLS. These monthly surveys are administered to a sample of the population scientifically selected to represent the civilian noninstitutional population of the United States. The survey is designed to ascertain the employment status during the calendar week containing the 12th of the month, of all the individuals 16 years of age and older residing in the interviewed household. Although a separate questionnaire is prepared for each individual, any adult member present in the household is requested to respond for those not at home at the time of the interview. Excluded from the regular monthly enumerations are inmates of institutions (such as prisons and mental hospitals), persons under 16 years of age, and members of the armed forces. Data on this latter group are obtained from the Department of Defense and are included in the published data in the categories "total noninstitutional population" and "total labor force."

As it would be financially prohibitive to conduct a complete enumeration of the entire population each month, a representative sample is scientifically selected. The first step in this process is the selection of a subset of areas from the 3,141 counties and cities in the country. The selected areas are comprised of 924 counties and independent cities and the District of Columbia. The sample is designed to reflect urban and rural areas, different types of industrial and farming areas, and the major geographic divisions of the country in the same proportion as they occur in the nation as a whole.

These areas are further divided into enumeration districts of about 300 households and then into small clusters of about four dwelling units each. From these clusters, the dwelling units to be surveyed are chosen by statistical selection and the households living at these addresses are interviewed. Each month approximately 47,000 households are interviewed in this manner, or approximately one household for every 1,300 in the country.

In order to avoid placing too heavy a burden on the selected families, one-fourth of the sample is replaced each month. The procedure consists of interviewing a household for 4 consecutive months, dropping it for 8 months, then interviewing it for 4 more months before permanently dropping it from the sample. This procedure also facilitates year-to-year data comparisons and month-to-month continuity of the sample.

The questionnaires obtained from these interviews are transferred to the Washington office of the BLS by the end of the week following the enumeration. There the data are put on computer tape, checked for consistency and completeness, and adjusted for the fact that no response was received from some of the occupied households. The proportion of sample households for which interviews are not obtained varies between 3 and 5 percent depending on factors such as weather, vacations, and simple refusal to respond. Following other procedures to improve their reliability, the data are tabulated and released by the Department of Labor in its monthly publication, *Employment and Earnings*.

The Current Population Survey: Origin and Evolution

The CPS was begun in 1940 as a direct result of the Great Depression. Prior to the 1930s, there was no direct measurement of unemployment. However, as labor market conditions continued to worsen in the early 1930s, many *ad hoc* measures of unemployment, frequently at great variance with each other, began to emerge. Dissatisfaction with these results, in turn, led research groups and some state and local governments to experiment with direct survey techniques.

In these early surveys, the unemployed were generally identified as those persons who responded that they were not currently working but were "willing and able to work." This definition, however, was judged to be too dependent on the interpretation and attitude of the interviewee and further experimentation continued. In the late 1930s, new concepts were developed which sought to meet these criticisms. Under these new concepts, an individual's classification depended primarily upon his actual labor market activity during a specified time period. Some examples of labor market activity were whether he was working, looking for work, or doing something else. In 1940, these concepts were adopted by the Works Progress Administration for the national sample survey initiated in that year.

Since the survey's inception in 1940, a continuing effort has been under way to clarify and refine the various manpower concepts and to improve available labor market data. Most of the changes which have been introduced to date are a direct outgrowth of suggestions made by the President's Committee to Appraise Employment and Unemployment Statistics (The Gordon Committee) in 1962. The Committee was appointed principally due to public pressure to examine labor market concepts in the light of high unemployment and a second recession within 3 years. In its final report, it gave unanimous approval of the scientific objectivity, reliability, and professionalism of the concepts and organizations involved in the collection and publication of U.S. labor market statistics. It further made a number of recommendations for improving these statistics, most of which have already been incorporated by the BLS.

The Household Survey: Current Classification Methodology and Definitions

As noted above, each month the Department of Labor releases statistics derived from the household survey (CPS) conducted in the previous month. The most widely quoted of these data pertain, of course, to the number of persons employed or unemployed and to the rate of unemployment. These and other important concepts can best be understood in terms of how they are generated from the survey itself.

Perhaps the most important point to emphasize is that interviewees are never asked to classify themselves nor, in fact, are they directly classified by the interviewer. Instead, a carefully structured questionnaire is filled out for each eligible person, with the final classification done by computer according to official criteria. What then, are the criteria for this classification?

The survey is designed to ascertain the principal activity or labor market status during the week containing the 12th of the month (survey week) for all noninstitutionalized civilians 16 years of age or older. The central goal is to delineate persons as either Employed, Unemployed, or Not in the Labor Force. The sum of these three categories constitutes the Civilian Population while the sum of the Employed and Unemployed comprises the Civilian Labor Force. Thus, the Civilian Population consists of persons either in the Civilian Labor Force or Not in the Labor Force. Those in the labor force are also said to be labor force participants and the ratio of the number of participants to those in the population is referred to as the Participation Rate. Similarly, the Unemployment Rate represents the number unemployed as a percent of the Civilian Labor Force.

At the simplest level, employed persons are individuals with jobs, while unemployed persons did not work during the survey week but are both looking for and available for work. Clearly, many people are easily classified under these definitions. For example, a person who reported working 40 hours as a carpenter for a construction company in the week of the 12th was clearly employed. Similarly, an assembly line worker who lost his job when the factory he worked at closed and who has been visiting other local factories recently seeking employment can be classified as unemployed. Finally, a woman who reports that she worked as a housewife and did not seek outside employment is thus not in the labor force.

However, a great many cases are not so easily classified. Some persons have more than one "labor market status" during the survey week, as for example, a man who works part time and attends school the rest of the week. How are such persons classified?

The Employed

The method used is one which sorts people *not* by hours spent in a particular status but, rather, by a pre-established priority system. Thus, people who did *any* work at all during the survey week for pay or profit, irrespective of time spent in any other status, are counted as employed. Similarly counted as employed are persons who worked 15 hours or more without pay in a family operated enterprise. These persons are known as "unpaid family workers" if they held no other paying job. If a person worked less than 15 hours in this activity and was otherwise neither employed nor unemployed, he is counted as outside the labor force.

Finally, five other categories of persons are counted as employed. These are individuals who held a job but did not work during the survey week because they were either (1) on vacation, (2) temporarily ill, (3) involved in a labor dispute, (4) prevented from working due to inclement weather, or (5) taking time off for various personal reasons. These persons are counted among the employed and tabulated in the category "with a job but not at work," which is presented separately in BLS publications.

Persons who are not employed must be classified as either Unemployed or Not in the Labor Force, and it is the first of these categories which has the higher classification priority.

The Unemployed

The unemployed may be divided into two basic groups. The first consists of persons who are either waiting to start a new job within 30 days or workers waiting to be recalled from layoff. Each of these criteria alone is sufficient to classify a person as unemployed.

The second and far larger group consists of individuals neither on layoff nor waiting for a job to start who satisfy three specific criteria which are identified through a series of questions on the household questionnaire. These criteria are first, not having a job during the survey week; second, actively looking for work during the past 4 weeks; and third, being available during the survey week to accept employment. Actively seeking work consists of at least one of the following specific activities: (1) registering at a public or private employment office, (2) meeting with prospective employers, (3) checking with friends or relatives, (4) placing or answering advertisements, (5) writing letters of application, and (6) being on a union or professional register. If a person is found to have searched for work through one of these specific activities within the past 4 weeks, he is then asked whether there was any reason he could not have accepted a job during the survey week. If no reason (other than temporary illness) is given, the person is then counted as unemployed. The process of classifying a person as unemployed is therefore seen as consisting of a series of questions, all of which must be answered appropriately. If any of these conditions are violated, the person is counted as Not in the Labor Force.

Not in the Labor Force

Persons identified as Not in the Labor Force are further divided into four groups: "in school," "keeping house," "unable to work due to disability," and "other." This last category includes mostly retired persons or persons reported as too old to work; seasonal workers who are not reported as unemployed and are in the "off" season; unpaid family workers who worked less than 15 hours in the survey week; and persons who choose not to work, referred to as the voluntary idle. The significance of this latter group shall be discussed later in the section entitled "Discouraged Workers. . . ."

Recent Developments in the Household Survey

This multi-step determination of unemployment was one of several important changes in the CPS introduced in January 1967 as an outgrowth of recommendations made by the Gordon Committee. Prior to this time, a single question, "Was . . .looking for work?" was asked to interviewees about persons who were not employed. An affirmative answer was sufficient for the persons to be counted as unemployed.

The new procedure introduces three new elements into this process. Not only must a person be looking for work, but he must have done so during a specific time period of 4 weeks. Furthermore, he must have *actively* attempted to find work and lastly, he must have been *available* for work if a job had materialized.

These changes were introduced for several reasons, but most generally, they were introduced in order to eliminate some of the ambiguity from the classification process. For example, the 4-week period was included because respondents to the previous single question "could have interpreted 'looking for work' to imply either 'last week' or some vague earlier period. Similarly, the introduction of the specific jobseeking method requirement (not asked, of course, of persons on layoff or those waiting to begin a new job within 30 days) was designed to screen out those for whom jobseeking is more a state of mind rather than an overt action." Finally, the availability criterion was introduced principally to correct for the fact that a number of high school and college students who began to look for summer work in April or May were counted as unemployed at that time although they were not available for employment until June or July.

Some of the other important additions and changes introduced in the January 1967 *Employment and Earnings* were as follows:

1. Persons with a job during the survey week who were absent because of strikes, bad weather, etc., are now classified as employed even if they were looking for other employment at this time. Previously they were classified as unemployed.
2. New probing questions are asked to increase the reliability of information obtained on duration of unemployment, number of hours worked, and self-employment status.
3. Additional information is now being obtained which permits in-depth analysis of several important characteristics of persons both within and outside the labor force.
   a. A new question collects information on the reason for unemployment, i.e., whether the person lost his job, quit, or entered the labor force either in search of employment for the first time or after a period of nonparticipation.

b. Much more information is obtained for persons not in the labor force. Data are now collected on when they last worked; their reasons for leaving employment, and the industry and occupation in that last job; whether they want to work at the present time and, if so, why they are not seeking employment; and their intentions for seeking work in the next 12 months.

4. Finally, the new definition of unemployment *excludes* individuals who report that they would have looked for employment except for their belief that none was available in their line of work in the community. Previously, though no specific question was asked, persons who volunteered this information were included as unemployed in an attempt to capture what was referred to as "discouraged workers." Now recorded among the voluntarily idle, this group is excluded from the unemployed by means of the 4-week and active search criteria discussed above. This is done because of the very subjective nature of worker "discouragement." Instead they are included among persons Not in the Labor Force, while information on the reason for nonparticipation is collected and analyzed.

Discouraged Workers Among the Voluntarily Idle: The Hidden Unemployed

The special survey questions probing the reasons why persons outside the labor force did not participate in the job market were introduced in response to one of the Gordon Committee's strongest recommendations. The committee noted in 1962 that "the relatively simple dichotomy between those in and out of the labor force . . . (no longer provides) . . . a satisfactory measure of labor supply."

This conclusion was based on empirical evidence for the post-World War II period which showed that millions of persons entered and left the labor force each year and that the labor force expanded more slowly during economic downturns than it did over the long run. This slowdown in labor force growth, the result of an increased number of dropouts or a decreased number of entrants into the labor force, or some combination of the two, was interpreted as the "discouragement" effect of the cyclical downturn. The possibility that vast numbers of "discouraged workers" languished outside the labor force in a pool of "hidden unemployment" caused the committee to recommend that special efforts be made to collect detailed information on persons not in the labor force, with emphasis on the so-called "discouraged workers."

The introduction of the probing questions in the January 1967 CPS and their quarterly publication since late 1969 provided an important opportunity to examine this issue directly, through use of the survey technique. Though major difficulties exist in the identification of subjective phenomena like "worker discouragement," the methodology adopted by the BLS has provided much useful information since the initial publication of these data in late 1969. Basically, a person not in the labor force is identified as a discouraged worker if he "wants a regular job now, either full time or part time" and if his principal reason for not looking for work is that he either (1) believes that no work is available in his line of work or area, (2) had tried but could not find work, (3) lacks necessary schooling, training, skills, or experience, (4) employers think he is too young or too old, or (5) has other personal handicaps in finding a job.

The first two of these factors are generally referred to as "job market factors" and the remainder as "personal factors," and, as might be expected, it is this first series which appears to be directly related to cyclical changes in the labor market. In particular, a high correlation has been found between this series and changes in the rate of unemployment. Contrary to conclusions drawn from earlier econometric analyses, however, the survey results do not indicate the existence of large numbers of discouraged workers. Furthermore, only a small percentage of discouraged workers are adult males, with the great majority consisting, instead, of teenagers, housewives, and the elderly.

Research into the phenomenon of worker discouragement has revealed some interesting results for the interpretation of labor market behavior. Studies have shown that in the face of cyclical downturns, the growth of the labor force has slowed while the number of discouraged workers has risen. Contrary to expectations, however, this shrinkage or slowdown in labor force growth has been due primarily to reductions in labor force entries and reentries rather than to increases in labor force withdrawals. Furthermore, while the number of discouraged workers generally increases in cyclical downturns, a countercyclical flow of "added workers" is always present. For example, in families whose heads are unemployed, the rate of participation of other family members increases more than in households whose heads are employed. Generally, though, the discouragement effect is the dominant one.

If economic conditions develop, however, where this cyclical behavior is changed, and participation remains high in the face of recession, the rate of unemployment can be expected to worsen relative to previous experience. This, in fact, appears to be the case with the present "stagflation." In the present economic downturn, as in the past, increased unemployment of household heads has stimulated some "added" secondary worker participation. In addition to this, the high rate of inflation has also stimulated greater participation as families attempt to maintain their level of real income. In a period when employment is falling, however, this increased participation can only result in greater unemployment. One important indicator of the existence of this trend is continuing high rates of participation among women and teenagers in the face of high and rising unemployment. Another is the atypically small number of persons currently classified as discouraged workers. Thus many persons who, under ordinary recessionary conditions would be outside of the labor force, possibly as discouraged workers, now appear to be entering or remaining in the labor force in an attempt to circumvent the negative effects of recession and inflation on real family income.

Employment and Unemployment: The Doughnut or the Hole?

Julius Shiskin

The Employment Act of 1946, one of the landmark pieces of legislation in the history of our country, specifically provides that ". . . it is the continuing policy and responsibility of the Federal Government to use all practicable means . . . for creating and

Reprinted from the *Monthly Labor Review,* February 1976, pp. 3–10.

maintaining . . . conditions under which there will be afforded useful employment opportunities . . . for those able, willing, and seeking to work, and to promote maximum employment, production, and purchasing power." Among these goals, the one which has probably received the greatest attention over the three decades since the passage of this legislation is that of maintaining maximum employment. This attention has been magnified in the past year as unemployment rose to record levels last spring before showing some improvement in recent months.

The recent recession has also heightened public awareness of the fact that, while there has been widespread agreement on the need for full employment, there has been little agreement on just what full employment is, how unemployment should be defined, or of what specific data should be used in judging the performance of the economy. There is even disagreement on whether the focus should be on the employment or unemployment statistics. The media—as well as the professional literature— have focused mostly on unemployment. This has led analysts who believe the emphasis should be placed on employment to entitle the debate as "the doughnut or the hole?"

More specifically, it is the problem of measuring employment (the doughnut) and unemployment (the hole)—and the use of these measures in assessing economic performance—with which this article is concerned. Unemployment and the problems associated with its measurement are discussed first, because this area has received the most attention over the years; a discussion of measures of employment, which has recently received more intensive study and analysis, follows.

Measures of Unemployment

While both the developers and users of labor force statistics agree that no single unemployment measure can serve all the purposes for which such data are needed, there is much diversity of opinion about the most appropriate overall measure. The reason is that the unemployment figures are used by many persons for different purposes. Many use them to assess current conditions and short-term prospects, that is, as a cyclical indicator. Others use the data as a measure of how well the economy relieves the economic and psychological hardships experienced by jobseekers. But judgments as to what constitutes hardship arising from unemployment vary greatly among different political, social, and economic groups. Some view economic hardship in terms of the three basic elements of food, clothing, and shelter; others consider it in terms of relative standing in the income distribution, with all persons who fall in, say, the lowest one-fifth of the range classified as experiencing economic hardship. Still others consider those unemployed with adequate income from sources other than employment to be experiencing psychological hardship if they cannot find a job and, therefore, are denied an opportunity for a fuller life in some sense. Further, many believe long spells of unemployment for teenagers to be especially damaging to their development as responsible members of society.

This problem should also be approached from the viewpoint of economists, who are concerned with the overall performance of our economy in achieving vigorous economic growth. Looked at in this way, a measure which is geared strictly to economic hardship will necessarily be too narrowly based to give a good picture of the total, immediately available labor supply. Conversely, a measure which attempts to reflect the sum total of the underutilization of all potential manpower resources will undoubtedly include many persons with fairly comfortable levels of living.

Thus, no single way of measuring unemployment can satisfy all analytical or ideological interests. To meet the multiple needs of data users, the Bureau of Labor Statistics regularly publishes a wide variety of unemployment rates and indicators in its Employment Situation press release and the monthly publication, *Employment and Earnings*. It also publishes separate data on persons involuntarily working less than full time and on discouraged workers, which can be added to the figures on the unemployed by those who wish to do so. In general, it can be said that these published statistics are not specifically designed to measure economic hardship, but rather derive from an activity concept in which persons working are considered to be employed, persons looking for work are unemployed, and persons doing neither are not in the labor force at all. Finally, a distinction must be made between the use of the various unemployment series as cyclical indicators and as measures of the economy's performance.

Table 1 presents a grouping of unemployment indicators, or categories of the unemployed, identified by the symbols U–1 through U–7, which carries the process of presenting the unemployment statistics one step further. This relatively small array of unemployment measures illustrates a range of value judgments on the hardship that is experienced by the unemployed, going from a very narrow to a very broad view. Others could, of course, make their own selection of such indicators. The data compiled by the BLS make it possible to construct a very large number of different measures of unemployment. The ones presented here were chosen because they are representative of differing bodies of opinion about the meaning and measurement of unemployment, because they are meaningful and useful measures in their own right, and because they can generally be ranked along a scale from low to high.

No approval or disapproval of the value judgments implicit in the selection of these series is intended here. All series are regularly published by the BLS with the exception of U–6 and U–7, and in these cases the components are published, so they can easily be calculated by anyone who wishes to do so.

The first series, U–1, is the number of persons unemployed 15 weeks or longer as a percent of the civilian labor force. The rationale behind the selection of this series is the belief that unemployment is a more severe problem when it has lasted long enough to cause substantial financial hardship. The assumption is that shorter periods can be handled by unemployment compensation plus the use of savings and, in some cases, assistance from other family members.

The second series, U–2, is the number of persons who lost their last jobs, taken as a percent of the civilian labor force. The implication of this series is that unemployment is more serious for experienced workers, from whom the loss of a job leads to significantly lower income. Here unemployment which accompanies entry or reentry into the labor force and voluntary job-leaving would appear to be considered an inevitable but less serious matter.

U–3 is the number of household heads unemployed as a percent of all household heads in the civilian labor force. In this case, it is assumed that unemployment is more serious when it affects breadwinners. Other jobseekers, secondary workers, would presumably be supported by the heads of households while seeking employment.

U–4 is the number of unemployed persons seeking full-time jobs, as a percent of all those in the full-time labor force (including those employed part time for economic reasons). The assumption here is that a measure which is limited to those unemployed who are strongly attached to the labor force is more meaningful than one which also

TABLE 1 Range of Unemployment Indicators Reflecting Value Judgments about Significance of Unemployment, 1974–75 (Percent)

U–1 through U–7	Annual averages		Seasonally adjusted data	
	1974	1975	October 1973 (cyclical low month)	May 1975 (cyclical high month)
U–1—Persons unemployed 15 weeks or longer as a percent of total civilian labor force	1.0	2.7	0.9	2.7
U–2—Job losers as a percent of civilian labor force	2.4	4.7	1.7	5.1
U–3—Unemployed household heads as a percent of the household head labor force ..	3.3	5.8	2.7	6.1
U–4—Unemployed full-time job seekers as a percent of the full-time labor force (including those employed part time for economic reasons)	5.1	8.1	4.1	8.5
U–5—Total unemployed as a percent of civilian labor force (official measure)	5.6	8.5	4.7	8.9
U–6—Total full-time job seekers plus half part-time job seekers plus half total on part time for economic reasons as a percent of civilian labor force less half part-time labor force	6.9	10.3	5.9	10.9
U–7—Total full-time job seekers plus half part-time job seekers plus half total on part time for economic reasons plus discouraged workers as a percent of civilian labor force plus discouraged workers less half of part-time labor force .	7.7	11.5	6.6	12.0

Note: Reflects recent revisions of basic data, including seasonal experience through December 1975.

includes more casual and marginally attached workers. Unemployment is likely to be more serious for full-time than for part-time workers because the former are more likely to be breadwinners, will lose more income through inability to find work, and are more committed to the labor force.

U–5 is the official, regularly published unemployment rate for all workers age 16 years and over. This series represents the total number of persons not working but available for and seeking work, as a percent of the civilian labor force. It can be viewed as the base series from which each of the other six series discussed in this article is constructed through the addition or subtraction of various labor force and unemployment components. In a sense, this series reflects a consensus among the many different user groups; it involves no value judgments regarding a person's family or marital status, relative need for work, or personal characteristics. It only requires that jobseeking take place. It has had widespread support from various study groups and was recommended by the Committee to Appraise Employment and Unemployment Statistics (Gordon Committee) established by President Kennedy in 1961.

U–6 includes, as a percent of the labor force, the number of unemployed persons seeking full-time work, plus one-half of the number of unemployed persons seeking part-time work and one-half of the number of those involuntarily on part-time work schedules but desiring full-time employment (with the part-time labor force given only half weight). The rationale behind this series is that involuntary part-time workers should be counted as at least partially unemployed, and their loss of working time should be reflected in the overall measure. Similarly, it is felt that unemployed persons seeking only part-time work should be given only half weight because their employed counterparts—those employed part time voluntarily—work about half a full-time workweek; the voluntary part-time employed are also given half weight. (This indicator is comparable to the "percent of labor force time lost" series, which *is* regularly published.)

The final series, U–7, is the same as U–6 except that the number of discouraged workers is added to both the unemployed and labor force components. This series is based on the idea that the situation of discouraged workers is essentially the same as that of the unemployed—they are jobless, want work, and presumably are available for work. The only difference is that they are not looking for jobs because they believe no work is available for them. It should be noted, however, that specific information regarding their work history and prior job-search activity is not now collected, and many of them could be reflecting only a casual interest in entering the labor market or maintaining an unrealistic desire for a prestigious job paying a high salary.

As can be seen from the foregoing discussion, the data available from the BLS allow interested persons to construct unemployment series that range from those using very narrow definitions of unemployment to those based on extremely broad criteria. The series selected depends largely on the particular use to which one wishes to put the data, and on the attitudes held concerning the nature and severity of unemployment.

In table 1, the 1974 and 1975 annual average values for each of the series U–1 through U–7 are shown along with the values for the cyclical high and low months of the recent recession. In 1975, as the table indicates, the series ranged from a low value of 2.7 for series U–1 to a high of 11.5 for series U–7.

Each of the series is also plotted on chart 1 on a quarterly basis from 1953, or the first year the data for a particular series are available, through the fourth quarter of 1975.

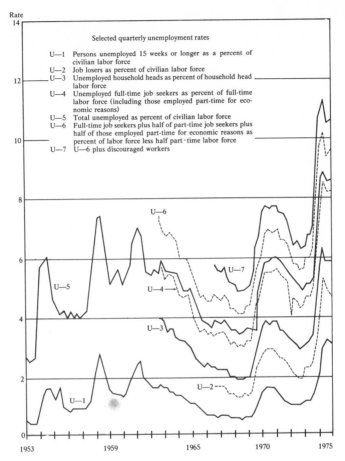

CHART 1 Unemployment Indicators, 1953 through 1975

Note: Trend lines do not reflect recent revisions in basic data.

The chart clearly illustrates the successively higher percentages of unemployment reflected by each of the series.

Measures of Employment

We now turn to the employment statistics, to consider two alternative employment measures and the information that they provide for economic analysis and interpretation.

First, it should be pointed out that the employment figures have numerous statistical advantages over the unemployment figures.

Under the survey procedures, every person 16 years or over in the civilian noninstitutional population is classified as employed, unemployed, or not in the labor force. With few exceptions, a person who during the survey week did any work at all for which he or she was paid is considered to be employed. Persons are unemployed if they did not work at all during the survey week, were available for work, and actively tried to find work during the past 4 weeks. All others are classified as not in the labor force.

Employment, therefore, is a firmer and more objective concept than unemployment; consequently, it is easier to define and measure. In measuring unemployment, uncertainties can arise, such as in the determination of whether jobless persons are actively seeking work or whether they are currently available for work. The identification of employment, on the other hand, is relatively straightforward.

Next, employment, a much larger figure than unemployment, is subject to a relatively smaller measurement error. To illustrate, in the fourth quarter of 1975 there were 85.4 million employed and 7.8 million unemployed.

Additionally, the seasonal adjustment of employment is more accurate than that of unemployment. The reason is that seasonal changes in total employment are relatively small, as are changes in the level from one period to another. In contrast, unemployment is subject to large seasonal swings as well as dramatic changes in level over short periods of time. As a result, the multiplicative seasonal adjustment method, which BLS uses and which has almost always worked well for economic series, introduces distortions into the seasonally adjusted unemployment series when the level changes dramatically. There are no similar problems in adjusting the employment series.

The employment series is not without statistical and definitional problems, however. Some analysts believe allowances should be made for part-time workers, underutilized workers, and workers with earnings below the poverty threshold.

Employment-Labor Force Ratio

The first employment measure to be considered is the employment-labor force ratio, or the percentage of the civilian labor force that is employed. Thus, it is simply the complement of the familiar total unemployment rate. It provides a measure of actual employment as a percentage of that part of the population which has met the market test of working or actively seeking work.

Despite the use of a more solid figure in the numerator, the advantages of the employment-labor force ratio over the unemployment rate are dubious. The major public concern lies with trends in unemployment. The reason that a series such as the jobless rate is constructed in the first place is to focus on a problem. This is similarly true for statistics on illness, crime, poverty, and other areas. Thus, public attention has not been directed to the percent of people in good health, of those who have escaped crime, or of those who are above the poverty threshold. Rather, attention is centered on the percent of persons who are ill, who have been victims of crime, or who have incomes below the poverty level. And such statistical series are compiled to provide data for those concerned with social or economic problems.

Although BLS receives occasional requests that the employment-labor force ratio be featured in press releases and public discussions, this measure has not received widespread acceptance for use as an economic or social indicator. The ratio itself is not regularly published by the Bureau of Labor Statistics, but it can easily be calculated by subtracting the unemployment rate from 100.

Employment-Population Ratio

Another employment measure, and one which seems to be more useful than the employment-labor force ratio, is the employment-population ratio. It is derived by dividing the total civilian employment by the civilian non-institutional population age 16 years and over. It is a measure of employment as a percentage of the population, which is the group that is available for work in the broadest sense. This kind of measure was suggested to BLS in March 1970 by Professor Milton Friedman of the University of Chicago and had been used by some labor market analysts during the previous decade. It has been published by the BLS in *Employment and Earnings* on a quarterly basis since April 1973. Monthly data are published in that periodical for the total employment-population ratio only, but the data needed to calculate the major age-sex ratios are also published there. All of these data are also published quarterly in the BLS press release, Labor Force Developments. (See chart 2.)

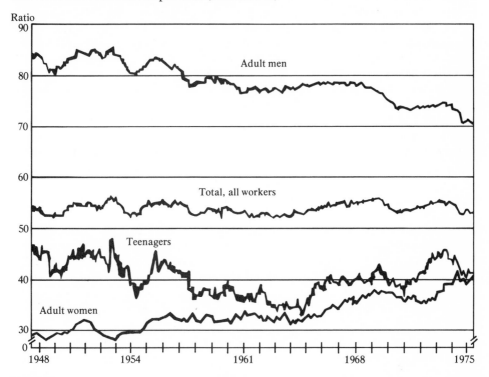

CHART 2 Employment-Population Ratio by Age and Sex, Seasonally Adjusted, 1948–75

For certain purposes of economic analysis, the employment-population ratio may provide a better measure of labor market conditions than either the unemployment or employment rate, which use the civilian labor force as the base. The reason is that the labor force itself may expand or contract in response to changes in the pace of economic activity, in contrast to the greater stability of the population.

To the extent that persons leave the labor force during an economic decline—that is, lose their jobs and do not seek others—the reduction in employment will exceed the increase in unemployment. Similarly, if there is a rapid growth in the labor force during the expansionary phase of the business cycle, employment will increase more than unemployment will decline—that is, persons enter and reenter the job market at the same time that many job losers return to work. The potential expansion and contraction of the labor force is illustrated by the data which show that more than 10 million out of a total of about 59 million persons not in the labor force during the fourth quarter of 1975 worked at some time during the preceding 12 months. Most of those leaving the labor force were housewives and students, who wanted only seasonal or other temporary work, and older persons who retired or left because of disability. About 700,000 workers were squeezed out because of slack in the economy; about two-thirds of them were women.

Further perspective on the potential expansion of the labor supply is provided by the data on discouraged workers. In the fourth quarter of 1975, about one million persons reported that they wanted jobs but did not seek them because of discouragement over job prospects. Two-thirds of this group were women. A larger group, 4.3 million persons, reported that they wanted jobs but did not look for them for a variety of reasons, such as school attendance, family responsibilities, or illness. Some of these nonparticipants might be drawn into the labor force if jobs suddenly became readily available, even at a relatively low wage. These groups not in the labor force represent a reserve which could substantially shift the size of the labor force under changing economic conditions—for example, in the event of a Federal job guarantee program or the elimination or reduction of the Federal minimum wage for teenagers.

The behavior of the labor force in the current recovery appears to be somewhat different from that of earlier recoveries. In the past, the labor force has grown very little during the first 9 months or so of cyclical recoveries. During the first 9 months of the current recovery (dating from March 1975) labor force growth has been substantial—1.2 million, compared with the median path of virtually no growth in prior recessions. There are several plausible explanations for the larger than usual cyclical growth in the labor force during 1975. According to one theory, it reflects the changing role of women in society; in fact, adult women have accounted for about half the above-normal cyclical growth this year. Another hypothesis is that the combination of inflation and unemployment has put severe financial pressure on many families and induced an unusually large number of family members to seek jobs. Still a third possible reason advanced is that some people who otherwise might have left the labor force may be staying in because of the extension of unemployment insurance benefits. Eligibility for these payments requires the beneficiary to be seeking work. In any case, and for various reasons, we have seen an unusual cyclical growth in the labor force during the recovery in 1975.

Thus, while the unemployment rate is potentially subject to wide variations as a result of special developments leading to growth or contraction in the labor force, the employment-population ratio includes a more stable base for a measure of labor market activity, one that is undisturbed by the shifts of workers into or out of this labor force.

There are measurement problems in estimating monthly population totals, but these are relatively minor, especially for age groups 16 years and over. A more serious problem is that there are no comparable population figures upon which to base trends in full- or part-time jobs, as well as in employment by occupation or industry.

Since about 1948, the employment-population ratio appears to have held about steady, except for a slight upward tilt from 1970 to 1974. (See chart 2.) However, this overall trend masks important changes in the age-sex composition of the ratio over this period. The ratio for adult men has trended gradually downward, primarily in line with increasingly early retirement. On the other hand, there has been a pronounced secular increase in the ratio for adult women over this period. Teenagers showed a dual pattern over the period, as their ratio declined between 1948 and 1964 and rose in the subsequent decade. Trends in an aggregate, made up of components which are moving in different directions, are difficult to interpret. Furthermore, aggregate employment is a simplistic measure which does not take into account variations in skills, earnings, and hours of work. Hours of work may be especially important in this context in view of the increasing proportion of part-time workers in the labor force over the last two decades. A more sophisticated measure taking such factors into account might reveal a different trend.

Like other economic indicators, the employment-population ratio should be used in conjunction with the broad range of indicators of labor market activity currently available in order to develop a balanced and accurate picture of actual labor market conditions. It should be noted, for example, that an expansion in the labor force could result in an increase in both the employment-population ration and the unemployment rate. The two measures, examined together, can be more revealing of underlying labor market developments than can either measure by itself.

It is important, as it is in assessing an economic indicator, to be wary of using *one* number without any breakdowns, as has been done by some advocates of the employment-population ratio. The BLS has repeatedly stressed in the analysis of its unemployment statistics the importance of using the wide range of detail available in order to make a sound judgment of what the underlying economic conditions are. It is equally important that this be done with the employment-population ratio. Finally, it is important to continue research into the historical and current behavior of this ratio and its many components. The Bureau of Labor Statistics will try to do further research on this subject, within the limits of our research resources, and we encourage others outside the Bureau to do further work in this area as well.

Ratio and Unemployment Rate Compared

It is useful to distinguish between a "cyclical indicator" and a "measure of performance," as already noted in the opening section on unemployment. A cyclical indicator shows what stage of the business cycle the economy is in or what stage it is likely to be in soon: thus, "coincident" indicators describe the current cyclical stage, and "leading" indicators, the stage that is likely to be reached in the period immediately ahead. The classification of economic indicators according to the sequence in which they move over the business cycle can be carried out in a reasonably objective way. On the other hand, measures of performance of the American economy reflect value judgments on the goals of economic policy—for example, high employment (or low unemployment) and stable prices. The distinction between cyclical indicators and measures of performance is emphasized by the fact that neither the unemployment rate nor the Consumer Price Index, two principal measures of economic performance, are included in the new National Bureau of Economic Research (NBER) short list of cyclical indicators. (It is also to be noted that the new NBER short list omits real gross national product (GNP), the most comprehensive measure of economic output and one of the most important measures of economic performance, because it is not available monthly.)

In its assessment of cyclical indicators, the NBER has devised a method of assigning to them numerical scores, or weights, ranging from 0 to 100. The scoring plan covers six major elements: economic significance, statistical adequacy, historical conformity to business cycles, cyclical timing record, smoothness, and promptness of publication. The ratings throw into clearer perspective the characteristic behavior and limitations of each indicator as a tool in short-term economic forecasting.

When the employment-population ratio is tested by these standards, it comes out with a score of 76, compared with 87 scored by the top cyclical indicator, nonagricultural payroll employment. The principal reason for its lower score is that the employment-population ratio has a poor cyclical timing record at business cycle peaks. Consequently, the employment-population ratio could not be classified as leading, coincident, or lagging at business cycle peaks, and it lagged at business cycle troughs. In addition, this series is fairly erratic over the short-run and, therefore, receives a relatively low score for smoothness. For these reasons, the employment-population ratio did not qualify for inclusion in the NBER short list of cyclical indicators. The total unemployment rate received a slightly higher score—78—but did not qualify for the new short list because of differential timing at peaks (led) and at troughs (lagged). While neither the unemployment rate nor the employment-population ratio was selected for the new NBER short list, they both scored fairly high. The unemployment rate, in particular, must be rated as a good cyclical indicator. If the fact that it leads at peaks and lags at troughs is borne in mind, it can be put to good use in cyclical analysis.

The unemployment rate and the employment-population ratio must both receive high ratings as measures of performance (along with real GNP and the Consumer Price Index). With this standard in mind, it should be noted that the unemployment rate reached a very high level over the course of the most recent business cycle and attained a postwar record during the 1974–75 recession. While the employment-population ratio showed a sharp drop during the recent recession, it had also indicated prior to the downturn that a slightly larger percentage of the U.S. population has been working during the past 5 years or so—the most current complete cycle—than in previous postwar cycles. (See table 2 and chart 2.) Further, the average for the full 1970–75 business cycle is higher than for any previous business cycle. Thus, in terms of the goal of promoting maximum employment, the employment-population ratio would appear to give a higher rating with respect to the performance of the American economy during the 1970s than the unemployment rate.

TABLE 2 Cyclical Trends in the Unemployment Rate and the Employment-Population Ratio since 1945

Business cycle dates (trough to trough)	Duration (months)	Unemployment rate			Employment-population ratio		
		Cyclical average	Cyclical high	Cyclical low	Cyclical average	Cyclical high	Cyclical low
			(3–month average)			(3–month average)	
(1)	(2)	(3)	(4)	(5)	(6)	(7)	(8)
October 1945–October 1949[1] ...	48	4.7	7.0	([2])	56.1	56.9	55.3
October 1949–August 1954	54	4.0	5.9	2.5	56.7	57.9	55.1
August 1954–April 1958	44	4.6	7.4	3.8	56.8	57.7	55.3
April 1958–February 1961 ...	34	5.9	7.0	5.1	55.9	56.4	55.2
February 1961–November 1970 ..	117	4.7	6.0	3.4	56.5	58.0	56.5
November 1970–March 1975	52	5.6	8.9	4.7	57.2	58.1	55.9

[1] Data are not available prior to January 1948; therefore, averages are computed for the period January 1948 to October 1949.
[2] Not available.

Note: The high and low dates used to compute the values shown in cols. (4), (5), (7), and (8) are those for the specific series rather than the general business cycle turning dates designated by National Bureau of Economic Research. The 3–month average is the mean of the high or low month, the month preceding the high or low month, and the month following the high or low month.

How can these apparently contradictory trends be explained? The answer appears to be that there are changes in the labor force participation rate—a greater percentage of the population wants to work than in the past. Thus, a greater percentage of the population is in the labor force, both as employed and also as unemployed.

For the present, we can say that the employment-population ratio and the unemployment rate are both useful cyclical indicators, though neither ranks among the very best. However, both measures rank close to the top as measures of performance. Both illuminate different aspects of labor market conditions, and both are necessary for a balanced view of the overall employment situation. Thus, I would say the answer to the question, "The doughnut or the hole?" is the doughnut *and* the hole.

Unemployment

Recent Developments in the Theory of Unemployment

Steven P. Zell

Over the 40 years since the Great Depression, economists have developed a variety of theories to explain the phenomenon of unemployment. Many of these explanations are products of their time, emerging as the result of major social and economic developments. Yet, all such models have at least one thing in common. They represent attempts by their proponents to provide a theoretical framework within which policy prescriptions can be developed.

This article examines four recent theoretical explanations for the problem of unemployment: the theory of structural unemployment, the job search labor-turnover theory, the theory of human capital, and the dual labor market hypothesis. These alternative approaches are examined with particular emphasis on their respective views of the structure and behavior of the labor market, and especially on the policy prescriptions which follow from these different views.

Inadequate Demand or Structural Unemployment?

Given the experience of the Great Depression, there understandably has been much interest in diagnosing the causes of unemployment. From a policy standpoint, however, the most important question is why workers who lose their jobs are not quickly reemployed, and why many new entrants or reentrants to the labor force remain without jobs. As noted by Gilpatrick, if reemployment is assured, the reasons for the original unemployment are of little interest. Thus, "the causes blocking reemployment are the proper targets for policy." [1]

One long-standing controversy over the persistence of unemployment developed in the late 1950s and early 1960s between the advocates of the inadequate aggregate demand theory and the proponents of the school of structural unemployment. This controversy arose at a time when the national unemployment rate seemed to lose its

Reprinted from the *Monthly Review,* September-October 1975, pp. 3–10, with the permission of the Federal Reserve Bank of Kansas City, Missouri.

resiliency. From 1951 through 1957, the unemployment rate exceeded 5 percent of the labor force only in one year, 1954. Then, after reaching its recession high of 6.8 percent in 1958, the unemployment rate did not fall below 5 percent for 7 years.

In 1961, the Joint Economic Committee conducted a series of hearings[2] to try to determine whether structural factors or inadequate demand were responsible for the high unemployment the country had been experiencing since the closing months of 1957. The distinction between these two explanations for the persistence of unemployment appeared crucial from the viewpoint of policy. The advocates of the inadequate demand theory, most notably Walter Heller, then chairman of the Council of Economic Advisors, tended to dismiss the significance of structural unemployment. They argued instead that the persistently high unemployment was due to the incomplete recovery from the 1957–58 recession. The solution therefore lay in more expansionary fiscal policies such as lower taxes and greater government spending.

The structuralists, on the other hand, viewed the unemployment as arising from a change in the composition of labor skill requirements relative to labor skill availability. They argued that the structural mismatch could arise in several ways, regardless of the level of aggregate demand. For example, technology may change, the demand for certain products may disappear, raw materials may be used up in a given geographic area, a factory or industry may change its location, or the proportion of different skill groups in the population may change over time.

As long as the labor force is able to adapt to these changes, said the structuralists, no problem exists. But if people are unwilling or unable to move to a different geographic area where workers with their qualifications are in demand, if their skills have become obsolete, or if their skills are of limited transferability and their numbers in the labor force increase without a concomitant increase in the demand for their services, structural unemployment is the result.[3]

Arguing that a combination of these developments was at the root of the persistently high unemployment, the structuralists claimed that a policy of adapting the unemployed to available job openings would substantially reduce the unemployment rate at the *current* level of national income. Because they believed the problem to be structural in nature, they further claimed that an attempt to reduce the unemployment through increasing aggregate demand would only succeed at the cost of substantial inflation as bottlenecks appeared.[4]

Following extensive debate, the inadequate demand view prevailed in Washington, and the 1964 income tax cut was passed in an attempt to stimulate demand. This provided a test of the two alternative theories which seemed to substantiate the inadequate demand position. In 1965, the unemployment rate fell below 5 percent and then remained below 4 percent from 1966 to 1969.[5] Nevertheless, a great deal of interesting work has been done on the concept of structural unemployment, and it remains a potentially useful tool for explaining certain occurrences of unemployment, especially when the economy is functioning much closer to full employment than was the case in the late 1950s and early 1960s.[6]

Some New Theories of Unemployment

Since the structuralist-inadequate demand controversy of the early 1960s, economists have generally agreed about the cause of the increase in unemployment and its persistence during and following a recession. The recession falloff in the demand for goods and services leads to a rise in the unemployment rate, while the uncertainty of a recovery, the increased productivity of those already employed, and the knowledge of the availability of a pool of unemployed workers delays rehiring once the economy begins to turn around. Yet even when the economy was functioning near the limits of its capacity, as in the late 1960s, the overall unemployment rate still hovered just below 4 percent of the labor force, while for some population groups, it was considerably higher.

Observing this phenomenon, several economists attempted to answer what has become a central question in current unemployment theory: "Why is the unemployment rate so high at full employment?" [7] Three important theories which deal directly with this question are, respectively: the job-search, labor turnover theory; the theory of human capital; and the dual labor market hypothesis.

The notion of the level of "full employment" unemployment is not unambiguous. One approach suggests that the level of "full employment" unemployment in the United States is a rate of unemployment (say, 4 to 5 percent) which, if maintained permanently, is compatible with some steady rate of inflation (say, 3 or 4 percent per year). [8] When the economy is operating at full employment (as defined in this way), an increase in aggregate demand can lower the unemployment rate further, but only at the expense of higher and higher rates of inflation. The question that the various theories of unemployment must deal with is why the full employment level of unemployment (resulting in a steady and relatively low rate of inflation) is reached at so high a rate of unemployment.

The Job-search, Labor-turnover Theory

Of the three theories of unemployment noted, the formal search-turnover model most directly draws a functional relationship between unemployment and inflation. [9] Characterized as a "rigorous theoretical development of the traditional notions of frictional unemployment," [10] the search-turnover theory views unemployment as the result of a search process, where both employers and workers have limited information about the opportunities in the labor market. According to this explanation, when a worker begins looking for a job, either from a state of nonparticipation or previous employment, it is generally not in his economic interest to take the first available position. Lacking basic information on the opportunities in the labor market, the worker instead searches for information on the types of jobs, level of wages, and working conditions available to a person of his qualifications. He therefore spends time unemployed while learning about jobs and waiting for better job offers.

Thus, according to the search-turnover theory, unemployment represents a type of investment by workers in obtaining information about the labor market. Unemployment persists because the labor market is inefficient in providing this information and thus fails to quickly match workers and job vacancies. Taking the existing patterns of labor supply and demand as given, the proponents of this theory suggest that unemployment can be substantially reduced through a comprehensive program of manpower policies. In particular, this would include a several-fold expansion in the Federal-State Employment Service to improve the quality and speed of worker-job matches and to reduce turnover; improved vocational counseling and expanded job opportunities for youth to reduce their high turnover and to increase their future productivity; training and job restructuring to reduce skill shortages in certain occupations; support of geographic mobility to reduce pockets of high unemployment while good jobs remain unfilled elsewhere; and elimination of institutional barriers, such as union restrictions on entry and occupational licensing, which increase unemployment by reducing the efficiency of search. All of these policies are based on the belief that an improvement in the inflation-unemployment trade-off can only be achieved by reducing the "frictions" within the labor market and thereby improving its efficiency.[11]

There is much to be said for this view of the labor market with its emphasis on turnover as the principal element in unemployment. Data on duration of unemployment in the United States indicate clearly that the Keynesian view—that high unemployment is caused by the long-term inability of some fraction of the labor force to find jobs—is invalid in the United States when it is functioning near "full employment." Instead, the high unemployment rates are the result of frequent, generally shorter spells of unemployment.[12]

Nevertheless, Hall and other economists find fault with the implicit premise of the search theorists that "every person who finds himself out of work is spending a few weeks between jobs in the normal advancement of his career."[13] This, they feel, incorrectly represents the labor market situation of teenagers, of women, and, in particular, of the unskilled and uneducated segments of the labor force.

> The central problem seems to be that some groups in the labor force have rates of unemployment that are far in excess of the rates that would accord with the hypothesis that the unemployed are making a normal transition from one job to another. Some groups exhibit what seems to be a pathological instability in holding jobs.[14]

Both the theory of human capital and the dual labor market hypothesis represent attempts to explain this seemingly pathological job instability. Yet, because they represent very different viewpoints as to the nature of the problem, their respective analyses and policy prescriptions differ greatly.

The Theory of Human Capital

In many respects, the theory of human capital is simply a logical extension of the underlying assumptions about human behavior on which most of modern economic theory is based. According to these assumptions, economic man is rational man, and all of his decisions are based on deliberate economic calculations.

The theory of human capital extends this concept to the determination of the distribution of income and unemployment. Emphasizing individual choice, this theory concludes that the existing distribution of income and unemployment reflects differences in the level of education and training, which, in turn, are the direct result of decisions by individuals whether or not to invest in themselves.[15] From this premise it follows that the unemployment problem of disadvantaged workers is a problem on the supply side rather than the demand side of the labor market. That is, because these workers lack the basic skills necessary to make it worthwhile for employers to hire them at the prevailing level of wages, the amount of labor they are willing to supply at this wage level exceeds the demand for their services by employers, and unemployment results. Thus, the inability of these workers to find and hold stable employment is due to insufficient investment in their own human capital. This theory suggests, then, that the appropriate policy to reduce the unemployment of disadvantaged workers consists of extensive manpower training and skill upgrading.

In many respects, this policy prescription is very similar to that of the structuralists, and both of these schools strongly influenced the format of the great majority of modern Federal manpower programs. These programs began in 1961 with an emphasis on training unemployed workers in regions with high unemployment, but gradually shifted their focus from regional unemployment to unemployment of specific groups of disadvantaged workers.

The theoretical foundation for the earliest of these programs was provided by the theory of structural unemployment. Holding that structural factors and wage rigidities prevented employers from hiring poorly or inappropriately trained workers, this theory suggested that training would raise the productivity of these workers to a level where they could obtain employment. Thus, though the structuralists viewed the unemployment as arising from a structural disequilibrium in the labor market, while the human capital school saw the problem as one of inadequate personal investment in individuals, both agreed the solution lay in expended training for unemployed disadvantaged workers.[16]

In the late 1960s, however, it was observed that despite substantial labor market tightening and numerous low-paying vacancies, disadvantaged workers continued to experience high rates of unemployment. As correctly noted by the search theorists, the problem was clearly not one of a chronic job shortage for disadvantaged workers, but rather a situation of excessively high labor turnover. Nevertheless, the human capital approach still appeared to be relevant if its emphasis was changed from merely qualifying these workers for any job, to qualifying them for high-paying jobs at which they might stay.[17]

The Dual Market Hypothesis

To another group of economists, however, both the human capital and search-turnover approaches seemed seriously flawed. While these two theories differ in many respects, they share the belief that labor markets are shaped by economic motivations within an essentially competitive framework. "Relative wages are assumed to be flexible, employers are believed willing and able to adjust their employment in response to changes in wages and productivity, and workers are assumed to make training and information investments easily in response to changes in relative wages."[18]

Claiming that these premises were unrealistic and misleading, these economists developed an alternative view of labor market behavior which has come to be known as the dual labor market hypothesis. An outgrowth of both the civil rights and anti-poverty experience of the 1960s, this school views unemployment as "rooted less in individual behavior than in the character of institutions and the social patterns that derive from them."[19] Much more of a "sociological" and "institutional" approach rather than a purely economic approach to the labor market, it deals specifically with trying to explain the seemingly excessive job turnover in what its proponents call "the secondary sector."

As advanced by Peter B. Doeringer, Michael J. Piore, and others,[20] the hypothesis views the economy as being conceptually divided into a primary and a secondary sector. The *primary sector* is characterized by good jobs, high wages, satisfactory working conditions, employment stability, and prospects for promotion. The *secondary sector,* its antithesis, is characterized by bad jobs, low wages, poor working conditions, layoffs, little chance for advancement, and high turnover. When a primary sector worker becomes unemployed, he is unemployed in the involuntary, Keynesian sense. He is out of his accustomed place in life, and though he may temporarily accept other, less attractive work, he is essentially waiting to regain his lost position. Unemployment in the secondary sector, however, is not at all like this. Rather than consisting of people waiting to regain a lost position, it is more a process of shuttling from one low-paying position to another.[21]

According to this theory, while adult white males are usually employed in the primary sector, women, teenagers and, in particular, minority groups are generally confined to the secondary sector. But because secondary firms provide little specific on-the-job training, because there is only a limited chance for advancement, and because a worker's current wage is unlikely to differ widely from that available in a great number of other similar jobs, a worker finds little incentive to either stay on the job or to perform particularly well at it. Hence, once a worker is in the secondary sector, the unstable work environment encourages the adoption of certain poor working habits: "casual devotion to job, reporting to work late or not at all on some days, and quitting without good reason often within months of taking the job."[22] It is these habits which most clearly distinguish the primary and secondary sectors and which make movement into the primary sector so much more difficult. In addition, this vicious cycle is reinforced as secondary sector employers are unwilling to invest heavily in the training of a work force which is prone to high turnover, and simultaneously, are less reluctant to fire a worker in whom they have little invested.[23] These factors, thus, tend to result in entrapment in the secondary sector.

Above and beyond this entrapment, which helps to perpetuate the low productivity of secondary sector workers, the dualists identify two principal explanations for the continued duality in the face of labor market forces which would tend to eliminate the wage disparity between the two sectors.

The first of these explanations, restrictive practices, represents legalized barriers to the occupational mobility of workers. The prime example of this is occupational licensing by the state, where access to the skilled trades is often controlled by license boards composed of licensed members of the supervised occupations. These persons have strong economic incentive to keep the number of workers permitted to practice their trade at an artificially low level in order to raise the wages of those already licensed. A similar restrictive practice is followed by unions who can maintain an artificial scarcity of good jobs either through a close control of the number of apprentices (as the craft unions) or through negotiating so high a wage that employers decide to hire fewer workers than are willing to work at that high a wage level.[24]

The second explanation for the continued duality, discrimination, is viewed as operating in two ways, through statistical discrimination, and discrimination pure and simple. Statistical discrimination represents an attempt to simplify the hiring procedure by assuming that certain poor work habits are closely related to personal characteristics such as race, age or sex. Under this procedure, a number of job candidates may be wrongly rejected even though they are actually qualified. This kind of discrimination, in conjunction with outright discrimination, enlarges the secondary work force while reducing the supply of labor to the primary sector. It thereby gains the economic support of both secondary employers, who now pay a lower wage, and of primary employees, who now receive a higher wage. Furthermore, although primary employers receive no economic gain from outright discrimination, the higher wages they must pay are compensated by the reduced costs of screening job candidates through the use of statistical discrimination.[25]

If this dual labor market schema is correct, then the potential effectiveness of the skill training programs proposed by the human capital school is open to serious question. The dualists have noted that a great part of the training necessary for workers to satisfactorily perform in the primary sector cannot be purchased in schools or elsewhere. Rather, it is only available on the job, and, in order to acquire this training, the worker first must be hired, and then must be accepted by the established group of workers who must teach him what they are doing. In other words, "social acceptability," which is directly related to such characteristics as race, sex, and shared social beliefs, is a key factor in obtaining "primary-sector" skills and a job in the primary sector, and this "social acceptability" cannot be purchased in the usual sense.[26]

Within this framework, the proponents of the dual labor market hypothesis develop a number of policy options which focus on the *institutional* forces they feel underlie the structure and behavior of the labor market. In particular, they propose policies to eliminate discrimination and restrictive practices which have kept people out of the primary sector, and policies to shift the demand for labor, and thus jobs, out of the secondary and into the primary sector.

While their anti-discrimination policy calls for an intensive, but straightforward, use of instruments like civil rights legislation and Federal contract compliance programs, the dualists' proposals for shifting jobs from the secondary to the primary sector are more complicated. Basically, the dualists suggest a two-pronged attack: (1) having the government impose the characteristics of the primary sector on the secondary sector through expanded coverage of social legislation; and (2) adopting a long-run, stable, full-employment policy.

The first set of programs is designed primarily to convert secondary sector jobs into jobs with primary-type characteristics. Some examples of occupations which, to some extent, have already undergone this type of conversion are longshoring, unskilled construction labor, and office cleaning. It is assumed that these policies, which, in effect, are designed to legislate higher wages, would also tend to stabilize employment and develop promotional ladders as the alternative, secondary job structure becomes more costly for employers. Hospital and hotel jobs, for example, might be particularly susceptible to this kind of conversion.[27]

The second type of program, adopting a long-run, stable, full-employment policy, is directed at significantly expanding the primary sector. While acknowledging that the full-employment policy which has been followed in this country has not accomplished this goal, the dualists claim that this has been due to its stop-and-go nature. Employers who believe an expansion to be temporary, say the dualists, are reluctant to admit workers to the primary labor market. Rather than incur the costs of training and providing career benefits, and the problems which might arise from the structural changes involved in this expansion, employers would rather rely on subcontracting and temporary employment from the secondary sector. If, however, employers can be convinced of a strong public commitment to stable full-employment, corresponding to an unemployment rate of between 3 and 4 percent, they would then be much more likely, claim the dualists, to significantly expand the number of jobs in the primary sector.[28]

Conclusion

The dual labor market approach, with its emphasis on the interrelationship between economic, sociological, and institutional variables, has attracted considerable attention in recent years both within and outside the economic profession.[29] Nevertheless, neither it alone nor the alternative theories of human capital and search-turnover present a complete picture of the problem of unemployment. Due to the complexity of the labor market, all three theories fail to consider important aspects of the problem, and all three necessarily incorporate simplifying assumptions about the structure and behavior of the labor market.

Thus, for example, the dualists, in their policy prescriptions, implicitly assume that secondary workers have all of the necessary human capital needed to succeed in primary-type employment. To the extent that this assumption is incorrect, their proposals to legislate higher wages in the secondary sector and to expand the primary sector could lead to both higher unemployment and inflation unless also coupled with programs to encourage formation of physical and human capital, improve job matches, and discourage turnover. Therefore, rather than choosing between the alternative theories, it is more instructive to view them as an important set of complementary perspectives on the nature of unemployment, which, when taken together, correctly portray the problem of unemployment as a complex interrelationship of supply, demand, informational, and institutional factors.

NOTES

1. Eleanor G. Gilpatrick, *Structural Unemployment and Aggregate Demand* (Baltimore: Johns Hopkins Press, 1966), p. 2.

2. U.S. Congress, Joint Economic Committee, Subcommittee on Economic Statistics, *Higher Unemployment Rates, 1957–60; Structural Transformation or Inadequate Demand*, 87th Congress, 1st Session (Washington: U.S. Government Printing Office, 1961).

3. Gilpatrick, pp. 4–5. Also Barbara R. Bergmann and David E. Kaun, *Structural Unemployment in the United States*, U.S. Department of Commerce (Washington: U.S. Government Printing Office, 1966), pp. 4–5. The classic example of workers' unwillingness to move to another geographic area is the case of the unemployed coal miners in the 1950s and 1960s. Similarly, railroad firemen represent persons whose skills have become obsolete, while minority teenagers with skills of limited transferability have increased their labor supply in excess of the increase in the demand for their services.

4. Richard Perlman, *Labor Theory* (New York: John Wiley and Sons, 1969), p. 167.

5. Besides the tax cut, spending for the Vietnam war greatly stimulated the economy during these years. While the resulting fall in unemployment supports the view that demand had been inadequate, the accompanying climb in the rate of inflation, to a level consistently above 3 percent since 1966, points to the existence of inflationary bottlenecks which arise when the economy is subjected to a too rapid rate of expansion.

6. Gilpatrick, *Structural Unemployment and Aggregate Demand* and especially Perlman, *Labor Theory*, ch. 7, present strong evidence of the existence of structural unemployment and argue convincingly that "much of the confusion in evaluating the impact of structural aspects has resulted from illogical or loose definitions of the term. . . ."

7. This is the title of a study by Robert E. Hall, "Why Is the Unemployment Rate So High at Full Employment?" *Brookings Papers on Economic Activity* (No. 3: 1970), pp. 369–402.

8. Hall, "Why," p. 370. It has been suggested that because of changing age-sex composition of the labor force, the trade-off between the rates of unemployment and inflation may actually be worsening over time. See George Perry, "Changing Labor Markets and Inflation," *Brookings Papers on Economic Activity* (No. 3: 1970), pp. 411–41.

9. See, for example, Charles Holt and Associates, "Manpower Proposals for Phase III," *Brookings Papers on Economic Activity* (No. 3: 1971), pp. 703–22.

10. Robert E. Hall, "Prospects for Shifting the Phillips Curve Through Manpower Policies," *Brookings Papers on Economic Activity* (No. 3: 1971), p. 660. Frictional unemployment is temporary unemployment which arises due to the time required for finding or changing jobs.

11. Holt, "Manpower Proposals," pp. 712–16. Along the lines of the first of these proposals, the U.S. Manpower Administration has recently initiated a 15-state, Federally funded program designed to encourage both employers and employees to register their manpower needs and skills with their state office of employment security. . . .

12. Hall, "Prospects," p. 660. Also see Hall, "Turnover in the Labor Force," *Brookings Papers on Economic Activity* (No. 3:1972), pp. 709–56, and Steven P. Zell, *A Comparative Study of the Labor Market Characteristics of Return Migrants and Non-Migrants in Puerto Rico* (Commonwealth of Puerto Rico, Puerto Rico Planning Board, Bureau of Social Analysis, 1974), chs. 6 and 8.

13. Hall, "Why," p. 389.

14. Ibid.

15. Peter B. Doeringer and Michael J. Piore, "Unemployment and the Dual Labor Market," *The Public Interest,* No. 38, Winter 1975, pp. 69–70.

16. While one policy prescription of the search-turnover approach also stresses job training, this is done as part of a multifaceted program operating on both the demand and supply sides. Thus, in addition to providing job training for workers, it is also proposed that employers be aided in restructuring their jobs to better fit available manpower. The emphasis is not one of upgrading the skills of the disadvantaged *per se,* but rather one that concentrates on eliminating skill mismatches in sectors of the economy which contribute excessively to inflation. "The unskilled and disadvantaged . . . will benefit disproportionately from the vacuum effects of general upgrading and the overall reduction of unemployment that can occur." Holt, "Manpower Proposals," pp. 720–21.

17. Hall, "Prospects," pp. 661, 674–81.

18. Doeringer and Piore, "Unemployment," p. 71.

19. Ibid., p. 72.

20. Peter B. Doeringer and Michael J. Piore, *Internal Labor Markets and Manpower Analysis* (New York: Heath, 1971), and Michael J. Piore, "Jobs and Training," in Samuel Beer and Richard Barringer, eds., *The State and the Poor* (Cambridge, Mass.: Winthrop, 1970).

21. Doeringer and Piore, "Unemployment," pp. 70–71.

22. Hall, "Prospects," p. 683.

23. Doeringer and Piore, *Internal Labor Markets,* pp. 165–72. Also Michael Wachter, "Primary and Secondary Labor Markets: A Critique of the Dual Approach," *Brookings Papers on Economic Activity* (No. 3:1974), p. 651.

24. Hall, "Prospects," p. 684.

25. Piore, "Jobs and Training," p. 56.

26. Doeringer and Piore, "Unemployment," p. 72.

Stagflation

Abba P. Lerner

Stagflation sounds like a particular type of inflation—a new addition to the growing list of different types. It is one that occurs at a time of economic stagnation; but the emphasis is on the "flation" part of the word, giving the impression that the real problem is inflation rather than stagnation.

The basic picture of inflation in almost everybody's mind shows the economy working at full capacity but still unable to satisfy the demand for output. There is not enough to go 'round. "Too much money is chasing too few goods"—excess demand bids up prices and wages, raising costs and money incomes.

It is this picture, in which *excess demand* and capacity output are integral elements, that makes it sound paradoxical to have inflation coupled with conditions of *deficient demand.* The idea that there may be too little money or too little spending

Reprinted from the *Intermountain Economic Review,* Fall 1975, pp. 1–7, with the permission of the publisher and the author.

for the proper working of the economy (which is what causes stagnation) is therefore inconsistent with the basic picture of inflation and creates a tension in the mind—a mental dissonance—and a paradox is born.

For the inflationary process to continue for long, the quantity of money must also be increasing so as to serve the increased volume of payments for current output at rising prices. Full capacity production being assumed, *physical output* will rise at a rate equal to the steady increase in manpower plus the increment in output per man— a total of about 4 percent a year (disregarding outside influences such as variations in harvests and import/export price changes). The *value* of the physical output and the volume of spending will be increasing at this 4 percent rate, *plus* the rate of increase in prices. So if prices are rising at 10 percent, spending must be rising at 14 percent and the quantity of money must be rising at some similar rate, allowing for changes in its velocity of circulation.

Continuing a long tradition of contributions to the growing list of definitions of inflation, I shall now try to limit the word "inflation" to conditions of *excess demand*— the excess demand being the wind that blows up or inflates the economy-balloon. With no excess demand, there is no blowing up of the economy. Stagflation is thus a misnomer. It is not a kind of inflation. It is a *stagnation* of the economy during which prices are rising. However, no harm is done if rising prices is called price inflation, since this does not imply that *the economy* is being inflated by excess demand.[1]

The Classical Approach

The original pre-Keynesian "classical" approach to the problem of unemployment was to apply to the economy the standard Supply and Demand proposition for the determination of the price of a particular good with constitutes only a tiny part of the economy. An excess of demand over supply causes the price to rise; a deficient demand causes it to fall. A rise in price increases the quantity supplied and decreases the quantity demanded; a fall in price does the reverse. These adjustments thus bring supply and demand into equality at an equilibrium price.

Applying this to the economy as a whole, an excess of total demand—which means a level of spending *more than enough* to buy the potential output—should cause prices to rise until the demand is no longer excessive but is just enough to buy the full-employment output at the higher price level. Conversely, if total spending is insufficient to buy the whole full-employment output at the current price level, prices should fall until the same volume of money expenditure *is* sufficient to buy the full-capacity output. The solution requires only that the authorities keep their hands off the rather stable quantity of money based on the rather stable accumulated stock of gold.

Unfortunately, the micro-economic Supply and Demand proposition does not translate properly into the macro-economic environment. For this there are a number of reasons:

1. In the case of a single commodity, a fall in its price causes consumers to buy more of it, substituting it for other goods; producers supply more of it instead of other goods. The converse holds for a rise in the price of a single commodity. In the case of the economy as a whole, however, when prices rise or fall, *there are no other goods* from or to which consumers and producers can switch!
2. Since any reduction in the price paid is a reduction in the price received, any

decrease in total spending in the economy is a decrease in total money income earned in the economy. If total money income falls just as much as prices, there is no increase in real income so that the fall in prices does not stimulate any increase in total demand. The deficiency of demand and the depression continue.

If total money income falls less than prices, there will be an increase in output and employment. But income can fall less than prices only if output and employment increase. Similarly, if income falls more than prices, output and employment will fall. Anything can happen. In the translation, the micro-economic proposition loses its cogency.

3. The decrease in overall spending does not as easily lead to a fall in prices. Wages and other costs are rigid downward, hence the response of the producer is to reduce output. This can be a life-saver for some producers but it does not help the economy as a whole. The reduction in output means employing fewer workers and reducing the demand for materials and other factors of production. Total income and costs are therefore reduced equally. This is why excellent micro-economic advice to families, firms and even whole industries as well as cities and states is macro-economic poison for the economy as a whole. Retrenchment and belt-tightening may be eminently reasonable policies for the individual, but they are at the same time immensely efficient recipes for widening and deepening a recession into depression and slump.

4. A policy of passive dependence on the automatic self-curing of depression by the operation of the micro-economic Supply and Demand mechanism could have a happy ending, but only after resistances to prices and wage deflation are overcome. This would occur only after a long delay and, for a considerable time, only in some especially depressed parts of the economy. Distress sales, as well as wage cuts for workers whose savings and credit are exhausted, constitute the belt tightening that spreads to the other sectors. This establishes an *expectation* of falling prices. Buyers then cut their spending still more while waiting for even greater bargains. With the ripple effect of successive belt-tightenings, a depression can degenerate via panic into a catastrophic slump like that of the 1930s.

There does exist a bottom to such economic collapses. Even when wages, costs, prices and income all finally fall together, they cannot help each other. But the quantity of money does not automatically fall with these. When the fall in prices has sufficiently increased the purchasing power of the money stock, some of the money thus made surplus, or idle, begins to be spent. Total spending increases and *ipso facto* total income increases. We then have some "belt-loosening" and this has the same kind of effect as belt-tightening, only, of course, in the opposite direction. It increases output and employment and could indeed start a movement towards prosperity. There is only one question: is all this suffering really necessary? Can we not avoid the accompanying injustices, resentments and the danger to the continuance of a free society?

The Keynesian Approach

The essential function of the Keynesian Revolution was to redirect the attention of some economists from concentrating on full-employment equilibrium to considering states of the economy with less than full employment. Two lessons for practical policy emerged:

1. It is not necessary to suffer long and severe depression as a means of increasing real spending (by increasing the real value of the money stock through depression-induced reductions in prices). The same end can be achieved painlessly by increasing the *number* of dollars instead of the *purchasing power* of each existing dollar.
2. Increased spending can be achieved even more directly by expansionary government fiscal policy—larger government expenditures or reduced taxes. The deficit must, of course, be financed by an increased money supply or by increased government borrowing.

The Keynesian economists did not succeed in persuading the government in the 1930s to increase total spending enough to restore prosperity. Similarly, Wladimir Woytinsky and other "premature-Keynesians" in Germany did not succeed in persuading the Weimar government to restore prosperity by deficit financing—policy which could well have prevented the rise of Nazism and the Second World War. But the war did bring about sufficient spending, full employment and economic prosperity.

The one Keynesian lesson that seemed to have been fully absorbed by all economists, and even by most politicians and bankers, is that the authorities should not permit the quantity of money to be decreased in a recession. The story of stagflation is the story of the *unlearning* of this lesson.

Expectations and Rising Prices

Since the essence of stagnation is *deficiency* of demand, and since stagflation is a species of stagnation, the rising prices cannot be due to *excess* demand. The cure for inflation calls for a *reduction* in excessive spending. But if there is already insufficient spending, a reduction in spending only transforms stagnation into depression.

The key to the puzzle of what makes the prices rise is in *expectations.* The Supply and Demand analogy leaves out expectations—or rather, assumes a special state of expectations. If prices are expected to rise at, say, 10 percent a year (perhaps because they have been rising at that rate for some time) a deficiency of demand will not tend to cause prices to fall. It will tend to cause expectations to be *revised downward,* perhaps to a rate of increase of 8 percent. An excess of demand will cause expectations to be revised upward, perhaps to 12 percent. The new expectations will tend to decrease or increase the actual rate of price rise until a new excess or deficiency of demand causes a further revision. Only if the previous expectation happens to be of price level stability—or zero change in price—does the standard law of Supply and Demand turn out to be correct.

Expectation of rising prices is the cause of rising prices in stagflation. Workers demand increasing wages to maintain their real income in the face of a rising cost of living. Their employers grant the increasing wage rates. They are not particularly moved by the justice of the demand, but they expect to be able to pass on the increasing costs to their customers in the rising prices. The customers can pay the rising prices because *their* wages and other incomes are also rising.

One must not complacently forget that some incomes will rise much more than the average, while others rise less, or even fall. This can entail great injustice, deprivation and suffering. But what can and should be done to correct this is part of another story.

Stagflation Policy

Just as in the case of genuine inflation of the economy—demand inflation—rising prices require a proportional increase in spending if output and employment are to be maintained. A less than proportional increase in spending will only reduce sales, output, real income and employment instead of mitigating the excess demand inflation. This constitutes the difference between true inflation of the economy by excess demand and the "expectational" rising prices previously described. Keeping the increase in spending below the increase in prices, instead of mitigating the inflation, only accentuates the "stag" in the stagflation. This is exactly what our government is doing and it has increased the unemployment rate to 9.2 percent.

Why the government proceeds in this manner is the subject of many explanations. Here I must limit myself to one over-simple and one over-sophisticated theory.

The simple theory states that the authorities *identify* rising prices with demand inflation. Unable to distinguish between these, they hope to cure rising prices by reducing the demand for goods and services. But by preventing spending from rising as much as prices, they have succeeded only in intensifying the recession. They have also committed the sin of reducing the quantity of money during depression—not the number of dollars (this number has been increasing) but the quantity of *real* money. The total purchasing power of the money stock has been permitted to decrease significantly.

Keynes avoided the problem of rising prices by conducting his analysis in terms of "wage units." The wage unit is the average money wage; if wages, prices and income all move together there is no change whatever in terms of the wage unit. My own "Functional Finance" popularization and development of the Keynesian revolution also disregarded rising prices other than those caused by demand inflation. In this I followed Keynes' implicit assumption that only when we have more-than-full employment—as a result of excess demand—will prices in general rise.

High Full Employment and Low Full Employment

Around 1947 I became concerned about prices rising even when the economy is producing less than its capacity output. In my *Economics of Employment,* published in 1951, I split the full employment concept into "Low Full Employment" (symbolized by 6,000,000 unemployed) and "High Full Employment" (symbolized by 2,000,000 unemployed). Low full employment (it does not really deserve to be called full employment) was the level of employment beyond which prices begin to rise. High full employment was the level beyond which the economy could not work properly. It would lack the minimum number of people who must be between jobs in a free economy continually adjusting to changes in demand and in technology.

At less than low full employment, wages and prices would fall. Beyond high full employment, wages and prices would rise in a true demand inflation. Between low full employment and high full employment we had less than satisfactory employment together with rising prices. This was later called Stagflation. The remedy I tentatively suggested is what later came to be called "incomes policy."

A Natural Level of Employment?

The over-sophisticated rationalization of the government's policy of keeping stagflation at 8 or 9 percent unemployment is based on Milton Friedman's theory of the "natural level of employment." This theory is indeed based on expectations. It says that there is one level of employment (or unemployment)—the "natural" level—at which the actual and the expected rates of price inflation coincide. At the natural level of employment, and only at the natural level of employment, can we have a constant, unchanging rate of price inflation. This includes the zero rate of price inflation if expectations happen to be of a stationary price level.

Any attempt to increase employment beyond this "natural" level would result in an acceleration of the price inflation; and the increase in employment could survive only as long as the expectations lagged behind the accelerating increase in actual prices. The acceleration could be stopped only by bringing employment down to the natural level again.

From this it followed that any attempt to increase employment at the cost of a somewhat greater rate of rising prices would have to be abandoned in order to check a runaway escalation of price inflation. That would mean a reduction in employment back to the natural level, but now burdened with higher actual and expected rates of price inflation.

It is possible, however, according to this theory, to achieve a lower rate of price inflation by using the strategy in reverse, imposing for some period a "lower than natural" level of employment and thereby reducing the actual and expected rates of price increase. There could then be an increase in employment back to the "natural" level with a slower, possibly even zero or negative, rate of actual and expected price increase.

This seems to be the strategy of the White House in presenting us with a prospect of 8 or 9 percent unemployment. The "natural" level of unemployment is apparently envisaged as about 7 percent. This is safe enough since nobody knows where the natural level of employment resides. Indeed it can have no fixed abode since we have enjoyed higher and lower rates of price increases at both higher and lower levels of unemployment.

A Stagflation Range of Employment

The "natural level of employment" theory is a remarkable example of ingenuity in mobilizing considerations of expectations to construct something very similar to the classical theory of "full employment" equilibrium. But like Keynesian or functional finance, full employment is fated for fission. It too must be split into a high level of employment and a low level of employment. Between them, and limited by them, is a *"natural range"* rather than *level* of employment within which we enjoy stagflation.

If we imagine employment measured along a line from left to right (or unemployment measured from right to left) the upper limit of the "natural range" is to the right and the lower limit to the left. It is only to the right of the upper limit that the automatic escalation of inflation is plausible. There we have over-high full employment and the excess demand that legitimizes the use of the word inflation.

Only to the left of the lower limit is the automatic deceleration of the price rise plausible. Here we have the region of severe recession which has lasted long enough to create vast chronic unemployment, business collapses, bankruptcies of cities, states, pension funds and unemployment compensation funds, enough starvation and despair to break down the pressures to make wages keep up with prices. It is this catastrophe-induced slowdown, and then fall, in wages, costs and prices that ultimately increases the value of the money stock enough to start an automatic upward movement of spending, output, and employment. Fortunately we do not know and hope never to know, this lower limit to the "natural range of employment." Even the Great Depression of the thirties did not reach this breaking point. That dive in economic activity was arrested by the New Deal, but prosperity was restored only by the great increase in wartime spending which was sufficient to yield full employment *at the current prices.*

The intensity of depression required to hatch the automatic recovery is also dependent on its duration. But it does seem that unemployment between 15 percent and 5 percent is within the "natural range." We have neither runaway inflation from excess demand nor complete economic collapse with implosion of the price level.

In this stagflation range (where we currently find ourselves) between economic collapse and excess demand inflation, the state of expectations determines the rate of price increase, and the rate of spending, in terms of the current price level (or the wage unit), determines the level of employment. We stay within this range because stagflation strategy will be abandoned by any government whenever double digit unemployment rates threaten. This was recently demonstrated by President Nixon eating his words in a 179 degree turn from increasing taxes and reducing spending ("fighting inflation," as if we were suffering from excess demand) to reducing some taxes and increasing some spending to prevent catastrophic intensification of the depression.

Until we can induce a change in expectations by some form of the unpopular incomes policy, or until we are blessed by serendipitous accidents, such as a substantial fall in the price of fuel, or unexpected increases in harvests or in industrial productivity, we will continue to have rising prices, wages and incomes. Authorities will provide the fiscal and monetary expansion required to prevent catastrophic depression. But in their eagerness to gain immunity from the charge of being responsible for the rising prices they will not increase spending enough to maintain full employment. We will continue to suffer from random ups and downs of employment in a protracted stagflation.

Special Groups in the Labor Force

Special Problems of Women Workers

Manpower Report of the President, 1975

Despite the greatly increased labor force participation of women since 1950 and their changing work profiles, women are far from achieving equality in terms of occupational status. . . . The earnings differential between men and women has remained substantial over the last two decades, and women are still concentrated in the lower paid, traditionally female occupations and industries. . . .

Barriers to the entrance of women into skilled craft jobs or into certain professional occupations are often based on outmoded concepts of the degree of physical strength required or on outmoded ideas about women's worklife expectancy and, by implication, the value of providing educational and training opportunities to women. . . .

Below the professional level, skilled trades and apprentice-type jobs have been projected for the 1970s as an area of rapid employment increase. This area is also one in which women are greatly underrepresented, although Federal executive orders and regulations calling for equal employment opportunity and affirmative action to eliminate sex discrimination have opened many doors formerly closed to women. Data from the 1973 Current Population Survey show 561,000 women employed as craft workers (about 4 percent of the total), compared with 277,140 in 1960 and 494,-871 in 1970. Another positive trend is reflected in vocational school enrollment data for 1972. In that year, 33,006 women enrolled in technical programs, up from 22,890 in 1966–67. The increase was even greater among women enrolled in trade and industrial training courses, rising from 155,808 in 1966–67 to 279,680 in 1972. . . .

Poverty and Female-Headed Families

Half the women who head families are divorced or separated, and growing rates of divorce and separation make the existence of female-headed families an increasingly common phenomenon. However, the responsibility for supporting a family is a difficult one for a woman, who often faces severe obstacles in her job search.

Reprinted from *Manpower Report of the President, 1975,* pp. 69–75.

Dependent children require support but make full-time labor market activity a special problem in the one-parent family. Among female-headed families, 37 percent of the women heads are widowed, 13 percent are unmarried, and the remaining one-half are divorced or separated. The presence of young children is a critical factor in determining labor force participation, particularly among women heads aged 25 to 44, nearly half of whom have three or more children. High child-care costs and low earnings potential reduce the feasibility of paid employment and in many cases make it uneconomical. Indeed, 61 percent of female heads of poor families do not even seek outside employment—some through discouragement and others through a reluctance to surrender child-care responsibilities to others. Moreover, divorced and separated women are often ill-equipped for market occupations other than those requiring a minimum of education and skill.

Long Term Unemployment

A reflection of these problems is the fact that of the 4.2 million women heads of families who worked or looked for work during 1973, 17.1 percent experienced some unemployment. About one-fourth of these women did not work during the year. For over another fourth who did work, their unemployment totaled over 6 months in one or more spells of joblessness.

It is essential to note that two-thirds of all female heads of families have less than a high school education. Nearly three-fourths of women family heads who are employed work in clerical, operative and service positions. Private household and part-time occupations predominate, but earnings and benefits in these areas remain exceptionally low. Median earnings for year-round, full-time household employment in 1971 were $1,926 with few paid vacations or sick leave and almost no protection via unemployment benefits or workers' compensation.

As a result of obstacles such as these, poverty is widespread among female-headed families. While a large number of families were able to move out of poverty in the decade of the 1960s, the proportion of poor families with a female head rose from less than 1 in 4 to more than 1 in 3 over the decade. In 1972 the median income was $4,469 for female-headed families with children under 18 years of age and $3,351 for those with preschool children. The poverty threshold for a four-person nonfarm family headed by a woman in 1972 was $4,254. While fewer than 1 out of every 10 male-headed families had income below the poverty threshold in 1972, more than 5 out of every 10 female-headed families fell in that category.

Alimony, child support, welfare, and social security provide a large source of income for female-headed families. But the preponderance of poverty among women in this group indicates that these payments represent only a partial solution to their multiple problems.

Denial of Credit

Apart from the difficulty of gaining adequately paid employment, female heads of families face other obstacles to gaining economic independence. Traditionally, for example, women have experienced difficulty in achieving the financial security needed to obtain credit (particularly mortgage credit). Women who are single, divorced, separated, or widowed may be refused credit simply because of marital status. When a woman is divorced, separated, or widowed, she may be denied credit on the grounds that she has no established credit record, even when she applies to the same companies where she has held accounts with her husband. Similar problems also arise in such areas as automobile and medical insurance. Although recently passed Federal and State laws have lowered some of the barriers preventing equal access to credit, discriminatory practices continue.

Black Female Family Heads

Within the category of female heads of families, black and other minority women constitute an even more economically disadvantaged group. Nearly one-third of all families headed by women are black, and 1 out of every 3 black families is headed by a woman compared to 1 out of 10 white families. The 1972 median earnings of black female family heads was $3,370, only three-fourths that of white female family heads and $884 below the poverty threshold for a four-person nonfarm family headed by a woman. Larger numbers of children, lower levels of education, concentration in low-skill low-paying jobs, and high rates of unemployment combine to produce poverty for black families dependent on women.

Intermittent Labor Force Participation

For the majority of women, high school is the only time that formal career planning takes place. Generally, such plans have been geared to preparation of women for a short period of employment in anticipation of an extended or even permanent withdrawal from the labor market—but, with a growing proportion of women continuing to work or reentering the work force after childbearing, the disadvantages of such shortrun planning have become clear. Reentry into the jobs held before withdrawal is often unsatisfactory, even impossible, since many of the earlier positions no longer exist. Yet little attention has been given to the need for retraining for new occupations.

Widening Occupational Choice

Women's need for a wider range of occupational choice remains acute. It is not surprising, therefore, that continuing education programs have been highly successful during the past two decades, in part because they were aimed at meeting the critical needs of women to develop the skills required for reentering the work force on a permanent basis. The desirability of such retraining is illustrated by the fact that in the longitudinal survey of women aged 30 to 55, more women retrogressed in their careers than progressed.

Since most women complete high school, there is an obvious need for college-level course offerings that allow older women some flexibility in entrance requirements and class schedules. Restrictions set by the woman's location and her domestic responsibilities have been mitigated somewhat by the growth of community colleges, but there is a need for consideration of additional steps aimed specifically at easing the labor force reentry problems of women.

Reentry into the work force might be eased by programs designed to employ women on a part-time basis as a prelude to full-time work. The object of such programs would be to enable women to recover skills during a period of readjustment to full-time labor market activity. The extent and nature of part-time jobs could be negotiated according to the amount of retraining required. Where the period of absence from work has been relatively short, problems of retraining may be secondary to lack of promotional opportunities. Childbearing may necessitate an absence of only a few weeks or months. Yet restrictions on leave and the frequency with which promotions are based on continuous work experience make it difficult for a woman to pick up her career where she left off. Childbearing still leads to resignation in many cases and resignation necessitates a reentry, compounded by all the problems of an initial job search and acclimatization.

Maternity Leave

A variety of maternity leave provisions exists in the United States; in the majority of cases, however, coverage is quite limited and the availability of maternity leave is growing only very slowly, even though EEOC guidelines are encouraging provision of these rights. Still, a 1973 University of Michigan survey showed that, over the preceding 3 years, the availability of full reemployment rights increased by 14 percent and the availability of leave with pay by 12 percent.

The notion that fathers might care for infants is beginning to spread in the United States. Several schools and public agencies have provisions for parental leave without pay for periods of 30 days to 4 years. However, most union labor agreements provide fathers with no more than 1 to 3 days of paid leave when children are born.

Since more and more women now intend to continue their careers after giving birth, the possible loss of job security or consideration for promotion because of short absences on maternity leave is becoming an important issue in many private firms and public sector institutions. More than 90 percent of today's women expect to have one, two, or three children. These family-size expectations need to be taken into account, but can no longer be viewed automatically as the cause of long interruptions in the worklives of American women.

Mobility Problems

In addition to the intermittency associated with childbirth and early childrearing, women workers also face a special constraint imposed by mobility factors. The relocations required by the demands of a husband's job can interrupt a woman's career, greatly reducing her possibilities of progress and even of maintaining employment. Migration of husbands causes considerable interruption in the employment of wives, according to recent studies. Wives' jobs, on the other hand, appear to be little hindrance to husbands' job change and movement, since the rates of interstate moving for married men with wives employed in 1965 and 1970 were only slightly below those for married men with wives not employed in either year.

In every age category, the proportion of wives working in both 1965 and 1970 was much lower when relocation had occurred. Thus, the geographic mobility of the household tends to disrupt the worklife of the married woman. On the other hand, a married woman suffers from a lack of geographic mobility in her own job. While husbands appear relatively unhampered by marital ties in their ability to migrate, wives appear to have the opposite problem.

Minimizing the undesired mobility or immobility faced by working wives involves some compromise arrangements within businesses and within families. While no agreement among members of a dual-career family can achieve the mobility that could be available to each member operating independently, considerable flexibility can still be attained.

Unemployment Compensation

Related to the issue of labor force participation by working wives is the question of the fairness of unemployment compensation laws. In the past several years, substantial improvements have been made in eliminating statutory discrimination against women unemployment insurance claimants. Three areas in particular have registered important advances, although complete equality is still unrealized.

A major area of improvement involves disqualification from benefits solely because of pregnancy. In January 1973, 37 State unemployment insurance laws contained this provision, and, of these, only 3 permitted rebuttal. The others flatly denied benefits for a certain number of weeks before and after childbirth, required subsequent earnings to requalify for entitlement, or delayed entitlement for a period after ability to work had been reestablished—action comparable to that taken in the case of a "voluntary quit without good cause." Nevertheless, the number of States denying benefits because of pregnancy alone has been steadily declining to 31 by July 1973 and to 24 by October 1974.

Leaving work because of marital or family obligations—moving with the spouse to another area, for example—constitutes another reason for disqualification from benefits in several States. Such terminations usually raise the issue of availability and willingness to work after the job separation. At one time, 23 States denied benefits for this reason, and 7 restricted application of the provision to women. In about half of these 23 States, subsequent employment or earnings were required to requalify for benefits. At the present time, only 13 States disqualify claimants on this basis, and, in all cases, the provision is applied equally to men and women. Nevertheless, since women are more likely than men to follow their spouses to a new job location, in practice such provisions still disqualify women more often than men.

Finally, in the 11 States that offer dependents' allowances as part of their regular unemployment benefits, statutory provisions are no longer more restrictive for women claimants than they are for men. Nevertheless, because such allowances are usually limited to the individual who provides at least 50 percent of the total family support and the laws generally exclude parents from dependent status, the proportion of women claimants is much lower than that of men claimants.

Dual Careers

Nearly two-thirds of all women who work have childrearing responsibilities in addition to their jobs. The presumption that women have the major responsibility for child care and household maintenance, whether or not they work, means that women with family responsibilities who enter the labor force usually undertake a new role in addition to their many other tasks.

Arranging Child Care

When a wife takes on paid employment, her husband's contribution to the work of the household tends to remain unchanged. A study by the Organization for Economic Co-operation and Development found that total workloads for married women increased by an average of 13 hours per week, while the total workload of their husbands actually dropped by an average of 1½ hours per week. But regardless of the amount of additional work the married woman entering the job market is willing to undertake, there is no way that she can provide full-time child-care services. In households where both parents work, the necessity of having someone else assume a major responsibility for the care of young children raises important questions regarding the availability of child-care facilities.

In the Ohio State University National Longitudinal Survey of women aged 30 to 44, a mid-1967 survey of the types and costs of child-care arrangements found that about 7 out of 10 children were cared for in their own or in relatives' homes and almost 1 out of 4 in other private homes, usually in pooled neighborhood arrangements. Relatives were the most frequent source of child care, while group care in day-care centers, nursery schools, and the like accounted for fewer than 1 out of 10 children, as shown in table 1.

TABLE 1   Child-care Arrangements of Employed Women Aged 30–44 Using Child Care, 1967

TYPE OF ARRANGEMENT	PERCENT DISTRIBUTION[1]	
	White	Black
Total	100	100
In home:		
By relative	24	31
By nonrelative	25	11
In other private home:		
By relative	18	28
By nonrelative	24	19
In group center	8	12

[1]   Detail may not add to totals because of rounding.
SOURCE: Computed from *Dual Carreers*, vol. 1, table 4:13, p. 123.

On the other hand, a 1971 survey of child-care arrangements of working mothers in New York City found that up to 13 percent of all child care was undertaken by such group facilities. Comprehensive national figures are still unavailable, however, and it is not clear whether the increasing use of child-care arrangements is tending more toward group care than private arrangements.

The question of who should bear the cost of providing day care for children remains unanswered. From the parents' point of view, the higher the child-care costs, the fewer the job opportunities that are economically viable to the family. Although in many cases such costs do not pose severe limitations (in the National Longitudinal Survey about half the relatives provided the child-care services free of charge), the cost of care provided in the home of a nonrelative or in a group facility is significant. More than half the woman using these arrangements paid between $2 and $4 a day in 1967. Even more costly was the care provided in the child's own home by a nonrelative; here nearly two-thirds of the women paid $4 or more per day for the service.

Such institutional developments as the industry subsidized creches of Japan and the governmentally provided "ecole maternelle" system for 3- to 6-year olds in Belgium and France remain rare in the United States. Nevertheless, the number of American preschool children with mothers in the work force has risen dramatically from about 4 million in 1960 to more than 6 million in 1973. Although licensed day-care facilities more than doubled their estimated capacity between 1965 and 1973, the space available could at most accommodate only 1 out of every 6 preschool children of mothers in the work force at the end of this period.

Scheduling Market Work

Women's responsibility for household services often precludes full-time employment, Notwithstanding remarkable advances in household technology, cleaning, laundry, and food preparation are still time-consuming tasks that impede women's attempts to handle full-time employment. The fact that 1 out of every 4 women workers had part-time jobs in 1973, while another 1 out of every 4 worked only part year, reflects the problem many women have in taking on a full-time job in addition to household duties. (It also reflects the difficulties many experience in obtaining full-time jobs even when they would prefer such employment.)

Some believe that variations in work schedules can provide a partial solution to this dilemma. The traditional approach has been for the woman to take a part-time job that allowed her to continue providing the domestic services needed by the family. However, part-time employment that fully utilizes the capabilities of women is quite scarce. The consequent loss suffered by both women and the society has been described by the Department of Labor's Women's Bureau:

> . . . many women who have skills in demand in the labor force are unable to find part-time jobs which would permit them to make a contribution to family income or to the economy as well as to handle home responsibilities, including the care of school-age children.

Reallocation of domestic responsibilities between husband and wife and a re-scheduling of hours in industry to allow for these shifts in responsibility might well improve human resource allocation. Some movement in the latter direction is beginning to occur in the United States, but recent developments in rescheduling working hours have placed major emphasis on compressing the workweek to 4 days. In the course of these changes, both management and labor organizations have expressed concern that such compression of work schedules could be particularly hard on married women with families—yet surveys of married women workers reveal that they prefer the 3-day weekends these timetables allow. At present, however, less than 1 percent of all workers in the United States are on a 4-day workweek.

Rather than compressing the workweek for all, European experiments have stressed "flexitime," an arrangement that permits workers to set their own arrival and departure hours within a prescribed band of time in the morning and afternoon. The workday can vary in length as well as starting and finishing times, as long as workers complete the total number of hours required in a given period, usually a month. . . . One of the main advantages for workers lies in the fact that flexitime exables a variety of personal and family matters to be undertaken that were previously difficult to arrange in the context of a rigid work schedule. Still, legal and contractual provisions for overtime pay after 8 hours a day or after a 40-hour week might well hamper the introduction of flexible schedules into the United States. In addition, it is difficult to apply such a scheme to service workers and blue collar workers in production jobs which require certain hours of performance or a high degree of worker coordination. Nonstandard, part-time arrangements have usually offered few of the job options or fringe benefits, even on a pro rata basis, that full-time occupations provide. Along with these problems, women face a number of statutory provisions that explicitly or implicitly exclude them from any form of unemployment insurance.

Changes in standard work practices will not be achieved without experimentation; nevertheless, the opportunities such changes could offer husbands and wives to arrange compatible careers could be crucial to women's market work.

Questions for the Future

During the last quarter of the 20th century, woman's commitment to market work, traditionally limited in duration and significance, is likely to grow. Declining birth rates, along with rising levels of education and career aspirations of younger women, suggest that the future worklives of the two sexes will come to resemble each other more and more, both in terms of occupational distribution and time spent in the labor force. Women's employment problems now lie in an inability to find or take jobs commensurate with their abilities and rising expectations. For many reasons—stereotyping in education, training, and hiring practices; intermittency; immobility; the demands of a dual career; discrimination—there appears to be a wide discrepancy between the career aspirations of younger women and the realities of the labor market.

The situation raises important policy questions whose implications warrant some review. For example, can education, training, and employment practices be revamped to offer a wide range of occupational choice to both men and women? Can part-time and other flexible work arrangements be made in order to permit a more even distribution of market and nonmarket work? What kinds of child-care plans will meet the needs of a family in which both parents are at work, or only one parent, a working one, is present?

Admittedly, these questions are not easy to answer. But the search for answers deserves nationwide attention—for workable responses can bring about substantial improvement in individual fulfillment, the family's well-being, and the nation's productive capacity.

The Economic Situation of Spanish Americans

Paul M. Ryscavage   *Earl F. Mellor*

Approximately 10 million Americans with a Spanish background lived in the continental United States in the early 1970s. They represented about 5 percent of the U.S. population and were composed of several ethnic groups.

Included in 1972 were 5.3 million Mexican Americans, 1.5 million Puerto Ricans, and 600,000 Cubans. The remainder were Central Americans, South Americans, and others of Spanish origin.

Most Spanish Americans are relative newcomers to this country. In 1970, the great majority of Puerto Ricans were either born in Puerto Rico or had parents who were born there. Nearly half of the Mexicans were of Mexican birth or parentage.

Spanish Americans are concentrated in certain parts of the country. Mexican Americans live primarily in the five Southwestern States—Texas, New Mexico, Arizona, California, and Colorado—although significant numbers have moved to other parts of the country. Puerto Ricans are most commonly found in the New York City area and other large cities of Pennsylvania and New Jersey. Cubans are located, for

Reprinted from the *Monthly Review*, April 1973, pp. 3–9.

the most part, in Florida. In 1970, about 84 percent of all Spanish Americans lived in metropolitan areas compared to 68 percent of the total white population.

In varying degrees, these Americans are often beset by many of the same problems blacks face, such as low family income, high unemployment, job discrimination, and lack of adequate education and skills. In addition, they face a language barrier hindering their efforts to achieve economic parity. This article discusses the economic situation of Spanish Americans as a whole and of each of the three major ethnic groups.

Identifying the Group

This article is based on data from the 1970 Decennial Census and three recent supplements to the Current Population Survey (CPS). The two principal definitions of Spanish Americans used in this article are as follows:

Spanish origin or descent. This includes persons who identified themselves as Mexican, Puerto Rican living on the mainland, Cuban, Central or South American, or other Spanish origin or descent. This is the definition used in the Current Population Survey.

Spanish heritage. This is a summary definition used in the 1970 Census. It includes persons of Spanish language and others of Spanish surname in the five Southwestern States of Arizona, California, Colorado, New Mexico, and Texas; persons of Puerto Rican birth or parentage in the three Middle Atlantic States of New Jersey, New York, and Pennsylvania; and persons of Spanish language in the remaining 42 States and the District of Columbia.

These definitions overlap greatly, yielding similar population counts and similar social and economic characteristics.

Our discussion relating to the specific ethnic groups is based on Census and Current Population Survey definitions. The Current Population Survey identifies groups as to whether they are of Mexican American, Puerto Rican, or Cuban origin; the Census identifies these three major ethnic groups only on the basis of their current location. Hence, Mexican Americans are represented by those persons of Spanish language or surname in the five Southwestern States; Puerto Ricans, by those of Puerto Rican birth or parentage in the three Middle Atlantic States; and Cubans, by persons of Spanish language in Florida.

Income Profile

Regardless of the specific income measure used—family income, per capita income, or the proportion with low incomes—the incomes of Spanish American families as a group fall far below the incomes of all white families. The discussion that follows is based on total family income, that is, the combined income from all sources of all income recipients in families of two persons or more. National data show that:

Median income for families of Spanish origin in 1971 amounted to $7,500, about $3,100 below that of all white families and $1,100 above that of black families.

Mean income per family member among those families of Spanish heritage in 1969 averaged $2,000 compared to nearly $3,300 for whites and $1,700 for blacks.

One-fifth of all families of Spanish origin had incomes below the low income threshold of the Federal Government in 1969 compared to 10 percent of white families and 30 percent of black families.

Some caution should be exercised in generalizing about Spanish Americans as a group because there was considerable variation in the incomes of Mexican, Puerto Rican, Cuban, and other Spanish American families. Nevertheless, the income of none of these major ethnic groups equaled the median income for all white families, and Puerto Rican family income was lower than that of black families. Median income for all white families was $10,672 in 1971; for families of Cuban origin, $9,371; for Mexican Americans, $7,486 and for Puerto Ricans on the mainland, $6,185.

The median income of Spanish Americans ranged from 89 percent of that of all whites for Cubans, to 70 percent for Mexican Americans, and 58 percent for Puerto Ricans.

Of all major Spanish groups, Puerto Ricans had the lowest income in 1969—29 percent were below the Federal Government low-income threshold, about the same as among blacks. The incidence of low income was 21 percent among Mexican Americans and 14 percent among Cubans.

Factors Affecting Family Income

There are many factors leading to the lower average income of Spanish American families. They earn less income and also receive smaller amounts from most other sources such as interest, dividends, and retirement income. The discussion that follows is focused on earnings (wages, salaries, and self-employment income) because earnings account for about nine-tenths of aggregate family income both among Spanish Americans and the total U.S. population. The gap between the incomes of Spanish American and other white families reflects primarily the lower earnings of Spanish American families.

Family earnings, in turn, are the product of the average number of workers per family and the average earnings of individual workers. Except for Puerto Ricans, the average number of workers per family is the same for Spanish Americans as for other white families. The crux of the income problem for Spanish American families, then, is the fact that average earnings per worker, and particularly of primary workers, are lower than those of other white workers. In the case of Puerto Rican families, the primary worker was often a woman.

The earnings of Spanish American workers vary somewhat in different parts of the country, depending on the general level of wages. For example, generally lower pay scales in the South have some effect in holding down the earnings of Cubans in Florida. But much of the difference between the earnings of Spanish American and other white workers remains even when comparisons are made within the same States and regions.

Another factor contributing to lower annual earnings among Spanish American workers is their lack of skills, which together with discrimination in hiring and promotion, lead to their concentration in low paying jobs and to higher rates of unemployment. Underlying part of this problem is their lack of formal education and their difficulty with the English language.

Labor Force Participation

Spanish American families, excluding Puerto Ricans, and other white families both had an average of 1.7 workers in 1971; among Puerto Ricans, there was an average of 1.2 workers per family. This difference reflected lower labor force participation among both men and women workers in Puerto Rican families. Low rates of labor force participation among Mexican American women were offset by participation of other family members besides the chief breadwinner.

Except for Puerto Ricans, the overall labor force rate for Spanish American men was essentially the same as for all white men, around 80 percent. In March 1972, only 73 percent of the Puerto Rican men were in the labor force, partly because of health problems. Around one-quarter of all Puerto Rican men under 65 and outside the labor force were disabled.

Rates of labor force participation are comparatively low among Mexican American and Puerto Rican women. Little more than a third of the Mexican women and a fourth of the Puerto Rican women were in the labor force in March 1972. Labor force participation among all white women was 43 percent at that time.

The effect of large families and child rearing on labor force activity are important factors in the low participation rates of Mexican American and Puerto Rican women. The average family size of Mexican American families in 1970 was 4.4 members and of Puerto Rican families, 3.9 members; in contrast, the average size of all white families was 3.5. In addition, while only one-fourth of all white families had children under age 6, 44 percent of the Puerto Rican families and 40 percent of the Mexican American families had children this young.

Social attitudes which discourage wives and mothers from seeking jobs outside the home may also be important. The labor force participation rate of Puerto Rican women with children under age 6 was only slightly more than half that of all white women with children of the same age. As their children reach school age, the proportion of Puerto Rican women in the labor force increases somewhat, but remains significantly below the rate for all white women.

Mexican American women with children under age 6 enter the labor force to about the same extent as all white women, but as their children grow older, labor force participation does not rise so fast as that for all white women. Nevertheless, in families where there are no children under age 18, the labor force activity of both Mexican and Puerto Rican women nearly equals that of all white women.

The comparatively small number of working wives in Mexican American families was offset by other secondary earners drawn into the work force to supplement the low earnings of the primary breadwinner. In 1970, only about 39 percent of the Mexican American wives had any work experience, while 50 percent of the other white wives did. But 51 percent of the Mexican American children and other relatives worked compared with 39 percent in other white families.

Labor force rates for Cuban women in Florida were above those for other Spanish women and also of all white women, regardless of the presence or absence or the ages of children in the family. The following tabulation shows labor force participation rates for women age 16 and over in April 1970, by race, ethnic group, and number of children:

	Total	Children under age 6	Children under age 6–17	No Children under 18
White	40.6	28.4	49.0	41.5
Negro	47.5	47.6	59.8	43.4
Spanish heritage, total	38.1	28.4	43.5	41.7
Mexican	37.8	29.8	43.3	40.1
Puerto Rican	29.9	16.6	30.5	39.9
Cuban	47.1	38.6	59.7	45.1

Earnings and Occupations

The earnings of Spanish American workers in 1969 were lower than those of all white workers. This was true among both men and women and held for all three major ethnic groups. Among men, the largest deviation from white workers' earnings was among Puerto Rican workers, the smallest among Cuban workers.

Median earnings for all Puerto Rican men were only two-thirds those for all white men from the Middle Atlantic States ($5,500 and $8,300). Mexican men earned about three-fourths that of all white men from the Southwest ($6,000 and $8,100). Median earnings for Cubans ($5,600) were nearly 80 percent as high as those of all white workers in Florida ($7,200). (Because of regional wage differences, the earnings of Mexican men were slightly higher than those of Cubans even though the relative earnings differential was smaller for the Cubans.)

To a large extent, these earnings patterns reflect the occupations of Spanish American workers. They are found in disproportionately great numbers in the poorest paying jobs with the least prospects for advancement, including such jobs as food service worker, freight service handler, cashier, and cleaning service worker. Of all the employed men of Spanish origin in April 1970, 19 percent were in the 10 lowest paying occupations at that time, while only 10 percent of all employed white men were in these occupations.

As their earnings position might indicate, Puerto Ricans were the most concentrated in low-paying jobs. About 3 out of 5 Puerto Rican men in April 1970, for example, were employed in operative (semiskilled), laboring (unskilled), and service occupation. Half the Mexican Americans and two-fifths of the Cubans were so employed.

Some Spanish American men, however, had good jobs. Nearly 1 out of 5 employed men were skilled craftsmen in 1970, almost the same proportion as for all whites. Spanish American men also were employed in the professional, managerial, and sales occupations, although Mexicans and Puerto Ricans were especially underrepresented in these jobs relative to white men as a whole.

Even when Spanish American men obtained jobs in the professional, managerial, and craftsmen occupations, however, their earnings were significantly lower than the earnings of all white men in the same occupation group and same locality. The greatest earnings difference occurred among Puerto Ricans.

Most Spanish American women were also employed in relatively low-paying jobs—clerical, operative, and service occupations—with a few noticeable exceptions. More of the Puerto Rican women were in operative jobs because of the concentration of Puerto Ricans in the northeastern cities with large manufacturing industries. Mexican American women, on the other hand, more often held service jobs than did either Puerto Ricans or Cubans. Overall earnings of Mexican, Puerto Rican, and Cuban women were lower than for all white women, but in general earnings differences were not so great as among the men.

Because of the lower average earnings of women, the income position of Spanish American, and especially Puerto Rican, families is affected by the relatively high proportion headed by women. About 14 percent of all Spanish American families were headed by women in 1970 (slightly higher than that for all whites); among Puerto Ricans the proportion was 27 percent.

Women heading Puerto Rican families must rely on public assistance or on their own low earnings. In 1970, only about a fourth of the women heading Puerto Rican families had any work during the year. Average annual earnings for those who did work were under $4,000.

Unemployment

Unemployment affects Spanish American workers to a greater extent than other white workers and accounts in part for the former group's low annual earnings. In March 1972, the latest date for which unemployment data are available for this group of workers, their jobless rate was one-third higher than for all whites (8.1 percent and 5.6 percent, respectively). Jobless Spanish Americans totaled a quarter of a million at that time. Unemployment is much less severe among Cuban workers than among other Spanish American groups. In April 1970, the rate of unemployment was 4.4 percent for Cubans, slightly above the rate for all white workers in the nation. Among the Mexicans in the Southwest and Puerto Ricans of the Northeast, however, jobless rates were more than 1.5 times as high:

	Both Sexes	Men	Women
Total	4.4	3.9	5.2
White	4.0	3.6	4.8
Negro	7.0	6.3	7.7
Spanish heritage, total	6.6	5.8	8.1
Mexican	6.9	6.1	8.5
Puerto Rican	6.7	6.1	8.1
Cuban	4.4	3.2	6.2

Unemployment rates for Mexican and Puerto Rican women were particularly high. The job-finding difficulties of Mexican and Puerto Rican women in the labor force are probably due in part to their especially low level of education. In contrast, the job-finding success of Cuban women clearly reflects their distinct educational advantage.

Spanish American workers are less likely than other white workers to be employed throughout the year. Special tabulations from the Current Population Survey for 1970 reveal that a larger proportion of the husbands in Spanish American than in other white families had less than year-round, full-time employment. In addition, only a small proportion of Spanish American working wives had full-time, year-round work experience.

Formal Education

Spanish Americans lag far behind other Americans in educational attainment. Median years of school completed by persons 25 years and over averaged 9.6 for Spanish Americans compared with 12.1 for the total population. This low level of education has hampered many from qualifying for higher paying jobs and has had a significant impact on family incomes.

One out of every five persons of Spanish origin age 25 or over in 1972 lacked the 5 years of schooling generally thought necessary to achieve literacy, four times the corresponding proportion for the entire population. However, younger Spanish Americans generally have completed more years of schooling than older Spanish Americans.

Substantial differences exist in the educational attainment levels of the major ethnic groups. Again Puerto Ricans generally lagged behind their counterparts. For this group, median years of education completed in 1970 ranged from 8.0 years in Pennsylvania to 8.6 years in New York, compared to 11 years for Cubans in Florida.

For Mexican Americans in the five Southwestern States, the range was from 7.2 in Texas to 10.6 in California.

In part, these differences in education reflect differences in the education of different Spanish American groups when entering this country. Many Cubans who recently arrived in this country already had relatively high educational attainment levels. Puerto Ricans and Mexican American immigrants, on the other hand, were mainly low-income persons coming in search of jobs and livelihood, with relatively little education at the time of entry.

Spanish American women, on average, have less education than men. The median level of schooling completed by the women was 9.4 years compared to 9.9 years for men. The difference may be linked to the more traditional role assigned to women in the Spanish family. The Spanish tradition of male dominance and the prevalence of large families have probably contributed to the lag in the acquisition of formal education and English language skills of women of Spanish background.

Low incomes among Spanish Americans limit their expenditures for higher education. The proportion of Spanish American youth attending college and universities is clearly below that of other whites. Equality of opportunity in this area is critical for the Spanish Americans, because higher education is an important long-run factor in the improvement of their economic situation.

But the problem is not limited to higher education. Although Spanish American youth is better educated than the adult population, there is still a significant gap between Spanish American youth and all youth at all levels of schooling. For example, two-thirds of all young people, but only half of Spanish Americans age 18 to 24, completed high school. Fewer 16- and 17-year-old Spanish Americans were enrolled in school compared to all youth of the same age. And a greater proportion of 16-year-old Sanish Americans had not even entered the junior year of high school compared to other white students of the same age (62 percent compared to 45 percent).

Improvement in the use of the English language is a key element in the advance of the educational level of Spanish Americans and their upgrading in the job market. It is encouraging, therefore, that the inability to read and write English is declining among young persons of Spanish origin. Although only 3 out of 4 adults, age 25 or over, reported that they could read and write English in 1969, 9 out of 10 young Spanish Americans age 10 to 24 reported that they could do so. (Differences, of course, existed among the separate ethnic groups.) But until the substantial deficiencies can be overcome, the economic status of Spanish Americans will continue to lag that of the labor force as a whole.

The Changing Economic Position of Black Urban Workers

Jack E. Nelson

Data from the 1970 Census indicate clearly that a major restructuring of residence patterns along racial lines is taking place in the nation. Whites are moving to suburban areas and Blacks are concentrating in the nation's inner cities. Blacks have made significant economic gains by inheriting a piece of the nation's cities, but if current trends continue, the economic growth potential of these areas from a long range perspective is questionable. As the opportunities gained from the out migration of white workers taper off and as natural economic growth in inner cities continues to wane, unless action is taken to the contrary, the dramatic gains in employment evidenced by black workers in the sixties will trail off severely. This paper attempts to shed some light on these important issues in the hope that it will help spur the national debate—particularly in the black community—over strategies to continue the advancement of black Americans.

Blacks Inherit Inner-city Jobs

In the turbulent years between 1960 and 1970, 2.6 million whites left the nation's inner cities (Table 1). Most of the exodus consisted of adults between the ages of 25 and 44 years and children under 14 years. The movement among whites, from both urban and rural areas, was primarily to suburban areas. By 1970 the white suburban population had increased 32 percent over 1960, and nearly 4 in 10 whites lived there. As whites migrated to suburban areas, the black population in inner cities increased by 3.1 million. In percentage terms, 70 percent of the growth of the black population took place in the nation's inner cities. By 1970, 55 percent of all Blacks lived in urban centers and constituted 22 percent of the total inner city population—up from 16 percent in 1960. The black population in several major cities—such as Atlanta, Washington, Gary and Newark—approached or topped the 50 percent mark.

TABLE 1   U.S. Population Changes by Race, Age and Residence: 1960–1970

	Central City		Suburban		Nonmetropolitan	
	1960	1970	1960	1970	1960	1970
Whites						
All ages	47,638	—2,550	51,793	16,746	59,267	4,535
13 years and under	12,177	—2,188	16,311	3,045	17,590	—630
14–24 years	6,920	1,581	7,077	5,724	9,163	2,548
25–44 years	12,511	—2,468	14,861	2,864	14,334	178
45 years and over	16,030	527	13,544	5,114	18,180	2,439
Median Age	32.9	—.2	28.6	—1.3	29.2	.1
Blacks						
All ages	9,480	3,107	2,430	1,106	6,481	204
13 years and under	3,228	1,046	859	458	2,451	—66
14–24 years	1,437	1,121	415	278	1,147	340
25–44 years	2,701	235	630	240	1,240	—46
45 years and over	2,114	707	526	130	1,643	—25
Median Age	25.5	3.0	23.1	.5	24.9	—5.2

SOURCE: U.S. Bureau of the Census, *Current Population Reports,* Series P–23, No. 37, "Social and Economic Characteristics of the Population in Metropolitan and Nonmetropolitan Areas: 1970 and 1960," U.S. Government Printing Office, Washington, D.C., 1971.

Reprinted from the *Review of Black Political Economy* 4, no. 2 (1974), with the permission of the publisher.

The cross-migratory pattern of whites to suburban areas and Blacks to central cities is the greatest single factor contributing to the general improvement in economic opportunities for Negro workers in the decade of the sixties. There were a total of 1,153,000 jobs held by white males in inner cities in 1959 that were not held by them in 1969 (Table 2). Increases primarily in the professional and technical and managerial occupations reduced the net loss of jobs by white males to 900,000, but, overall, the gross number of jobs vacated by them in central cities totaled 1,153,000.

The vacuum created by the large exodus of white males from inner city labor forces resulted in greater employment opportunities for minority workers. Jobs held by Blacks in inner cities increased by a phenomenal 1.2 million between 1960 and 1970—an increase greater than the total net growth of 1.1 million jobs for all races in the inner city. Blacks on the other hand obtained only 4.2 percent of the increase in jobs in suburban and 3.9 percent in rural areas. A preponderate 70 percent of the total increase in jobs in the black work force occurred in the nation's central cities.

TABLE 2   Net Changes in Employment Levels in Central Cities: 1959–1969

| | Total Employment (000) | | Total Net Change | Net Change by Race and Sex | | | |
| | | | | Whites | | Blacks | |
	1959	1969	Change	Males	Females	Males	Females
Professional & Technical	2,783	3,350	568	137	193	97	109
Managers & Officials	1,986	2,247	261	74	87	71	24
Clericals	4,452	5,088	636	—134	339	74	330
Sales	1,745	1,513	—232	—261	8	—3	30
Craftsmen	2,953	2,799	—154	—295	—4	166	5
Operatives	4,452	4,120	—332	—442	—165	174	99
Laborers	1,089	1,095	6	—5	—12	2	12
Service Workers	3,028	3,368	340	41	231	—46	73
Farmers	75	53	—22	—16	—3	—3	—
Total	22,562	23,638	1,076	—900	674	530	682

SOURCE: U.S. Bureau of the Census. "Social and Economic Characteristics of the Population in Metropolitan and Nonmetropolitan Areas: 1970 and 1960."

The number of white males in urban work forces either decreased or increased at a substantially slower rate than for black males in every major occupation group with the exception of service workers. Consequently, large numbers of black workers were able, with the general exception of sales jobs, to capitalize on the tight labor market created by the flight of white males to the suburbs. A visual survey in most large cities will show a complete racial metamorphosis in high visibility jobs such as bus and taxi drivers, delivery men, postal carriers and municipal clerks. There were important changes in other jobs vacated by white males as well. As the employment data in Table 2 indicate, the increased representation of black workers in inner cities equaled over 100 percent of the decrease in the number of white male clericals, 58.0 percent of the decrease in white male craftsmen, and 61.8 percent of the decrease in white male operatives. White females and non-black minorities also benefited from the out-migration of the white males.

Blacks are concentrating in inner cities where they are experiencing short-term gains filling jobs vacated by white males. But the inner cities are no longer growth centers and because the settlement of large numbers of Blacks, Puerto Ricans and Chicanos there is considered anathema by much of the white establishment, the economic deescalation of central cities will probably continue unchecked. The number of jobs in inner cities increased by a paltry 4.8 percent in the past decade. This compares unfavorably with increases of 44.2 percent in suburban and 20.4 percent in rural areas. Between 1959 and 1969, 92 percent of the growth of jobs in the economy took place in suburban and rural areas. The black population is becoming increasingly urban, but the uncertain fate of inner cities as economically viable entities threatens to undermine the long range prospects for continued advancement of the black work force. Employment opportunities for black workers will show severe moderation in the future as the turn-over of jobs held by whites drops off. Reliance for new jobs will then depend upon expansion of the inner city economy, which in fact will undoubtedly be declining.

There appears to be little prospect for significant job expansion for Blacks in non-metropolitan areas. In 1969, 51.5 percent of the black population in rural areas lived in poverty. Roughly every other rural Black was impoverished, compared with only 14 percent of rural whites. Poverty, of course, translates into employment patterns and while approximately 3 in 10 Negroes live in rural areas, only 1 in 10 of the increase in jobs for Blacks in the sixties occurred there. Employment opportunities for Blacks in urban areas increased by 36.5 percent; the increase in rural areas was a modest 9.9 percent. Employment opportunities for whites in rural areas, however, increased by 21.5 percent and accounted for 35.2 percent of the nationwide total increase. Of the Blacks that were able to obtain jobs in rural areas, most still are confined primarily to the lower paying, lower status jobs. In 1969, for example, only 20.3 percent of rural Blacks held jobs in the better paying professional and technical, managerial, clerical and craft occupations, compared with 50.2 percent of rural whites and 37.5 percent of urban Blacks.

The Quality of the Black Work Force Improves

Irrespective of whatever else may be said about the economic trends of the sixties, Blacks made very dramatic gains. Between 1959 and 1969, the number of black professionals and technicians increased from 277,000 to 582,000 (110 percent); black officials and managers increased from 66,000 to 222,000 (236 percent); and black craftsmen increased from 374,000 to 631,000 (69 percent). The portion of the black work force performing these better paying, higher status jobs increased from 12.1 percent to 18.8 percent (compared with 35.0 percent and 37.8 percent, respectively, for whites). There were also significant changes in Negro participation rates in nearly every occupation, including decreases in the proportion of Blacks in the laborer and service occupations (Table 3).

The decrease in the participation rate of black service workers is subject to interpretation. Although Blacks have traditionally performed menial tasks as service workers, the service industries are among the fastest growing in the economy and offer many well-paying jobs. Most of these new jobs are being created in suburban areas where Blacks generally do not work. Therefore, while the number of Negro male service workers decreased during the decade by 10.9 percent, the number of white male service workers *increased* by 12.3 percent. The decrease in black male service workers was accompanied by the elimination of large numbers of poorer paying jobs in the occupational grouping, many as a result of technological innovations. Accordingly, the relative earning position of black male service workers was substantially improved over 1960 although their number decreased. In 1960 black male service workers earned 64.2 percent of the wages of white male service workers, but in 1970

TABLE 3 Negro Occupational Participation Rates and Occupational Distribution

	Employment (000)		Participation Rates		Occupational Distribution	
	1959	1969	1959	1969	1959	1969
Professional & Technical	277	582	3.7	5.2	4.7	7.6
Managers & Officials	66	222	1.2	2.9	1.1	2.9
Clericals	402	998	4.1	7.3	6.9	13.1
Sales	88	150	1.9	3.2	1.5	2.0
Craftsmen	374	631	4.1	6.3	6.4	8.3
Operatives	1,280	1,867	10.3	13.4	21.9	24.6
Laborers	875	841	28.8	24.5	14.9	11.1
Service Workers	2,033	2,102	27.5	21.6	34.7	27.6
Farmers	458	209	11.5	7.2	7.8	2.7
Total	5,853	7,603	9.2	9.7	100.0	100.0

SOURCE: U.S. Bureau of the Census, "Social and Economic Characteristics of the Population in Metropolitan and Nonmetropolitan Areas: 1970 and 1960."

the percentage increased to 79.4. Similarly, black male service workers earned 78.5 percent of the median earnings of all black males in 1960, but 80.6 percent in 1970.

Earnings

Statistics for the period 1960–1970 indicate that a pervasive restructuring of the national work force was (and presumably still is) taking place. In the decade of the sixties the population became more metropolitan, and in metropolitan areas the work force became more white collar. The average worker was richer and better educated, and there occurred an upward shift in family earnings in nearly every income bracket. The employed black population shared in the prosperity of the sixties, but because their participation in the economy at the outset of the decade was so limited, the relatively modest changes in actual numbers appear astronomical when expressed in percentage terms.

TABLE 4 Distribution of Family Income

	1959		1969	
	Whites	Blacks	Whites	Blacks
Under $3,000	14.0	40.9	8.1	21.4
$3,000 to $5,999	22.0	31.4	15.2	28.7
$6,000 to $9,999	35.2	20.5	28.1	28.1
$10,000 to $14,999	19.3	6.1	27.9	14.7
$15,000 and over	9.5	1.3	20.6	7.1
Median	$7,360	$3,721	$9,793	$5,998

Table 4 shows that Blacks have made qualified gains with respect to their general earning capacity. Black family income increased by 61.2 percent between 1959 and 1969, while white incomes increased during the same period by 33.1 percent. In 1969, the earnings of black families on the average equaled 61.2 percent of white family income compared with 50.5 percent in 1959. These percentage gains, however, tend to becloud the actual change which occurred. The difference in the increase in wages between Blacks ($2,277) and whites ($2,433) widened the gap in their median incomes by 7 percent. This indicates that the rate of change for the Blacks, though improving, has not occurred at a pace which would bring parity with whites at any future point of time.

The greatest change in the family income profile for Blacks occurred in the $3,000 and under bracket which decreased by 19.5 percentage points, nearly all of which is counter-balanced by increases in the $6,000 to $15,000 middle income range. The data indicate substantial upward movement throughout the lower income brackets for black families while white families generally showed movement from the middle to the upper income brackets. In 1959, for instance, roughly 30 percent of white families earned $10,000 or more, while in 1969, about 50 percent earned this much. By comparison, in 1959 about 8 percent of Blacks earned $10,000 or more and in 1969 nearly 22 percent (less than the 1959 distribution for whites) were in this upper income range. So there is improvement in the earning capacity of black families, but parity is the goal and that is still a long way off.

Educational Training

The average educational level of black workers increased during the sixties. There was, in fact, greater upward movement in the median years of schooling for Blacks than for whites (Table 5). Between 1962 and 1970 the gap in years of school completed between black and white male workers was reduced in every major occupation group except service workers and nonfarm laborers. In 1970, nonwhite workers slightly exceeded the average educational level of white professionals and technicians and educational parity was reached between white and nonwhite clerical workers.

TABLE 5   Median Years of School Completed by Occupation Group of Employed Persons

| | Males | | | | Females | | | |
| | 1962 | | 1970 | | 1962 | | 1970 | |
	White	Nonwhite	White	Nonwhite	White	Nonwhite	White	Nonwhite
Professional & Technical	16.4	16.2	16.5	16.6	16.0	16.2	16.4	16.3
Managers & Officials	12.5	10.7	12.8	12.4	12.4	n.a.	12.6	n.a.
Clericals	12.5	12.4	12.6	12.6	12.5	12.5	12.6	12.6
Sales [1]	12.7	—	12.8	—	12.1	—	12.4	—
Craftsmen	11.3	8.9	12.1	10.5	9.9	10.0	11.0	11.6
Operatives [2]	10.4	8.9	11.6	10.6	—	—	—	—
Service Workers [3]	10.7	9.4	12.1	10.5	11.3	10.7	12.1	11.2
Farmers [4]	8.7	5.7	9.4	6.6	9.2	n.a.	10.4	n.a.
Nonfarm Laborers [2]	9.4	8.1	11.0	9.2	—	—	—	—
Median	12.1	9.0	12.4	11.1	12.3	10.5	12.5	12.1

1. Nonwhite sales workers are combined with the statistics for clerical workers.
2. Female operatives and nonfarm laborers are combined with the statistics for craftsmen.
3. The data for female service workers do not include private household workers.
4. Does not include farmers and farm managers in 1962.
SOURCES: U.S. Department of Labor, Bureau of Labor Statistics, *Educational Attainment of Workers, March 1962.* and *Educational Attainment of Workers, March 1969./1970.* Special Labor Force Report 125.

From an educational standpoint the labor force is becoming more and more homogeneous. Nevertheless there still exists a significant gap in the average wages per *educational background* between the races. In 1959, the average schooling of black workers 18 years and older was 8.7 years or 72 percent of the average for whites; in 1969, the corresponding figures were 11.1 years or 91 percent of the level for whites. On the other hand, in 1959 a black worker with 1 to 3 years of high school earned 63.5 percent of the salary of his white counterpart, and in 1969 the earnings of Negro workers with this range of education increased to only 68.2 percent of the wages of white workers with equal schooling (Table 6). These figures indicate that the value of black education is improving in the labor market but the demand for higher educational training outpaces the wages employers are willing to pay for qualified

TABLE 6 Black/White Earnings Ratios by Years of School Completed

	1959	1969
Elementary	57.2	65.8
Less than 8 years	61.4	71.2
8 years	64.5	63.7
High School	63.0	68.3
1 to 3 years	63.5	68.2
4 years	65.0	70.1
College	60.8	72.2
1 to 3 years	64.1	75.5
4 years or more	58.7	70.2

SOURCE: U.S. Bureau of the Census, "Social and Economic Characteristics of the Population in Metropolitan and Nonmetropolitan Areas: 1970 and 1960."

black workers. Negro college graduates, for example, still earn less than white high school graduates. But the gap is closing too. In 1959, Blacks with 4 or more years of college earned 81.9 percent of the wages of white high school graduates, in 1969 this gap was narrowed to 98.2 percent.

There is evidence that employers are "skimming" among the black work force—the superstar syndrome—where primarily the most talented are accepted and the mediocre and below average workers are routinely rejected. Such discriminatory hiring practices are borne out in educational statistics on white collar workers. In 1970, a substantial 42.1 percent of black employed males with high school diplomas or better held white collar jobs, compared with 58.0 percent for white males. However, on the other side of the educational coin, only 8.8 percent of black employed males with 3 years of high school or less held white collar jobs while 18.5 percent of similarly educated white male workers held whitecollar jobs. Employers, then, hire Blacks with high school education or better for the presumably more desirable white collar jobs at rates roughly comparable with white workers. But they hire lesser educated Blacks at less than half the rate of similarly educated whites for white collar jobs.

Long-range Trends

Despite rather substantial economic gains during the sixties, Blacks in the long run have not been able to maintain a proportionate share of jobs in the economy. Since 1940 the nonwhite population 14 years and over has consistently increased at a faster rate than the white population. But the increase in the black civilian labor force has been consistently less than the expansion of the black working age population, while this relationship has been positive for the whilte population (Table 7). In 1970, for example, the black population had grown over the decade by 28.8 percent, but the black labor force increased by only 23.4 percent. By contrast the white population grew during the same period by 17.1 percent, but the white labor force increased 18.2 percent.

In addition to the increasing number of Blacks not taking part in the work force, those who participate are experiencing greater difficulty in finding and holding a job.

Unemployment rates for nonwhites continue to run consistently higher than for whites with the result that nonwhites make up a disproportionate share of the workers on unemployment roles. In fact, 1970 was the first decade in 30 years in which Blacks did not show a substantial increase in their proportion of the total unemployment

TABLE 7   Labor Force Trends: 1940–1970 (%)

	1940	1950	1960	1970
Decade Increases: Blacks				
Population		13.8	18.2	28.8
Labor Force		7.9	18.5	23.4
Decade Increases: Whites				
Population		10.9	11.3	17.1
Labor Force		13.1	14.5	18.2
Labor Force Participation				
Blacks	58.1	55.0	55.2	52.9
Black Males	79.8	74.6	69.9	62.7
Whites	51.3	52.3	53.8	54.3
White Females	24.1	28.1	33.6	38.9
Unemployment Rates				
Blacks	16.8	7.8	8.7	6.9
Whites	14.2	4.5	4.7	4.1
Black Share of Total Unemployed	12.8	16.8	18.0	17.3

statistic (Table 7). The proportion remained roughly the same between 1960 and 1970 at about 18 percent—an increase of 5 percentage points (or more than two-fifths) over the 1940 level. The unemployment problem is particularly acute in inner cities where unemployment rates among Blacks of 40 percent and higher have not been uncommon in the last few years. And so, the general manpower trends of the economy continue to reflect unfavorable treatment of Blacks despite the substantial gains of the sixties.

Conclusion

Overall, the employment profile of black workers in the decade of the sixties showed a mixed picture. Adverse trends indicate that downward participation in the labor force continued through the sixties but Blacks within the labor force showed general improvement. The education between Blacks and whites was substantially narrowed between 1960 and 1970, but the wage gap continued. The employment situation for rural black workers showed little improvement.

The gains made by black workers in the sixties were due primarily to the out-migration of whites—especially white males—from the nation's central cities. As these migratory patterns become more stabilized in the future, the byproduct in the form of employment opportunities for Blacks can also be expected to taper off. Consequently, the current rate of rapid growth for black workers cannot be expected to continue beyond the next few years.

The centrifugal movement of the economic base to suburban areas has revolutionized the urban concept in America. Our cities have been supplanted with metropolises radiating out from core cities. This outward movement resulted from growth patterns and development opportunities which have been bolstered by the social problems of central cities. Central cities have a certain economic inertia by which they will continue to exist, but the cross-migratory patterns of middle class whites and lower class minorities is taking its toll. The social and the economic are inextricably related, and the economic opportunities of inner cities which now invite heroin peddling, thievery and racketeering to an unprecedented extent are declining in more conventional economic activities.

The employment data presented here outline the need for national policies which will effectively deal with the urban crisis. If the black workers currently concentrating in the nation's cities are to continue progressing toward a fair share of the American economic pie, then federal policies must be directed to insure that the cities remain economically viable. Equally important though as more and more businesses relocate or otherwise become established in the suburbs, opportunities for Blacks must be opened there through federally sanctioned activities such as affirmative recruitment efforts by suburban employers to hire inner city Blacks, improved means of transportation between the inner city and the suburbs, and open housing opportunities in areas near suburban work sites. Black America is taking its stand in the central cities at this point in history. If the cities are not able to continue functioning as viable economic communities capable of producing middle class inhabitants, they will alternatively become containments within affluent suburban shells and their inhabitants will increasingly face the prospect of becoming wards of the state.

New Perspectives on Youth Unemployment

Manpower Report of the President, 1972

High teenage unemployment, particularly among black youth, is one of the country's most critical manpower problems. Young workers aged 16 to 19 have for years had an unemployment rate four or five times that for adults aged 25 and over. . . . Black teenagers have had a rate of joblessness more than double that for white youth. In the summer months, teenagers' job-finding problems have been much intensified, as both students and new high school graduates have flooded into the labor force. The inevitable result has been a great number of dissatisfied, discouraged young people— of whom many have given up looking for jobs and as a result are without constructive activities.

Youth unemployment is not a single problem but many. . . . It affects—in different degrees and in different ways—in-school and out-of-school youth, younger and older teenagers, high school graduates and dropouts, boys and girls, blacks and whites. All groups of youth face rates of joblessness far above that for adults. But minority group members and those handicapped by limited education are the ones most severely affected. There is a pronounced inverse relationship between the number of years of school young people have completed and their rates of unemployment. In particular, high school dropouts have an unemployment rate nearly double that of graduates.

The very considerable change that has occurred in recent years in the composition of the teenage labor force is another factor which must be borne in mind in analyzing the problems of joblessness among the young. Students, predominantly interested in

Reprinted from *Manpower Report of the President, 1972,* pp. 77–90.

part-time jobs, accounted for 56 percent of the teenage labor force in October 1971 compared with only 41 percent in 1960. The proportion of students among the teen-aged unemployed had risen to 54 percent by 1971, from 30 percent in 1960. Policy measures designed to alleviate youth unemployment must take account of this change, which greatly affects the kinds of jobs needed by young people. And finding work is often critical for students as well as out-of-school youth; it frequently deter-mines whether they can manage to stay in school.

The high rates of joblessness among teenagers, in large measure, reflect their fre-quent exposure to unemployment as they enter and reenter the labor market after periods devoted to military service, schooling, or vacation or as they change jobs, try-ing to find a more satisfactory field of work. Once young workers are established in jobs, their risk of unemployment is only moderately higher than that of adults. But many barriers stand in the way of their obtaining steady jobs. Some employers are reluctant to hire youth for more than casual work because of their lack of training and work experience and the very fact of their frequent movement between jobs and into and out of the labor market. The requirement of a high school diploma, even for many jobs not actually demanding this level of education, is a barrier to employment of in-school youth and school dropouts. And legal minimum wage standards may bar youth from some jobs because of their inexperience, consequent need for training, and initially low productivity.

For some youth, frequent changes of low-level jobs accompanied by spells of unem-ployment may not have long-term negative effects. Recent research indicates that a considerable number of young people are able to improve their economic position, with time and additional experience as they change jobs. But for substantial numbers, particularly among the disadvantaged, haphazard, discouraging early work experi-ences can establish a pattern very difficult to overcome in later life.

For these young people, a variety of special measures may be needed. A differential minimum wage which would allow employers to pay youth less than adults might get young people off to a faster start in finding employment. Federal manpower programs can help to reduce the number of jobless, discouraged youth and to give those who have dropped out of school another chance to equip themselves for a life of productive work. But in the long run the need exists for more career-oriented education, so that young people not bound for college will be prepared for an occupation upon leaving high school, and for adequate guidance and job placement services to aid the transi-tion from school to work.

That measures such as these will not, by themselves, solve the problems of unem-ployed youth goes almost without saying. In the absence of a high rate of economic growth and a high general level of employment, efforts to improve young workers' job qualifications and remove the special obstacles to their employment cannot be counted on to open up many more opportunities for them. But the reverse is also true. To bring youth unemployment down to more satisfactory levels will require *both* stimulation of employment demand by general fiscal and monetary measures and policies specifically designed to reduce the structural barriers which impede young workers in locating jobs. . . .

The Groups Most Affected by Unemployment

Though all groups of teenagers have relatively high jobless rates, Negroes have been by the far the hardest hit. In 1971 white youngsters had an unemployment rate of 15.1 percent, less than half the rate for black youth (31.7 percent).

Extraordinarily high Negro unemployment is often explained in terms of the disadvantaged environment from which this group comes. However, even within urban poverty areas, there is a vast gap between whites and Negroes in the extent of unemployment; Negroes in such areas had more than twice the unemployment rates of whites in 1970 (35.8 percent and 16.3 percent, respectively).

Among whites as well as Negroes, 16- and 17-year-old workers have higher unemployment rates than 18- and 19-year-olds. The differences are not large, but they are very consistent by sex as well as by color. Thus, in 1971, white boys aged 16 and 17 had an unemployment rate of 17 percent; those 18 and 19, 14 percent. For Negro boys of these ages, the rates were 33 percent and 26 percent, respectively. The unemployment rates for girls showed a similar pattern.

The rate of unemployment is slightly higher among teenagers who are out of school than among those still students. This was true in 1971 and during most of the preceding decade. The divergence in unemployment rates between high school graduates and dropouts is far more pronounced. Among out-of-school teenage workers, those who failed to complete high school have had nearly twice as high an unemployment rate as those who had at least a high school diploma (23.3 percent as compared with 14.4 percent in October 1971).

With rates of unemployment as high as this, it must be assumed that many other jobless young people have given up the search for work and so are not counted among the unemployed. This assumption is supported by statistics on labor force participation, which show that the groups of young workers with the highest rates of unemployment tend to have the lowest participation rates. Thus, Negro boys, with an unemployment rate nearly twice that for white boys, were significantly more likely to be out of the labor force in 1971.

That teenagers' job-finding difficulties affect their labor force participation rates is indicated also by the changes in these rates in response to cyclical fluctuations in the economy. As employment rises and unemployment falls, the number of teenagers in the labor force tends to increase. Furthermore, during recessions the teenage unemployment rate understates the number of frustrated would-be employees to a greater extent than in more prosperous periods. . . .

Students in the Labor Force

The number of young Americans who work while still in school rose sharply during the past decade. Students in the teenage labor force more than doubled in number between 1960 and 1971, whereas young workers not in school increased by only about 13 percent. As a result, students accounted for 56 percent of the teenage labor force in October 1971, compared with 41 percent in 1960.

Growth of the student labor force stems from the much larger number of teenagers in the population and in school, as well as from increases in the labor force participation rates of in-school youth. The latter development is, of course, intensified by the tendency for young people to remain in school longer. These trends are likely to persist in the foreseeable future. Projections show a growing proportion of youngsters, both white and Negro, completing high school and going on to college in the near future while, at the same time, teenage labor force growth is expected to continue through 1980, though at a much slower rate than in the 1960–70 decade.

White youngsters are more likely than Negroes to be working or seeking work while enrolled in school. In 1971, 40 percent of all white teenage students were in the labor force, compared with 24 percent of the Negro students. It is also likely that the generally high unemployment rates among Negroes deter some students from seeking jobs.

Although information about students' need for work is limited, a Department of Labor study conducted in October 1969 concluded that part-time job opportunities were of great importance for many students. This was shown by the fact that of the 16- to 21-year-old unemployed students, 29.5 percent experienced difficulty in paying school expenses and 26.9 percent had to stop or decrease financial assistance to their families. Furthermore, 8.9 percent of those not in school said they had to leave school because of unemployment. The proportion who said they experienced no adverse effect from unemployment was very small.

These conclusions are corroborated by a survey of Neighborhood Youth Corps enrollees which found that inability to meet school expenses was an important reason for dropping out of high school. Of the dropouts in the sample, more than one-third said that they left school for economic reasons.

But financial need should not be the sole criterion in judging the importance of adequate employment opportunities for students. Youngsters in all income groups derive advantages from early in-school job experience. They learn work discipline and job-hunting methods and acquire knowledge of the labor market, all of which help them to make a better adjustment to a full-time career in later life.

Out-of-School Youth

Out-of-school youth, including both high school graduates and dropouts, now constitute less than half of the teenagers in the labor force, but they numbered over 3.1 million in October 1971. Their unemployment rate was over 17 percent.

The approach to work of out-of-school students is basically different from that of students. Jobs are a primary and crucial concern for these youngsters. They are at a critical point in life when their labor force record is being shaped and when the jobs they take may have major influence on their future work experience. They are much more likely than students to look at jobs from a long range point of view.

Despite the importance of employment to many students, there can be little doubt that the job-finding problems of young workers who are out of school—and for whom the alternative to work is often destructive idleness—is a policy objective of even greater urgency. For this group particularly, it is important that the jobs provided afford learning experience and opportunities for upward mobility.

Job-finding difficulties are compounded for those out-of-school youth who failed to complete high school. In October 1971, the unemployment rate for school dropouts aged 16 to 19 was 23.3 percent, while for graduates it was 14.4 percent. Whereas 90.4 percent of male high school graduates were in the labor force, this was true of only 80.3 percent of the boys who had dropped out. And of the young men aged 16 to 21 employed in October 1969, only half of those without high school diplomas were earning $2 or more an hour, compared with 7 out of 10 of those with a high school education (and no college).

The importance of high school graduation is also reflected in the occupational status of youth aged 16 to 21. The proportion of young people who find their way into clerical and, to a lesser extent, other white-collar occupations is much higher among high school graduates than among dropouts. The latter are more concentrated in operative, service, labor, and farm occupations. . . .

In spite of the difficulties school dropouts face in the labor market, some 655,000 young people aged 16 to 24 left school between October 1970 and October 1971 before completing high school. Half of these were 16- and 17-year-olds; under most State laws youngsters may leave school at age 16. . . .

In view of the importance of a high school diploma as an employment credential, the reasons for dropping out of school were explored in a recent longitudinal study. It was found that deep-seated problems—such as the low socioeconomic level of a youngster's family and his past school failures, rebellious and delinquent behavior, and ability limitations—make it likely that particular young people will quit before graduation from high school. Dropping out, therefore, is a symptom of a youngster's troubles, not the basic cause.

As a result, the authors of this study reject any implication that if potential dropouts could be made to stay in school, they would be just like the rest of the graduates. By the time a potential dropout reaches the 10th or 11th grade he usually has personal problems that will not be resolved by another year or two of high school. The authors conclude that more attention should be given to intervention in the lives of troubled youngsters at an early age. . . .

Causes of High Teenage Unemployment

A wide variety of factors have combined to put today's teenagers in a particularly disadvantageous job market position. Their age group is exceptionally large, owing to the high birthrates of the early 1950s. Their typical pattern of entry and reentry into the labor force, with intervening periods of withdrawal from the labor force, means repeated exposure to the risk of unemployment. They have met increasing resistance from employers to the hiring of young workers as educational standards (and thus age levels) for employment have gone up. And they have encountered added competition for jobs, particularly from middle-aged women returning to the labor force.

Labor Force Patterns of the Young

Since first-time entry into the labor market and subsequent withdrawal and reentry play such an important part in the employment history of the young, teenagers always have higher overall unemployment rates than adults. Data on the reasons for unemployment show that in 1971 the proportion of the teenage labor force unemployed because of job market entry and reentry was over 12 percent, out of an overall youth unemployment rate of 16.9 percent and in contrast with only 1.6 percent of all adult workers. Unemployment for other reasons—i.e., layoffs and quits—was only moderately higher for youth than adults. . . .

Work Attitudes of the Young

The negative attitudes of young people toward work have often been mentioned as one of the main reasons for teenage unemployment. Unrealistic expectations are cited with respect to wages as well as hours, working conditions, and responsibilities. Concrete information on this subject is very thin and somewhat contradictory. According to a longitudinal study, in process at Ohio State University, young men's occupational aspirations are high though eventually adjusted downward. Some individuals, particularly Negro youngsters, tend to have aspirations higher than are warranted by their backgrounds, as well as the general odds against achieving the desired status in life.

But an examination of young people's actual job-hunting experiences in the summer of 1969 raises some doubts about the "unrealistic expectations" argument. Of the approximately one million 16- to 21-year-olds who looked for work but did not find it, 51 percent of the whites and 42 percent of the Negroes indicated that no jobs were available. Only 12 percent of the whites and 14 percent of the Negroes said they refused jobs because they did not like the kind of work or working hours involved or because the pay was too low. . . .

Employers' Attitudes Toward Young Workers

Whenever older, more experienced workers are available, employers generally hire them in preference to the young. Some of their reasons for doing so are that young people are more likely to change jobs frequently and usually require more training than persons with more substantial labor market experience, thus making them less productive, at least in the short run. Some employers are unable to hire youngsters because of the child labor laws and others, confused about the laws, simply prefer not to get involved. . . .

Child Labor Laws

Legislation designed to protect young people from exploitation or from work which might impair their health or interfere with their educaion has also put restrictions on their employment. The Fair Labor Standards Act (FLSA) sets 16 years as the basic minimum working age for non-agricultural occupations in interstate commerce but bars workers under 18 years of age from employment in occupations stipulated as hazardous by the Secretary of Labor. Fourteen and fifteen-year-olds may be employed on a more limited basis, with greater restrictions on occupations and hours. Their work is generally limited to non-school hours.

Since State laws supplement Federal legislation, employers are bound by at least two sets of regulations, and experience has shown that frequently employers are poorly informed as to what the child labor standards are. Research on the importance of child labor laws in decisions not to hire the young is lacking. There are indications, however, that employer confusion with respect to the content of the laws is a handicap to youth. Many employers do not realize, for example, that only 5 percent of all jobs are covered by the Nonagricultural Hazardous Occupations Order issued under the FLSA and that, therefore, 16- and 17-year-olds may be employed in most occupations. If it is true that "Employers are confused about, and have little grasp of, the child labor laws and that they refuse to hire young workers out of fear that they may get into trouble with the law," then it is more important to improve employer education in this respect than to consider revisions of the child labor laws.

Hiring Requirements

As average levels of education have increased, employers have raised their requirements for many blue-collar as well as white-collar positions. The high school diploma is widely used as a criterion in hiring, even for jobs which can be performed satisfactorily without this level of education. As a result, youngsters who have dropped out of high school, and those who have not yet finished, are in a poor position to compete for the better jobs, as are adults without a high school education. Yet a study of 10 clerical, sales, operative, and service occupations in various industries found no relationship between educational attainment and the degree of job success. It is noteworthy also that in 1967 about half the workers in the skilled trades were not high school graduates.

Occupational licensing is another form of "credentialing" which may keep young workers from having access to jobs. They are precluded from working in many occupations where skills could be learned through practice by licensing requirements specifying training in "approved" programs or institutions. The fees imposed in licensing could also constitute a hardship for young disadvantaged workers. . . .

Competition for Jobs

Women who enter or reenter the labor force in their thirties or later may often compete with their sons and daughters for the part-time, low level, neighborhood jobs sought by those in school, as well as for the full-time, entry level or low skilled jobs desired by many out-of-school youngsters. Married women 35 years of age and over tend to have occupational patterns very similar to those young people; 75 percent were employed in clerical, sales, service, or operative jobs in 1971. Since the proportion of women aged 35 and over in the labor force increased from 36.9 percent in 1960 to 39.9 percent in 1971 (or from 14.5 million to 17.8 million), the competition that youngsters face in seeking employment has stiffened. . . .

Young People in Jobs

The average American youngster goes through several periods of job search. He tends to look for "youth jobs" until leaving school and "career jobs" after that.

Young people usually make their initial entry into the labor force as part-time or summer job seekers. They are not generally available for career jobs but, instead, look for work which will provide some income but little long-range occupational commitment. In fact, a youth's total part-time experience is likely to have little if any impact on his industrial affiliation in his first full-time job. Since teenagers who are still in school do not offer much in the way of education, training, and experience, they typically find work of limited responsibility in small nonunion firms. They are likely to function as salesclerks, busboys, short-order cooks, and stock clerks and serve on store and office cleaning crews.

This picture changes considerably when youngsters leave school, look for full-time jobs, and start to think in terms of status and advancement prospects. They are then interested in getting on the first rung of a job ladder—i.e., in obtaining career type jobs. Thus, out-of-school youngsters are more often found in manufacturing establishments, offices, and large stores, in which employment is more likely to be permanent and to lead to promotions.

It is not surprising, therefore, that students and nonstudents, regardless of age, were employed in quite different proportions in various industries and occupations in October 1971.

The vast majority of those in school—about 4 out of every 5—were to be found in trade and service industries, where there are many part-time jobs. The occupations employing the largest number of students were service work, and clerical, laboring, sales and operative jobs. In contrast, only about half of those out of school were in trade and service industries and a sizable number (over 1 out of 4) were in manufacturing. The occupations with the largest groups of out-of-school workers were clerical and operative jobs.

There were also differences between Negro and white youngsters in industry and occupational employment patterns. Negroes were more likely than whites to work in service industries and substantially less likely to be employed in trade. Relatively more Negroes than whites were employed in manufacturing, but this applied only to the manufacture of nondurable goods. Negroes were more likely than whites to be service workers, and only about a third as likely as whites to be in sales occupations.

The well known tendency of young people to change jobs frequently has again been confirmed by the longitudinal study at Ohio State University. This study also shows that, among young men, blacks are more likely to change jobs than whites, even after allowance is made for differences in their occupations and educational attainments. . . .

Rates of job change decline substantially with advancing age, and by their middle twenties most men have settled down. By this time, they have either found work in line with their aspirations or have arrived at a more realistic assessment of their labor force potential. The fact that at this age many have acquired family responsibilities contributes to this settling down process.

Long-range Consequences of Early Work Experiences

What are the effects of the rapid change of low-level jobs which characterize the transition from school to work in this country? Do young people prefer to experiment, to look for work best suited to their momentary needs, and to change jobs as their requirements change? Do they tend to gain the type of work experience which will be useful in later life, or is their initial contact with the labor market likely to create frustration, disillusionment, and an unfavorable attitude toward work?

Clearly the results of early work experience are different for different youngsters. But the available evidence suggests that for many teenagers employment experience while still in school may be helpful in establishing work habits and making it easier to obtain subsequent employment. The Ohio State study shows, for example, that in 1967, out-of-school white boys who had worked while in school the preceding year had an unemployment rate only one-fifth that of out-of-school youth without previous work experience. The same research indicates that changes made after leaving school have generally been to the economic advantage of the young men involved, while at the same time providing an opportunity to correct inappropriate job choices. The advantage from job changing appears to be greater and more consistent for Negroes than whites, probably because Negroes are likely to start work at lower levels.

The fact that unemployment decreases consistently and substantially as young workers reach the next older age groups is evidence that most of them achieve a progressively better integration with the world of work. In 1971, the average rate of unemployment of 16- and 17-year-olds was 18.7 percent and for 18- and 19-year-olds, 15.5 percent.

For workers in their early twenties the jobless rates were substantially lower—11.8 percent for those aged 20 to 21 and 8.9 percent for those 22 to 24. But even this last rate was more than twice that for workers aged 25 and over. The settling down process and decrease in job changing among older youth and their consequently lessened exposure to the risk of joblessness are clearly reflected in these unemployment figures. Many workers in their twenties also benefit from added education and training and employment experience, which improve their competitive position in the job market.

It is undoubtedly true that many young people suffer little if any disadvantage from their early, haphazard labor market experiences. These are the strong individuals who are able to experiment in the job market and benefit from doing so and those who successfully hunt short-term jobs to earn money for temporary needs while they prepare themselves for careers at higher levels.

There are, however, other youth who never emerge, or emerge only with great difficulty, from their early experiences of unemployment and marginal employment. Negroes and high school dropouts stand out prominently among them, but current information is not adequate to isolate other specific groups, such as whites from low income families. Furthermore, it is not known how many of the youngsters who were effectively integrated into the world of work had to adjust their sights downward from career goals they might have attained had they benefited from better and more extensive counseling.

It is obvious, however, that the process of making the adjustment from school to work is a very long one for many youngsters, if judged by their disproportionately high unemployment figures. For those who do not consider early unemployment purely temporary, discouragement is obviously involved in the continuing spells of unemployment. And though many youngsters who quit jobs find new ones relatively quickly, others are not so fortunate. A surprising 23 percent of the unemployed out-of-school 18- and 19-year-olds had been out of work for 15 or more weeks at the time of the October 1971 labor survey.

The relatively low labor force participation rates for out-of-school teenagers also indicate that the youth labor market, as it currently functions, leaves many teenagers behind. In October 1971, 30 percent of all teenagers not in school were also not in the labor force. For Negroes the proportion was 38 percent. . . .

There can be little doubt that those who do not make a satisfactory labor market adjustment while young are subsequently likely to be found among the large pools of disadvantaged middle-aged for whom special programs need to be developed or welfare provided. By reexamining the school-to-work transition process in the light of those who appear to be left behind and by providing more intensive special services—including guidance and education geared to the very young in the early years of school and continued until they are successfully placed—efforts to ease the youth unemployment problem may go hand in hand with reducing the numbers who need public assistance at a later stage in life.

It would seem from the European experience that a rate of youth unemployment far above that for adults is not inevitable in an industrialized society. Thus, a closer examination of this country's institutional arrangements for absorbing into the labor force youth not bound for college is in order. It would be unfortunate if the high educational sights which the United States has set for its population were to work to the disadvantage of those who either cannot or do not wish to go on to higher education.

Manpower Policy

The Uses and Limits of Manpower Policy

Lloyd Ulman

Policies that had been billed in the 1960s as specifics against inflation, unemployment, or poverty can hardly expect many enthusiastic endorsements today. Certainly, criticism of the so-called manpower policies, which had been touted for all three jobs at one time or another—and whose financial support from the federal government had increased tenfold over the decade—should come as no surprise. On the other hand, the criticism seems to have come most strongly and with equal fervor from the opposite ends of the political spectrum; and some readers may wonder whether any policy that has become the target of such wide-angle cross fire can—like the man who hates children and dogs—be all bad.

Public manpower policies have come to embrace a wide range of personnel activities including (but by no means restricted to) counseling, training (in both educational institutions and on the job), the provision of better and cheaper information to employers and job seekers, and financial subvention of employers and trainees. Yet this broad range of activities constitutes only a subset of what a group of economists in the Swedish Confederation of Trade Unions (or LO), termed "active labor market policies." By the end of the 1940s, Sweden, like other countries in Western Europe, began to experience the unemployment-inflation dilemma, which was often posed most acutely during crises in the balance of payments. Since wage determination in Sweden has proceeded under a highly centralized system of collective bargaining, the LO responded to one such crisis by accepting a wage freeze, only to see its collective sacrifice nullified by extra wage increases (or "drift") at the local levels, and a subsequent "wage explosion." This sorry sequence of events—which unfortunately, was to be replicated in other countries in subsequent years—left the Swedes disenchanted with wage and price controls as an instrument for containing inflation at high levels of employment.

Reprinted with the permission of Lloyd Ulman from *The Public Interest*, No. 34, Winter 1974. Copyright © 1974 by National Affairs, Inc.

Particularly disillusioned were the trade union leaders. As bargainers, they, like their counterparts in the Employers' Confederation, felt that collective bargaining could be effective only in the presence of employer resistance sufficient to preclude local wage drift. Yet they rejected completely the creation of excess capacity and unemployment as a means of generating such resistance and reducing the rate of inflation. Moreover, as egalitarian Social Democrats, they aimed at a policy of income redistribution through "wage solidarity" or the narrowing of wage differentials through centralized bargaining (among other policies); and such solidaristic bargaining would also be frustrated by local side deals that permitted occupational or industrial groups held back under the central negotiations to restore their traditional favorable differentials.

The Swedish Approach

How, then, might what *The Economist* in the early 1950s called the "uneasy triangle" of full employment, price stability, and collective bargaining be made more tolerable? And how, at the same time, might the cause of greater economic equality be served and economic growth promoted? A hopeful answer begins with the observation that the sum total of unemployment in a country at a point of time is not uniformly distributed among all industries, occupations, and regions, but tends to be concentrated more heavily in some labor markets than in others. Indeed, at levels of unemployment, that, while relatively low, are still short of what the public and the policy makers would regard as "full" employment, some markets would experience even shortages (or bottlenecks).

A lower overall unemployment rate could be achieved by conventional measures that would increase aggregate demand through some combination of tax reductions, increased government spending and easier money. But under such aggregate expansionary measures, demand for labor (and for capital as well) would be increased indiscriminately in bottleneck markets and slack markets alike. This would be undesirable on one and quite possibly two counts. In the first place, while excess supply of labor would be reduced, the rate of absorption of labor in excess supply might be limited by bottlenecks in other types of labor (used with more plentiful varieties in the same process of production). Indeed, excess demand would be increased by such blunderbuss measures, as existing bottlenecks grew larger and new ones emerged in markets that previously had been close to a balance between supply and demand. As a result, the rate of inflation would be increased while the economy remained short of its overall employment goal.

To be sure, bottlenecks tend to shrink and disappear as businessmen expand their training programs and seek ways to economize on the use of scarce labor, and also to the extent that consumers find substitutes for goods the prices of which have risen especially rapidly because their rates of production have been retarded by shortages. However, such corrective processes may be associated with (and, indeed, partly rely upon) exceptionally big wage increases for workers in short supply who, if skilled, tend to have relatively high wages to begin with. This would constitute a second reason why a union movement committed to a narrowing of wage differentials would oppose exclusive reliance on general reflationary measures. Such a union movement could, and in fact would, attempt to maintain preexisting differentials by bringing up the wages of the groups still in plentiful supply, but this would merely accelerate the overall rate of wage and price inflation without redressing the imbalances in various labor markets.

An alternative approach consists of a variety of selective measures that the Swedes have subsumed under the rubric of "active labor market policy." Some active labor market policies would be aimed directly at concentrating a desired increase in demand in the labor surplus markets—e.g., by financing investment in less developed regions and by the creation of jobs in the public sector and in sheltered workshops for people of relatively low employability. Other labor market policies would be aimed directly at specific areas of excess labor supply by increasing the mobility of labor through manpower policies, including training and relocation assistance. At least in principle, substitution of the laser beam for the blunderbuss would enable a given reduction in unemployment to be secured with a smaller increment in aggregate demand and, therefore, with a lower rate of inflation. At the same time, conditions would be less conducive to wage drift and hence more conducive to the reduction of wage differentials through central bargaining.

The Swedes believed that active labor market policy was superior to wages and price controls under the conditions of excess demand caused by the application of conventional "Keynesian" aggregate demand policy for two broad reasons. In the first place, they felt that employment could be expected to respond more promptly to policies that were aimed directly at the specific loci of employment than to general policies that depended more heavily on secondary multiplier or trickle down effects (although this is not to suggest that large-scale application of selective policies would not also generate secondary effects). In the second place, they saw that wage and price controls under conditions of very high employment frequently fail because they have to work against market forces. Conversely, to the extent that they are able to keep the lid on, controls reduce economic efficiency and inhibit growth. Active labor market policies, on the other hand, should make the market work more effectively than it otherwise would. Left to itself, the wage structure may respond only sluggishly to changes in demand and supply; and workers whose mobility is often impaired by financial as well as other barriers to the acquisition of skills, job information, and geographic relocation tend to respond only sluggishly to changes in the wage structure.

The idea behind active labor market policy generally has been either to redirect market forces, as with some demand policies like regional assistance or public works programs for "the hard to employ," or (more frequently) to move the markets more efficiently in the directions indicated by existing concentrations of bottlenecks and unemployment. In all cases, however, the object is to make the market work in the direction desired by the policy maker rather than, as in the case of controls under full employment, to seek to frustrate the operation of a set of preexisting market forces which are left in place under the policy.

A good example might be found in the different means often employed by incomes policy (or direct restraint of money wage and price movements) and manpower policies in pursuing the objective of improving the relative position of low-paid groups. Incomes policy seeks to grant these groups exceptional treatment, or at least partial exemption from the general "norm" for wage increases, but it has often been frustrated when higher-paid groups demanded the same favored treatment for themselves to restore or maintain what they regarded as "equity." Manpower policy, in contrast, should increase the supply of the more highly trained workers relative to the supply of untrained workers. Thus manpower policy should tend to raise the wages of the unskilled by making them relatively scarcer at the same time it inhibits the rise of wages in the more skilled groups by making them more abundant. To the extent that there has been unsatisfied demand for skilled labor, the policy increases total employment without adding to aggregate demand. (The same strategy was pursued in a related area: the great post-War expansion of college education in Sweden has been motivated in good part by the Social Democratic governments' desire to facilitate income redistribution by increasing the relative size of the highly educated sector of the population.)

The U.S. Response to "Creeping Unemployment"

The United States introduced its modern manpower policies at a later point in time than Sweden, but also at what the Swedes and all Europeans would consider an earlier stage in economic evolution. The federal government began granting financial aid to the states for vocational education during the First World War (under the Smith-Hughes Act of 1917); it established what is now known as the Federal-State Employment Service and also an apprenticeship policy in the 1930s (under the Wagner-Peyser Act of 1933 and the Fitzgerald Act of 1937 respectively). However, it did not directly establish occupational training programs and subsidies until the early 1960s, with the passage of the Area Redevelopment Act in 1961, the Trade Expansion Act in 1962, and most important, the Manpower Development and Training Act (MDTA) that same year. Moreover, when the MDTA was passed, inflation was not a current concern, while unemployment was much more severe in the United States than it was and had been in post-War Europe. In 1961, the first year of recovery from a recession, unemployment averaged 6.7 percent, and in 1962 it stood at 5.5 percent, while price levels remained virtually stable.

Nevertheless, these levels of unemployment were diagnosed by some as "structural" in nature. Many people were impressed by the observation that, whereas unemployment in the peak (or final) year of the upswing in 1949–53 had fallen to 2.7 percent, it went no lower than 4.2 percent in the peak year of the 1954–57 upswing, and in the following cyclical rise of 1958–60, its downward progress was arrested at 5.1 percent. Apprehension over "creeping inflation" in the early and middle 1950s had to make room for apprehension over the trend of "creeping unemployment" in the late 1950s and early 1960s.

Concern over creeping unemployment was shared by a fairly odd assortment of bedfellows. At one extreme were the economic conservatives, including those in the Federal Reserve Board and the Treasury, who opposed the tax cuts and other deficit-increasing measures advocated by the "new economists" in the Council of Economic Advisers and the academic community. The former argued that the unemployment was structural in nature and coexisted with job vacancies elsewhere in the economy; hence, expansion of aggregate demand would simply generate more inflation than employment.

At the other extreme were various groups, notably the Ad Hoc Committee on the Triple Revolution, that were mightily impressed by automation. They regarded automation as a radical departure from conventional technology which was causing a quantum jump in the rate of increase in productivity in the economy. Unemployment resulted from two properties of this phenomenon: (a) widespread technological displacement of labor and (b) a growing satiety of demand caused by the economy's capacity to satisfy existing private consumer wants more rapidly than (employed) people were able to develop new wants.

Under such dramatically changed circumstances, unemployment could not be reduced by fiscal-monetary measures designed to increase the level of private employment because the level of private employment could not be increased. Demand creation would have to take the form of public spending, which could increase employment because, it was alleged, non-market communal needs were still unsatisfied. For the most part, however, unemployment would have to be reduced, not through the expansion of employment, but by providing the unemployed and the poor with enough income to induce them to withdraw from (or not to enter) the labor force, i.e., to stop looking for remunerative employment. A radical redistribution of income thus would be required because "the traditional link between jobs and incomes is being broken."

The middle ground of structural diagnosis was mainly occupied by labor market economists in the Department of Labor, in the trade union movement, and in the academic community. They were impressed with the decline in the proportions of non-skilled blue-collar jobs in the economy, and they were deeply apprehensive over technological displacement. Unlike the conservatives, they were not particularly inhibited by the prospect of budget deficits. Nor did their opposition to the proposed tax cuts—which it should be noted, was not shared by all in this group—dwell on the alleged inflationary effects of such measures. Rather, it was based on the opinion that tax cuts could not reduce unemployment to the level of 4 percent which the Council of Economic Advisers had proclaimed as an "interim target." Like the radical structuralists, the moderates did believe in the efficacy of job creation in the public sector. But they did not particularly subscribe to the glut hypothesis and they did believe in the unemployment reducing potential of retraining programs. They were the chamions of the Manpower Development and Training Act.

The Council's Position

It should be noted that the Council was not averse to manpower policy, although it did reject the structuralists' interpretation of the economic evidence. It subscribed to the view that the slowdown in the rate of economic growth and the "creeping unemployment" during the Eisenhower years resulted from failure to maintain adequate levels of demand in the economy rather than from any *increase* in the degree of structural unemployment over the preceding decade, which, it was claimed, did not occur. And the Council reasoned that the injection of more money demand would be both necessary and sufficient to move the economy from 5.5 percent unemployment to 4 percent without sacrificing price stability. In essence, these economists claimed that the problem was a "Keynesian" problem and not a "post-Keynesian" problem—and, it might be added, they had their hands full teaching the Keynesian lesson about unbalanced budgets to parts of the Administration, to the Congress, and to the public at large. At the same time, they were far from oblivious to the trade-off problem. However, they addressed it through the advocacy of incomes policy (or wage and price guideposts). Hence they implicitly took issue with the Swedes who had regarded incomes policy as unnecessary when the economy is operating well below capacity, as well as an inferior competitor to active labor market policy under full capacity utilization.

Although the various structuralist arguments were presented with less than compelling rigor, they did call attention to certain phenomena and they did foreshadow some concepts which were later to assume considerable significance for the development of manpower policy in this country. (We shall return to this point.) Meanwhile, however, two events—or rather one non-event and one event—tended to cast some doubt on their anlaysis of the unemployment problem and on their policy prescription.

The non-event was the failure of the manpower administrators to uncover significant numbers of skilled workers who had been displaced from their jobs by technological change and who, as a consequence, were suffering prolonged spells of unemployment. By 1963, according to Stanley Ruttenberg, then Economic Advisor to the Secretary of Labor, "it was already evident that we were working on the wrong woodpile."

The event which did occur was the enactment of major tax cuts and the development of an inflation-free upswing that lasted until 1965 when the interim target of 4 percent unemployment was reached. This association sufficed to vindicate recourse to broad macroeconomic policy for the purpose at hand in the minds of the public and of most professionals, although dissenting interpretations also were advanced by "monetarists" and by some "structuralists." (The latter pointed to the role of increased Vietnam involvement in directly increasing public expenditure and in withdrawing young men from the civilian labor force.) But the less advertised part of the Council's analysis was also roughly confirmed by events, in that once the interim unemployment target was passed, price stability rapidly began to give way to inflation. In the mid-1960s, the high-employment, inflation-prone economy returned to the United States after a decade of relative price stability. This was the type of economy for which the Swedes had developed manpower policy, and it was also the type of economy which the American Keynesians believed called for structuralist measures (among others) to improve the trade-off between unemployment and inflation. It might also be added that their "monetarist" adversaries also believed that structural reforms were necessary, in order to reduce the "natural rate of unemployment" (i.e., the minimum unemployment rate sustainable without an accelerating rate of inflation), and that such measures include improved labor information services.

The New Structuralism

The prospects for manpower policy seemed further improved by analysis which revealed the occurrence and significance of large-scale changes in the composition of the labor force and unemployment in the 1950s and 1960s. In particular, attention was drawn to the great increase in the proportion of women in the labor force and an associated rise in the unemployment rates of women relative to those of men in the same age groups. Concern was also voiced over the great increase in the teenage portion of the labor force and in teenage unemployment relative to adult unemployment. There was no evidence of increase in the occupational or geographic dispersion of unemployment; and this has been construed as inconsistent with the earlier structuralist position, which stressed technological displacement and related changes in the composition of demand.

Structural unemployment can be increased, however, by an increase in the supply of labor in a particular market as well as by a decline in demand for that sort of labor; and the number of vacancies can be increased by a reduction in supply as well as by an increase in demand. Of course, changes in relative labor supplies (e.g., in the age or sex composition of the labor force) do not necessarily result in more unemployment together with more shortages. This unhappy outcome can be produced, however, in one or more of the following circumstances: (1) when the labor that has become more plentiful is inferior in quality to the labor that has become less plentiful, in the opinion of employers of the latter variety: (2) when wage structures are sufficiently sticky so that wages of the groups which had grown more plentiful cannot be reduced relative to the others by enough to offset their lower efficiency; (3) when changes in the composition of demand for labor do not fortuitously match changes in the composition of supply, so that new arrivals might find employment in the same lines of work and at the same relative pay as their predecessors.

Unfortunately, all these conditions (including the last, negative one) seem actually to have prevailed in the post-War period. First, youthful and female labor has been regarded by employers as less productive than so-called prime-age male labor, the former because of lack of experience, and the latter due to less steady attachment to the work force. Second, institutions such as minimum wages and collective bargaining have made for wage rigidity; under collective bargaining, entry rates rose relative to the minimum wage, and, at least until the late 1960s, skill differentials generally failed to narrow (in some cases they widened) despite a relative surplus of unskilled labor. Both of these conditions tended to make the increased youth and female work forces rather imperfect substitutes for men between the ages of 25 and 64, whose unemployment rates fell sharply relative to the national average, and even absolutely, over the last two decades. Finally, occupational and industrial shifts in the demand for labor were not very congruent with demographic changes in the composition of the labor force. In the post-War period, the demand for unskilled blue-collar labor in the high-productivity, manufacturing sector no longer exerted a "pull" on the low-productivity, agricultural sector (as it has in such rapidly industrializing countries as Japan, Germany, Italy, and France). Agriculture, however, under the stimulus of very rapid technical change, supplied a powerful "push." Farm employment fell from 9.9 million in 1950 to 4.5 million in 1970; and the shrinkage of this sector, a heavy employer of teenagers, was superimposed on a bumper crop of youths. Yet there was a gap to be bridged between technological displacement and unemployment; and it must be remembered that the disproportionate decline in the demand for production labor in manufacturing was accompanied by dramatic increases in employment in the service sector and in white-collar occupations. Moreover, if the demand for inexperienced workers in manufacturing had grown apace with the supply, the demand for more experienced labor would have expanded even more rapidly than it did.

The American Rationale

To the extent that limited substitutability of youthful and female labor for experienced male labor has accounted for the widening of unemployment differentials among demographic groups, it has tended to make the American economy more inflation-prone. Economists have established that the greater the dispersion of unemployment rates among the various "compartmentalized" or "segmented" labor markets in an economy, the greater the rate of inflation that is generated at any given rate of overall unemployment; and econometric studies have suggested that the increased spread of unemployment rates among age and sex groups has indeed tended to worsen the inflation-unemployment trade-off in the United States. Presumably, therefore, any policies that are designed to reduce the watertight integrity of various compartments—in the case of manpower policies by increasing the efficiency of less productive labor and by improving the flow of information about job openings—can potentially improve this trade-off and thus appeal to policymakers and others concerned with overall demand management. This might be regarded as an American version of the rationale for manpower policies originally provided by the Swedes.

Moreover, it must be noted that benefits can result from improving the occupational or geographic mobility of labor in *any* compartmentalized markets and not simply in markets where supply has been increasing relative to demand. Mobility-improving policies could potentially be productive when applied in markets where unemployment rates are relatively *high* whether or not they have been relatively *rising*. This is of particular significance in the case of the non-white groups whose unemployment rates might actually have improved relative to the national average toward the end of the last decade. (However, this improvement might have been more apparent than real since the proportions of black men reported as actively seeking work also declined during the same period, which might indicate growing frustration and despair.) But even if non-white unemployment has not been growing faster than the over-all rate, it has certainly been relatively high—over twice as high for non-white men as for white men.

Support for manpower policy might be provided by post-War innovations in the economies of education, as well as by the structuralist refinement of the aggregate trade-off analysis referred to above. The economics of "human capital" regards the acquisition of information as an investment, since it involves incurring present costs (both direct and indirect in the form of earnings foregone during the learning period) in exchange for future returns (in the form of increased earnings for the individual and greater productivity and output for the community). Such investments are made by the student or trainee himself (or by his family), by the employer, and by the general public.

The provision of public support for education has been defended on the grounds that poor people are less able to incur the costs of education than others since, even if they sought to borrow for that purpose, their own human capital could not be held as collateral by the banks. Moreover, because they are poor, each dollar of income diverted from present consumption represents a greater sacrifice for them than it does for others; hence the poor may be less willing to invest in education. The same could be said of all expenditure made by poor people, but the public is presumed to have a special interest in the spread of education. Thus, in the absence of public support, the community's total investment in education would be too low, and its productive capacity would be correspondingly reduced. Public provision for support of training might be defended on similar grounds, given that the formal education provided to the poor—especially the non-white poor (and particularly those in the rural South)—is lower in quantity or quality than the community average, and given that on-the-job training can be viewed as a sort of postgraduate extension of institutional education, building on the latter. Employers are willing to incur training costs to the extent made profitable by their employees' expected quit rates (which in turn vary inversely with the wages paid), but they can economize on their training outlays by hiring better educated—hence better "prepared"—workers. Therefore, public support or subsidization of training for the educationally disadvantaged could compensate for their lower trainability on the job.

The results should be greater equality of opportunity and of unemployment rates, more training provided, and a less inflation-prone and more productive economy. Moreover, this line of argument can possibly lend support to the existence, and conceivably the extension, of public employment exchanges. Like education and training, the acquisition of information about jobs, workers, and terms of employment can also be regarded as an act of investment, and outlays on "search" should be increased as long as they are exceeded by increased flows of income resulting from increased mobility of labor (and capital).

Thus, manpower policy in the United States could find some intellectual support both in the new structuralist approach to inflation and unemployment and in the human capital approach to information and work. This, however, does not imply that the development of manpower policy in the 1960s was in sole and direct response to these economic analyses. In the next section, we shall find that other influences were predominant. Nor is it suggested that all those who erected the theoretical constructs were strong advocates of manpower policy, let alone that the policy has gone without serious challenge. We shall consider some of the main lines of criticism in the two sections following the next one.

Manpower Policy Meets the War on Poverty

Having discovered that they were "working on the wrong woodpile" in 1962, the Manpower Administration did not require much analytic guidance to find the right one; in 1963, resources were switched from unemployed family heads with work experience to programs designed to reduce youth unemployment. Then came the Johnson Administration's war on poverty, with the passage of the Economic Opportunity Act in 1964 and subsequent amendments in the three following years, passage of the Civil Rights Act in 1964 and the Elementary and Secondary Education Act of 1965, and the amendment of the Social Security Act in 1967. Broadly speaking, these legislative developments, together with a torrent of administrative initiatives, might be regarded as having impinged on manpower policy in two ways.

In the first place, manpower programs were regarded by the anti-poverty warriors as part and parcel of a wider complex of approaches and activities directed to such areas as education (including pre-school and remedial education), legal aid, social services, anti-discrimination and affirmative action, welfare reform and income maintenance, and community action. (The latter can be regarded as both a form of group therapy for the demoralized and a way to create pockets of political power for minority groups whose only source of leverage on the white middle-class electoral majorities seemed, at the time, to be a disposition to lay waste their own neighborhoods.)

In the second place, the inclusion of manpower programs in the anti-poverty complex resulted in a broadening and redirection of manpower policy itself. To attempt a catalogue of such modifications fortunately is unnecessary for the purpose at hand, since such a task lies beyond my own capability. But even superficial observation supports certain summary observations.

First, the clientele of manpower training was broadened to include not only the young, but individuals from the most disadvantaged groups in the community, including welfare recipients (notably under the Work Incentive Program) and the handicapped. This required an attempt to redirect two older state-controlled activities, vocational education and the provision of labor market information. The share of funds allocated to institutional training, which was carried out by the vocational education system under the MDTA, was greatly reduced in the second half of the decade in favor of the subsidized On-the-Job Training (OJT) program; and the Secretary of Labor was empowered to select both the occupations for which training would be offered and who the trainees would be. The Employment Service was instructed to redirect its efforts to serve disadvantaged groups. It was supposed to change over from "screening out" to "screening in," since two thirds of the training slots were reserved for the disadvantaged.

Second, accommodation of the disadvantaged meant that relatively more resources had to be devoted to subsistence allowances and to other subsidies to the trainees as well as to private employers (as in the On-the-Job program under MDTA and in Job Opportunities in the Business Sector). Sometimes it was difficult to ascertain whether the main thrust of the activity was training or subsidy. (The summer program of the Neighborhood Youth Corps was charged with being primarily a device to buy civic peace in the ghettos rather than seriously fulfilling its stated objective of providing teenagers with work experience and earnings that would induce them to remain in school.)

Third, the establishment of community action agencies was supposed to result in a sharing of the authority to design and administer programs with representatives of the communities from which the trainees or clients were drawn.

Although the war on poverty clearly helped to redirect the manpower programs, the multiplicity of legislative and administrative authorities, coupled with the absence of a clear notion of what everybody was supposed to be doing, helped to produce a bewildering variety of programs. Many of these trod on one another's jurisdictional toes; many died young, only to be reincarnated in some different form. Some of the administrative disputes involved differing objectives and concepts, as evidenced by the bruising triangular struggle between the state-based Employment Services, an old-line bureaucracy with an undistinguished reputation for effectiveness, the Manpower Administration in the Department of Labor, which sought to divert funds to training the newer client groups, and the Office of Economic Opportunity, which represented the local Community Action Agencies. Disputes such as these, involving federal agencies, state governors, mayors, and neighborhood organizations, led to the establishment of still more administrative structures designed to coordinate fragmented activities. These were generally unsuccessful. As a result, few programs were able to operate as efficiently as one might otherwise have expected; this was especially true where there were competing programs in the same locality, with each being run on a small and inefficient scale.

The Sympathetic Critics

Although the war on poverty broadened, redirected, and complicated the administration of manpower policy, it left intact, and indeed strengthened, its emphasis on unemployment, and the unemployed. This emphasis was further reinforced at the end of the decade by legislation of a "trigger clause," whereby additional funds would be released once unemployment had reached and remained for three months running at (or above) a level slightly exceeding 5.5 percent. But in neither its modified nor its pre-war on poverty form has the policy escaped criticism. And the criticism has emanated from sympathetic as well as skeptical quarters.

The sympathetic critics themselves are in two camps, one housing those who believe in a grand policy aimed primarily at the macroeconomic targets originally specified by the Swedes, and the other characterized by the belief that the policy should be directed and restricted to such high-unemployment groups as non-white minorities, women, young people in their late teens, and the aged unemployed. Both groups agree on the desirability of improving administration and efficiency through some "decategorization" and "decentralization"—i.e., reducing the number and halting the proliferation of specifically legislated and separately administered programs, and granting local authorities more discretion in determining the mix of the manpower programs in their respective communities. Both groups call for at least a partial return to "creaming," or selecting the more promising or better qualified applicants for training. This practice was largely abandoned during the war on poverty in favor of concentrating on the most disadvantaged individuals in the disadvantaged groups. But the latter practice tended to produce more trainee dropouts and, even in cases where the training was completed, to result in the displacement in dead-end jobs of the unskilled people who did not go through the public manpower programs by those who did.

However, the trade-off-oriented critics want the policy directed to job bottlenecks as well as to disadvantaged people; they would extend "creaming" to cover admission of employed people as well as the unemployed, so that, as the more advantaged trainees move up the ladder to the unoccupied rungs, their places at the bottom could be filled by more marginal workers. By the same token, they would have the policy to devote more resources to subsidizing private employers to provide training for their own skill requirements. On the other hand, less ambitious critics—including observers with greater familiarity with the actual operation of the American programs—feel that subsidy funds have already supported training that would have been provided by employers in the absence of such support.

Finally, the big-policy buffs believe that the American policy is carried out on too small a scale to be effective, and that substantial enlargement would yield significant results. They are undeterred by the record of growth—with training enrollments rising from 34,000 in 1963 to 1.4 million in 1971, as federal obligations climbed from $56 million to $1.5 billion for training, and from under $300 million in 1961 to $4.8 billion in 1972 on the whole array of programs. They would place this in perspective by pointing out that the tax cut in 1964 released some $14 billion, or noting that manpower programs cost only about a third of one percent of GNP in the United States compared to 1.5 percent in Sweden. The more cautious critics point out that the Manpower Development and Training Program's efforts in the past to train for skill shortages have not been very successful. Moreover, they fear that a magnification of such efforts under a large-scale, demand-oriented policy would more likely than not result in the planners' nightmare, i.e., the attempt to forecast trends and changes in occupational demand.

The Skeptics

To the skeptics, the growth of manpower policy means simply that an ugly duckling has been turning into an ugly duck. Their skepticism about even the potential effectiveness of manpower policy derives primarily from their views of the nature of post-War unemployment and poverty, although not all who share these views in fact reject all labor market policies. Their analyses lead them to reject the structuralist diagnosis, at least to the extent to which active labor market policy is indicated as a prescription. On the other hand, these analyses differ among themselves in various important respects, so that different skeptics find different reasons for their skepticism. We might distinguish at the outset two main sources of skepticism. The first is the view that much of the unemployment at which manpower policies are aimed has been voluntary and socially useful in nature. The second is the view that such unemployment is socially undesirable and is caused by various barriers to mobility, but that the barriers in question will not yield to the application of manpower policy.

The argument that much contemporary unemployment is voluntary, and that it might be socially useful, is related to the inability of the manpower administrators in the early 1960s to find long-time unemployed married men in large numbers. Instead, unemployment was found to be concentrated increasingly among women, the young, and the non-white, and to be predominantly characterized by short duration and high (and for some groups, increasing) incidence, including high quit rates. (Indeed, the high levels of unemployment that have prevailed in the United States, relative to other industrialized countries such as the United Kingdom and Sweden, have been traced to relatively high quit and layoff rates, which have helped to make the trade-off between inflation and unemployment more adverse on this side of the Atlantic.) There are two main reasons for holding that such unemployment is voluntary in nature and that it does not constitute as serious a social problem as unemployment of middle-aged family men. In the first place, it is pointed out that married women and teenagers may become unemployed more readily than married men because they have more useful alternatives to paid work, either at home or in educational institutions. As the representation of such secondary groups in the labor force increases, the proportion of total unemployment motivated by such relatively productive alternatives likewise rises.

In the second place, it is maintained that, as individual and family incomes and assets increase, individuals find it profitable to spend more and more time in job search activity, taking more time between jobs (or before accepting a first job) and possibly quitting one's job more readily in order to get a better one. Training programs are inappropriate solutions under such conditions. Lack of skill is not the problem, for there really is no problem at all. In fact, to the extent that such programs lure employed or voluntarily unemployed people out of the labor force into the programs (either as trainees or instructors), they might even be a counterproductive source of inflationary bottlenecks. But it will be recalled that a case might be made for improving the quality of information about the labor markets; this would reduce the costs of search to employers and employees and hence would presumably lower the duration of both unemployment and job vacancies. Actually, efforts are being made to improve the Employment Service by establishing "job banks" and by planning for their conversion into a computerized system of job-matching. But such efforts also could be counterproductive, since they could induce workers to quit their jobs and look around more frequently. What is gained on the swings (lower duration) is lost on the roundabout (higher incidence).

The second body of skeptical opinion emanates from an analysis that posits the same characteristics of unemployment as the first: short duration and rapid turnover. It differs from the first, however, in maintaining that such unemployment is essentially structural rather than frictional in nature, resulting not from the purposeful pursuit of superior opportunity but rather from frustration and apathy induced by the existence of barriers to opportunity. But manpower policies are rejected as a corrective device since, it is maintained, the barriers are not caused by lack of education or information. One cause of immobility is discrimination based on color and sex, which has the effect of reducing the economic value of education to those discriminated against. Thus individuals with identical educational attainment can earn significantly different incomes. Lower rates of return on education in turn might well discourage investment in education by individuals in the groups concerned, who thus might indeed suffer from an educational deficiency. But compensatory training could not improve the situation substantially as long as discrimination remains to depress the return on training.

Discrimination, however, is not always regarded as a sufficiently powerful influence to create important or lasting barriers to mobility and opportunity all by itself.

According to the neo-classical economists, the least bigoted employers in the dominant groups would be willing to hire discriminated-against labor at lower rates of pay, and thus enjoy and exploit a competitive advantage over their more bigoted rivals and drive them out of business. Hence discrimination is usually regarded as working in concert with other barriers to mobility. The latter, according to the "dual labor market" theory, have the effect of dividing the work force into two groups, one employed in sheltered markets—characterized by systems of internal training and promotion, great job security, and high wages—and the other crowded into "secondary" markets with low-wage, dead-end, short-term jobs. Since the number of entry-level jobs in the preferred sector is small relative to the supply of potential applicants from the secondary sector, employers might resort to racial or sex discrimination as a cheap means of screening some applicants out (just as they might use educational credentials as a cheap way of screening others in).

The theory is rather vague in its attempt to specify factors which make for "primary" internal markets in some industries and not in others, but technological considerations are supposed to play an important role. In this sense, this market segmentation approach is in the tradition of the early structuralists. But the newest structuralists part company with the oldest in at least one important respect. They regard unemployment as a quit-and-layoff phenomenon in secondary markets rather than as a displacement phenomenon; to them the main problem is not lack of job openings but low wages and dead-end jobs which induce frequent quitting as a symptom of poor morale. Training would not yield a satisfactory answer to a problem characterized by lack of motivation. Instead they have emphasized affirmative action measures to compel "primary" employers to abandon screening by sex or color; and they have advocated the negative income tax or similar transfer policies that would have the effect of supplementing the depressed incomes earned in the secondary sectors. On the other hand, advocacy of income redistribution in this context might be regarded as in the tradition of the Triple Revolutionaries who first insisted that income be divorced from work.

The Question of Efficiency

In the light of the administrative misadventures of manpower policy and of the strong *a priori* criticism reviewed above, one might have been led to predict a dismal performance on the part of the manpower programs. It certainly is true that the developments which inspired the policy persisted long after the policy's introduction and expansion had occurred. Manpower policies did not reverse the rise in unemployment among women and youth, nor did they prevent the nation's inflation-unemployment dilemma from deepening. Big-policy advocates, as we have noted, would object that active labor market measures have not been deployed on a sufficiently large scale to affect large-scale economic developments. However, in Sweden, where the policy has been developed on a scale that is quite large by United States standards, it has not been able to prevent adverse movements in the Swedish Phillips Curve.

In an attempt to determine whether some of the programs actually introduced in this country have been effective and hold promise for the future, numerous benefit-cost studies have been made. With benefits measured as some type of post-training differential in incomes, most of the studies of MDTA programs indicated very high rates of return. There is some indication that on-the-job-training programs, which cost less than institutional training, have yielded higher rates of return than the latter.

It was also found that training exerted a greater impact on the most disadvantaged individuals—those with the lowest levels of education or of pre-training earnings or with the worst records of unemployment. For the Neighborhood Youth Corps programs, which offered more subsidy than training, results were rather mixed and did not unequivocally indicate a record of overall effectiveness either in increasing the earnings of enrollees or in reducing high-school dropout rates. Studies of the effectiveness of the Job Corps (an expensive residential training and rehabilitation program for underprivileged school dropouts with bad work experience) yielded mixed results. A rather rough study of JOBS (or Job Opportunities in Business Sector, under which training programs were carried on by private employers, with or without subsidy) indicated large apparent increases in earnings between 1966 and 1968. The Work Incentive Program, designed to provide training and placement in public employment to welfare recipients, was misnamed, because the welfare system's eligibility requirements have constituted a notorious disincentive for recipients to strive for gainful employment. Predictably, its record of completions and placements was very poor.

Critics of labor market policy have included critics of the research on policy effectiveness. Since some of them are proponents of human capital analysis, which relies heavily on empirical benefit-cost research, it might appear that they were gently hoist with their own petard. They claim, however, that these studies did not yield accurate assessments of benefits. Perhaps the criticism most strongly advanced is that most of the studies were characterized by the absence of adequate reference or "control" groups (or of any at all). This is an important consideration; however, the difficulty in obtaining a control group which is the identical twin of the target group in every relevant respect save that of completion of the program in question is so great as to raise a serious question of operationality. Even among people alike in respect to education, age, sex, and color, there are motivational and other differences between those admitted and those who were not, between those who completed the course and those who dropped out. Another criticism of most studies is that they assumed that the income differentials observed a short time after completion of the course (the benefits involved) would persist over a 10-year period. In at least some instances, however, it is more reasonable to believe that the magnitude of such benefits would dwindle over time, since the higher earnings of the trainees reflect more aggressive placement efforts on their behalf as well as the acquisition of skills. A third line of criticism is that some programs train and place people in high-turnover, unskilled occupations, raising the possibility that the trainees might merely be displacing previous job applicants. Related to this is the observation that, even where earnings were significantly raised by the programs, they remained below poverty levels, so that manpower training cannot be regarded as a substitute for direct income redistribution. Finally, some of the studies were made when the administrators were still "creaming" the pool of applicants for the most able and qualified individuals; moreover, the instructors themselves might have been the cream of their own crop. Hence attempts to expand the programs could run into diminishing returns.

Proponents of manpower policy have also criticized the evaluations. They object to inclusion of support payments to trainees, which are transfer payments, among costs properly chargeable to manpower programs. This implies agreement with the assertion that manpower development cannot be regarded as a substitute for direct income supplementation. However, the proponents of course believe that manpower development is worthy in its own right. This view is implicit in another caveat—that it might be desirable to retain a program which yields significant benefits in the form of increased earning power even if its costs, which are borne by the public, exceed those benefits which accrue to the disadvantaged groups. By the same reasoning, they would reject the position that direct income transfers are preferable to manpower development programs because the cost of the latter is greater; they would hold that such cost differentials are overwhelmed by the extra social benefit derived from improving the employability of people. Also, as a counterpoint to the diminishing returns argument, it might be maintained that costs in the early period covered by the studies reflected the administrative growing pains referred to above, and that costly duplication and overlapping could be reduced as the manpower programs develop in the future.

A Place for Manpower Policy

Although favorable (as well as unfavorable) results yielded by benefit-cost studies must be interpreted with great caution, they might also justify reexamination of the analyses which imply that all manpower policies would be largely ineffective. In fact, some interesting current research challenges the hypothesis that much of the unemployment, especially around cyclical peaks and among disadvantaged groups at such times, is either voluntary or frictional in nature. While awaiting publication and evaluation of this new work, we might give some thought to an old finding. In 1955, when unemployment averaged 4.4 percent, 55.5 percent of those who changed jobs (or 4.6 out of 8.2 million people) experienced no unemployment at all. (Another survey of the labor force, in 1961, revealed that 60 percent of the people who made only one job change that year had experienced no unemployment, that 80 percent of those who changed jobs once in order to improve their status did so without incurring unemployment, and that among male job changers 40 percent of those without unemployment landed a higher-paying job, as compared with only 26 percent of those who experienced some unemployment between jobs. In 1961, however, the unemployment rate average was 6.7 percent.) This casts some doubt on the assumption that job search is carried on most efficiently when the individual is not working and hence on the conclusion that unemployment is mainly voluntary. If unemployment is indeed voluntary, it does not follow that diversion of unemployed (and under-employed) individuals from the labor force into training programs would generate inflationary pressure on wages.

Nor does it follow that training programs need be ineffective in situations where barriers to mobility are thrown up by discrimination or even by a shortage of good jobs. Recourse to educational credentials as a cheap screening device (provided at public expense) by high-wage employers in protected labor markets suggests that at least some of the qualified applicants may be educated beyond purely economic requirements. If so, even relatively short compensatory training courses might bring those with educational deficiencies up to entry levels. Moreover, the social pressure on employers to hire duly certified graduates of public training programs could constitute a salutary dose of compensatory credentialing. Certainly, the criticism that benefit-cost studies are likely to overstate the payoff to training per se, because they do not take into account the effectiveness of aggressive placement efforts, is wide of the mark.

It is true, of course, that merely lengthening a queue of qualified job seekers does not increase the number of jobs which they are qualified to hold. However, the number of good jobs annually available is greater than suggested by the dual market theory. The latter suggests, as a stereotype, two compartmentalized sectors; in the high-wage internal labor markets, all are protected by non-academic tenure, and turnover is negligible; in the unprotected, low-wage sector, quits and firings are the order of the day. In fact, all the theory really requires is that turnover in the good-job sector be significantly lower than in the bad-job sector; and in this respect it can claim anticipatory confirmation in long-standing findings that high-wage industries tend to have lower quit rates than low-wage industries (even after allowance for differences in skill levels).

However, the *absolute* levels of separations—including layoffs, discharges, and retirements, as well as quits—are quite high even in industries whose relative quit rates are low, and whose wages are relatively high. Thus in 1967 petroleum and coal products ranked first among 29 industrial categories in average hourly earnings, and last in separations of production workers, but the latter still averaged 2.2 percent a month. This means that in a year of high employment (unemployment was 3.8 percent in 1967) this industry had to hire about 125 persons to keep an average of 100 on the job. Figuring this way, the eight highest-paying industries in 1967 (the lowest wage was 6 percent above the average for all manufacturing) turned over about 3 million production employees (out of a combined work force of about 6 million). Of course, if the ranks of qualified and credentialed job applicants were swelled by an expanded manpower development system, quit rates could be expected to fall. And if the overall unemployment rate were allowed to rise, fewer vacancies would be created on a replacement basis.

Nevertheless, the order of magnitude suggests that some potentialities for upward mobility exist, even within protected sectors. Some elbow room exists for labor market policies. It would permit the latter to contribute to a reduction in the spread of unemployment between the disadvantaged groups and the rest, and to a reduction in the concentration of employment of the disadvantaged in the secondary sectors, although the major problems in lowering the barriers to mobility would remain.

Although spreading the misery more evenly would serve the cause of distributive equity, that cause could better be served if there was happiness to spread around instead of misery. This could occur if the major barriers to mobility are greatly reduced *and* if, as they are being reduced, the total number of good jobs grows rapidly enough to absorb the unemployed and the underemployed. Experience has taught that the economy has tended to produce such a happy outcome when operating close to capacity or approaching that neighborhood. At such times, the maintenance of high and rising levels of demand acts like a giant suction pump as the relatively great growth in employment in the high-wage sectors forces wages up more rapidly elsewhere and results in a reduction of unemployment, both recorded and "hidden," which is especially great in the high-employment groups. Thus more jobs are created in the protected sectors, while more jobs elsewhere have their wages raised.

The trouble with this story, however, is that it does not end at this point. The process is invariably accompanied by inflation, which tends to perpetuate itself, and even accelerate, as unions in the protected sectors seek to make up ground lost while their employers have been raising prices to lift profit margins from pre-expansion levels. To counter these inflationary pressures, demand is then deflated, the suction is turned off, and wage and unemployment differentials widen again. This is the unhappy sequel which manpower policy was originally designed to prevent; and if it could reduce inflationary tendencies at high levels of employment, it could also indirectly reduce barriers to economic opportunity and equality—including barriers which might not have originated in lack of skill or information at all.

Moderate Expectations

Few believe that manpower policy could satisfactorily perform either of these tasks unaided, even if it were scaled up to Swedish proportions. It is highly doubtful whether it alone could increase mobility and otherwise improve the trade-off sufficiently to induce employers to resist cost push, and to prevent them from "administering" price increases when they are still operating well below capacity. It is highly doubtful whether it alone could level barriers to mobility sufficiently to effect a satisfactory redistribution of employment, unemployment, and income, or to significantly reduce poverty levels. That is why most observers, proponents of the policy as well as critics, now agree that manpower policy cannot be regarded as an alternative to direct wage and price restraint, to efficient enforcement of anti-discrimination legislation, and to direct income transfers to the poor. The proponents would agree that these other policies would be necessary as a complement to manpower policy.

But they might also maintain that manpower policy complements the other policies, too. It could increase the efficiency of wage-price restraint (which certainly could use all the help it can get) by removing inflationary bottlenecks, which often fuel union demands for more widespread wage increases in order to maintain or restore traditional relationships. It could help anti-discrimination policy by compensating for deficiencies in worker training and education that might have resulted from past discrimination. However, with respect to anti-discrimination policy, and even more with respect to direct income redistribution, political complementarity is of greater importance than technical complementarity. The day may come when the egalitarian spirit of the American public might drive it to embrace policies that would divorce income from work as a general principle. But as the Presidential election of 1972 made plain, that day is not at hand. (Nor is the era of consumer satiety, on which the divorce was originally predicated, about to dawn.) The so-called work ethic still dominates, and it is held strongly not only by the white tax-paying middle classes but by the underprivileged and the poor themselves, who want intensely to enhance their sense of worth along with their incomes. Policies designed to help the individual achieve these two objectives range from counseling-training-placement through public employment to wage subsidies or supplements. The exact mix will vary in response to changing needs and the relative efficiency of the different approaches. But some programs to improve and equalize work opportunity must be offered, if only as a condition for the provision of separate income supplementation for those among the poor for whom income must truly be divorced from work.

If the existence of a battery of manpower development policies is essential to the development of more thoroughgoing and effective policies of income supplementation, the latter are also conducive to the efficiency of the former. In the first place, a more effective division of labor between the two types of policy would be feasible, so that the training and information programs could concentrate more exclusively on their more narrowly defined functions. In the second place, the training programs, even if concentrated on the groups with the greatest problems of unemployment and deprivation, would be able to select the more promising individuals in those groups for training or placement. This would minimize the "displacement" problem. Such "creaming" of the more trainable individuals, in turn, would permit training—even when conducted in educational institutions—to be geared more closely to ladder-job openings, whether in the private sector or in public service.

Manpower policies with these attributes could avoid much of the administrative inefficiency which has been experienced to date, including the wasteful overlapping and duplication of activities. "Decategorization" and decentralization through revenue sharing have been officially proposed as a means to the same ends. A concluding note of caution, however, should be clearly sounded. Revenue sharing is unavoidably susceptible to the diversion of federally-generated resources away from activities designed to increase the economic potential of the disadvantaged, and in the direction of more well-to-do groups with superior economic and political power in the local community—whether through public works, lower taxes, or negotiated wage increases. From the viewpoint of manpower policy, revenue sharing is not an efficient instrument. Efforts to promote local autonomy and flexibility cannot dispense with federal guidance and direction to the degree required to secure an acceptable level of efficiency in policies designated to further the agreed-upon objectives of manpower policy. For it is at levels of government farther removed from local grassroots that such worthy interests of economically weak minorities can be more decently and efficiently promoted.